Guidance and Counselling

Guidance and Counselling

A K NAYAK

A P H PUBLISHING CORPORATION
4435-36/7, ANSARI ROAD, DARYA GANJ
NEW DELHI-110 002

Published by
S.B. Nangia
A.P.H. Publishing Corporation
4435–36/7, Ansari Road, Darya Ganj,
New Delhi-110002
Phone: 011–23274050
e-mail: aphbooks@gmail.com

2026

Rs. 1695/-

Typeset by
Ideal Publishing Solutions
C-90, J.D. Cambridge School,
West Vinod Nagar, Delhi-110092

Printed at
RD DIGITAL PRINTERS
Ansari road , Daryaganj, Delhi-110002

Preface

Surveying the faults and conflicts in society obscures many strengths and advantages and seems to put undue stress on the negative. But these are the factors that must be highlighted. There are shortcomings that demand immediate and comprehensive remedies. Guidance and counseling obviously cannot solve everything alone, but they can play a major role. Guidance workers can reach individuals who need assistance, help modify conditions that call for improvement, change institutions that are failing in their missions, and take steps to reverse destructive trends.

Problems and needs in society are nothing new, but today they seem to be proliferating at an unprecedented rate. Problems once hidden have become visible; new ones arise. All are given extensive coverage by media. No area of life is taboo. But rapid and unexpected local, national, and international changes give rise to needs and challenges qualitatively and quantitatively different from those of the past.

The book will be of use to graduate and post graduate students in education and to practicing teachers, administrators, librarians and planners. The chapters and the further sources of information cited in this book should lead the reader to thousands of people and documents for either research or programme planning purposes.

Editor

Contents

1

Guidance and Counselling: Nature and its Functions

Nature of guidance

To define guidance in clear-cut words is not easy. It has been defined in varied ways: Crow and Crow write, :Guidance is not direction. It is not the imposition of one's point of view upon another. It is not making decisions for an individual which he should make for himself. It is not carrying the burden of another's life. Rather, guidance is assistance made available by competent counsellors to an individual of any age to help him direct his own life, develop his own point of view, make his own decisions, carry his own burdens". Hamrin and Erickson define guidance as "that aspect of educational programme which is concerned especially with helping the pupil to become adjusted to his present situation and to plan his future in the line with his interests, abilities, and social needs."

Mathewson believes that "guidance is the systematic professional process of helping the individual through education and interpretative procedures to gain a better understanding of his own characteristics and potentialities and to relate himself more satisfactorily to social requirements and opportunities in accord with social and moral values". Traxler considers guidance as a help which enables "each individual to understand his abilities and interests, to develop them as well as possible and to relate them to life-goals, and finally to reach a state of complete and mature self-guidance as a desirable member of the social order."

According to Jones, "Guidance involves personal help given by someone; it is designed to assist a person to decide where he wants to go, what he wants to do or how he can best accomplish his purpose; it assists him to solve problems that arise in his life."

An analysis of the above view-points shows that guidance has the following main characteristics:

i. *It is a process:* It helps every individual to help himself, to recognise and use his inner resources, to set goals, to make plans, to work out his own problems of development.

ii. *It is a continuous process*: It is needed right from early childhood, adolescence, adult-hood and even in old age.

iii. *Choice and problem points are the distinctive concerns of guidance* as here the individual's unique world of perceptions interacts with the external order of events in his life context.

iv. *It is assistance to the individual in the process of development rather than a direction of that development*: The aim is to develop the capacity for self-direction, self-guidance and self-improvement through an increased understanding of his problems and his resources as well as limitations to solve the problem.

v. *Guidance is a service meant for all:* It is a regular service which is required at every stage for every student, not only for awkward situations and abnormal students. It is a positive programme geared to meet the needs of all students.

vi. *It is both generalised and a specialised service:* It is a generalised service because everyone-teachers, tutors, advisers, deans, parents-play a part in the programme. It is a specialised service because specially qualified personnel as counsellors, psychiartists, psychologists join hands to help the individual to get out of his problem.

Guidance and counselling differentiated

Very few terms have been more loosely or interchangeably used than the terms 'guidance' and 'counselling'.

According to Tolbert, "Guidance is the total programme or all the activities and services engaged in by an educational institution that are primarily aimed at assisting and individual to make and carry out adequate plans and to achieve satisfactory adjustment in all aspects of his daily life. Guidance is not teaching but it may be done by teachers. It is not separate from education but is an essential part of the total educational programme. Guidance is a term which is broader than counselling and which includes counselling as one of its services."

Bulter makes a logical separation of the counselling process discerned as having two phases called 'adjustive' and 'distributive'. In the *adjustive* phase, the emphasis is on the *social personal* and *emotional* problems of the individual; in the *distributive* phase the focus is upon his *educational, vocational* and *occupational* problems.

According to Arbuckle, Butler's *distributive phase* can be most aptly described as 'guidance' whilst the *adjustive phase* can be considered as the description of 'counselling'.

Principles of guidance philosophy

According to Hollis and Hollis, there are eight principles on which any guidance programme should be based. They can be modified to fit locally accepted beliefs. The principles are:

i. The dignity of the individual is supreme.

ii. Each individual is different from every other individual.

iii. The primary concern of guidance is the individual in his social setting.

iv. The attitudes and personal perceptions of the individual are the bases on which he acts.

v. The individual generally acts to enhance his perceived self.

vi. The individual has the innate ability to learn and can be helped to make choices that will lead to selfdirection consistent with social improvement.

vii. The individual needs a continuous guidance process from early childhood through adulthood.

viii. Each individual may at times need the information and personalised assistance best given by competent professional personnel.

Function of guidance and counselling

Guidance and counselling have three-fold functions: *adjustmental, orientational and developmental.*

Guidance and counselling are *adjustmental* in the sense that they help the student in making the best possible adjustment to the current situations in the educational institution and occupational world, in the home and the community. Professional and individualised aid is given in making immediate and suitable adjustment at problem points. At the same time, the adjustive attitude in the spirit of Reinold Neibuhr is to be developed in the individuals:

> God grant me the serenity,
> To accept the things, I cannot change.
> The courage to change the things I can
> And the wisdom to know the difference.

Guidance and counselling have *orientational* function also. They orientate the students in problems of career planning, educational programming and direction towards long-term personal aims and values. Awareness of the need to plan in the context of the complexity of the world of work is an essential prerequisite of going through education and preparation for after-education career. Guidance and counselling have another important function-*developmental function*. They should try not only to cure when the problems have occurred and done their damage, rather they should begin before the problems arise and maladjustments occur. If unsolved problems re allowed to accumulate, their total effect may lead the student to the point where his capacity for growth is blocked. In such cases, guidance and counselling have a very important developmental function for helping the students achieve self-development and self-realisation. Guidance and counselling also have to discharge the important function of furthering the welfare of the society and be important instruments of national development.

Scope of guidance and counselling

The scope of guidance and counselling is extremely comprehensive. As the life is getting complex day by day, the problems for which expert helps is required are increasing proportionately. The scope of guidance, per necessity, is extending horizontally to much of the social context, to matters of prestige in occupations, to the broad field of social trends, and economic development. Guidance is assuming more and more responsibility for the individual in every direction-it helps in the selection of educational courses, and profitable occupation, in job placement; placement in the next stage of education and training; occupational surveys; improvement of study skills, maintenance of mental health; counselling regarding personal adjustment problems; identifying the gifted, the backward and help them achieve the maximum. In short, educational, vocational, avocational, social, personal, moral and even marital problems of individual are the concerns of guidance and counselling. Their scope is indeed very vast.

Need of guidance and counselling

A cursory glance at our seats of higher learning will show the imperative need of instituting in them a well-organized programme of guidance and counselling. Education is expanding its frontiers making it well-nigh impossible for an individual students to make a choice of courses and careers without expert guidance. Occupational scene too is changing so rapidly that yesterday's rocket circuitry electronics specialist considered as highly prized as a marks-man on the old frontier is to-day's unemployment statistic. One of the great stories in out midst is the dramatic increase in jobs.

Not only that quite a big number of students at the threshold of a college or university are in for compelling and difficult life situations-they are shy, fearful, gullible, not skilled in managing their own affairs. They lack self-acknowledge which may enable them to form realistic life-goals and plans. They lack both focus and meaningful direction. Occasionally they lose their way in the dark labyrinths of adolescence and do not know how and when to act. They have a grapple with complex social problems-living with and sharing facilities with peers, such as living in hostels and sharing extra-curricular experiences, adjustment to heterosexual relationships etc. Surveys of Indian students and alumni document the widespread feeling of dissatisfaction with college and university life.

A survey was conducted by the All India Educational and Vocational Guidance Association for gauging college student's needs. Three thousand students from seventeen Indian universities responded. The survey revealed student's felt needs. Eleven problems were marked by more than 50 percent of the respondents:

1. I cannot do as well in my studies as other people expect me to do.
2. I do not know enough about the qualifications needed for different kinds of worked or careers.
3. I worry too much about what my future will be after I have finished my studies.
4. Even though I force myself, my attention will not remain on my assignments long enough to finish them.
5. I do not know how to make froemds among the opposite sex.

6. I do not have sufficient information about matters on sex.
7. I do not know enough about my aptitudes and abilities for different kinds of work or careers.
8. It is difficult for me to get the books I need for study.
9. I cannot read fast enough to complete my studies in time.
10. I do not know proper methods of study.
11. I have more difficulty in forgetting my mistakes than I believe I should have.

The eleven areas may be summarised under four headings *Study habits and skills, Career choice, Knowledge of aptitudes and abilities, Sex education.*

The respondents reported that their *parents were the only source of help they received, if any, along these lines and practically no help had been forthcoming from college personnel!*

Eighty per cent of respondents expressed the need of such assistance from their non-parental source. The bigger the college, the bigger the campus, the more the need for personalised student services, else the student will merely feel a small cog in a huge machine!

Another survey of the educational, vocational and personal problems was conducted by Umrudin and Gadri Widespread maladjustment was rated among hostel residents who showed much concern over problems connected with *study habits, vocational choice, family relationship and mental hygiene.*

All these emerging issues and problems make it

obligatory for our educational planners and administrators to build into our higher education an appropriate guidance and counselling programme for the development of the individual student into an adult personality, imbued with social and occupational awareness, intellectual and functional proficiency, discipline and confidence. The classroom activities, however well-conducted and well-organised, alone are not in a position to accomplish all this.

It is true that provision of guidance and counselling services in the colleges and universities cannot be seen as a panacea for all our educational ills nor can a counselling officer hope to give students a trouble-free or problem-free life, but where possible, he can help them to resolve their difficulties, or if that is not possible, to live with them. To help them resolve the stresses and strains does not require a nosey-parker intrusion of privacy but the response of an understanding and empathic person and an atmosphere of understanding, faith and sincerity. And this is what is needed.

Guidance and counselling programme needs to be introduced in our colleges and universities to meet the varied needs of the educational system, administration and students:

To help in the total development of the student: The emphasis on intellectual development through the teaching of subjects alone cannot help in the total development of the students. We have to evolve some method of helping students understand themselves and helping teachers understand the students. There has to be a basic and fundamental change in our entire system of education, change which recognises that matter how well a human being is educated in chemistry, physics, economics, history or literature, he remains a barbarian unless he knows something about himself. Self-knowledge in depth which has been the forgotten factor in our educational system must become its primary focus-and this is what can be done through a programme of guidance and counselling. Total development of the students are expected, accepted, understood and planned for and all types of experiences in an institution are so organised as to contribute to the total development of the student. That, all that a student needs in an educational institution is good teaching, is an exploded myth. Something much more and beyond this is needed to produce competent, mature and well-rounded citizens.

To help in the proper choice of courses: Everyone knows that so far our educational system has grown up in a higgledy piggledy fashion. The subjects which are the least wanted humanities and the liberal arts-have been those most frequently offered and taken, both in the colleges and the universities because they were the oldest and relatively inexpensive areas of knowledge, taken because they require to specified intellectual equipment. No wonder, the turnout of graduates and post-graduates in Arts in the year 1973 Annual and 1972 supplementary is 2,47,948 and 64, 465 respectively, while in all the other faculties put together it is 2,83,471 and 33,333 respectively. Hence, thousands of youngmen educated in these liberal arts are without jobs.

Turn-out of Graduates and Post-graduates: Facultywise 1973 Annual and 1972 Supplementary

Faculties	*Graduates*	*Post-graduates*
Arts	2,47,948	64,465

Science	1,06,695	17,433
Home Science/Arts	1,393	276
Commerce	66,899	7,758
Eduaction	53,676	1,604
Engineering	13,198	982
Technology	927	427
Medicine	13,167	2,139
Agriculture/Dairy Sc.	4,723	1,517
Veterinary Science	907	195
Law	19,504	390
Oriental Learning	448	60
Music-Fine Arts	176	150
Others	1,758	401
Total	5,31,419	97,798

The problem is grave in another way also. In an article on 'Unrest on Campus', Piloo Modi, M.P. wrote, "Our student population reaches the university level, having made up their mind broadly about the courses that they may have-a decision, which in almost all cases, is taken by unthinking and unsympathetic parents and relatives with an eye on a more lucrative profession. It is great tragedy when a potential poet becomes a chemical engineer.. Many a mute inglorious Milton is languishing in the dark engineering world." This entire process of herding our youths into educational disciplines unconnected with their aptitudes needs to be checked through a scientific process of guidance and counselling for the best development of individuals and growth of society.

To help in the proper choice of careers: We are living in a highly complex and rapidly changing world of work. There are changing requirements in industrial jobs, altered market conditions for professional manpower, the development of para-professional occupational selection more difficult than eve. The young students in colleges and universities need to be informed about various jobs and openings available to them and the requirements, responsibilities and the nature of work involved in them so that they could measure themselves up to them and develop and crystallise their occupational goals. They need to be helped in making meaningful occupational selection and preparation for an entry into them to have a fulfilling and rewarding career.

The need for helping the students in the choice of a proper career is further enhanced due to the fact that majority of our students in colleges and universities are the first generation learners. In their family, they have no one with an experience of college or university education background to guide them in the choice of a career. With a right to the best education available, and a wide range of jobs open them, these students need mature help in making a judicious occupational choice. Hence the need of adequate guidance and counselling arrangement in our colleges and universities.

To help the students in vocational development: The process of vocational development covers almost the entire span of life on an individual. It begins quite early in one's life and continue till sometimes after retirement. In this process, the individual passes through various stages—growth, exploration, maintenance and decline. Guidance services need to be provided to the colleges and universities to help the students in the process of vocational development-particularly the stage of growth and exploration, by making it possible for them to gain knowledge about themselves-their abilities, interests and needs on, the one hand and knowledge about the world of work on the other. By providing them opportunities for self-exploration as well as exploration of the world of work while they are still in an educational institution, their transition from education to work can be facilitated.

To develop readiness for choices and changes to face new challenges: In a paper entitled The Need for counselling in Higher Education, presented at the Third International Round Table of Educational Counselling and Vocational Guidance, Miss New some, Counselling Officer at the University of Keels, North Strafford Shire, England, writes, "For the students of higher education the demands of life are likely to be great, in a most different way from the exacting demands of education itself. On graduating he will be called upon to make use of the kind of person he has become as much if not more than what he has learnt in his course of study-not only to make an initial choice of what he is to do on graduating but will be called upon to change his occupation several times in a life time. Readiness for these choices and changes is essential, not only to the student himself but to the society as a whole. To the extent to which he is able to capitalise on his experience and face new challenges with a realistic expectation of success, to that extent he will benefit society. If he is unable to meet the changing demands, not only of the working world but also of his other roles of life, to that extent he will be a liability and will fail to fulfil the expectations which society has for its most able people." Guidance services are needed to develop in the students the ability to cope with their new problems and concerns in such a way that they become more competent to meet the demands which will continue to be made upon them in the future.

To minimise the mismatching between education and employment and help in the efficient use of manpower: The latest analysis done by Planning Commission reveals that the educated youth between 15 and 29 years of age constituted 11.5 per cent of the corresponding labour force but they accounted for 33.2 per cent of the total unemployment in the country. According to the Planning Commission's labour force projections, the total number of educated unemployed at the beginning of 1980 was estimated at 3.47 million. If there is no further deterioration in the unemployment rate, this number is likely to go upto 4.66 million in 1985. And this is the challenging situation we have to face.

It needs to be pointed out that the hiatus between education and employment has rarely been as wide and as disturbing as it is today. Higher academic education, as very well pointed out by Mr. L. K. Jha, Chairman of the Economic Administration Reforms Commission, is far too general and diffused to be of practical value to the vast majority of youngmen and women. Most of our young men and women have no clear objectives or career targets. They amble through university courses of learning without acquiring much knowledge of preparing themselves for an uncertain future.

Every 12 months, our colleges and universities disgorge thousands of hopeful youngsters into the labour market who are virtually unemployable-despite their fancy degrees and diplomas. In fact, employers often complain that of the hundreds of applications that come in response to a single vacancy, at least 80 per cent have no relevance to the job specifications whatsoever. Few students pursue their education with a clear idea as to what they would eventually like to become. People even register at the employment exchange with scant idea about the sort of work they would like to be employed at. No wonder while jobs go abegging the youth go begging for jobs. Not only that, the employment of workers ill-suited to their jobs generally leads to a higher rate of labour placement or to the retention of persons who are inefficient. All this is a huge wastage of our scant resources. Guidance facilities can help in reducing this wastage and thus ensure efficient use of manpower.

To motive the youth for self-employment: Considering the magnitude of educated job-seekers flowing into the job market in India every year, it is essential that a sizable fraction of enterprising youth is initiated into careers of self-employment. Some arrangement needs to be instituted in the colleges and universities to identify the deserving cases fit to take up self-employment, educate them on how to proceed about the job of setting up a venture, help them through the cooperation of the concerned agencies in this sphere to prepare technically sound and economically viable projects; sponsor their cases to the banks for loan assistance and guide them to overcome the teething troubles effective follow-up after the commencement of the venture.

To help freshers establish proper identity: In our country the youngmen entering colleges and even universities are comparatively young in years. Young adolescents s they are, they are passing through a stage between childhood and adulthood, between the morality learned as a child and the ethics to be developed by the adult. They find it extremely difficult to establish a satisfactory identity. Such failure or delay leads to what can be called "role diffusion". This crisis in role identity is perhaps very acute today. The uncertainties of the future, the conflicts in languages, culture, regions, castes, etc., and the erosion of traditional values has rendered Indian youth rootless.

Fuster did a small study with Bombay college students, both men and women. The strongest needs, as reported by the students themselves where they were requested to indicate rank orders, were for achievement in life, self-reliance and a sense of security, success in college and university, to have an understanding friend and (for the males) *money.*

Guidance and counselling programme is needed to help students deal effectively with the normal developmental tasks of adolescence and face life situations boldly.

To identify and motivate the students from weaker sections of society: Students from weaker sections have their own problems and needs. They experience difficulty in adjustment with the peers, teachers and the environment. To communicate, make friends, utilise the time profitably, make the best use of lectures, make an effective use of library and other facilities available all pose problems for them. Guidance facilities are urgently needed for such type of students to enable them to adjust and utilise the available facilities properly.

To help the students in their period of turmoil and confusion: The students undergo a great deal of turmoil and searching to give meaning to their lives. They have their conflicts and anxieties. They feel disillusioned regarding higher education. They find that colleges and universities, instead of imparting them education, just enable them to pass examinations-they feel sunk and cheated. When this education does not enable them to get immediate employment, they feel lost and bewildered.

Similarly, they have their personal conflicts and anxieties. They have the problems about their parents and family, their relations to boy and girl friends. They have the problems of adjusting their personality to the world of people, of ethical ideas and of goals and situations. For tacking all these situations successfully, they need someone to sort out the strands-they need some strong, tactile presence of a hand guiding the anxious and enabling them to develop realistic expectations.

To help in checking wastage and stagnation: The average pass percentage at the graduate and post-graduate level is about 50 to 60. Thousands of our students, unfortunately, drop out, get pushed out, and fall out of the system. This problem is becoming more serious day by day.

There is another unfortunate side of this problem-majority of our students as the Table 2 shows pass in third division, which is a low qualification for the world of work.

This poor achievement may be due to so many reasons lack of proper study skills and effective study habits, lack of the knowledge for making full use of the facilities provided and so on.

Also, the majority of our students do not fulfil the promise indicated by the Secondary School leaving examinations and do not utilize their professional qualifications after graduation.

A study of the years 1950 and 1954 alumni of Delhi University where approximately 1800 alumni were interviewed revealed:

i. In general, these students did not fulfil the promise indicated by secondary school leaving examinations, since about 45 per cent received a lower university rating at graduation.

ii. Many graduates do not use their training occupationally.

Percentage Distribution of Successful Candidates According to Divisions Awarded: B.A, B.Sc., B. Com., and M. A., M.Sc., M. Com. 1973 Annual and 1972 Supplementary

Examination	I Division	Turn out II Division	III Division	Total
B. A.	2,214	43,562	1,69,496	2,15,272
	(1.0)	(20.2)	(78.8)	(1000.0)
B. Sc.	12,780	40,960	41,238	94,978
	13.5)	(43.1)	(43.4)	(100.0)
B. Com	939	15,467	45,488	61,874
	(1.5)	(25.0)	(73.5)	(100.0)
M.A.	3,170	28,792	26,322	58,284
	(5.4)	(49.4)	(45.2)	(100.0)
M. Com.	393	4,202	2,202	6,797
	(5.8)	(61.8)	(32.9)	(100.0)

A study conducted by D.G.E and T., Ministry of Labour, 1962 on the graduates of the year 1950 revealed the percentage of graduates in clerical work-commerce 67 per cent, B.Sc. Pass 63 per cent. B.A. Pass 64 per cent, Proficiency in Law Certificate 48 per cent, M.A. Arts 31 per cent, B.A. Honours 25 per cent, etc. It is obvious that sizable percentage of alumni obtaining professional qualifications have to work as clerks. The report also gives evidence of much aimless and unrealistic vocational choice.

Higher education is a very costly enterprise. Much of the money wasted on these poor and low achievers could be saved by a policy of prevention. Just as preventive medicine is sounder economically and more humane than remedial medicine, so too is preventive education more sound economically than remedial education. There is thus a clear need for developing better professional services of a counselling kind to check the huge wastage of student time and money and also huge state expenditure on education. Miller, in this connection, said so well, "If one counsellor could prevent the wastage of only four student years each costing - 800 to -1200, he would be earning his keep. Similar savings of graduate salaries foregone as a result of failure or delay would benefit student as well as the taxpayer."

To identify and help students in need of special help: There are such students as the gifted, the backward, the handicapped who need special opportunities. Some arrangement needs to be provided in our colleges and universities to identify them and provide them with help according to their requirements.

To ensure the proper utilization of time spent outside the classrooms: It is common knowledge that students in the colleges and universities spend two to three times as many hours outside classrooms as in them. And the manner in which students spend their non-class hours clearly affects their success in achieving both academic competence and personal development of all types. It is, therefore, essential that institutions of higher learning provide positive direction to students by influencing how they can use those non-class hours. They programme of guidance and counselling can meet this need.

To help in tackling problems arising out of student explosion: Increased demand for higher education is outstripping the growth of facilities in the seats of higher learning. Resultant unfortunate qualitative changes in the nature of entire educative experiences are creating innumerable problems. The students population is highly affluent and extremely poor, educated in convents and ordinary schools and colleges, rural and urban areas, students from our own country and different foreign countries are attending colleges and universities. When students from a broad range of families and educational and social backgrounds meet in classes for instruction, in hostels for housing, in cafeterias and mess halls for eating, numerous problems crop up. Guidance and counselling facilities need to be provided for helping them tackle these diverse and complex problems.

To check migration: There is an unhealthy trend among the youth of migrating from rural to urban areas and from our own country to foreign countries. Unless migration is checked by proper guidance and counselling, cities will continue to swallow the rural talent and foreign countries the national talent and thus render both unproductive.

To make up for the deficiencies of home: A large number of students come to institutions of higher learning from homes which are not able to assist them adequately in dealing with their life problems. Because of various factors such as rapid industrialisation, political and social changes in the occupational structure of the country and the growing complexity of life there are greater pressures and strains in the family. They home is not able to provide the kind of support and help it did in earlier days. Also, there is a gap in the range of sympathetic adults who could be turned to in need, which formerly was filled by adult who could be turned to in need, which formerly was filled by adult brothers and sisters, friendly aunts and grand parents when communities and families were more intimate.

Also our homes are not equipped to be the source of information concerning the qualifications required for different kinds of courses or careers. Such information can come from agencies which make a full time job of supplying adequate and up-to-date materials. Similarly, home is not equipped for studying future labour shortages and the labour supply and demand situation. Besides, many parents are not trained for helping their grown up children to develop sound study techniques, and obtain reliable information in matters of sex etc. Seth collected a sample of students at Allahabad University. The parents were indicated as the most usual source of help. Forty per cent of student respondents said that they could not discuss their problems with their parents. There is a strong evidence that professional help could be well-used.

To minimise the incidence of indiscipline: Majority of our students lack a sense of direction, a sense of purpose and a sense of fulfillment. They indulge in destructive activities which lead to social damage and loss. This educated proletariat, so to say, is a time bomb in the heart of the nation that can explode any time if immediate care is not taken to inactive it. Adequate guidance and counselling facilities is the only answer-to help and guide the youth to worthwhile channels and help them realise the goal of optimum academic, personal and social development.

2

The Need for Counselling

There are no accurate figure of the number of counsellors in our educational institutions. Under the umbrella of the British Association for Counselling, the National Association of Counsellors in Education and the Association for Student Counselling are the two groups particularly appropriate for people who work in educational settings. Their membership consists perhaps at most, of a thousand people who are sufficiently interested in counselling in education to join an appropriate association. Some members of the National Association of Careeres and Guidance Teachers may consider counselling as part of their work. It seems unlikely that there are more counsellors throughout the country than the number of people in these groups, certainly not a number to be justifiably considered a multitude.

The advent of professional counselling as a supplement to pastoral care has had a very mixed reception. There has been hostility and resentment from those teachers, tutors and parents who see the counsellor as one who is making a take-over bid for the personal relationships with children and students which hitherto have bee their concern. Others feel antagonistic towards the counsellors' acceptance of children as they are and towards the counsellor's effort to help young people to make their own choices and decisions and, within limits, to take responsibility for their own lives. I remember being sharply taken to task by a school governor because I said that children should not have freedom to choose anything. Perhaps a look at some of the objection to counselling which people raise may be appropriate as an introduction to the needs.

Some objections to Counselling

Not a great deal is known about counselling in education in this country, and one of the aims of this book is to provide an introduction to the work which may help people to decide what counselling can and cannot do in diverse educational settings. Among those people who know a little about counselling and among those who know nothing there are some who raise strong objections to the introduction of counselling as a specialist activity in schools and colleges, which is what I advocate. Some of these objections merit attention, because they arise from very real fears and firm beliefs about the meaning of education and of life, and they are helpful in the sense that they enable counsellors, indeed sometimes force them, to re-examine their own beliefs and acknowledge their defences.

1. Counselling is of no value

This view is representative of those who believe that any helping relationship is detrimental both to individuals and to society because to need help is a sign of weakness and to provide it fosters deficiencies in charter; adversity is the means to strength and people should counter it along and unaided. Leona Tyler argues that 'Counseling is still to a large extent an art, dependent more on shared experience than on reported experiments..' and counsellors need to 'distinguish between the things we do simply because they seem to work well and things we so because of some definite research evidence'. Nevertheless counsellors can and should assess the value of what they are doing.

2. Counselling fosters conformity

This objection to helping professions is being voiced increasingly by some students, who suggest that the counsellors manipulates people for example, into taking up safe, secure occupations instead of 'doing their own thing', which seems to ignore the fact that for some people 'doing their own thing' lies in a secure occupation and conformity. It is true that counsellors encourage people to take into account the cognitive and affective aspects of a decision or problems and the likely consequences, which does to some extent encourage caution. The alternative is action by impulse, which in certain circumstances, such as immediate danger, or in response to another person's distress, may be appropriate.

3. Counselling perpetuates the myth of freedom

Those who object to the self concept theories of counselling suggest that counsellors deceive themselves by talking about freedom of choice, for in reality life is deterministic and each step affects the direction of the next one. Someone described the importance of previous experience by saying that 'as we walk into the future we come face to face with the past'. In suggesting that we have a human capacity to choose between two or more genuine alternatives we should acknowledge that the choice is always limited and freedom have been compared to a game of cards, in which the limits are imposed by the cards which you are dealt and the freedom comes in the way you choose to play those cards.

4. Counselling is not a discipline

At the present time in this country, counselling is not a discipline; it draws upon knowledge from many areas but its main subject is people, and to may knowledge there is no subject which attempts to concern itself with people in the way in which counselling does. Psychology is concerned with behaviour, not so much with the people who do the behaving, and sociology seems concerned to a large extent with people in groups and the problems which society creates for them, but not with solutions. Between psychology and sociology there seems to be a gap in our knowledge and our concern which social psychology to some extent may close, but into which counselling is a study of interpersonal relationships, their effects, their development and practice in education may grow. Much depends upon the activity of counsellors and counsellors educators and the importance that they themselves attach to the study of their subject. However, in America Brammer and Shostron suggest that 'there is an identifiable body of fairly valid techniques and progress for counseling and psychotherapy'.

5. Counsellors are inadequately educated.

The objection that counsellors are inadequately prepared for their work must inevitable in these early years have some validity. It is of vital importance to assess the needs in a particular school or college which a counselling service may realistically be expected to meet and it is essential to appoint a counsellor who is trained and capable of running the type of service needed. Of course counsellors are indequately prepared to perform as psychiatrists, as educational psychologists, as nurses, as mind readers or as magicians. Trained counsellors should be adequately educated to counsel students who may wish to talk with them about personal, educational or vocational problems, but they are not trained to solve all these problems; they should be adequately educated in the administration and interpretation of certain tests, and in their liaison work with outside social services and with school staff. Counsellors are always learning and one of the things that a few years' experience as a counsellor reveals very painfully is that the counsellor who tries to be many things to many people sometimes ends up being nothing to anybody.

6. Counselling is not universally available throughout a school

The objection that in theory counselling is available to all children or students but in practice is limited (usually because of the size of the school population and the counsellor's own temperament and preferences) is a valid one. Counselling is often regarded as a source of help for those with problems or crises, but it can have a preventive as well as a remedial function, and it is only one source of help; students and children alike will turn for help to any one of a number of people within the institution, according to their temperament and inclination. The relationship and help provided by a counsellor are not for everyone and cannot compensate in the long term for other relationships which may be inadequate.

7. Counsellors pamper people and make them dependent

The charge that counsellors pamper students often arises from those who equate understanding with softness and over-indulgence, and acceptance with the sanctioning of any kind of behavior, The understanding and acceptance offered by a counsellor are an attempt to encourage constructive ways of copying with problems rather than the negative or destructive ones which often seem to occur as a result of the blind application of moral judgements.

8. Counselling is an unwarranted invasion of privacy

'We are, I fear, getting to know one another. Reticence, secrecy, concealment of self have been transformed into social problems; once they were aspects of civility'. The right to privacy is fundamental to adults and children, and certainly pupils and students should be free to reject our concern, but in most circumstances counselling is not imposed, and therefore privacy should not be invaded without agreement. I think Rieff is right to point out the danger in the increase in over-solicitousness and I hop that counsellors may have the experience to help to balance this rather than to add to it.

Social factors in the development of post-war education

Since the end of World War II the majority of West European countries have revised their educational systems, attaching greater importance than ever before to the problems of guidance (of which counselling is a part) in schools. The introduction of comprehensive education is a development with which, in principle, I am in agreement, and I am aware that change is never made without inconvenience, even when it is a change is never made without inconvenience, even when it is a change for the better. Several years ago I worked in a school which was one of three to be reorganized and transferred to a new, purpose built, pleasant comprehensive school. The reorganization of the three schools tool place some eighteen months before the new building was completed and during this interim period the schools was housed in three separate buildings some distance apart, not an uncommon situation in reorganization schemes. The transfer to the new building was organizationally fairly competent, considering the size of the enterprise and the inexperience and lack of training of teachers in such undertakings, and the school is now well established and bursting at the seams. Yet when we consider the cost of that experience in terms of human distress we have difficulty in justifying it. Everything seemed to be considered except the people; provision was made for the timetable, the furniture, the books, the equipment, but there was no one in a sufficiently detached position to consider the situation and say, 'Look at the way these children are behaving. What are we doing to them?'. or 'This arrangement has placed these teachers under intolerable stress, what can we do to help them?' A counsellor is one of those who can be in a position to consider the 'people problems' of educational development.

> There is a significant association between the system of school authority as perceived by the class teachers, both as person and professionals. In other words, where teachers feel either that they have a hand in the internal running of the school, or that its outside directors are aware of their internal problems, they tend to be both liked by their pupils and to be seen as effective teachers. If the teachers see their superiors as remote or dictatorial, they, in their turn are seen by their pupils as unfriendly and in their turn are seen by their pupils as unfriendly and ineffective.

Awareness of the existence of this kind of situation could lead to an easing of the problem, and a counsellor is an appropriate person though not the only one to develop this awareness and to help people to cope with the resulting change in relationships.

Communication between home and school

The teacher/parent relationship is sometimes another difficult part of school life which could be made smoother with the help of a counsellor. In evidence given to the Plowden Committee on Primary Education, the Association of Educational Psychologists suggested that many teachers show defeatism in their attitudes towards parents, pleading that the parents who need to become involved in their children's education are the very ones who do not attend meetings, which of course is often the case. Schools must be encouraged, says the Association, 'to go out into their areas and ensure these contacts, without which much educational effort will be wasted'. Suitable teachers ought to be given the job of developing effective liaisons with parents and welfare, industrial and commercial interests in their areas, for 'with rare exceptions, there is a gross under-functioning of the school as a focal point for community interest and activity'.

Whilst I would not dispute this, I would like to suggest to the educational psychologists that to except a teacher to spend the day with some classes and then seek out parents in the evening is tantamount to inflicting the worst of tortures, and if they do not believe this, they are very welcome to test it empirically by doing it. I am not saying that teachers should not visit the homes of children, but I do think it is an advantage for schools to have a counsellor or social worker to provide a regular means of communication. Joan Clerk, in describing her work as a Home School Liaison officer, gives her impression of the unwillingness of some parents to visit schools: 'Parents who had never visited the school at all, one found, were very often people who were genuinely scared of teachers. They felt that teachers "looked down" at them, and however wrong this may be, that is the way that they perceived the situation.

Pressure of diffuse role expectations

Daws suggests that the teachers' professional image is one of the most demanding of all the professions, requiring, as it does, that a teacher have a knowledge of his subject and a knowledge of his pupils and that he teach both it and them well.

The increased pressure on teachers to be all things to all children, which is often self-inflicted and which, of course, is impossible, nevertheless indicates that it is becoming increasingly desirable for a teacher to have as great a knowledge of himself as he has of his subject and his pupils. This applies equally to the counsellor, but she is given the opportunity to gain self-knowledge during her training an opportunity not often presented in the course of teacher training.

Social and geographical mobility

This is not suggest that the socialization of children is solely the job of the schools. It is initially the job of the parents, and most of them succeed, but where they fail or are inadequate then teachers and counsellors can be the safety net between the potential delinquent and his determined drive to self-destruction against the bulwark of society. Bryan Wilson suggests that the creation of large housing estates, large schools and the promotion of social mobility have all weakened community allegiances, and that the important aspect of this development has been the breakdown of the nexus between home and school.

> Once the school ceases to belong to the community, parental moral training is much less reinforced by school training. As education is shorn of its moral concerns, and as teaching becomes subject to greater professional specializations, so the personal knowledge of particular children by teachers becomes less intense. As school size increases, so this context becomes increasingly impersonal. The individual child learns to look out for himself: if he acquires independence, he also learns the ropes according to the values of the peer groups and - increasingly evident-of the entertainment dominated youth culture.

This impersonal effect is also increased by the greater mobility of teachers, It is not too uncommon for a child to be taught a particular subject by two or three different teachers in one year. The reputation of teachers comes to depend increasingly on their ability to further their own interests by manipulating a fluid job situation, whereas formerly their reputation depended largely on their role in the community as respected persons.

Parental needs

Many adults are well meaning considerate of and anxious for the welfare of children, particularly their own. However, parents are exhorted on all sides by child care experts, psychologists, women's magazines, newspapers, radio and television to treat their child in this way or that way, to feed him this food or that food in order that he may develop into a strong, healthy, stable-minded adult. So much so that the child is likely to need all these assets by the time he reaches maturity in order to cope with his neurotic parents.

Some timely words of comfort for bewildered parents were give by Alexander Thomas, Associate Professor of Psychiatry at the Nes York Medical Centre, in presenting the finding of his New York longitudinal study:

1. Children have their own characteristics of individuality from early infancy onwards. Healthy child development can best be fostered by approaches that are congenial and appropriate to the child's' temperament. Most parents will have little difficulty in recognising their child's individual characteristics once they free themselves from the stereotyped view that there is only one kind of normal child and only one good way to bring up a child.

2. Any specific temperamental characteristic is in itself no guarantee either of healthy or disturbed development. Some children are easier to handle than others but the course of psychological development always depends on the specific character of the temperament-environment interaction.

3. Parents are not responsible for their child's' temperamental characteristics. A 'difficult infant' or a 'slow warmer-up' may require extra attention from the parent but can develop in as healthy a fashion as any other child. To label such children as anxious and insecure, and to blame the parents for this, as is often done by professionals in the child care field, is to stigmatise the child incorrectly and to burden the

> parent destructively with unnecessary guilt. Currently popular theories that consider behavior problems in children to arise exclusively from pathological attitudes in the parents are a source of guilt and anxiety for any parents. The fact is that many, many problems can develop in children even with mature devoted parents who have not appreciated the implications of their child's' temperament as a guide for themselves. Such parents need insight into their children's' characteristics rather than into any presumed 'unconscious' pathological attitudes within themselves.

It is possible that a counsellor may help parents to see their children differently? Not an easy task by the time adolescence is reached, but not, I think, necessarily too late for some mutual readjustment to take place, as Joan Clerk proved in her work with parents.

Need of adolescence

The need of some young people to have the opportunity to talk to someone like a counsellor was emphasized by James Hemming in his Book *Problems of Adolescent Girls* in which he made a study of the letters written to the 'problem page' of a magazine for girls. He studied 787 letters and divided the problems they contained into four main categories instancing the percentage of enquiries about each as follows:

> Friendship 36.1%; Personal 30.1%; Home 21.9%; School 11.9%.

One example from the mail letters he quotes reveals several difficulties, none of them desperately serious to the onlooker but each sufficient to case a sensitive adolescent a great deal of worry and pain.

> My mother doesn't like us to love my father and tells us things about him like him betting his wages away, really it is my mother who makes all the bothers. My life is all worries as I am not nice looking either and the boys call me skinny legs. When we were doing the Merchant of Venice I was chosen for Shylock and I learn it all and at the last somebody else was put in and I cried every night in bed and I shall never forgive her.

Hemming suggests that we seem to be taking to much for granted in assuming that adolescents will find people to give them help when they need it. He points out that there is a gap in the range of sympatric adults who can be turned to in need which formerly was filled by adult brothers and sisters, friendly aunts, uncles and grandparents when communities and families were more intimate.

> 'Lacking in their own community the support they need, adolescent girls turn to the impersonal friendliness of advice columns. We can hardly be satisfied with this state of affairs. What adolescents seek to gain through writing to a paper should be available to them in a personal relationship.'

The vagaries and ambivalencies of this stage of life are well described by Anna Freud, who says:

> Adolescent are excessively egoistic, regarding themselves as the centre of the universe and the sole objects of interest, and yet at no time in later life are they capable of so much self-sacrifice and devotion. They form the most

> passionate love-relations, only to break them off as a bruptly as they began them. On the one hand they throw themselves enthusiastically into the life of the community and on the other, they have an overpowering longing for solitude. They oscillate between blind submission to a chosen leader, and defiant rebellion against any and every authority. They are selfish and materially minded and at the same time full of lofty idealism. They are ascetic but will suddently plunge into instinctual indulgence of the most primitive character. At times their behavior to oter people is rough and inconsiderate, yet they themselves are extremely touchy. Their moods veer between light-hearted optimism and the blackest pessimism. Sometimes they will working indefatigable enthusiasm and a other times are sluggish and apathetic.

What do young people themselves feel about their own difficulties?

Here is a plea from a girl for the opportunity to talk to an adult who is willing and has the time to listen.

> '"School days are the happiest days of your life," they tell you complacently. But you're bored sick of school, you want to get out into the "big world outside", but you're scared. It would surprise a lot of adult (who seem to have forgotten their own youth) how many of the swaggering and self-confident teenagers they see around are really scared for long stretches at a time. If only we could reach out more, express our feelings and thoughts aloud. But who will

> listen? Only other teenagers, and they're in the same boat as us!'

The need for realistic expectations

Some bewildered criticism from a university student which expresses the disillusionment and demineralization that a number of them feel when it becomes obvious that their expectations of university life are a long way from reality.

> The trouble with our educational system is that you enter the upper sixth and they say you are going to go to university. They plan your life out. You don't' really know what you want to do, so they give you a choice.. a very limited choice at that.. Going to university is considered a good thing, everyone's proud of you. But I'm disillusioned. In a rut. When I went to university I thought I would get an education but all they do is to teach you a pass exams. I feel cheated!

Not all young people go on to higher education and of the majority who do not, some find jobs and others are unable to do so. A nineteen-year-old boy from Middlesborough describes his feelings about being unemployed:

> I'm on the dole, I have been out of work for four months. I want to work, I feel guilty about not working because I'd like to bring money into the home, to make life easier for my mother. When you leave school you don't think of the responsibility of being on the dole. I worry about a job for myself but I feel even worse about men with wive and families to keep.. People don't' realise how hard it is up here, they think I'm a lay about. But I do want work. I am desperate about it!

Indeed, he is desperate, for without work his identity as a man in the north-east is negated. As he says, you do not think about the responsibility when you leave school, and there have not been many people who regard it as important to help you to think about it.

Sexual needs

Coming to terms with one's own sexuality is not an easy process for many young and some not so young people, particularly in the face of the unrealistic romanticizing of the advertising media and the facade of many adults.

> 'My first experience was with an old woman, she was about twenty-five. I am not really attracted to older women, I prefer beautiful young girls and young boys... I didn't get any pleasure from it at all. I was only fifteen.'

> 'When it comes to it you're scared because they've told you, the other girls have, that it's painful. And you don't really feel anythings for the body, except as a means of getting this wonderful experience that everyone talks about.'

Ambivalence

Ambivalent feelings and attitudes are another difficult area of acceptance for all of us, but educators in particular seem to have a great dread of ambivalence and to deny its existence. It is much easier if things are either right or wrong, good or bad, yeas or no, do or don't, and people know their own minds. The failure to recognize and accept ambivalence as normal is perhaps one of the most prejudicial factors against making choices and decisions to which we can have some commitment.

'I was frightened of failure, yet very ambitious. I resented authority because I referred it, and I hated convention, partly because I had a fear of not being accepted.'

Counselling development in response to needs

The extent to which counselling is accepted and developed depends very largely on the work that counsellors themselves do to counteract the inertia of public opinion and/or the apathy of local and government authority, Perhaps the most useful contribution to the growth of counselling will ultimately be found to be the publicity that counsellors themselves give to their own work and problems, and the energy with which they emphasize those important economic, social and above all human issues for which their work is vital.

The quality of life in many of our school and colleges is sufficiently inadequate to arouse anger in the mildest of counsellors, and as people who are in everyday touch with the plan that this inadequacy creates for children, students, and staff, we could use some of that anger in a constructive enhancement of our own profession.

The provision of counselling services in education is not seen as a panancea for all or educational ills, nor does a counsellor hope to give children and students a trouble- or problem-free life, but where possible to help them to resolve their difficulties, or if that is not possible, to live with them. I believe that we should help children and young people to cope with their everyday problems, for all lives bring crises which may be unexpected-illness, a death in a family, a missing parent- and most of us at some time suffer shattered dreams and frustrating or distressing experiences. Being aware of a child's stress situations and being sensitive to the individual thresholds of stress within human beings can be a complex and subtle process which requires not a 'nosey parker' instrusion of privacy but the response of an understanding and empathic person. Teachers and tutors have an important task here in knowing when to try to decrease a child's internal burden by reducing his workload or whn to recognize that disturbed behaviour may be his way of asking for help. Pain, hardship and failure can offer valuable learning experiences, but not in the negative way in which they are often used in education.

Need for a shared approach

This does not imply that teachers or counsellors should attempt to be amateur psychiatrists or substitute parents, but that they should work together in an attempt to find educational answers to those psychological problems whicharise in the educational setting, for even when children are referred for psychiatric help they usually remain in attendance at school and have to cope with and be accommodated by the school community, except for the hour a week which they spend at the Child Guidance Clinic.

The National Association for Mental Health in its proposal to involve schools in a positive mental health approach drew atention to the potential of the school as being of central importance in preventive measures because it is a community which caters for the total population of young people, it can compel their attendance over a long period of their childhood, and it more or less has a commitment to mental health goals.

The N.A.M.H. Working Party set up to review the purposes of counselling and its development in schools offered the following opinions:

1. that schools, because they have a concern for the entire child, should take some responsibility beyond that for the intellectual and scholastic development of children;
2. that current changes in society and in the educational scene, particularly the development of large socially heterogeneous comprehensive schools and the steady postponement of the school leaving age, will create for the school and the steady postponement of the school leaving age, will create for the schools problems which will emphasize the need for teachers to be actively concerned with the childs' total personal development;
3. that, because of the needs for pastoral care and a growing awareness of them by the schools, the services of trained counsellors will be increasingly necessary as an additional resource;
4. that the schools' counselling practices will need to find more explicit emphasis on the timetable and in the activities of the school; and that more time must be devoted, both in initial training and in subsequent in-service courses, to giving teachers the skills to discharge these responsibilities;
5. that nearly all school activities, whether pedagogic, organizational or social, both these internal to the school and those related to the external community, have their influence on the personal development of the child. Furthermore we are of the opinion that ways can be found of achieving this state of affairs which will enhance the efficiency of the school in serving its traditional objectives.

The changing family: On nothing has there been so great an impact as on the family. A recent feature article in Newsweek raises the question, "Who.. is raising today's childern?" and cogently points out that parents lack time and commitment to serve as models for their children. But these are not the only family problems. The home, once regarded as the ideal setting for bringing up children, is being disrupted by divorce and separation. The institution of the family is being disrupted by divorce and separation. The institution of the family is being attacked by critics who decry its deficiencies and suggest alternative life-styles. Working parents face hectic schedules. Another *Newsweek* article concludes that "the emotional demands in a two-career family are profound."

Geographic mobility, changing housing patterns, and the establishment or retirement communities have contributed to the erosion of the extended family. Far fewer grandparents and other relatives live in the home or nearby and now baby-sitters and day centers give children the personal attention once provided by relatives.

Cities in upheaval: The plight of cities of becoming commonplace. Financial pressures are accelerating the decline of the quality of life in large urban areas.

Cities were once favourable environment for education and personal development, but social conflict, economic crises, loss of family ownership of property, street crime, and deteriorating neighborhoods have spoiled many of them. Vandalism in schools has increased, and in some areas teachers and pupils alike are assaulted by youth gangs. The inner city has been hit hardest, but crime has also been moving to the suburbs. In many regions, the stabilizing effects of work are missing; unemployment rates are high, particularly among minority youths.

Family and community life exert a reciprocal influence on each other; as the neighborhood deteriorates, the positive contribution of the family diminishes. Even though efforts are being made to rehabilitate blighted communities, many families move out, thus accelerating the negative trend.

Conflicts in values, attitudes, and morals: The unprecedented spread of therapies points to a widespread sense of life as meaningless and deep conflicts of values. Psychiatry has been called the new religion.

Much of the present unease and uncertainty began in the 60s, a decade in which traditional morals. Ethics, and values were profoundly challenged. The 70s is a period of searching for meaning and purpose, and is marked by a new media-wide openness about changing patterns of values. The cover of *Time* shows a sergeant in the Air Force saying "I'm a homosexual.." A few years ago, the topic could not have been discussed in the general press. This new frankness reveals issues that must be faced, and confronts young people with complexities once relatively known.

There are other equally striking examples. The daily newspapers carry frequent reports on the behavior of government officials that would have been called sensationalized, improbable fictions only a few years ago. Stories about cheating scandals on college campuses appear with almost monotonous regularity. Drinking has increased among the young studies reveal that one out of every four 13-year-olds is a "moderate" drinker. Cohabitation is a widely accepted life-style for many college students. Many high school students drop out because of unwanted pregnancies.

3

Guidance: Scope and Challenge

Contemporary society: Needs and trends

Surveying the faults and conflicts in society obscures many strengths and advantages and seems to put undue stress on the negative. But these are the factors that must be highlighted. There are shortcomings that demand immediate and comprehensive remedies. Guidance and counseling obviously cannot solve everything alone, but they can play a major role. Guidance workers can reach individuals who need assistance, help modify conditions that call for improvement, change institutions that are failing in their missions, and take steps to reverse destructive trends.

Problems and needs in society are nothing new, but today they seem to be proliferating at an unprecedented rate. Problems once hidden have become visible; new ones arise. All are given extensive coverage by media. No area of life is taboo. But rapid and unexpected local, national, and international changes give rise to needs and challenges qualitatively and quantitatively different from those of the past.

But traditional values have strong supporters. In the search for ways to build moral awareness, schools and professional colleges are introducing new courses in ethics. Secondary schools stressing traditional standards of discipline, dress, and manners have waiting lists. A well-known psychologist has advanced the point of view that the ethical and moral values that have evolved in human societies have a scientific basis.

The new cynicism about politics: Distrust of politicians and the political system is not new, but in the previous and current decades they have reached unprecedented intensity.

The Vietnam War threw the issue of credibility into sharp relief. In this decade Watergate, revelations about CIA and FBI intrigues, and invasions of privacy have multiplied the questions. Lurid sex episodes have surfaced about members of Congress. National government, however, has not been alone in provoking distrust. Governors, judges, and legislators have been convicted of minor and major violations of the law.

People have growth doubtful and cynical about the sincerity of the government's concerns for the welfare of the individual. Social services, education, and programs for those in need have been cut back. Moreover, the public is convinced that the government is more keenly aware of the problems and needs than at any time in the past and that ignorance is not the reason for neglect. As a result, many feel overlooked and powerless to take action in matters that deeply affect their lives.

Economic factors: Much of what constitutes the "good life" is tied to the state of the economic. Inflation erodes resources for education, travel, and improved living conditions. Unemployment and underemployment caused by economic slowdowns wreak havoc on family life, particularly for women, minority group members, and people who are just catching up in the job market.

The very economic conditions that aggravate social problems also necessitate reductions in services to those most several affected. An enormous burden rests on helping agencies and educational institutions, which must cope with long waiting lists and overcrowded classrooms.

The most destructive effects, however, are psychological-the feelings of apprehension, uselessness, and selfishness generated by depressed economic conditions. Capable people with much to offer give up looking for work. Students spoil each other's experiments to improve their own chances of getting into highly competitive medical schools. Only a few businesses and industries agree to reduce wages so that no one will laid off.

The changing role of work: Many young people are uncertain and confused by the conflicting attitudes about work. They hear that the work ethic is disappearing, that most jobs are demeaning and destructive, that technology will replace large numbers of workers, and that in many specialties a flooded market will cause unprecedented unemployment. But they also hear the unemployed asking for a chance to work, that work is the path to equality for minorities, and that you have to develop salable skills to meet the demands of a technological society.

Many young people worry about the future. Realistic and accurate occupational information is lacking and rumors of shortages and overcrowding proliferate. Career plans can change in a day. In case after case , individuals who have spent years preparing for a specific occupation suddenly realize they must find employment in an unrelated field. Many programs are restricted to avoid projected worker surpluses. Freedom of choice dwindles.

Automation and technological advances have reduced the number of low-skill entry jobs, and have also lessened the worker's pride in his share in producing a finished article. Efforts to establish new procedures to give employees more status and control have met with limited success.

New pressure and demands on school: Problems, issues, and trends in public education figure prominently in this book. They are in fact often the same as those in guidance and counseling. The most pressing are listed below; others will be covered later. The list touches on aspects of all the problems previously mentioned; school problems reflect the problems of society.

1. Writing skills and achievement in science are declining.
2. The quality of preparation of entering colleges students is declining.
3. New workers can except considerable difficulty in finding jobs.
4. There is a growing concern about pupils' moral development.
5. The rights of pupils are being violated.
6. School vandalism is costing taxpayers over half a million dollars a year.
7. Violence in schools is increasing.
8. Lack of discipline is considered a major school problem; many parents would prefer stricter schools.

9. Schools have taken over responsibility after responsibility and raised unrealistic expectations in the minds of the public.

10. Questions are raised about the value of increased funds for schools.

11. Schools do not provide an effective learning environment. As much as 95 percent of current educational practice is of questionable value.

12. Schools need to be dejuvenilized. Break down the isolation of the school subculture, treat pupils more like adults, and make the educational institution more integral a part of life.

Problems of young people: Difficulties for school-age youth and young adults are inherent in the conditions already described. But some particularly pressing ones need to be emphasized. Social and academic pressures on youth have caused increased drug use, running away from home, emotional disturbance, and suicide. Lack of involvement and commitment to meaningful work, education, and social activities leads to isolation and alienation. Difficulties in role identity arise, as typified by expressions like "I don't' know who I am"; "I've got to find myself'. Family mobility generates feelings of rootlessness and lack of community identification among the young, some of whom seek a sense of belonging in allegiance to strange or destructive cults and groups. But the end of high school, the typical teenager has watched 15,000 hours of TV, and TV is acknowledged to breed a fascination with violence and a craving for instant success.

Changing sex roles pose problems for all ages, but particularly for the young experiencing conflicts about work, sexual freedom, and family responsibilities. For example, the girl or boy who has learned the traditional sex roles with respect to careers may, because of both personal values and societal pressures, find it difficult to choose a nontraditional occupation.

The increasing average age of the population will also affect the young. More concern is being expressed for problems and needs of older Americans. Major changes in social, economic, and political policy that will touch young people include, for example, increased taxes for services. The proportionally fewer young persons will wield less influence and therefore receive, for example, less attention from consumer markets.

This is only a sampling. Other changes could be listed; and it is likely that even more pressing ones are just over the horizon.

Guidance today

A report of the contemporary status of guidance coming after a review of societies' need might seem to suggest that the profession will supply all answers. But although the guidance profession is a powerful force, its focus must necessarily be limited to appropriate high-priority targets. Trying to do everything for everybody will result in frustrations for workers, gaps in coverage, and thin or invisible effects. The following description of guidance today will help identify priorities and outline the most important factors to weight when considering the occupation and the life-style it involves.

The prospective counselor should be aware that counseling is at a crossroads. Demands of the people served and developments within the profession have led to differences of opinion about strategies, needs, roles, priorities within the population, work certification, and degree of support. Each issue is complex; all defy a brief summarization. In chapters that follow, they will be examined in depth, but at this point it is important to note a handful that have major implications for opportunities and limitations in the field. First, there is the issue of serving as an agent of change-how actively should the counselor be involved in altering customs, lows, and established patterns of society? Some want to help the individual adjust to what exists; others want to taken an active role to alter prevalent conditions, for example, current attitudes towards minority groups. Second, there is a trend towards developing large-scale programs and strategies; one-to-small-group counseling is being replaced by training and preventive activities. Third, new standards for preparation are emerging. Finally, among other issues and dilemmas, two related matters stand out-accountability and the limitation of resources. Counselors, like other educators, are being required to demonstrate the difference they make in the lives of others, even though financial support may not match needs. There is a definite trend to require services for all sorts to prove their effectiveness; support is based on evidence. Moreover, counselors will be expected to produce more without increased support or to prove that higher levels of support will result in measurable and desirable change.

Still, it is apparent that counseling and guidance are well established him public educational institutions, community agencies, colleges, and universities. An impressive number of practitioners are currently employed in public schools. In 1970-71 there were more than 40,000 counselors in more than 90 percent of the schools. This is up from a little over 2,000 in the 1930s. The mission of providing developmental and remedial help to all pupils during the critical formative years is ambitious. The profession has enjoyed a position of prestige and status in time of critical national needs; its services are sought when human resources must be developed, social conflicts eased, and destructive behavior eliminated. Relatively new on the helping scene, it has matured to the point where hundred of graduate preparation programs are offered; standards, ethics, and local guidelined have been developed; and strong national organizations have emerged with an impressive, stimulating array of professional publications.

Guidance is longest-established and most prevalent in secondary schools. At latest count, nine out of ten school counselors were working at this level development at the elementary-school level has been more recent, but expansion has been rapid. From 1967 to 1971, the number of counselors more than doubled, reaching almost 8,000 in 1971. Growth in the middle/junior high school, post high school, community, and rehabilitation settings has also been substantial.

Guidance and counseling, grades K through 12, are characterized by common major themes. Among them are concern for the total person, the importance of collaborative work, similarities in helping procedures in all settings, and emphasis on development.

The chief theme is the importance of looking at the total person, rather than fragmenting services as if each need existed independently. Help is provided for educational, career, and personal development, thus the work of the counselor extends to all aspects of school, home, and community life. Emphasis varies with grade level. Parents play a larger role during the elementary years, but increasingly counselors in all grades are extending services to include work with the pupils' whole environment and with other significant persons in their lives. Help must be more comprehensive than that provided by individual conferences; consultation, coordination, and training are being added to the direct, face-to-face assistance of counseling.

A second theme of guidance is the use of a team approach. Counselors in elementary, middle, and high schools participate with a team of teachers, social workers, psychologists, and medical personnel to provide a comprehensive help system. Even of, counselors are unique members and occupy a key position. Being school-based, they can maintaining close contact with teachers, pupils, and administrators and emphasize a truly developmental approach. The counselor is the logical person to coordinate the work of all team members.

A third theme is establishing a common core of helping approaches and rationales applicable on all educational levels. There are differences due to pupil's ages, but theoretical concepts, human relations, skills, and other helping procedures are being developed and tested to build a body of professional knowledge of use to all guidance workers. A degree of specialization is needed, but the bases of guidance at different educational levels are more alike than not.

A fourth major theme, emphasis on development, is visible in the effort to facilitate pupil development rather than concentrating on remediation, and by the trend to link services at all educational levels. It has, for example, recently been recognized that the choice of an occupation is not a single event that takes place at the end of school or college-preparatory decisions are made as early as the first years of school, and each year confronts pupils with related new decisions and tasks. The developmental view has given rise to a sequential approach to guidance. The total K-12 program is integrated rather than broken down into elementary, middle/junior, and senior high school.

In addition to these four themes, a trend toward increased work with pupils with special needs has been set off by recent state and federal legislation. The new responsibility is mostly diagnostic and could have the long-range effect of blending the roles of the school counselor and the school psychologist,

Within the fields of guidance and counseling there is an ever-increasing professionalization. Statements by guidance organizations articulate roles and responsibilities. Ethical codes are formulated and put into effect. Preparation standards are upgraded to guarantee quality services. Licensure issues have recently arisen, and guidance organizations are striving to insure that counseling is represented in the formation of school policy. Taking over the destiny of the profession is an uphill battle, but leaders are making substantial progress. Much more needs to be done, but there is no doubt that guidance has established itself as a major helping profession.

4

Techniques

Counselling

"In education our goal is guidance; our technique among others is counselling"-has been aptly said by David V. Tiedeman. Counselling is said to be the core of the entire guidance programme. It is considered to be the most intimate and vital part of the guidance programme.

Counselling is as old as society itself. In every day life, we find, counselling goes on at many levels-in a family setup, parents counsel their children, in society doctors counsel patients, lawyers clients, teachers students. In other words, there is no limit to the problems on which counselling can be offered nor to the type of persons who can render this help.

Professional counselling, in its present form, is a recent development. Colleges and universities, industries an business establishments are becoming increasingly interested in counselling and its potential for improving interpersonal relationships. It is believed, where no counsel is, the people fall; but in the multitude of counsellors, there is safety. No wonder, counselling is being recognised as an important technique of guidance here, there are everywhere!

Before we discuss the how of his technique, let us try to know what counselling is?

Counselling has been understood and defined in a number of ways:

i. Webster's dictionary defines counselling as "Consultation, mutual interchange of opinions, deliberating together."

ii. Wren says, "Counselling is a dynamic and purposeful relationship between two people who approach to mutually defined problems with mutual consideration of each other to the end that the younger or less mature, or more troubled of the two is aide to a self-determined resolution of his problem."

iii. James Michael Lee and Nathaniel J. Pattan say, "Counselling is the relationship between two persons in which one of them attempts to assist the other in so organising himself as to attain a particular form of happiness, adjustment to a life-situation, or in short, self-actualisation. Counselling always involves a one-to-one relationship, that is one client and one guidance worker in a formal or an informal interview situation."

iv. Merle M. Ohlsen writes, "Counselling is an accepting, trusting an safe relationship in which clients learn to discuss openly what worries and upsets them, to define precise behaviour goals, to acquire the essential social skills, and to develop the courage and self-confidence to implement desired new behaviours."

v. According to Arbuckle, "Counselling is helping a

person to come to see who he really is, what he has and does not have; what he can do easily, what he can do with difficulty and what he probably cannot do at all...(It) is a close sharing of a human relationship with one who has form him a high regard; one who can offer him unconditional acceptance, but own who has no guarantees, no answers."

vi. Pepinsky and Pepinsky feel, "Counselling relationship refers to the interaction which (i) occurs between two individual called "counsellor" and "client", (ii) takes place within a professional setting and (iii) is initiated and maintained as a means of facilitating changes in the behaviour of the client. The Counselling relationship develops from the interaction between two individuals, one a professionally trained worker and the other a person who seeks his services."

vii. Hahn and Maclean define "Counselling as a process which takes place in a one-to-one relationship between an individual beset by problems with which he cannot cope alone and a professional worker whose training and experience have qualified him to help others reach solutions to various types of personal difficulties."

viii. Blocker explains it as "helping an individual became aware of himself an the ways in which he is reacting to the behavioural influences of his environment. It further helps him to establish some personal meaning for this behaviour and to develop and clarify a set of goals and values for future behaviour."

An analysis of the above viewpoints will reveal the major elements of counselling.

(a) Counselling involves two individuals-one seeking help and the other, a professionally trained person who can help the first.

(b) There should be a relationship of mutual respect between the two individuals. The counsellor should be friendly and co-operative and the counsellee should have trust and confidence in the counsellor.

(c) The aim of counselling is to help a student to form a decision, make a choice or find a direction at some important fork in the road such as that of planning a life career, a programme in college or university, or a campaign to obtain employment.

(d) It helps the counsellee acquire independence and develop a sense of responsibility. It helps him explore and fully utilise his potentialities and actualise himself.

(e) It is more than advice-giving. Progress comes through the thinking that a person with a problem does for himself rather than through solutions suggested by the counsellors.

(f) It involves something more than the solution to an immediate problem. Its function is to produce changes in the individual that will enable him to extricate himself from his immediate difficulties.

(g) It concerns itself with attitudes as well as action.

(h) Emotional rather than purely intellectual attitudes are the raw material of the counselling process. Information and intellectual understanding have their place in the counselling process. But it is the emotionalized feelings which are most important.

Counselling is a generic service of student personnel work having a wide range of activities and includes faculty advising, counselling in psychological clinics, mental hygiene and other specialised types of counselling. It is a body of techniques which helps young individuals to grow up normally through guided learning.

Counselling has proved to be very useful wherever the development of an individual student is cared for. It helps an individual to know himself better, gives him confidence, encourages his self-directiveness and provides him with new vision to grow.

What counselling is not

1. Counselling is not giving information **though** information may be given.
2. Counselling is not giving advice, making suggestions and recommendations.
3. Counselling is not influencing the client's values, attitudes, beliefs, interests, decisions, etc. with r without any threat or admonition.

The main objective of counselling is to bring about a *voluntary* change in the client. for this purpose, the counsellor provides facilities to help achieve the desired change or make the suitable choice. *The client alone is responsible for the decisions or the choices he make, though that counsellor may assist in this process by his warmth and understanding relationship.*

Counselling and psychotherapy

Counselling and psychotherapy are different. Although the psychotherapist uses counselling as one of the techniques of treatment, psychotherapy is concerned mostly with individuals whose behavioures are neurotic. It deals with repressed individuals but counselling is concerned mostly with normal anxieties. Psychotherapy operates in a medical setting whereas counselling operates in an educational setting. Psychotherapist uses play therapy, psychodrama, socio-drama, etc. as techniques; in counselling, such techniques are used as can be employed in educational institutions, industrial establishments etc. Psychotechnics is deeper in scope whereas counselling is broader in scope. A counsellor cannot be a psychotherapist, a psychotherapist can be a counsellor, being better and specially qualified.

Purposes of student counselling

Dunsmoor and Miller are of the view that the core of student counselling is to help the student to help himself. From this point of view they describe the following purposes of student counselling:

1. To give the student information on matters important to success.
2. To get information about student which will be of help in solving his problems.
3. To establish a feeling of mutual understanding between student and teacher.
4. To help the student work out a plan for solving his difficulties.
5. To help the student know himself better-his interests, abilities, aptitudes and opportunities.
6. To encourage and develop special abilities and right attitudes.

7. To inspire successful endeavor toward attainment.
8. To assist the student in planning for educational and vocational choices.

It is obvious that the goal of counselling is problem clarification and self-directed needs. The counselling officer helps the student to understand the problems and helps the student to help himself. In this process, the role or the student is objective self-assessment of the situation and the role of counselling officer is to formulate the decision making process and to act as the stimulator of insights and sensitivities of the student.

Counselling does not solve the problems but helps in solving and if solution is not possible to help face challenges and to live with them.

The fact is so well brought out in Hannah's Green-book. Here, the girl bitterly accuses her psychiatrist after an unpleasant incident-what good is your reality when justice fails and dishonesty is glossed over and the ones who keep faith suffer—what good is you reality then?

The response is "..I never promised you a rose garden, I never promised you perfect justice...and I never promised you peace or happiness. My help is so that you can be free to fight for all of these things. The only reality I offer is challenge and being well is being free to accept is or not at whatever level you are capable. I never promise lies and the rose garden world of perfection is a lie and a bore too."

Scope of counselling

Counselling has a vast scope. According to Williamson, "The techniques of counselling individual students may be observed in greatly modified form, in the individualized service; granting loans and scholarships; handling discipline cases; assignment of rooms and selection of room-mates in dormitories; advising on student activities and programmes; helping students choose vocational objectives; selecting optional courses of study; learning to read at college rate and comprehension."

Concerns about educational progress, course programme planning financial and health matters, and problems of family, social and emotional adjustment are commonly expressed in the context of counselling. Very often, many of these are closely intertwined in experience of the same student. In such instances, terms such as 'vocational problem' and 'emotional problem' are nothing more than convenient labels which serve as tentative and approximate methods of classifying counseling cases. It often happens that a problem which is initially expressed by the student as simply one of learning how to study better or of making a suitable vocational choice turns out to be much more complex than that.

Levels of counselling

Counselling is a term that is used quite loosely for face-to-face interviews in which the counsellor attempts non-coercively to help the counsellee or client, or a group of clients, to make personal decisions.

It may be helpful to differentiate three levels of activity related to training:

1. *Informal counselling*: It is any helping relationship by responsible person who may have little or no training for the work. For instance, ladies helping patients in hospitals through friendly conversation with them.
2. *Non-Specialist counselling by professionals*: It is the help

provided by physicians, lawyers, teachers, ministers, and others who do a great deal of face-to-face work with psychological problems in the course of their other work. Sometimes, special titles are used like "religious counselling" or "financial counselling".

3. *Professional counselling*: It is helping another person with decision and life-plans, whether personal or educational vocational, by a person specially trained for this work. Professional counsellors are usually psychologists, or educational psychologists. 'Professional' means among other things the possession of master's or doctor's degree with at least a year of supervision by a trained professional and the acceptance of a professional code of ethics. Training for psychologists, among other things, emphasises test interpretation, research, the psychology of personality, occupational information and experience with a variety of clients.

Classification of counselling

Counselling can be classified according to the nature of the problem, the complexity of treatment, and the competence of the counsellor.

Some writers classify counselling in terms of several factors. Lloyd Jones and Smith, for example, describe various levels of counseling with respect to the depth of the problem, length of contact, degree of need, and the skill of the counsellor.

At the Surface level is the counselling offered when the student wishes only some item of information. The counselling given may be casual; it is brief, and it may be superficial inn that it is not extensive or intensive. The need for help is important even though slight, and the relationship maintained through the brief contact should not be less than that maintained during the long counselling session.

Counselling at the next level requires a more prolonged contact because the counsellee needs more and complicated information. He may, for example, wish assistance in planning a programme of study for a two or four year period. As the problems became more complicated and as more intensive study of the case is required, and more specialised help is needed, counselling at deeper levels becomes necessary.

When the student is seriously disturbed, therapeutic counselling may be needed. Williamson feels that counselling is needed not only for helping individuals to gain insight into their emotional conflicts but also for helping them with problems stemming from lack of information, such as information about vocational aptitudes and interests or about work opportunities, so that they may conduct their future adjustments in such a way, that 'minimum of maladaptive repressions' occur.

When counselling is required?

The following are some of the situations in which counselling is needed:

i. When the student needs not only reliable information but an interested interpretation of such information as meets his own personal difficulties.

ii. When the students needs a wide, sympathetic listener with border experience than his own, to whom he can recount his difficulties and from whom he may gain suggestions regarding his own proposed plan of action.

iii. When the counsellor has access to facilities for helping in the solution of a students' problem to which the student does not have easy access.

iv. When the student is unaware that he has a certain problem but of his best development, must be around to a consciousness of that problem.

v. When the student is aware of a problem and of the strain and difficulty it is causing, but is unable to define and understand it, and is unable to cope with it independently.

Who should be counselled?

The following type of students are in urgent need of counselling:

i. Students who have a consistent record of under-achievement.

ii. Students whose scholastic achievement drops suddenly.

iii. Students who need financial aid in order to continue their studies.

iv. Students who find it difficult to participate in class and extra-class activities.

v. Students who use exhibitionism for gaining recognition or attention in class.

vi. Students who find it difficult to adjust to the college/ university.

vii. Students who suddenly decide to drop out of college/ university.

viii. Students who display unusual ability in any direction intellectual, artistic, musical, etc.

ix. Students who have behaviour problems such as drug addiction, aggressiveness, bullying, stealing, shyness, timidity, etc.

Different counselling techniques

There techniques are used for counselling. These are divided on the basis of the n nature of the counselling process an the part of the counsellor.

1. Directive or Prescriptive or Counsellor-centered counselling.
2. Non-directive or Permissive of Client-centered counselling.
3. Eclectic counselling.

Directive or prescriptive or counsellor-centered counselling:

E.G. Williamson is the chief exponent of this viewpoint. Such type of counselling involves six essential steps:

— *Analysis*-Collection from a variety of sources the data needed for a adequate understanding of the student.

— *Synthesis*- Summarising and organising the data so that they reveal the students' assets, liabilities, adjustments and maladjustments.

— *Diagnosis*-Formulating conclusions regarding the nature and the cause of the problems exhibited by the student.

— *Prognosis*- Predicting the future development of the student's problems.

— *Counselling*- The counsellor's taking steps with the student to bring about adjustment and readjustment for the student.

— *Follow-up*-Helping the student with new problems or with recurrence of the original problem and determining the effectiveness of the counselling provided to him.

Here the counsellor plays the major role; he does all that he can to get the counsellee to make a decision in keeping with his diagnosis. He tired to direct the thinking of the consellee by informing, explaining, interpreting and advising.

A considerably use of interpretations and direction by the counsellor has led to this type of counselling being described as directive or counsellor-centered or active approach technique.

Non-directive or permissive or client-centered counselling

Car R. Rogers is the chief exponent of this viewpoint. In this type of counselling, it is the client-the counsellee-who is the pivot. He takes an active part in the process of therapy. He gains insight into his problem with the help of the counsellor. It is he who takes decisions as to the action to be taken. The counsellor's role is passive. This type of counselling is a growth experience. The goal is the independence and integration of the client rather than the solution of particular problem. The principal function of the counsellor is not to cultivate self-understanding in the client but instead, to create an atmosphere in which the client can work out his own understanding. The emotional elements or the feeling aspects are stressed rather than the intellectual aspects and the counselling leads to a voluntary choice of action.

In this type of counselling, we make use of few or no diagnostic instruments, except in typical situations when the individual is handicapped due to certain limitations.

Eclectic counselling

Some psychologists like Bordin believe that Rogers and Williamson are towards opposite ends of the pole and the counselling methods may be evaluated along a continuum from non-directive to directive. When a counsellor deliberately tries to incorporate in his practice both directive and non-directive techniques, the result is eclecticism. F.C. Thorne, who is the exponent of this view, finds that it is possible for a counsellor to alternate between directive and non-directive methods even in the same interview without disrupting the non-directive permissive relationship with the client.

Here, the counsellor first studies the personality and needs of the individual. He then selects the technique that would be most helpful for the individual. He can start with the directive one but when the situation demands, the counsellor may switch over to the non-directive and vice-versa. The attempt is made to adjust the techniques to the requirements of the situation and the individual. Even techniques like reassurance, merely giving information, case history, testing, etc. can be used to achieve the purpose. The counsellor must be competent and proficient in the use of all available methods. The validity of the results is determined by the skill with which any method is used with reference to etiologic diagnosis and the indications of each individual case. The critical factor is not what method is used but rater the skill with which it is used.

The process of eclectic counselling proceeds somewhat along the following lines:

i. Counselling may be preceded by an intake interview.

ii. During the opening phase of counselling, the

counsellor tries to establish rapport and may have to do structuring so that the client understands what to expect of counselling.

iii. Often a tentative diagnosis is made which may include the collection of a case history and a plan for counselling is formulated.

iv. To enhance the client's self-understanding, information, about him and his background may be gathered form various sources. The client needs to be helped to assimilate this information.

v. Educational, occupational and social information, if needed by the client, may be supplied to him.

vi. The client achieves emotional release and insights, alters his perceptions and attitudes about himself and his situations.

vii. During the closing phase, the client makes decisions and plans, modifies behaviour, solves his problems.

vii. There may be follow-up contact, if needed.

No matter what method or view-point-directive, non-directive or eclectic is employed in the practice of interviewing and counselling, counselling should have developmental preventive and remedial values.

It is obvious that counselling process is viewed differently by different approaches, But in spite of the diversity in approaches to counselling, there are common factors which are:

i. All counsellors accept the importance of ideal counselling relationship.

ii. Interview is the basic tool of counselling.

iii. The counselling relationship is built during interviews.

iv. All counsellors realise the importance of acceptance of and respect for the counsellee.

v. "Honesty", "sincerity", or "Openness" of the counsellor is another common element with all counselling approaches. How the counsellee perceives the counsellor is more important than even the skills and the knowledge of the counsellor.

Types of counselling

Counselling can be:

1. Individual, and

2. Group.

1. Individual counselling tools

Individual counselling can be done through Interviews of different types.

(a) Interview

Interview is a give and take of views between the interviewer and the interviewee. It consists of consultation, mutual interchange of opinions and deliberating together. It can be used to get information, to give information and to change behaviour. Its purpose, thus is three-fold-it involves gathering all available pertinent facts, making a diagnosis on the basis of all the evidence and formulating an appropriate plan of action.

All problems may no be settled in the interview but to be successful, it should lead to some plan of action. Its aim should be to serve the individual even though the counsellor may do no more than present the facts in a more objective light, thus enabling the student to see himself, his asses, his liabilities and his opportunities more clearly than he cult see them unaided.

The interview may be used for any of several purposes, but a purpose it must have. It may be introductory, fact finding, informative, evaluative, therapeutic in nature and its use for any of these purposes should be clearly recognised by the counselling officer and his subject.

What are some of the specific practical questions which are likely to come up for consideration during an interview? There are a great many such questions of course and they are as varied and as individually coloured as the interviewee who seeks answers them. The student who feels a need to be better informed about his scholastic and vocational prospects may want estimates of his aptitude for college work, his intellectual promise for special fields of training, his disposition to favour or avoid various spheres of activity, and his emotional adjustment tendencies. He may wish to consider with his counsellor the questions as whether he should remain in college, how much additional training he should take, what course he should take and whether he should transfer to another institution. He may decide to ask about the duties and services performed by workers in a particular occupation and about employment requirements and opportunities in that field of work. There might be some difficulties at home or harassment by other students or he might find difficulty in his a adjustment with room-mates in the hostel.

It is obvious there is no simple answer to the question 'what problems should be discussed in an interview?' Perhaps the best rule of thumb is the any personal problem that generally concerns the interviewee or any question that bears upon his personal planning ad decision making activities is a legitimate matter for interview. What is a proper counselling topic for one student may not be suitable for another. There are a number of problems of the students-academic, disciplinary, economic, educational, emotional, residential, social, etc. which necessitate the use of this tool. Here is a suggestive list of problems on which students may seek interview:

Change of subjects
Guidance at bifurcating stage
Courses where available
Courses where available
Co-curricular activities
Free studentship, fee concessions, etc.
Unfair means case
Difficulties at home
Harassment by other students
Misunderstanding with some teachers
Love affair
Prospects after completion of studies
Living in the hostels
How to study?
How to prepare for examinations?

The fact that a student comes to a teacher occasions a meeting and may result into an interview. for some problems , interview may have to be arranged and the interviewee may have to the called for, as stated earlier, under the heading 'Who should be counselled?'

Types of interviews

Introductory interview

The first interview with a subject should be designed for the purpose of getting mutually acquainted and building rapport, so that follow-up conference and procedures sill be welcomed and appreciated. The counsellor may introduce himself, state the purpose of the interview and advise the subject about the procedures that will be used later. The short ten-to-fifteen minute introductory interview may end with an invitation to the subject to drop in at any time, with making a second appointment, with informing him about the time of the next conference, or with setting the data of the first administration of tests or of any other procedures that are to follow.

Expending of whatever time is necessary to establish happy relationship in this introductory interview, is justified. In the part of the counsellee, it involves developing a feeling of ease, born of growing confidence in the counsellors' competence, interest, knowledge, and skill, and a feeling of freedom to reveal both facts and emotions. On the part of the counsellor, it entails treating the student as a responsible adult, being considerate of all attitudes and feelings.

The introductory interview should be held very soon after the students enters the college. If the first interview is delayed until the student runs into difficulty, fails in some subjects, breaks a rule, has trouble with other students or, the like, the counselling officer may not find it easy or possible to establish good relations with the students.

The counselling officer should make notes about this introductory interview after the subject has left the conference room. It is not advisable to take or recommend any action on the basis of data obtained in the introductory interview, as there will usually be little information to justify action.

Fact-finding interviews

These interviews may be designed to discover the intensity of a counsellee's attitudes towards persons and situations which he cannot or will not reveal in writing or in response to formalised questions which do not allow for indication of strong feelings. Thus interview may reveal interests that had no previously been noted, and it may allow the counsellor to determine their strength and their source. It can be used to obtain information concerning relationships with other persons and about activities that are carried out with them.

Informative interview

A counsellee may be interviews for the purpose of informing him about data that have been obtained form other sources, for providing information to answer question that he has raised or of passing on some decision that has been made about him by a person in a position of authority. The counselling officer may also inform a student about such matters as his performance in tests and their interpretation; the acceptance or rejection f an application for a position or for permission to a change in courses, the decision of the principal/head of the department concerning his success in an examination.

Many educational-vocational problems of the students are solved by acquisition of new and accurate information about themselves and the world of work or by discovering a different orientation to information which they already possess.

Therapeutic interviews

Interview may be used for therapeutic purposes. All of us like to discuss our problems, dreams and aspirations with others in whom we have confidence ad with whom we have rapport. Interview gives a chance to the counsellee to talk about himself, his past, his wishes and fears, his hopes and aspirations. The process of talking things over bring new clarity of thought, relief from over-tension, and a new objectivity. We can know a lot from what the counsellee says, from how he behaves in the interview situation, by noting what the student is not inclined to talk about, what he speaks of with the most satisfaction and the most distress, what are the topics which when mentioned cause him the most embarrassment or inhibition. In other words, it often happens that how a thing is said, seems just as important as what is said and it is only in the interview that this aspect of the counsellee's revelations can be appraised. When through interview the counsellee is permitted to "think aloud" in the presence of a sympathetic listener, it can give a clue to a number of problems of the counsellee.

Interview procedure

1. Preparation

Interviewing is an art that requires careful planning and preparation for satisfactory performance and good results. Before the interview, the counselling officer needs to work out the entire interview procedure. He needs to be sure as to how is the going to initiate it, what responses are possible to his opening statement, which one of these responses does he want, how he can eliminate the unwanted responses and achieve definite objective.

The following hints can prove useful:

i. Decide what is to be a accomplished:

The interviewer knows the problem, when the interviewee comes for the interview, he has his own expectations and objectives. It is, therefore, important for the interviewer to be clear about what is to be accomplished. It will be desirable to write them down.

ii. Know the interviewee:

It is necessary to know the interviewee before he comes for the interview. This could be done from college records, test records, cumulative records, activity reports, from his friends and, if necessary, form his parents/ guardians, etc. This will help in two-ways-in giving a good start to the interviewer and in establishing rapport and in solving the problem. Such data can furnish a framework within which the students' problem can be advantageously surveyed.

iii. Make appointments:

When appointments are made, both the interviewer and the interviewee are prepared. It saves time.

iv. Provide for privacy:

Privacy is an essentials condition of interviewing. It is necessary that the student is in a proper frame of mind induced by privacy and respect for the counseling officer's competence. Interruptions during the course of the interview should not be there.

v. Practice taking the interviewee's point of view:

The interviewer must learn to step in the shoes of the interviewee. He must be able to see the interviewee's point of view, how he looks at the problem, how he reacts to the interviewing.

vi. Know your own personality:

The interviewer needs to be objective. He must be able to introspect, overcome or at least control his opinions, convictions, attitudes, preconceptions, prejudices, notions, etc.

The process

i. Establish rapport:

The interviewer should make all out efforts for establishing rapport relationship of confidence, trust and mutual appreciation which helps the counsellee to express himself without inhibitions and resistance. Building of this relationships helped by the atmosphere of the counselling officer's room, his attitude and the initial reception he gives to the counsellee. The room should be attractive and pleasing. The general atmosphere should convey an impression of friendliness and informality. By rising to meet the student as an expected guest, the interviewer may give an impression that he is welcome. By giving him full attention and avoiding a preoccupied manner, he can give to the student the impression that the conference is the most important thing he could be doing at the moment.

ii. Help the interviewee feel at ease and ready to talk:

The interviewer should being with topics which are easy to talk about and thus warm up the interviewee. After getting on the main topic, the counselling officer should make the interviewee talk freely. It is essential that the interviewee feels free to express his own ideas unhampered by the ideals, values and preconceptions of the interviewer.

He should give advice only sparingly. Even when

advice is sought, it would be better to avoid assuming responsibility for the decision which rightly should rest on the student himself.

iii. At the close of the interview, watch for additional information or new leads in the casual remarks of the interviewee:

The interviewer should be alert to catch the change of expressions which may drop after the interview has ended when the tension has been released and he is off guard, he may say things which he may have wanted to say earlier but which seemed to him irrelevant or too trivial to mention. The interviewer must always remember that the interview has not yet closed even when he has asked all his questions.

3. Interpretation

What the interviewee says is often a mixture of facts, his view of the situation as he sees it, and his feelings. Unless the interviewer has information from other sources, he is often unable to distinguish between fact and fiction. There is another difficulty arising out of the interviewer himself-his tendency to project his ideas and attitudes upon the interviewee. Without interpretation the counsellee may remain on a superficial level of self-understanding. The interpretation to students of the varied aspects of their emotional life is essential and it requires great skill and understanding.

4. Developing insights and putting them to work

The process of clarifying and gaining insight naturally leads to the making of decisions and the planning of courses of action. The successful interviewer is resourceful in making the counsellee reach his decisions and put them into practice.

5. Recording

There should be an efficient system of recording and maintaining the interview notes. If a complete record is desired, it may ;be necessary to keep a taper-recorder in the room. In cases, where good rapport has been established, the necessary notes can be taken without disturbing the subject.

In general, however, the interview will proceed better if no notes are taken. A summary must, however, be written, immediately after the interview, to make sure nothing of importance is forgotten.

Limitations

i. The validity of data obtained from interviews is always suspect because the results are contained in judgments made by one person.

ii. The validity and reliability ;of this technique varies with how well and skillfully the interview has been structured and who is conducting it.

iii. Interviewer's bias is another limitation of this technique. Researchers have pointed out the fact that the interviewers report a particular phenomenon according to their own interpretations, understandings, beliefs and attitudes. The validity studies of interviews have revealed very low statistical measures of validity when interview predictions have been compared n the principle of learning. The most important contribution to behavioural counselling has been made by. Pavlov, Skinner, Wolpe and John D. Kumhboltz who believed that neurotic behaviour is acquired and is subject to the established laws of learning.

Goal

The goal of behavioural counselling is to change particular behaviour efficiently and specifically.

The Counselling Process

Blackhom and Silverman have suggested the following steps of behavioural counselling:

i *Problem definition*: The counsellor should specifically define the problem-all the circumstances regarding the inappropriate behavivour should be identified.

ii Development and socials history of the problem should be prepared.

iii. *Specification of the Counselling goals*: The client and the counsellor should come to an agreement as to what the problem actually is. It is the counsellor's responsibility to decide if the goal is within his realm of expertise and in accordance with ethical behaviour.

iv *Selection of methods*: The techniques used in the counselling, consistent with the client's goals, need to be selected.

Techniques of behavioural counselling

Behaviourists use a variety of techniques to build new habits:

i. *Operant conditioning*: It is based on the idea that a person will learn to behave in a different way if the new behaviour is rewarded and the old behaviour is ignored.

ii. *Aversive conditioning*: It is technique for eliminating specific behaviour patterns. The therapist teaches the person to associate pain and discomfort with the response he wants to unlearn. This form of behaviour therapy has been used successfully to treat alcoholism, homosexuality, obesity and smoking. Dent treated alcoholics by giving them a drug that produces extreme nausea when mixed with alcohol in the stomach. The people were encouraged, infact, instructed to drink, and each time they did they became violently sick. Gradually they began to feel sick everytime they. even saw a bottle of whisky.

Desensitization- It is another technique for reducing irrational behaviour. In this technique if a client has described several anxiety producing situations, those situations are ranked from the lowest to the highest in terms of disturbance. The client is instructed in relaxation technique. When this is accomplished each anxious situation is presented starting with the one that produces the least anxiety. As the situation is recalled by the client he is reinforced by the relaxation process until there is no anxiety. Behaviourists have used desensitization to cure phobias about snakes, heights, closed rooms and sex.

Reciprocal Inhibition - There are individuals who feel anxious and unhappy most of the time. Wolpe feels behaviourists can treat diffused anxiety. Here the therapist establishes a hierarchy, from the least to the most anxiety, provoking situations. Next he teachers the client to clear his mind, release tense muscles and relax. In some cases, he may use drugs or mild hypnosis to produce relaxation. Once the client has mastered the technique of deep relaxation, they begin at the bottom of his anxiety hierarchy. The therapist asks the person to imagine the least threatening scene and to signals when he begins to feel tense. At the signal, the therapist tells him to forget the scene and concentrate on relaxing. After a short period, he instructs him to return to the scene. This process is repeated until the person feels completely relaxed. Gradually they move up the list until the client is able to imagine the situation he most learn to inhibit anxiety responses with incompatible, deep muscle relaxation.

It is obvious that the success of behavioural counselling depends upon the following:

i. establishing a valid hierarchy by ;the client and the therapist;

ii. discovering and adequate reinforcer (cooperant conditioning) by the therapist; and

iii. lack of counter conditioning outside the therapy sessions.

Some psychologists are critical of behavioural counselling. They feel that by concentrating only on behaviour, it presents an over-simplified version of human psychology. These psychologists feel that an individual's mental behaviour is just as important in therapy as his overt behaviour.

It is also felt that the behavioural counselling is symptom oriented. Effort is made to smother the neurotic symptoms, no effort is made to remove the conflict that caused them. There is always a danger of the client relapsing intuit to be educated about invite each student for an individual counselling interview, particularly so in case of freshmen, as TDC I year and MA/MSc First year students, who besides their educational and vocational problems, have their peculiar problems of personal and social adjustment as they are passing through the difficult and social adjustment as they are passing through the difficult phase of adolescence. What technique of counselling-directive or non-directive or a combination of both-would be suitable under our cultural set-up is a point that deserves careful consideration at the hands of counselling officers.

Group guidance

Group guidance is an important part of the guidance programme. It is true that the most important objectives in the guidance process are to help the individual achieve selfdirection, self-knowledge and self-realisation-these objectives cannot be achieved in a cultural vacuum. Many important experiences must take place in a group setting, since it is the only way they can be learned realistically.

Group guidance is that relationship in which a guidance worker attempts to assist a number of students to attain for themselves satisfactory development or adjustment to their respective individual or collective life situations. It occurs in a setting in which one or more guidance workers encounter students as a group.

Group are best suited for discussing educational and vocational plans, problems relating to adjustment to college and social situations, problems relating to choice of options and choosing a career, economic and occupational problems, personality adjustment problems, etc.

A number of techniques can be used for imparting group guidance:

i. *Informal Discussions* - Informal discussions, if done under the able and skillful leaders, can prove very helpful. These discussions should centre around desirable objectives and should be so guided as to result in conclusions that may be helpful to he group as whole.

ii. *Group Reports*- If the students are divided into groups which have certain specific problems to tackle and later these reports are presented in larger groups. They can help all the members of the group in gaining awareness of a number of problems and their solution.

iii. *Lectures* - Lectures delivered by experts on certain problems too can impart group guidance in an effective way.

iv. *Dramatics* This is another good techniqued of group guidance. If certain interesting topics are dramatised, the students can be given guidance in an interesting way. How to appear for an interview, how to prepare for an examination, how to prepare notes-all these can be dramatised land guidelines suggested to the students in an interesting way.

v. *Question box* - "Question - box" says Jones, "If carefully organised and not too frequently used, is also a desirable technique, for it gives the shy and retiring pupil and opportunity to propose a question that is bothering him without revealing that it is his question". Most of the times, we find the shy student remains buried with his problems as he is not vocal. It is also possible that there are quite a few students having the same problem. So if the question could be proposed in a silent way, the same could be discussed in a group and valuable guidance provided to the students.

vi. *The case conference*- Here the problem faced by the majority of the group is stated concretely by way of a case. Each member of the group reviews his own experience in a similar situation. The group is guided away from the more immediate and temporary advantages to be gained toward more remote and temporary values. Then the effect of the exceptions may be discussed. Some other conditions that should be considered in deciding a plan of action are also gone through. Some generalisations are also formulated which may prove helpful another situations. According to Jones, the entire process of the case conference is an experience in social thinking and it has positive and unique values in the group guidance program.

Kinds of groups for group guidance

various types of groups may be utilised for group guidance like;

i. Regular subject classes

ii. Special Groups organised for the consideration of special topics

iii Tutorial groups

iv. Advises under a particular adviser

v. Conferences such as career and educational conferences

vi. Clubs or other groups organised around some common interest

vii. Students with common adjustment problem and use all pertinent tools and techniques in its solution.

5

Theoretical Approaches to Counselling

Counselling is in many way a synthesis of approaches from related movements such as social casework, psychometrics, clinical psychology, and psychotherapy. Although human difficulties appear to lie in specific areas, for example vocational, personal or marital difficulties, it is people who need help. Consequently the person, not the problem, is the maintain focus of the counselling process. This applies even when the counsellor is using a behavioural approach, which is specifically problem centered.

To work effectively to help a person it is important that the counsellor should analyse what is happening in the counselling sessions. The theories upon which her approach to counselling are based offer the conceptual tools and provide a frame work for this thinking. Although theories provide a framework, this does not imply that they are rigid and inflexible; they are working assumptions which offer provisional ways of analysing and organizing evidence in a search for something better.

Theory helps to explain, predict, evaluate and improve what happens in the counselling relationship and to answer questions such as 'What is happening now?' 'What accounts for this?' Using her particular theoretical orientation with its underlying philosophical implications, each counsellor attempts to answer these questions with her own unique yet limited perception. Work on a satisfactory general theory of counselling is being done by Egan and by Carkhuff in his work on helping through human relationships.

Theories of counselling are drawn from a number of schools or approaches and although they differ in emphases, they all acknowledge acceptance, rapport, the need for support, some limits and the professional status of the counsellor.

It is possible to trace two historical bases for counselling theory, one depending on psychoanalytic principles and emphasizing the emotional 'feeling' aspects of personality, and the other on learning theory, concentrating on re-learning some adaptive ways of behaviour in response to the demands of life. Some writers such as Barclay trace learning theory back to psychoanalytic thinking.

Psychotherapy and counselling

It has been suggested that there are three elements which are either explicit or implied in all systems of psychotherapy or counselling: a theory of personality, a social philosophy concerning the relationship of individuals to society and a body of therapeutic skills which influence behaviour.

American writers vary in their approach to the problem of delineating the differences between counselling and psychotherapy. Some suggest that they are viewed as overlapping areas of professional competence, counselling being characteristically short term, educational, supportive, situational, problem-solving, with emphasis on conscious awareness and normal people, while psychotherapy is long term, supportive and reconstructive; it has a focus on the unconscious, and an emphasis on 'neurotics' or other severe emotional problems. The scope of both counselling and psychotherapy and be subsumed under the framework of therapeutic psychology, and the distinctions between them often seem to be quantitative as opposed to qualitative.

In the area of personal problems counselling and psychotherapy are most nearly synonymous.

> What is most likely to trigger the request for a counseling appointment is unhappiness or dissatisfaction with the course one's life is taking. Thee may be problems in relationships to other people. There may be feelings of boredom and general meaninglessness. There is likely to be anxiety, along with vague or well-defined fears about the soundness of one's own personality. The treatment given to persons in such states of mind has frequently been labelled psychotherapy: it is in such cases that therapy and counseling are indistinguishable. Most of he controversy that has arisen..over whether there is or is not such a distinction can be resolved if we think in terms of what a counselor is eligible to do.
>
> What a counselor should be equipped with, if he is to serve clients of this sort well, is some tools that will enable him to make visible in its main

> outlines the present patterns of a person's life and the possibilities this pattern provides for future development. Whether members of the professions giving such assistance decide to label such tools 'counseling; or 'therapy' is not really a very important matter.

The theoretical orientation of the counsellor may well have some influence on whether she calls her work counselling or psychotherapy. Some people working in student counselling base their approach on an analytically oriented theory, and frequently refer to their work in the Student Counselling Service as psychotherapy.

A thought-provoking comment suggests that

> It may be, however, that we no longer need to worry about what counseling is, or what psychotherapy is, or if and how they differ. There has been increasingly recognition that counseling or psychotherapy is not enough. It will not solve all our social problems. It is not applicable to many people, at least as presently practised or, more accurately, in the hands of our present practitioners.

There are several personality theories which have useful implications for counselling.

1. Psychoanalytic theory.
2. Self theory.
3. Trait theory.
4. Field theory.
5. Behaviouristic learning theory.

Not all these are applicable to the present approaches to counselling in this country, but 4 they are worth a mention, since no theory has been found as yet to explain completely the process of counselling. Some of the main points of each theory are suggested below.

Psychoanalytic theory

The 'talking cure', first used extensively by Freud, forms the basis of the counselling relationship for all the approaches, although they vary in the way in which they use it.

The psychoanalytic concepts of levels of awareness are significant for the 'dynamic' approaches to counselling, though not for the behaviourist or learning theory approaches which place no value on the concept of 'depth' of the unconscious. Both use the conscious level of awareness consisting of those ideas of which the person is at present aware, and both utilize the preconscious ideas which, although not in the individual's present awareness, can be recalled. Although Freud regarded the unconscious level of awareness as having a powerful influence on behvaviour, the behaviourists prefer to think that the explanations of and solutions to human problems are to be found within the perceptual capabilities of the individual without recourse to the depths of personality.

The Neo-Freudian theorists, Adler, Horney, From and Harry Stack Sullivan in American have moved away from traditional Freudian theory in so far as it postulates a personality based on a biological drive concept, mainly sexual in nature, the satisfaction of which is the goal to which all behaviour is directed. For the Neo-Freudians personality is a social product 'processing needs which arise as much from the individual's society as from his biology'. Whilst the American approach is sociological in the sense of approaching human problems and conflicts as social ones, European practice seems to have retained the biological individual approach: 'in Europe.. the approach is not only predominantly biological, but, under the influence of Melanie Klein and others, increasingly so'. The scientist's social background and his culture influence psychological theories but although the American approach is having an increasingly active influence on European psychology, the interest is selective rather than complete.

For example, Britain has been interested in behaviourist theory but accepted it from Pavlov rather than from Watson; the Neo-Freudians Horney and From have proved to be almost scientific best-sellers here-but were read by the intelligent layman rather than the analyst or psychiatrist.

The American approach to counselling in education may be added to this list of increasingly active interests from across the Atlantic, for 'the general acceptability of a scientific theory is not wholly dependent upon its validity as a science, because history shows that its relevance to the contemporary situation and the degree to which it conforms to the contemporary approach are equally important. In a world which increasingly sees all human problems as social problems, psychoanalysis as a method of treatment may well fall into desuetude, not because it does not work, but simply because it is inapplicable to the problems of the day'.

The use of a modern analytical approach to counselling in England is well described by Ellen Noonan in a recent book on different counselling styles.

Self theory

Self theories are much newer in counselling and psychotherapy than analytic theories. Carl Rogers is credited with having collected the most systematic assumptions and constructs on self theory and is recognized for his application of the theory to counselling ad psychotherapy in his client-centered or non-directive therapy, recently re-named experimental therapy. This is one of the main theories taught in the departments of counsellor education in American universities and it is one of the main approaches to counselling in American schools. It also has a strong emphasis in several such courses in English universities, although it is only one of the theories which are studied. It seems particularly appropriate for counselling in education because it was initially developed whilst Rogers, a psychologist, was Director of the Child Guidance Clinic at Rochester, Psychologist, was Director of the Child Guidance Clinic at Rochester, in New York State. He observed that certain administrative structures and policies in schools and colleges prevent maladjustment, while others contribute to it. It is important to know how to prevent maladjustment in school sand homes, in addition to knowing how to treat it. Rogers stressed the need for more concern with the teaching of reading to prevent the costly effects of reading disability, as well as emphasizing the psychological, social and economic loss which results from wrong vocational choices, and the consequent need for education about vocations and course choice.

Client-centered counselling derives from its time and its cultural setting, but Rogers acknowledges its debt to the appreciation of unconscious striving and the complex emotional nature of man contributed by Freud; to the therapy of Otto Rank; to the scientific method of psychology, which submits all hypotheses to a process of objective verification or disproof; and to Gestalt psychology for its relationship of the cluster, or various phenomena which make up the individual, to the whole. Rogers suggests that this approach is rooted in the educational, social and political philosophy of American culture, though he does believe that behaviour in the counselling relationship transcends to some extent the limitations of influences of a specific culture. To this list, Barclay adds the antecedents of liberal Christian theology, existentialism and phenomenology.

Carl Rogers is in some ways the Martin Luther of psychotherapy, not philosophically or temperamentally, but in the sense that he has challenged the dogma and extended the scope of participation in the work to make it available to a much wider range of people. Counselling is not the appropriate approach to the problems of all children or all parents, but it is one significant method of dealing with adjustment problems.

Adjustment begs the question 'adjustment to what?' but used in the context of self-theory is signified a person who is acting in accord with his self-concept, which is learned progressively form birth. When a person's awareness and experience are closely matched his behaviour may be described as congruent. Where there is incongruence between a person's awareness and his experience, if he is aware of trying to communicate a feeling of love but experiences hostility his communication is defensively distorted. The implication for counselling is that the communications of both counsellor and client should aim at a state of congruence.

A further assumption of client-centered counselling is that the individual's reality is that which he perceives, and external events are only significant in so far as the person experiences them as meaningful. Thus the counsellor must try to work from the client's 'internal frame of reference' if she is to accept his feelings and attitudes.

The most significant therapeutic element in this view of counselling is the emotional quality of the relationship. Information, diagnosis, historical understanding are all secondary to the climate created by the counsellor through her sincerity, warmth, acceptance and sensitive empathic understanding. The client is believed to have the capacity and motivation to solve his own problems and it is suggested that these will emerge in the freedom and safety of the counselling relationship.

Although Roger's early work was with children, adolescents and families he later moved from the Child Guidance field into the academic world, constantly researching the results of his counselling and revising his theory. Since then the scope of client-centered work has extended into hospitals and Rogers's present position is probably to be found in this comment on schizophrenia.

> What does the word schizophrenic mean to me? To the extent that it has any definite meaning at all, it means that there is a person who is highly sensitive to his own inner experience and also to interpersonal relationships with others, who has been so defeated and traumatised in endeavouring to make use of his sensitivities that he has retreated both from his own experiencing ad from any real contact with others. In addition to his fairly basic understanding, the work

> schizophrenic also means to me that anyone whose behaviour is deviant and who cannot easily be understood is tossed in this all encompassing basket. Subsequently Rogers concentrated his attention on encounter group work and then on relationships between couples. His latest work, Carl Rogers on Personal Power, focuses on the power residing in individuals rather than in traditional areas and the effect that people who are aware of their own power can have politically, in systems, institutions and societies.

Trait theory

The trait and factor theorists see personality as a collection of interdependent factors, abilities, attitudes, interests and values an temperament together with social traits. This approaches mainly used by counsellors working with educational and vocational problems, in which some prediction of success in school or job is of value, rather than by the therapeutic counsellor concerned more with feelings which have become debilitating. It is in this theory that the influence of psychometrics on counselling is greatest.

Williamson regards it as equally unfortunate to underemphasize the rational aspects of the counselling situation as it is to understress the emotional, for he believes that counselling should help people to learn to think logically and constructively about themselves, their relationships and their situation. He is an exponent of the directive counselling approach, which because of its emphasis on learning, the collection of information, diagnosis, prognosis, counselling and follow-up within a caring relationship, and his view that counselling follow-up within a caring relationship, and his view that counselling and discipline are not incompatible seems to offer a way of counseling appropriate to the dual role or teacher/ counsellor, which other approaches do not offer so readily.

Cattell's factorial work on the organization of personality, and Allport's psychology of the individual have both contributed to this approach to counselling; indeed it is perhaps more appropriate term this an approach to counselling rather than a theory of personality.

Field theory

Any theory of personality wide enough to encompass the vital aspects of man's behaviour was recognized by Kurt Lewin as one which would be multidimensional. Field theory revived the concept of man as a complex energy field, a set of forces operating in conjunction with an environment which is also a set of forces. Lewin's work on group dynamics, social conflicts and re-education has particular relevance for counselling.

Gestalt psychology, another approach to field theory, has made two main contributions to counselling theory through Gestalt therapy which applied the principles of Gestalt psychology to psychotherapy. One contribution is the principle of the organization of perception and the other is the 'phenomenon of insightful learning'.

The implications of these principles are that a person in a dis-organized state will organize his perceptions as completely as possible to reduce the tension. Behaviour is construed as a primary function of the person's present perceptions and it is therefore important first to understand a person in terms of his own unique perception or his phenomenological field, not in terms of his past history, as in the psychoanalytic approach, nor in terms of past learning, as in the behavioural approach.

Insightful learning is achieved in counselling by a 'reconstructing of the field', or a review of past experiences with a loosing of the rigidity of former thinking through re-experiencing past or present feelings and ideas, so that over a period of time the reorganization and freeing of perception which results in insight may take place. This is important for the self-theorists and the psychoanalytic orientation which lean heavily on insight. In Counselling Shop, Gaie Houston gives an indigenous view of Gestalt therapy.

Behaviouristic learning theory

The learning theorist is characterized by his assumption that most human behaviour is learned and can be modified. The stimulus response model is an important explanation of behaviour, and this approach is sometimes known as the stimulus-response theory of personality. Stated simply, in order to learn, a person must want something, notice something, do something and get something. It is the reward which acts as the reinforcement, so that the S-R pattern tends to be repeated under similar circumstances. A response which is not repeated and rewarded or reinforced from time to time tends to disappear, or be extinguished. Substituting one stimulus for another to get the same response is known as reconditioning or, when used in therapeutic terms, re-education.

This emphasis on how behaviour was acquired and how it can be changed offers a way of helping students with some practical difficulties, such as study problems. Whilst some students cannot study because other things worry them, there are students who cannot study well because in the past they learned to study badly.

Krumboltz is another theorist who sees behavioural counselling as the application of learning theory to counselling. He defines counselling somewhat broadly as 'whatever ethical activities a counselor undertakes in an effort to help the client engage in those types of behaviours which will lead to a resolution of the client's problems'.

Krumboltz considers that the goals of behavioural counselling can be achieved by the use of several approaches including the operant learning process, the use of imitative learning, classical conditioning and emotional and cognitive learning. He views the counsellor as an active helper in the learning process working towards specific and precise kinds of behaviour change through the use of techniques and procedures which are experimentally tested to determine their usefulness. The goals of counselling must be defined in terms of specific behaviour so that these behaviours may be recognized and reinforced when they occur. The counsellor is seen as one who arranges conditions so that the student may learn more adaptive ways of coping with his difficulties within the setting of a warn, friendly and secure counselling relationship.

Michael and Myerson relate the experimental analysis of behaviour to counselling an suggest that the phenomenon with which counsellors deal is behaviour and that the independent variable which controls that behaviour is the environment. They accept that behaviour derives from the interaction of hereditary and environmental variables, but point out that a behavioural approach attempts to specify those conditions and process by which the environment controls human behaviour. The example of students who discontinue their studies is used to illustrate that by their behaviour such students are showing that they are not being 'reinforced' by those influences which keep other students at college, or that the educational reinforcement they are receiving is weaker than reinforcement coming from other sources. In such a case, it is the job of the counsellor to discover what reinforces student 'drop-outs' and to make these reinforcements contingent upon learning. They make he provocative claim that 'Under appropriate environmental conditions, which man can create, almost anyone can be motivated to do anything'.

It is perhaps unfortunate that the vocabulary of behavioural theorists often appears to be so technical, and so removed from the experience which most of us have of human interaction. The behavioural approach has much to offer to guidance ad counselling.

Behaviour therapy as evolved in this country in opposition to psychotherapy. Hans Eysenck, Head of the Department of Psychology of the Institute of Psychiatry, London University, has written critically of the ineffectiveness of psychotherapy and has claimed successful outcomes for behaviour therapy.

Current approaches

New ways of helping people in difficulty have recently been developed in America. They are not new theories of personality and tend to be derivatives of some of the older approaches. However, there is no longer just a triadic conflict of psychoanalytic versus client-centered, versus behaviour therapy, but a series of new developments which have arisen in part because of a disaffection with existing methods and in part as a result of renewed efforts to provide help for the poor and the disadvantaged. role playing, psychodrama, sociotherapy and reality therapy-which seems to have been particularly effective amongst delinquents and in schools-are some of these newer approaches. There has been a change, too, in the range of people offering this therapeutic help. Whereas formerly the therapeutic role was held primarily by the psychiatrist, therapist, psychologist, counsellor or social worker, an increasing number of lay therapists or 'paraprofessionals' are working in hospitals, schools and in the local communities with heartening success: 'this burgeoning of new practitioners has presumably terminated the search for the "one" most effective way of helping troubled people'.

It is now possible to find an introduction to the theories and techniques of ten of the styles of counselling currently in use in this country in one volume. Brigid proctor's book Counselling Shop contains the comments of then practitioners working in England, each of whom represents a different approach to counselling. I think it will be helpful to note these in the detail.

Psychoanalytic/object relations	Ellen Noonan
Rogerian counselling	Pat Milner
Behavioural counselling	Dougal Mackay
Developmental counselling	Francesca Inskip
Transactional analysis	Michael Reddy
Gestalt therapy	Gaie Houston
Reality therapy	David Wilmot
Social functioning	Eugene Heimler
co-counselling	John Heron
A radical respective	Tom Osborn

Below is a brief routine of three of the newer American approaches which may be quite helpful in educational settings.

Developmental counselling

Developmental counselling is an approach which aims to change behaviour in order to facilitate human development and is based on the assumption that students are capable of choosing the desired direction of their own development. Blocher has suggested a number of basic assumptions about the nature of developmental counselling which are summarized as follows:

1. Students are not considered to be 'mentally ill', but capable of choosing goals, making decisions and generally assuming responsibility for their own behaviour and future development.

2. Developmental counselling is focused on the present and the future and is primarily concerned with where the client is going not where he has been.

3. The student is a client, not a patient. The counsellor is not an authority figure, she is a partner of the student as they move toward mutually defined goals.

4. The counsellor is not morally neutral or amoral, but has values, feelings ad standards of her own. She does not necessarily impose these on students, nor does she attempt to hide them.

5. The counsellor focuses on changing behaviour not merely creating insight. She is a helping person, a teacher, a consultant and a confidante as these functions are seen to be appropriate in meeting mutually defined goals.

Developmental counselling is educational and is based on the assumption that human personality develops in terms of a mainly healthy interaction between the growing person and the environment. It aims to maximize human freedom, whilst recognizing that such freedom is sometimes severely limited by reality, and that few people are prepared to exercise the freedom which they do have. It also aims to maximize human effectiveness and suggests that the effective human being strives for control over those aspects of his environment which he can manipulate and also for control over his effective responses to those aspects of his environment which he cannot change.

Blocher admits that the psychology of human effectiveness is a relatively neglected area and acknowledges that psychology knows little about the behaviours which thousands of people employ to lead satisfying and effective lives. Despite the poverty of knowledge about human effectiveness, this approach to counselling may have particular appeal to counsellors working in educational settings.

Leona Tyler points out that the dominant personality theories of our time have grown out of the intensive study of abnormal individuals. Analytic theories offer useful conceptual tools to consider what is wrong with a student and how it might be set right, but not consider what this person might do. Learning theories are useful when there is an identifiable behaviour which needs to be changed, but are perhaps not as helpful to the student who is not seeking obvious change so much as to plan his future. The increasingly popular counselling characteristic of promoting full potential ignores the closed so that a few may be actualized. None of us use our full potential and such an objective is in many way illusory.

Developmental counsellors may also help those who are not troubled by confusion or anxiety but who might benefit from doing some serious thinking before taking important steps in their lives such as choosing a college course or a career.

A theory made up of what we know about the way in which individuals use human possibilities leads to a definition of counselling as a process of helping an individual to make his choices in such a way as to maximize the probability that his future development will be satisfying to himself and useful to those around him. A counsellor is seen as a specialist in developmental possibilities.

Reality therapy

Reality therapy was developed by Dr William Glasser, an American psychiatrist, as a result of his dissatisfaction with what he saw as the ineffectiveness and unreality of those methods of counselling and therapy which dismiss morality from the focus of treatment. Reality therapy holds that people are responsible for their behaviour, and Glasser believes that man's basic problem is moral, in the sense that being responsible is the requirement for mental health. He defines responsibility as 'the ability to fulfil our needs and to do so in a way that does not deprive others of the ability to fulfil their needs'. Glasser postulates that all people who come for help have identified in some way with failure and that the way to help them is to try to involve them, through the counselling relationship, in behaviour which will lead to success.

Reality therapy is based on the need which people have for love ad constructive activity, and requires from the counsellor an involvement through which she confronts the student with what he is doing and helps him to plan better choices and obtains a commitment from him to work towards those choices. It says that people who are failing have chosen to fail. They have chosen to identify with failure because they believe that they have no other choice, and the counsellor has to try to help them to understand that a better choice is possible. It is a method which guides people towards making those choices of behaviour which help them to move in the direction of successful involvement with others.

Glasser quotes case-histories of seriously delinquent adolescent girls, of psychotics, including chronic schizophrenics, and of disturbed ex-servicemen and students, and indicates that discharge rates from mental hospitals have risen fairly dramatically following the use of Reality Therapy as a form of treatment. He was written of use of his approach in schools and believes that schools, more than anywhere, are places in which children become convinced that they are failures and locked in a failure cycle which is difficult to break.

This behaviouristic method of counselling has been criticized for its apparently naive approach to the subtle realities of human personality and motivation. I think that we would he ill-advised to be deceived by its simplicity for this is an approach to counselling which has proved that it can be effective ad its moral precept perhaps makes it more attractive to teachers and educators than other methods.

Rational-emotive counselling

The rational-emotive approach to counselling was developed by the American Albert Ellis. His theory is that everyone has emotions but that some of us have emotions which are either too intensive or last too long for our own good. He suggests that intense emotions should last only a few moments and if they are more enduring than this, then the person needs to look closely at his philosophy of life.

Ellis has evolved that he calls an ABC theory of events and emotions in which he suggests that events themselves do not cause emotions, it is rather what we learn to believe about these events which creates the emotion.

'A' represents the existence of a fact, an event or the behaviour or attitude of another person.

'C' represents the reaction of a person, perhaps an emotional disturbance of unhappiness which most of use presume to follow directly from 'A'.

'B' represents the self-verbalization of the individual about the event "A', his definition or interpretation of it as awful, or terrible.

Errils's theory is that 'A', the event, does not cause 'C', the emotion, but 'B', the interpretation, does. He further suggests that emotion which is so intense as to interfere with normal life for any length of time is sustained by some irrational belief about an event. Below are several examples of the irrational beliefs which most people commonly hold but are unable or unwilling to specify verbally, although they consistently behave as though they hold such beliefs.

1. It is essential that one be loved or approved of by virtually everyone in one's community.

Comment

It is desirable to be loved, but the rational personal does not sacrifice his interests and desires to this goal.

2. One must be perfectly competent, adequate and achieving to consider oneself worthwhile.

Comment

The rational person strives to do well for his own sake rather than to compete with others: to enjoy the activity rather than the results, to learn rather than to be perfect.

3. Some people are bad, wicked or villainous and therefore should be blamed or punished.

Comment

The rational person does not blame others or self. He tries to understand mistakes and top them, but if he cannot, he tries not to let it upset him.

The rational-emotive counsellor attempts to show the student that his thinking is illogical, to help him to understand how and why this is so and to demonstrate the relationship between his irrational ideas and his unhappiness. The aim is to help the student to change his thinking and to abandon his irrational ideas by directly contradicting these and by encouraging, persuading and at times insisting that the student try some activity which will counteract what Ellis considers is the nonsense the student believes. Although the counsellor attacks the beliefs of the student, this approach can be very supportive of the person of student and the getting the student to try new ways of thinking about himself and to examine the subsequent emotional and behavioural responses which occur. As in reality therapy, one of the main tasks of the counselling relationship is to encourage the motivation to try new behaviours.

There have been attempts to present a more unites front. Dollard and Miller have attempted to integrate

Freudian psychotherapy ad the behavioural drive theory of Clark Huli. Bronfenbrenner attempts to translate Freud into Lewin's field theory. Rogers has attempted to explain his construct of the self in terms of learning theory.

In view of this it might seem attractive for the counsellor to select appropriate parts from each theory of approach and use them as the thinks fit. Yet eclecticism can be superficial and is often a cul-de-sac approach, for it seems unlikely that concessions from various theories will result in truth. At the same time it seems equally inappropriate to disregard the work of counsellors of differing orientations, for even though we work form a basic theory of our own choice we have much to learn from each other.

What does seem to be meaningful is for counsellors and therapists, regardless of their theoretical orientation, to attempt to apply the principles of their approach more widely to the situation in which they are working. In a decade we have seen client-centered therapy develop from a method of counselling to an approach to human relationships. We have come to feel that it has as much application to the problem of employing a new staff member, or the decision as to who is to get a raise, as it does to the client who is troubled by an inability to handle his social relationships.

6

Guidance as a Profession

The meaning of a profession

The guidance worker needs to develop a sense of unique personal identity, and with it an awareness and appreciation of the meaning of a profession with all the specific guidelines, regulations, and policies that define the practice of the specialty. When one analyzes the definition of the term "professional", the importance of the aspects covered in this chapter is clear.

The major identifying characteristic of a procession is its knowledge base. Theory and research are organized to guide practice. Guidance, drawing on the disciplines of psychology, sociology, economics, and others, meets this criterion.

A second characteristic is a code of ethical practice. The counseling profession has for many years been concerned with ethical standards, and the American Personnel and Guidance. Association has formulated a comprehensive and well-designed statement. But it is up to the individual practitioner to observe standards voluntarily. Employers such as school systems may use the

APGA's ethical standards as guidelines, but often look to the local standards and ethics of the teaching profession when questions of improper conduct arise.

The control of preparation and practice are two further factors that help define a profession. Through establishing admissions standards for preparation programs and specifying what these programs should accomplish, the guidance profession does exercise some control. But the role of the profession is largely advisory, its recommendations have considerable influence but do not set the standards for all employers.

A fifth characteristic of professional identity is personal autonomy in the provision of service, the individual counselor exercises independent judgement, makes decision, and provides help. Counselors may have considerable freedom in the way they practice their profession, but little control over allotment of time for specific activities. Even so, there is adequate autonomy for the counselor to utilize professional expertise.

A final professional characteristic involves the function of service to others. Counseling and guidance qualify as a profession by this criterion more fully than by any other. There is room for improvement in the applications of standards for preparation and practice; but professional status is justified in all crucial respects.

Preparation

The American Personnel and Guidance Association has taken the lead in formulating standards for preparation for guidance at the elementary and secondary levels. The guidelines are clear-cut, specific, and constitute excellent models. The secondary school standards have been more extensively studied, reviewed, and developed than those for the elementary school, but the current guides cover all counselors regardless of educational level.

Before the most recent standards were adopted in 1973, an earlier set of guidelines had been widely used by counselor-education institutions and accrediting organizations for self-study and program improvement. A manual was also prepared to help counselor education staffs prepare for evaluations. The new revision brings together existing guide lines for all levels in a unified and comprehensive report. The Association for Counselor Education and Supervision carries on the development of standards as a continuous process; new revisions will be forthcoming.

The introduction to the new standards reflects many contemporary trends. First, it spells out the need for students to demonstrate competencies. Second, it assumes differential rates of student progress; some may take longer to acquire proficiency than other. Third, it considers various models that extend graduate preparation beyond a single year; one such program, for example, combines an undergraduate major in guidance with a year of graduate study.

The four major sections cover objectives; the program of studies and supervised experience; responsibilities concerning students in the program; and support for the counselor-education program, administrative relations, and institutional resources.

The opening section on objectives sets the stage for the program. The major emphases are on explicit, cooperatively planned objectives evolving from input of those involved-counselor educators, students, and practitioners. Objectives show sensitivity to needs, problems, and trends in schools; they are regularly revised and updated.

The program of studies calls for academic and practical work to enable students to move to increasing levels of competence and responsibility. There are opportunities for observation and involvement in guidance. Responsibility for working face-to-face with individuals and groups comes as competence is developed. Along with increasing competence in helping activities, the program fosters a spirit of inquiry, ethical sensitivity, and skill in self-evaluation. The practical-work component is given specific emphasis; in a one-year period, 60 hours should be spent in face-to-face individual or group work.

The third section deals with selection, retention, endorsement, and placement of students. It speaks to student rights, pointing out the need for making clear the criteria and procedures for admitting students, and retaining or separating them from the program. It also indicates the program's responsibility for endorsing and placing graduating students.

The final section covers institutional support for programs in guidance. Emphasis is on cooperative relationships with other college or university departments for courses, and with school settings for practical experience. It specifies a minimum full-time staff of three members and spells out the necessary professional qualifications for those working with students. These standards, which describe what the program should provide and define the professional competencies to be mastered, are of great significance to the beginning students.

The APGA standards require preparation to cover all

levels of the profession, added emphasis on specialized work settings is to be provided through courses and practical work. For example, students preparing for elementary school counseling would concentrate particularly on courses and practical work designed for this educational level. Preparation for career guidance and participation in career education would feature added emphasis on these areas.

Current standards are oriented to competency, as are several contemporary preparation models. The system-based approach and HRD, for example, emphasize specific competencies, systematic means of achieving them, and evaluation in terms of counselor effect on counselees. The ACES standards emphasize that programs are to be evaluated in terms of competencies of each student. Such competencies would be illustrated by specific items such as supervised practice in working with groups. Zifferblatt discusses the systems approach, in which specific skills are learned recycled until they reach an acceptable level of competency. Another illustration shows specific and measurable characteristics of many competency approaches in terms of the student's growing self-awareness:

> Given two hours with a group of fellow trainees, the trainee must be able to make five self-observation responses, the validity of which can be confirmed by a majority of group members.

Among other strategies recommended in preparing counselors is an experiencing-growing-sharing process between counselor educators and students, which stresses individual development.

There is certainly no dearth of models and Santoro, which is a very positive sign. The future of those now in use, however, is not clear. Kennedy described problems that could cause the competency model to fade from the educational scene; it may not be feasible, for example, to keep students in the program until competencies are mastered. Programs must, despite limited resources, prepare counselors to meet new demands for services and demonstrate effectiveness.

Legal status, certification, and licensing

These areas are among the must controversial and ambiguous in the counseling profession; they are of major concern to anyone planning to enter the field. Potential legal problems revolve around malpractice, right to privacy, serving as defendant tin criminal action, encouraging an illegal act, or involvement in civil disobedience. Certification poses fewer potential problems. Your program will probably meet requirements, but you should known not only the standards in your own state, but also those of any other state you may wish to move to. Licensure is of recent concern. Previously it was critical only for counselors in some nonschool settings, but it is now emerging as an issue for school counselors too. Currently the employees of an educational instruction are given sanctions to practice by virtue of their employment status; the institution authorizes their activity and assumes responsibility for performance. This may not be true in the future.

Legal status: An understanding of legal factors in essential both for day-to-day practice in conventional types of service, and for anticipating problems that may arise with changing conditions. For example a counselor may feel existing laws and regulations are harmful and ought to be challenged but must know the consequences of disregarding them and share this information with others who might need to know, particularly pupils. The processes one chooses to bring about changes are to some extent a function of one's political convictions. Counselors are entitled to their own views, but there are harsh realities to consider when changes involve committing illegal acts.

Counseling today has no specific legal status. It has only recently come to be recognized as a formal part of school programs. Few court cases have dealt directly with school counseling, and even fewer statutes specify legal obligations and responsibilities. The status of counselors must be clarified in the light of the few existing cases and statutes, and on the application of the law to people in general. Enough data are available t spell out some guidelines and to alert counselor to their responsibilities and limitations.

Increasing professionalizing has generated rising concern about legal issues. Counseling today amounts to a service of therapeutic intervention ant he pupils' lives. With the responsibility this implies, it is sometimes uncertain just how the counselor can offer most help to the counselee without violating civil and criminal law. As Burgum ad Anderson point out, counselors have no general immunity from criminal law and are subject to civil law. Moreover, while statutes give some general guidelines, state and local laws vary enormously.

These are some of the questions a practicing counselor might encounter on a perfectly routine day: Can I assure the counselee of confidentiality? How about in group work" Can I be held liable for malpractice? Am I likely to become involved in a civil suite for carrying out my assigned responsibilities? Are there counseling activities that might lead to criminal charges?

Questions about confidentiality are the most frequent of all. Can counselors assure counselees of confidentiality? Except in a state that has privileged communication statutes, the answer is no. Some states do have such statues, but policies are hedged with restrictions. There is no general privileged communication for counselors, although Burgum and Anderson suggest the federal courts could extend it to them through interpretations of rules of evidence.

Regardless of national statutes, however, state and local precedents should be examined before assuring counselees of confidentiality. When the counselor has determined these legal limits, they should be explained to the counselee. In general, these principle are helpful.

1. If the counselee is a clear danger to self or others, the counselor cannot maintain confidentiality. Steps should be taken to protect others if they are in danger.
2. Generally the counselor respects the rights of others to confidentiality.
3. If a counselee is the victim of a crime, there is no privileged communication.
4. School counselors in most states do not have privileged communication. Where they do, laws may over only certain types of information.
5. For school use the term "privileged communication" can be defined as information shared with the counselor by the counselee, which the counselor cannot release without the approval of the counselee.

6. An individual may subpoena personal case material in college files for use in other actions. In the Bates College case, for example, the court upheld the plaintiff's request to view information he though was hampering his admission to other colleges. The more recent Buckley Amendment deals more completely with the question of access to records.

The counselor must also be concerned with the right to talk to others about the counselee without danger of legal action for libel and slander. Usually if the counselor makes comments about pupils, sends reports to parents, etc., believing the reports to be true, acting without malicious intent, and communicating only with individuals entitled to such information, legal action for libel and slander would not be successful.

Civil liability was an issue infrequently raised in past years, but it is a problem causing concern today. There is no sure way to judge what could be construed as counselor malpractice. If, however, the counselor follows the ethics and standards of the profession, malpractice liability would likely not be incurred, even if counseling has not been successful. A key requirement is that the counselor makes a referral when a problem becomes too difficult to handle. Group counseling involves the same responsibility, except that the probability of malpractice increases-there are more counsellees to observe and understand. Some problems are more likely than others to raise the civil-liability issue, particularly those involving sexual relations and abortion. According to Burgum and Anderson, advice about abortions, including possible medical and psychological complications, are beyond the counselor's competency. Even so, counselors must deal with these problems every day.

The case of Bogust V. Iverson illustrates the extent to the counselor's liability. A counselor in Wisconsin worked with a girl, Jane Dunn, on career, educational, and personal problems for a period of six months. When he felt that she had made all the progress she could, he terminated the case. Six months later, she committed suicide. Her parents sued the counselor, but the court ruled that he was not liable for failure to inform parents of her condition, and in fact, his training did not make him competent to make a judgement about danger to herself. The six months interval also weighed against placing liability on the counselor. If the counsellee had become emotionally very upset at the termination of counseling, very likely the counselor would have been held liable.

With respect to libel, slander, and other area of possible civil liability, the counselor has no special privilege. It is true that the counselor can talk or write about a counsellee to those who are entitled to the information without liability for legal action. But giving information to those who are not entitled to it, or doing so with harmful intentions, could result in a defamation suit. The same principles apply to student records; the safest course of action is to include only factual information. Unversified damaging information may make one liable for a civil suit. Since parents can examine records, control release of information, and challenge the contents, civil liability can easily be incurred. Professionally, though not legally, it is the counselor's responsibility to make sure that all school personnel understand the meaning and use of data.

Although it is unlikely, a counselor can, with the best of intentions, become a defendant in a criminal case. Burgum and Anderson list four possible types of charges:

— Accessory to a crime after the fact
— Encouraging an illegal abortion
— Coconspirator in civil disobedience
— Contributing to the delinquency of a minor

Reading their discussions of each of these situations will add depth to your understanding of guidelines for practice.

Burgum and Anderson also describe an illustrative case relating to criminal liability in which the school counselor, who has developed a good relationship with a boy in the custody of the iuvenile court, inadvertently helped him avoid arrest. The boy, with two companions, robbed a service station and then, realizing the gravity of his actions, went to the counselor for help. The counselor convinced the boy that he should turn himself, in but it was late at night, and they agreed he would go to the police the following day. Meanwhile, however, the counselor committed a series of acts that could make him guilty of being an accessory to a felony. He denied to police that the boy was sin his house. He gave the boy money, which was found in the youth's possession when he tried to skip town the next morning rather than reporting to the police. The counselor would have been well advised to report the matter to the boy's juvenile office, which would have been in his favour in a trial.

Another area of local concern to the counselor relates to the rights of pupils. The Gault case brought about full guarantees of due process for minors. Counselors can help pupils by making them aware of their legal right to due process in education, free speech, and property ownership. Rights of the handicapped are emphasized by due process provisions of PL 94-142. As Nasman points out, due process is not satisfied by establishing a standard procedure including such steps as informing the individual of charges and providing for a hearing, but rather it demands protection of pupils' right under the Constitution, just as if they were adults involved in legal charges. Due process should fit the situation and protect the pupil from arbitrary, unfair, and autocratic rules and policies.

The Buckley Amendment, already mentioned, deserves special attention. This law restricts the use of information in personal records; enforcement involves the denial of federal funds if violations are allowed to occur. In the past, school records were not treated with respect for the individual's rights of privacy, nor have parents and pupils has access to most of the information contained in them. The Buckley Amendment has given parents and pupils of legal age the right to inspect records, including letters, comments, and recommendations. Besides opening up records to pupils and parents, the law restricts access of others to these data. In general, parents must give consent for information in records to be released. Nasman discusses the regulations in detail. The complete law appears in the *APGA Ethical Standards Casebook*.

Parts of the Buckley Amendment with specific applicability to counselors' use of student records are as follows:

> Each educational agency or institution except as may be provided by 99.12 shall permit the parent of a student or an eligible student who is or has been in attendance at the agency or institution, to inspect and review the education records of the student.
>
> The parent of a student or an eligible student who believes the information contained in the

education record of the student is inaccurate or misleading or violates the privacy or other rights of the student may request that the educational agency or institution which maintains the records amend them.

The legal status of counseling is being established through new laws, statutes, and court decisions. While relatively few cases directly affecting counseling have gone through the courts, more can be expected as counseling achieves greater status and visibility as a helping service.

Certification: All states regulate the practice of counseling through certification, licensing, or endorsement on a teaching certificate. Certification requirements of counselors in different states are more striking for uniqueness than for similarity, and certification standards are changing both in scope and nature.

The most innovative development is the competency-based program. Dudley and Ruff's survey included only one suggestion of this approach, and only one program of this type was reported in the literature. Now 50 percent of the states have, or are planning a competency-based program, while only about 7 percent are not considering it. Over two thirds of the counselor preparation programs intent to convert to this approach, even though only about 7 percent have actually done so. The Washington program started in 1971 is an example. Behavioural objectives were established through input of teachers, pupils, administrators, and counselors. Counselors have been certified at three levels of competency: preparation, initial, and continuing. The initial-level competencies are the type developed in a masters-level program. Six areas of competency are specified; major ones are counseling, information service, and placement. Deficiencies in any of the competencies must be remedied according to procedures spelled out in guidelines of the certification program.

Program accreditation is closely related to certification of individuals; it also gives students an important indication of the quality of a program and enhances job-getting potential If evaluation for accreditation is performed, it conforms to the counselor preparation standards already discussed. Shertzer and Stone envision a national system of accreditation by an organization such as the Association for Counselor Education and Supervision or an educational accrediting agency such as NCATE. There is no national accrediting system in operation today, but there are indications that one may eventually be established.

Licensure: This topic is relatively new for counselors, although psychologists have been active in formulating state licensure policies for at least two decades. School counselors have been concerned mainly with certification and have only recently become aware of the potential importance for their work of developments in licensure.

There are important differences between certification and licensure. Each provides a service to the users of counseling by indicating the adequacy of practitioners. Certification laws regulate the use of the title "counselor" and specify the amount and type of training required for practice. Licensing goes beyond regulating the use of the title and indicates the unique services and practices that fall in the domain of the profession. The term "credentials" is often confused with certification. "Credentials" refers to the degree to other certificate the individual has been awarded; the term is also used to indicate competence for a job.

Up to new, licensure has been a concern of counselors in community settings such s mental health agencies and private practice. To date only one state requires licensing for personnel and guidance workers. But recent licensure laws have alerted counselors to the potential for state regulation of some or all of their work. In Ohio, for example, licensing laws on the practice of psychology have been interpreted to limit the use of tests by a counselor in off-duty hours. In the case, City of Cleveland v. Cook 1975, a counselor who was not a licensed psychologist was arrested for testing. The court found in favour of the defendant; Ohio counselors are contesting this interpretation of the law. The APGA Model Licensing Law specified the points favoured by he counseling profession, including exemptions for those employed as school counselors. But as the situation now stands, school counselors who plan to enter private practice in states with this type of regulation come under the licensing laws for psychologists.

The implications, however, may of far beyond off-duty activities or future career plans. As Sweeney and Sturdevant point out, the Ohio law and other similar ones specify that helping by licensing. Besides, licensure and privileged communication give school psychologists more freedom and prestige than school counselors. Sweeney and Sturdevant see "the right for school counselors to practice at all as being challenged".

Only one state actually licenses counselors, and most experts do not predict that other states will soon follow suit. But the situation may change; both the American

Psychological Association and the American Personnel and Guidance Association are actively promoting licensing laws. If counsellors do not establish their own licensing criteria and procedures, others will do it form them. The American Personnel and licensing boards and that licensing requirements are designed for counselors.

Licensure gives every indication of becoming a major issue. Congress and federal agencies are showing increasing interest in occupational sensing. Present methods of licensure testing can be unfair to qualified persons, some, for example, do not perform well on standardized tests. Licensure can affect employment opportunities, status, and legal bases of counseling.

Effective and well-desinged licensure laws can enhance the counseling profession, project the public, and open up new work opportunities, restrictive and unfair ones will interfere with the contributions of many potentially well qualified to offer others assistance. Sweeney ad Sturdeant and Cottingham recommend that counselors keep up with what is happening in licensure and support favourable alternatives. Their advice points out a responsibility of all members of the profession.

One mark of a profession is a code of ethics. It serves as a guide for providing services and ensures legality in carrying out these services. The counseling profession has a comprehensive, well-developed code, as well as special guidelines for work in schools.

The main points of the section on measurement and evaluation are that the counselor should understand tests, be particularly cautious about their applicability or minority groups, and present or interpret results in keeping with test validity. The section on ethical standards for research and publishing identified the welfare of the individual as the primary factor to be considered; the counsellor should make every effort to avoid harmful effects of research and should take action to reduce or eliminate such effects if they occur.

The section on consulting and private practice deals more with the activities of the private consultant, although much of the counselor's work with teachers administrators, and parents would be based on consultation principles. The section on personnel administration covers organizational and administrative responsibilities in the school counselor's work setting, particularly the need to establish mutually agreed upon goals with administration for major aspects of the job.

The final section deals with preparation standards and their importance to the beginning student.

The school counselor code of ethics is uniquely helpful for the elementary and secondary level in that it identified responsibilities to self and those with whom the counselor works-pupils, parents, faculty, staff, the school, and the community. In all relations the counsellor respects pupils' dignity, individuality, and right to self-direction. Responsibilities to pupils and parents follow the APGA ethical standards closely, but those relating to staff, community, self, and profession give additional guidelines for cooperative work with colleagues and community agencies, for self-development, and for implementing a contributing role in the profession.

In the experience that follow problems are presented for discussion and solutions. Additional examples may be drawn from personal experience and from the casebooks already listed.

Organizations

Professional organizations provide counselors with support, facilitate professional development, bring together colleagues with similar interests, offer opportunities for active participation in leadership roles, and provide placement services. Counselors can help themselves by building a strong organization. Representatives of the profession are active at national, state, and local levels to promote favourable legislation and to obtain funds for improved services.

Participation can begin during preservice preparation. The American Personnel and Guidance Association, a federation of thirteen divisions, is the most important and best-known organization for counselors. APGA offers student memberships at reduced rates, and students can attend APGA national conventions and take part in programs.

The American School Counselor Association is the APGA division for school counselors, but others too relate directly to work in public educational settings. These are: National Vocational Guidance Association; Association for Humanistic Education and Development; Association for Measurement and Evaluation in Guidance; Association for Non-White Concerns in Personnel and Guidance; Association for Specialists in Group Work; National Catholic Guidance Conference; and an affiliate, International Association of Counseling Services. The five remaining division deal with particular work settings such as college, university, ad employment service.

APGA and each of its division publish newsletters and journals covering current development s in the field, research, practices, legislation, and sources of information and materials. *Personnel and Guidance of journal* and the newsletter Guidepost are distributed to all APGA members. The American School Counselor Association is the only division that publishes two journals, The School counselor and Elementary School Guidance and Counseling, in addition to a newsletter.

Many other useful materials are available from APGA. Program abstracts, published at the time of the national convention, give summaries of presentations. Educational aids ranging from brochures, reprint series, and books to cassettes and films, may be obtained at reasonable cost. APGA publications include Hosford and de Visser's book Behavioural Approaches to Counseling ad an accompanying series of eight films keyed to units in the book. The organization also offers a seven-unit interviewing and communication skills development program, Influencing Human Interaction, which includes films, cassette tapes, filmstrips, and books.

Students and counselors alike can participate in APGA by contributing to its many professional journals. Editors urge members who have something to say to submit material for publication. Journal staff members give helpful and detailed advice on how to prepare articles for publication, explain common faults that result in rejections, and describe the step-by-step process of editing and publishing a professional journal. Articles that pass the editor are given blind reviews, and evaluators' comments are passed on to the author. At regular intervals each journal prints guidelines for authors specifying length, format number of copies of manuscripts to be submitted, and other such details.

Collective bargaining: Counselors, like their teaching

colleagues, are using collective bargaining, to obtain better salaries, improved working conditions, and other benefits. Humes and Kennedy view the process as a means to gain a power base for achieving professional status in the school ad a full voice in decision making. Creange believes that building a strong, broad-based national organization is one of the most critical issues facing school counseling today. But the American School Counselor Association has found little interest among counselors in collective negotiation. Many counselors are concerned with the question of professionalism v. collective negotiations; thus there is a search for a strong organizational base to advance the status of the profession, to protect job security, and to ensure a voice in determining professional roles and responsibilities.

Colleagues in non-school settings

Counselors are employed in educational institutions, community agencies, business and industry, hospitals, and clinics. In their comprehensive monograph on employment opportunities, careers in Counseling ad Guidance, Stone and Shertzer identify eighteen settings: vocational and technical schools; community and junior colleges; colleges and universities; vocational rehabilitation; U.S. Employment Service; Veterans Administration; programs for the disadvantaged; correctional and penal institutions; community mental health clinics; family service agencies; child-guidance clinics; Hewish Vocational Service; Urban League,; marriage counseling; business and industry; adult education; pastoral counseling; and private practice. The divisions of APGA identify settings other than public schools such as colleges and universities; rehabilitation services; employment services; and correctional and penal settings. Another listing of opportunities in the counseling profession includes business and industry; employment; and higher education. The these could be added counseling older persons, and a variety of services in consulting firms.

These lists show mixtures of settings, programs, and specialties. This reflects the situation with actual job opportunities; counseling older persons, for example, may be done in colleges, businesses, and community settings,. In each setting, however, the basic competencies, ethical standards, and legal guidelines apply. Priorities vary, however. There may, for example, be more responsibility in one setting for face-to-face work, while in another higher priority goes to coordination services. The focus of the work may also differ; career and program planning may consume most of the counselor's time in one institution, while in another personal therapeutic help may be the major emphasis.

Counseling takes on somewhat different forms in such post-high-school educational settings as voc-tech centers, community and junior colleges, and four-year colleges and universities. In vocational and technical centers emphasis is typically on career planning and placement; the master's degree may be adequate qualification. The role and function statement for the voc-tech setting resembles the statement for the high school. Community and junior-college counseling more closely resembles counseling at the college and university levels. Emphasis is developmental, but career planning and placement are particularly important for students in terminal occupational-preparation programs. The work of community-college counselors ranges from therapeutic and developmental programs to programs emphasizing career guidance, counseling, placement, testing, and a variety of administrative duties.

The college and university level typically offers two major types of work roles-one in the counseling-center setting, the other in general student personnel. The counseling center provides individual and group counseling and is moving toward functions of influencing student life and intervening in the campus community. Placement offices, which in the past have emphasized interviews with prospective employers for graduating students, are now becoming involved in career development and guidance and may offer services to entering students. Student-personnel work is putting increasing emphasis on student development, establishing living-learning centers on campus, and outreach and consultation, and counselors are finding new areas to apply their skills and expertise.

Community agencies and services offer a wide variety of occupational opportunities for counselors. Interest in these settings and private practice is reflected in the increasing concern about licensure. Counselors work in community mental-health agencies, family-service agencies, crisis-intervention centers, halfway houses, drug-counseling centers, and a host of programmes set up for special populations, such as minorities, the disadvantaged, and the unemployed. Each of these services typically involves some counseling, particularly those that deal with interpersonal conflicts and emotional problems. Those for work problems may put more emphasis on placement and training.

Working with older persons is one of the major new opportunities for counselors. The need is apparent. Few services exist. Counselor-preparation programs have done very litter to develop competencies, but interest is increasing. The reasons for growing concern are not difficult to understand. IT is predicted that by the year 2000 one half of the U.S. population will be over 50 years of age and one third will be over 65. Also, there is increasing emphasis on providing counseling over the entire life span.

The Federal-State Employment Service is one of the largest employers of counselors in the country. Under the Comprehensive Employment and Training Act of 1973, many special programs for guidance and training were taken out of the Employment Service, but its major function has not changed. There is a trend to provide more counseling to job seekers and to upgrade the qualifications of counselors. The CETA program emphasizes placement for work and/or training, and thus is mainly concerned in helping individuals to understand their abilities and interests and to make decisions.

Rehabilitation counselors offer assistance to a wide range of handicapped individuals. Typically the master's degree is required. Work is making increasing use of a counseling approach rather than job finding and physical restoration, and its major aim is to increase the effectiveness of rehabilitation and job placement. Preparation is comparable to a school counsellors, with the addition of courses on medical aspects of disability, rehabilitation procedures, and agencies. Since the major emphasis is to get the handicapped individual into a suitable job or preparation program, the assessment of potential through tests and medical examinations is a major function. In helping the handicapped individual move into the new setting successfully, the counselor must know a great deal about environments and utilize counseling to deal with attitudes that could interfere with success.

Opportunities for counselors are also growing in correctional settings. Penal institutions offer jobs in which counselors serve as links t the community, and work with delinquents. This setting has expanded enough in recent years to merit a special feature section in the Personal and Guidance Journal and the establishing of a separate APGA division. Programs aimed at upgrading the skills of correctional staffs make use of counseling methods and offer a new consultation-training role for counselors in the correctional setting. In this approach, counselors use group methods to help correctional officers learn more effective ways to deal with inmates.

7

Groups in Guidance and Counselling

Group guidance

Guidance is concerned with presenting information in a way which will enable each individual student to find some personal meaning in what he has read, seen or heard. It is not sufficient to present information to students, and to assume that they have all heard and understood the same thing, for each one reads personal meanings in the what may be considered 'objective' facts. If we exclude group counselling, then group guidance becomes a set of activities used with a group of students to help each in his individual learning. It is mainly a cognitive process with little attention given to feelings or emotions and is concerned with helping people to discuss the meaning of various kinds of information. The focus is on ideas, explanations, and verbal expression as an aid to a personal understanding of information or to the completion of a set task.

The following purposes particularly emphasize group guidance in the secondary school setting.

1. To assist in the identification of common problems.
2. To provide information useful in the solution of adjustment problems.
3. To provide opportunities for group thinking in regard to various problems and experiences.
4. To provide opportunities for experiences that promote self understanding.
5. To lay the foundations for individual counselling.

There are certain problems which are common to adolescents as part of the developmental processes of the developmental process of this age group, there are also certain kinds of educational, vocational and social information which can be of help to young people as they grow up. These may be presented in a group situation and discussed with the realization that their difficulties are not peculiar to them as individuals, as they often think, but are shared by fellow students.

Choice and decision-making in a group context

There are essentially two types of information needed for intelligent decision-making: information regarding oneself as a person with assets and liabilities, talents and limitations; and information regarding the particular situation about which a decision is to be made, or to which the self is related. When a person has this information he needs some way of dealing with it.

There are various models of choice or decision-making used by people in making vocational or other choices, which vary according to the individual concerned and his circumstances.

Trait and factor model

The trait and factor model is based on the idea that any individual possesses a variety of traits and any occupation demands certain requirements of those who enter it. The individual can match his traits with the occupational or educational requirements and determine which job or course he is best fitted for. This model is often used in vocational guidance in our schools and its main disadvantage is that it is too static and does not take into account the changing and developing nature of neither the student or the environment to which he must relate.

Economic model

An individual using the economic model chooses an occupation or a college which will maximize his gain minimize his loss; for example, going to college might be a means of achieving greater status and mobility. The gains achieved are not necessarily economic or financial but may consist of anything which is of value to the person concerned.

Social structure model

The individual using a social structure model of choice is restricted in the decisions he can make because his knowledge of the various opportunities available is limited by family, social and economic circumstances. This is particularly so as disadvantaged students for whom narrowness of cultural or social class horizons places restrictions on their educational or vocational selection had often leads to the equally narrow perspective of immediate gratification as the basis for choice.

Information processing model

A person may be forced into using the information

processing model of choice when the facts necessary for him to make a decision are so overwhelming that he is pressured into a premature decision. Some students chose a particular college or job because their friends have done so, or because they are vaguely aware that a college has a particular college or job because their friends have done so, or because they are vaguely aware that a college has a particular reputation. This type of choice supports the individual's rationalization and reduces his anxiety.

Need reduction model

The need reduction model is a comprehensive one which subsumes certain elements of the other models. It assumes that an individual has a self-concept and that he implements this picture of himself in his choice of course or occupation, by gravitating towards a career, or a course of study which he sees as compatible with his needs and interests. This may be a result of unconscious motivation, or a relatively rational conscious choice. The advantage is that this provides for change in the person's behaviour, environment and expectations between the individual and his environment. It suggests that making decisions about important areas of one's life is a complex and on-going process forming part of a developmental sequence extending from childhood through adulthood and not an isolated event at a particular point in time.

Some ways of presenting information in group guidance

It is no good giving information to students who see no need for it, so motivation should precede instruction in group guidance. The presentation of information is only part of the process and must be followed by some feedback to ensure that it reached each student accurately.

Large groups or assemblies

Whilst large groups offer an economical way of disseminating information, large group audiences tend to be passive listeners, or merely passive. We need to supplement this type of presentation by work in smaller groups and with individuals in which there is more opportunity for interaction and feedback.

Tutorial groups

Unless tutors in school have one period each day with their students the tutorial group is not an effective way of providing information on which to base choices, or of providing help in other areas. Tutors also need training in group work, and the support of a carefully planned, effectively led guidance programme.

Orientation groups

Orientation usually takes the form of large group information giving, plus smaller orientation groups which continue throughout the year and are aimed at helping the students to develop independence. This applied at all levels of education, not just at the school level. American studies indicated that three out of the four college students had difficulties with the transition from the orderly, fairly directive secondary school to the non-directive environment of college. Some of the reasons given for these difficulties were unrealistic expectations of college social and education life; an inability to organize their time; going to college without a strong desire to attend; and financial difficulties. Closed circuit television can be a useful medium for orientation purposes.

Discussion groups

Guidance groups are concerned with effective discussion

about the impact of information and also about problems arising from some personal adjustment and difficulties. Affective discussion groups can be useful in this area, as they form a bridge between the purely intellectual discussion group and the counselling group with its emphasis on empathy. They need planning ad structuring, and some of the techniques for initiating affective discussion are role-playing, case-studies, role-models, literature and audio-visual media.

Anne Jones offers a useful description of their use in a secondary school in *School Counselling in Practice.*

Although the two concepts of group guidance and group counselling overlap to some extent in the area of affective discussion, group guidance tends to be more cognitively oriented and is usually used in an attempt to personalise information, whereas group counselling is used in an attempt to meet emotional needs and is often closer to group therapy it is to group guidance.

Group counselling

Group counselling is not simply individual counselling applied to groups, nor is it merely an economical use of counsellor time. Many of the features of group counselling are quite unique and it would be wrong to think of it as 'individual' counselling in the mass. Because of the differences in the two processes, a counnsellor trained in the skills of individual counselling might find herself in difficulty is she attempted group counselling without having some training in group interaction. It is essential that a counsellor wishing to work with individuals and groups should have a thorough theoretical and practical grounding in individual counselling theory and practice together with some experience of principles and practices of group dynamics.

The term multiple counselling is sometimes used to describe counselling carried out in groups. This seems a misleading term since it is not clear whether it is the counsellors or the students who are 'multiple'. It is used in this book to denote a situation in which there are two counsellors working either with one student, as in the chapter on training, or with a group. The term group counselling is used here to describe a situation in which there is one counsellor working with a group of students.

Group counselling is a relatively new way of working to help people ad although it has a unique contribution to make to our range of helping skills, it is not the complete answer for all psychological ills or needs.

> Carkhuff has written quite strongly that
> Group processes are the preferred mode of working with difficulties in interpersonal functioning.
> We can do anything in group treatment that we can do in individual treatment-and more. Since groups are inherently interpersonal, they offer the helpee the means not only to relate to the helper and himself wit the helper's guidance but also to relate to other members of the group and to the group as a whole. Group processes offer the prospect for the greatest amount of learning for the greatest number of people at one time.

I find Carkhuff's unqualified approval as inappropriate and potentially damaging as attempting to gather peaches with a combine harvester. Certainly group counselling is sometimes successful with students who have not responded well to individual counselling, and there are several combinations of group and individual counselling in use. The two extremes are to use either group counselling or individual counselling only as a main technique. Some counsellors feel that it is unwise to make the two methods available to the same students at the same time because students may not bring out their deepest problems in the group, reserving them for the individual counselling sessions, which could inhibit the work of the group. Other counsellors feel that individual counselling offered concurrently with group counselling gives opportunity for a student to discuss more deeply and extensively personal problem areas which they have been unable to bring out in the group, either because of their own inability or because of a lack of opportunity and a need to share the time of the group with other members.

Group counselling overlaps with group guidance in its partial cognitive and factual content and with group therapy in its emphasis on feelings and emotion, and it has some similarities to the individual counselling situation, with the addition of the interaction of other members of the group and the sharing of counsellor. The effectiveness of group counselling may be partly attributable to the fact that, theoretically, it makes available the services of a number of potential helpers in the form of other group members, one or several of whom may be able to offer more help to a particular person at a particular point than is the counsellor herself.

Group counselling is a particularly useful, way of helping adolescents for whom peer group values are important. The interaction which takes place in a counselling group offers the students a means of gaining insight and understanding into his own problems through listening to other students discussing their difficulties. Ideas and values which a student has previously found unacceptable may become more understandable and sometimes more acceptable. The counselling group not only helps the individual student to change, but also often encourages both his desire an his ability to help social situation, for any group is more than the sum of its members: it is also the sum of its interactions.

Some practical considerations in group counselling

The physical arrangements which are desirable for a counselling group are similar to those which pertain to the individual counselling situation namely, a warm, sound-proofed room with fairly comfortable chairs. It is difficult, though not impossible, to conduct a counselling group in the average classroom, and even more difficult to conduct it in a cupboard. It is helpful if the same room can be used each time the group meets, because of the effect of a changed environment on the functioning of the group if their meeting place is not a familiar setting.

The time factor in the group counselling situation is related to the purpose of the group. If it is intended that most of the 'work' of the individual members is to take place in the actual group counselling session, it is necessary for the group to meet more often than it would if the counsellor and the group members feel that the students need time between meetings to absorb and test some of the experiences learned. IT is usual for the counselling groups used in education to meet once, or perhaps twice a week. If the group meets too often, or example more than three times a week, there is the possibility that the frequency of sessions will restrict the group members' external social contacts and limit their opportunities for social reality testing outside the group. The length of each group meeting will be related to the age of the people involved, and the frequency with which the group meets, but sixty to ninety minutes is probably a reasonable time span for college students, thirty to sixty minutes for secondary school pupils and no more than thirty minutes for junior school children.

The composition of a counselling group is another practical consideration which is related to the purpose of the group. Sometimes it is felt that a homogeneous group consisting of students of the same age or sex, or students who seem to have similar problems is the most helpful, whilst other counsellors find that the wider talents of a heterogeneous group make for a better counselling situation. It is necessary to look carefully at the desired outcomes for the group, and to try to ensure that the purposes of the counsellor and those of the students are the same. It is important to recognize that groups can be homogeneous only in certain limited respects. A group chosen for homogeneity in sex or age is likely to be heterogeneous in other factors such as socio-economic background, maturity, motivation and, of course, temperament. It has been suggested that it is unwise to include in a counselling or therapy group people who are excessively aggressive or hostile because they are likely to destroy the atmosphere of a acceptance in the group; people who are psychologically sophisticated or those who are not sufficiently in contact with reality have also been seen as undesirable group members, but it is difficult for the school or college counsellor to exclude students on these grounds unless they know them personally. A preliminary interview can help, though this may be more appropriate as screening for therapy groups than as a means of choosing members for a counselling group in an educational setting.

The size of a counselling group, like that of any guidance group, is related to the methodology used. A directive counsellor or one who prefers task oriented discussion may choose to work with a larger action. A group of six to eight students is probably the best size for maximum group interaction.

The role of the counsellor in group counselling

There are two basic assumptions upon which a counsellor may choose to build her role. One is that it is the task of the counsellor to work with the group to encourage the students to be more self-sufficient and self-directed, so that the counsellor herself may then become another group member and the interaction of the group itself will provide any help which members need. An alternative assumption is that the counsellor works towards the development of the students' self-sufficiency, but because she considered that the group members are not always able to help each other she does not abdicate her special helping role.

Glantz and Hayes offer six phases which they believe are involved in group counselling, and offer a basis from which to consider the work of a counselling group:

1. rapport.
2. acceptance.
3. listening and observing.
4. promoting group and individual understanding.
5. problem solving skill development.
6. closing evaluation and procedures.

Whilst the counsellor's acceptance of all the group members and their problems is assumed in the nature of the role of the counsellor, as is the acceptance of the student in individual counselling, the creation of rapport and acceptance within and amongst the group members themselves, and between them and the counsellor, is a unique experience which differs from the one-to-one counselling relationship in its patterns of development.

Rapport involves the gradual building of an association of mutual respects and trust and it can be introduced by initial discussion of the group, whether the group should be 'open', so that members may leave when they wish or new members may be brought into the group as it proceeds, or whether it could be 'closed', retaining its initial membership for a specified period of time. Questions directed at the counsellor can be referred to the group for discussion and decision by means of a counsellor response such as 'What does the group feel about this?' If multiple counselling is being done, the role and function of the co-counsellor may be discussed. The structuring of the group by the counsellor in the early stages may also help in the growth of rapport. Structuring should be brief and should focus attention on th particular goals of the group, which may be self apprais to encourage the free expression of feelings by gr members to each other and to the counsellor, an avoidance of purely intellectual discussion. The li the group may be expressed, for example, in term permitting of verbal but not physical expression feelings. The emphasis of the observance b members and the counsellor of confidentiali proceedings of the group is also a part which can help to bring about trust.

Initial resistance is a natural phenc and the creation of an accepting cl process which the counsellor tries own acceptance of each student's feelings an his expression of them. From the counsellor the students learn to accept and help one another. Listening and observing actively and intensely are two of the essential skills of the counsellor, and a group situation gives an added complexity to the use of these in order to promote both group and individual understanding. 'The counselor's task is more complicated in group counseling. He not only has to understand the speaker's feelings and help him become aware of them, but he must also observe how the speaker's comments influence the group members. The counselor must not only be aware of the discussion, he must be perceptive of the interplay of relationships among the members.' The counselling group can make little significant progress in developing the skills for solving problems until the initial stages of rapport, acceptance, understanding and insight have been established. It may be that the process of group counselling itself will uncover more problems that it actually solves, but if it is effective it also helps to bring about the attitudes and draws out the resources which will enable students to work at these problems themselves once they have been brought to conscious awareness. Alternatively it may lead them to seek individual counselling help for these.

ome outcomes of group counselling

s a result of research carried out into group counselling nong pupils in a secondary school Ohlsen reports that, h varying degrees of depth, each client discovered:

the expressing his own real feelings about people, things and ideas helped him to understand himself;

hat at least one adult could accept him and that this lult, the counsellor, wanted to understand him;

3. that his peers had problems too;
4. that, in spite of his faults, which they wanted to help him ot correct, his peers could accept him;
5. that he was capable of understanding, accepting and helping others;
6. that he could trust others.

Group counselling in education is not group instruction nor is it group therapy, but it is an experience which uses peer group support and identification in the social setting of the group to encourage students to accept and to learn more about themselves and at the same time to learn to accept and help others. 'Group counseling is characterised by experience not by words, by *being* something not by talking about it. If one can experience sense of reality about one's self in the presence of others then a step forward has been taken in the realisation of emotional maturity and security.'

8

The Personnel for Counselling Programs

Teamwork is a popular American concept that appears to have been originally and still is prevalently associated with athletic teams. Coaches and sportswriters consistently extol the virtues of the cooperative enterprise known as teamwork. Even though individual stars are clearly identifiable in most team sports, they are always quick to acknowledge the contributions of their teammates to their stardom and the interdependence that each member of the team has on the others in the pursuit of their mutual goals. This harmonious working together to accomplish a mutual goal is also noticeable in such cooperative endeavors as musical groups, surgical team, army tank crews, and aircraft crews. One could almost conclude that we have become a nation of "teams" as recent generations have seen the concept of teamwork expanded to encompass many organizations as well as institutional and agency settings. It is no longer uncommon, for example, to hear industrial leaders talk about the labour management team or the school principal to commend his or her educational team or a community agency to refer to its psychological team.

Regardless of the fact that the terminology may be overworked at times, we must accept the concept of teamwork as an important one if we are to efficiently and effectively bring all the potential resources of the psychological community to bear on behalf of its clients. In advocating a "team" concept we note the following.

- Teams are composed of individuals who are bound together in the pursuit of a common goal. This pursuit is enhanced by their functioning together as a unit. Teams are most effective when members of the team learn mutually complementary roles in order that duplication, overlapping, and competitive activities may be minimized.
- Working together, sharing knowledge and teamwork, when feasible, permits each to use his or her unique talents while determining who will perform the shared talents
- There is no single "best" team system or pattern of team organization; rather, many variations may be anticipated, since a team presumes the best available combination of personnel for the task at hand. For example, some teams may include both community and school personnel, faculty and student representatives, and/or professionals and paraprofessionals.
- The counselor, as well as other professional helpers, may have a variety of roles and may be a member of a variety of "teams" within a specific setting. We recognize that the number and variety of these roles will vary from setting to setting, as on some teams, for example, the counselor will be expected to function as a leader, whereas on others, he or she will

function as a follower. Like the skilled magician or juggler, she or he must be adept in "wearing the hat" most appropriate to the immediate activity in which she or he is engaged.

The professional helping team for schools

The school counseling program is an integral part-an important "team" in the total educational enterprise. Whereas this very fact is one of the potential strengths of the program, since by implication everyone is thus involved, it is also at the same time, a complicating factor. If, in fact, everyone is involved, then roles and relationships must be clarified to the point that each recognizes not only his or her own role and function but also that of colleagues in the total counseling and educational effort. Thus, whereas the team concept for schools has long suggested that the school counselor, teacher, administrator, and other personnel specialists must work together to accomplish the objectives of the school counseling and guidance program, one of the perennial problems which countless studies have enumerated has been the failure to clearly define, in both theory and practice, roles and relationships in such programs.

Another contributing factor that must be taken into consideration is the continuous call for educational change and innovation which threatens to obliterate many of the traditional structures and roles within education. Thus, at a time when many counselors are still trying to clearly identify their roles and relationships within the educational framework as viewed traditionally, change are taking place that may very well make this attempt to specify roles in terms of job descriptions, it is more appropriate to examine the special contribution each member of the "team" may be reasonably expected to make.

The school counselors' special contributions

The school counselor is obviously the central figure on the educational guidance team, for she or he is the specialist who brings unique knowledge and skills to the program without which it could not function. More specially, the counselor is frequently the only professional in the school setting prepared to offer individual and group counseling to students, parents, and teacher. The counselor also posses special knowledge in the area of educational and career development and adjustment, future planning and placement needs.

In addition to these traditional skills and knowledge, school counselors have, in recent years, played increasingly significant roles as consultants to other adults both within and without the educational setting who are also concerned with the pupil's well-being and development. Counselors will recognize that on many occasions they will be more effective when working through and with other significant adults in the individual pupils' life, such as parents, other educators, ministers, and youth workers. This consultation involvement with parents, teachers, and other adults is receiving greater attention as "writers within the counseling profession indicate that all school counselors must conceptualize pupils not as isolated individuals but as members of systems; i.e., family systems, learning systems, and community systems.

> Several reasons can also be stated for the school counselor's choosing to use the school setting for increased involvement and counseling with family systems. First, many personality theories support the idea that family environment and child-rearing practices influence the developing

> individual. Second, there has been increased acceptance of the school's becoming more involved with the home environment. Third, schools are established by society to maximize the potential effectiveness of its children and youth-and the counselor, as a part of the school must accept this responsibility. Fourth, logic dictates that more information about the family can be obtained from first-hand observation of the family, rather than reports by the children. Fifth, efficient and proficient referrals of individuals and families by school counselors to community agencies maximize the assistance available and enhance the professionalism of school counselors. Finally, increased responsibilities of the school counselor necessitate that all counseling strategies be the most effective possible.

In the "learning systems", counselors should also more actively pursue their consulting roles with school administrators and classroom teachers in broad areas of student needs and concerns, such as course offerings, work-study programs, positive school and classroom environment, meaningful activities, and student representation in school affairs. In the broadening of their professional educational consultation responsibility.

> Counselors should also work closely together with curricular specialists to assist one another when curricular or guidance and counseling objectives are hindered or subverted by school structure and organization. Further, counselors and curricular specialists should develop strategies and tactics in concern to overcome

obstacles and rigidities in school structure and organization impeding legitimate outcomes for students. In so doing, counselors and curricular specialists realize that structural and organizational improvements in schools may frequently bring about desired student behaviors just as validly as curricular or guidance measures.

In community systems school counselors must frequently anticipate a role as career consultants. In this capacity the counselor will plan for the integration of school and community career development resources to ensure their efficient and effective utilization. This suggests that counselors assume a major role in the school's career education program. To this end, school counselors will need to consider the following recommendations.

a. Involve business, labour, community representative, and parents in the development of career education programs as teachers and resource people.

b. Introduce occupational coping skills seminars to assist students in the transition from school to work, e.g., job seeking, interviewing, resume preparation, and self-analysis leading to self-improvement.

c. Sponsor or teach career exploratory courses throughout the school year as a part of the total guidance program.

The effective school counselor in the last decades of the twentieth century must also be able to assess social and psychological characteristics and relate these to educational developments and individual adjustments: be able to identify and recognize the influences of cultures and subcultures on their members: and be prepared to functions as a human resources developer and agent of change in the educational-community setting. Podemski and Childers recommend that

> To establish more response by school, school counselors, as a result of their professional training, experiences and organizational placement in schools, are in a position to harness forces that can stimulate the change process and thereby make school systems better learning environments. At a time when counselors and other educators feel greater pressure for accountability than ever before, the counselor is in a unique organizational position to serve as an institutional change agent. In the change agent role, the counselor is concerned with organizational development as well as the shaping and reformulation of the school's curriculum, program, and the organization itself to meet more effectively the needs of students, parents, and the community.

As the counseling and guidance specialist on the guidance team, the school counselor *must* also function as the guidance team leader. The development of the school guidance program, while involving other educational professionals, must, by virtue of the special knowledge and skills required, be directed by a trained, professional, and certified school counselor.

Counselors often have difficulty distinguishing themselves from other helping professionals because their specialized skills and knowledge are not unique to counseling. As Pate notes

> Our knowledge and skills are shared by psychologists, educators, social workers, and other helping professionals. While we cannot

> claim that counseling has a unique knowledge base, counselor's interpretation of their knowledge and skills into service is an important aspect of our claim to professional status and suggests a place for counselors in a psychological society.

Pate goes on to suggest that

a. Counselors must continue to emphasize the developmental nature of counseling. Our unique contributions are the assistance we give counselees to realize their potential better and our interventions to remove institutional barriers to that realization.

b. Counselors should continue to recognize education as important to their profession, just as they so recognize the field of psychology. Much of what counselors do for counselees is education or reeducation. We teach counselees to use their resources and to develop new resources.

c. Certainly counselors can take pride in the profession's historical ties with vocational counseling. Although we should not be content to equate counseling with career counseling, we should remind our pupils that we have a long record of commitment to career counseling.

Other pupil personnel workers

Most comprehensive programs of pupil personnel services in schools will include other professionals whose training and anticipated role may share some similarities to that of the school counselor. These include school psychologist, psychometrists, psychiatrists, and social workers, as well as the personnel whose training is more distinctive, such as the school nurse, physician, dentist, and dental hygienist. Each of these professional specialists also has unique contributions to make to the achievement of the school's objectives. However, if each specialist is to make a meaningful contribution, she or he must have some recognition of the roles and specialities of other pupil personnel workers, as well as a recognition of the expectancies normally assigned to him or her. We now briefly examine the special competencies of the more popular of these other pupil personnel workers.

School psychologist: The school psychologist is an important and integral member of the pupil personnel team. In most school settings, the traditional responsibility of the school psychologist is to diagnose and study individual children, who are usually experiencing problems in their educational or personal development. In this role, the school psychologist evaluates various aspects of a child's experiences and behavior that are relevant to an understanding of the child's school difficulties and achievements. For this role the school psychologist is trained in the use of psychological tests and also is prepared to engage in individual or group therapy with disturbed children. The psychologist may also aid teacher and parents in understanding the implications of child's behavior. Although the school psychologist has often been thought of primarily as a problem diagnostician, there has been an increased effort in recent years to consider other options. For example, Granowsky and Davis suggested that the school psychologist has an option for three different roles; (1) the diagnostic approach. (2) the community-centered approach, and (3) the administration approach. Based on a rapidly changing society, the authors suggest that psychologists examine their role definitions and select the one that is most appropriate for their particular school. The traditional diagnostic role employs (1) diagnostic testing and reporting; (2) designing educational strategies for pupils and teachers; and (3) evaluating these strategies. Such an approach involves behavioral approaches and classroom intervention and service.

A second role model would be that of the community-based school psychologist. Such a person would operate from a mental health center, be administratively independent of the schools, and act as a consultant to the school staff. Granowsky and Davis state that this model allows (1) the school psychologist to place his or her allegiance with the child rather than the school; (2) direct and more intense contact with the parents; (3) expanded resources utilizing the total mental health center staff; and (4) dual therapy emphasizing educational remediation plus individual growth. The psychologist would, in addition, provide the school with traditional services.

The third role model views the school psychologist as a part of the central administration. The psychologist (1) facilitates the group process and interchange among the professional staff; (2) identifies high priority problems; and (3) organizes an effective team of psychological specialists. The author believe that the school psychologist in this role would be proactive rather than reactive.

Based on his or her skill in diagnosis, the school psychologist can assist the school counselor and other pupil personnel workers in gaining a better understanding of individual students and their problems. The school psychologist can also serve as a resource person for case studies and as a source for referral for certain categories of disturbed pupils.

The school psychometrist: The school psychometrist is a pupil personnel worker whose training, background, and job functions are in many instances so similar to the school psychologist that little besides their job titles distinguishes them. However, the school psychometrist is often more limited in training and, as a result, is also more restricted in the kinds of activities in which she or he engages in the school. The major emphasis in the training of psychometrists and on their job performances is usually in the area of psychological measurement. In some school settings, the major contribution of the psychometrist to the school pupil personnel and guidance program may be in the organization and administration of the school's standardized testing program.

The School social worker: The role and function of the school social worker, like those of the school counselor, have evolved and broadened from its beginnings in the early 1900s, and have been influenced in heir development by compulsory education laws, new knowledge about individual differences among children, and a recognition of the impact of education and the school on school-aged youth. Today, the school social worker works to eliminate the social-emotional influences that handicap the students's formal education. To this end, the social worker actively workers with the family, school, and community, and seek the involvement and cooperation of parents in facilitating the development of their children. This may involve interpreting to the family their child's behaviour as the school views it and, in turn, receiving information regarding the child's behavior at home. The end goals is to have the parents participate positively in the school-child-parent relationship. The school social worker also functions in a liaison role between the school and community, and is particularly interested in eliminating the community causes of school problems rather than treating the results. In working with the family, school, and community, the social worker seeks to identify and eliminate the base cause of problems. Primary services of the social worker include case studies, group work, and consultation. In the school setting, the social worker is a valuable "Team" member who can make a significant contribution to the in-depth understanding of an individual student's problems through case studies and who also provides significant linkages between the school, home, and community.

School medical personnel: Most school systems employ medical personnel on at least a part-time basis. These personnel consist typically of the school physician, school dentist, school nurse, school dental hygienist, and school psychiatrist. These personnel can contribute to achieving a better understanding of the pupils' physical or clinical problems. The school counselor can, in turn, give to these personnel a better understanding of the causative factors of the students' physical and mental well-being. Medical personnel can also contribute to increased counselor understanding of pupil adjustment needs through in-service case studies and consultation.

The potential interrelationships between school health services and school guidance services was noted in the publication *Suggested School Health Policies*, prepared by the National Committee on School Health Policies of the National Education Association and the American Medical Association in 1966. This publication suggested four important aspects of the school health service: health appraisal, health counseling and interpretation, emergency care for injury and sudden illness, and communicable disease-prevention and control. Among the techniques suggested were; continuous observation, particularly by teachers, screening tests; psychological and social evaluation; and health records. The publication also suggested the importance of interpreting pupil health needs to parents, pupils, and teachers. It was also recommended that health personnel be aware of the influence of the teacher and other educators on the aware of the influences of the teacher and other educators on the emotional and social environment of the pupil. Thus, these commonly expressed concerns of both school counselors and school medical personnel indicate their natural allegiance in the development of cooperative programs for the development and adjustment of the individual.

Other pupil personnel assignments: In addition to the previously described professionals who, by nature of their training and certification, are specially prepared for their contribution to pupil adjustment and development, others, by virtue of their assignment, are also often members of the pupil personnel team. These individuals most frequently have the titles of attendance worker, dean, director of student activities, and placement director.

Attendance Worker: The attendance worker is probably the oldest "traditional" pupil personnel worker. Although most schools no longer label this individual "truant officer', the basic responsibilities of this individual is still in pupil accounting. The emphasis in pupil accounting, however, has gradually changed from threats and punishment to encouragement and remediation. In this role, the attendance officer and the counselor can each provide valuable information and consultation to each other. As an example, it is particularly important that the attendance officer and counselor coordinate important that the attendance officer and counselor coordinate their efforts in seeking solutions to the perennial dropout problem, identifying its causes, consulting with parents of dropouts, and encouraging the reentry of dropouts into school.

Student Deans: Whereas student deans have been more traditionally associated with college student personnel services, some high school and junior colleges often employ pupil personnel workers designated as deans of students, deans of boys and girls, or deans of men and women in addition to school counselors. The function of these individuals has often appeared to be one of administering student facilities, activities, and regulations. As a result, they are frequently viewed more as administrators than personnel workers. Students deans have also been frequently cast in the role of the disciplinary agents for the school. In this role, their potential contribution to the school guidance program is discounted by many who contend that guidance and discipline are poor "mix". A number of programs utilize the title of "dean" for their counselors, and traditional "deans" in other programs are trained counselors.

Student Activities Director: The director of student activities, as the title implies, is primarily responsible for the administering of the student activity programs within the school. In this capacity she or he may regulate and coordinate student group activities, identify and plan for needed activities, and assess or evaluate the individual activities and the activity program in general. Through cooperation with the school counselor, students may be assisted in participating in activities that will promote their growth and adjustment, serve their interests, and develop their special abilities. At the same time, coordination of guidance activities with other student and school activities can be facilitated.

Placement directors: Placement directors are most likely to be found in large secondary schools and institutions of higher education, where their role is primarily on part-time and/or full-time career placement. In addition, at the secondary school level, placement personnel will also be frequently concerned with the placement of students in post high school educational institutions. The increased emphasis of career guidance in the 1970s resulted in a corresponding emphasis on, and an increase in the number of, placement specialists in high schools. Cooperation with the school counselor and school psychologist will enable those responsible for pupil placement more effectively to *coordinate* pupil in terest, abilities, and experiences with placement opportunities and needs. A few schools also have college counselors or placement specialists whose major function is to facilitate the placement of interested and qualified students in a college of their choice.

The school administration

As indicated earlier in this chapter, the guidance team for schools consists not only of the professional counseling staff and other trained pupil personnel workers but also the school administrator. The school administrator, who may be a superintended of schools, junior college president, or building principal, is justified in expecting the staff of the school counseling and guidance program to contribute to the achievement of the institutions' objectives. The administrator must also recognize that this contribution will be severely handicapped if she or he fails to realize his or her important responsibilities in the success of this program.

The school administrator represents the educational leadership both in the community and in the specific educational institution as well. In this capacity, it is the administrator's responsibility to give open and recognized support for the school counseling and guidance program. The administrator should also provide advice and direction on budget expectations, physical facilities, ancillary professional and service personnel, and policy guidelines. The school administrator is also responsible for indicating to the school counseling and guidance activities which she or he views as mandatory or desirable in facilitating he goal attainment of the total educational program. In most setting, the administrator will have the primary responsibility for communicating program characteristics, achievements, and needs to school boards and other within the educational system and to the tax-supporting public.

The classroom teacher

With the exception of the home, pupils spend a far greater portion of their crucial developmental years in school than in any other type of institution. During these years, pupils obviously spend a far greater portion of their in-school time with the class-room teacher than with any other professional educational personnel. The teacher-pupil relationship is the central, or key, activity in the educational endeavor. It is therefore obvious that other activities in the educational setting which are concerned with the pupils development, adjustment, and total growth must, of necessity, involve those who work closest with them and, as might be anticipated, usually know them best. This means that the classroom teacher is an indispensable member of the guidance team.

The classroom teacher at every educational level has the opportunity to fulfill his or her important role in the school guidance program through functioning in the following ways.

As a Listener-Adviser: Mary had been increasingly distracted from her schoolwork and in a rather absent-minded manner se had been inattentive in class for more than a week. This was unlike the vivacious, energetic, and capable student Miss Jones decided that at the first opportunity she would examine Mary's record and consult with her school counselor prior to initiation any discussions with Mary. Miss Jones is an example of a guidance oriented teacher who is alert to the needs of her students and aware of the valuable assistance that the school counselor may be able to provide in helping her met these needs. Miss Jones and her fellow teachers at every educational level have countless opportunities to advise, consult, or just act as receptive adult listeners to students and their problems, concerns, decisions, achievements, and failures. This, then, is a primary role and function of the classroom teacher. This role of a listener-adviser does not suggest that the classroom teacher is a counselor in the professional sense (for counseling is a complex, special skill which requires specialized training), but does recognize that she or he is in the front line of the school counseling program.

As a Referral Agent: If, in our previous situation, it became apparent that Mary's difficulties were too complex for Miss Jones to handle, a guidance-minded teacher like Miss Jones very likely would discuss with Mary the possibility and advantages of talking with Mr. Haseley, In this capacity, Miss Jones would illustrate the important function of the classroom teacher serving in a referral role in the school guidance program. It is obviously impossible for the school counselor in is or her limited contacts with the total student population to be personally aware of all or even a small portion of students who may be in need of counseling assistance. Therefore, the alert classroom teacher in his or her role as a referral agent can ensure that students with significant problems will not go unnoticed and uncounseled.

As a Human Relationship Facilitator: When Johnny entered Miss Jone's class this morning, another pupil in the class spoke a ceery hello to which Johny replied, "Shut your damn mouth" Johny ten proceeded to shove his way ;rudely through a group of girls who were standing near his desk. Coming to his desk, Johny noticed some books of another student on his seat. He kicked them on to the floor saying" They aren't mine! What the hell are they doing here? The classroom provides an interesting have come to recognize the importance of the classroom setting for the development of human relationship skills in the individual student. The classroom teacher then, as the normally recognized leader of the classroom group, as another important role-i.e., that of a human relationship facilitator and developer. This means, first of all, that the teacher reflects and demonstrates good human relationship before and with her or his students. It also means that the classroom teacher plans and directs group interactions which promise positive human relationship experiences for each individual participant. Further, many students will need individual tutoring in developing and mastering these skills, just as in any other type of learning. In the case just cited for example, the ever-alert Miss Jones might plan a strategy for improving his relationships with his fellow students. Even though the teacher is the focus of human relationship development activities in the school, the school counselor should be viewed and used as the human relationship consultant in the educational setting.

As a Career Educator: Another important role and function of the classroom teacher, which is emphasized by the national career education movement, is the planned contribution in every subject matter class for ;the pupil's overall career and related educational development. In this role the teacher has the opportunity to provide a data base from which pupils will make their eventual career decisions and to understand the relationships between education and career planning. Indeed, at every educational level, the teacher has the opportunity to provide for career-oriented experiences that are appropriate to the levels of readiness of their students. The classroom teacher must also provide the student with opportunity to examine and develop various careeroriented skills and examine roles that may have career applications for him or her in the future. The school's program of career guidance must be centered in the classroom and integrated into the ongoing and total educational program of the institution. Since the total development of the individual is vital, the career aspects of this development cannot be separated from the whole.

For the classroom teacher's important role as a career and educational developer, the school counselor can again function as an expert consultant. The counselor can also assist the classroom teacher in securing appropriate educational and occupational development materials and can take responsibility for planning special activities that are related to the ongoing classroom experiences of the student.

Whereas the preceding paragraphs have described at the over all role and function of the classroom teacher as a guidance -minded teacher of guidance team, the classroom of the guidance-minded teacher offers the most natural, consistent, and effective setting from providing pupils with developmental guidance. We, therefore, encourage teachers to seek preparation for their important role on the school guidance team.

Paraprofessionals

In recent years education has witnessed and increase in the utilization of individuals who are not by training or experience classified as professional educators. These individuals, who have been labeled most commonly as paraprofessionals or educational aides, have served in a variety of capacities, such as providing clerical assistance to classroom teachers, supervisory assistance to study groups, tutorial assistance to younger and often "Slow" learners, and various service activities, i.e., cafeteria and transportation. Although the coming of the paraprofessional has not been without attending controversies, the economic and facilitative advantages appear to be slowly winning over the opposition that still exists to their employment.

The utilization and related controversies of the employment of paraprofessionals in school guidance and counseling programs has closely paralleled that of other areas of education. However a study by Guidance Committee of the North Central Association of Colleges and Secondary Schools seems to indicate both acceptance and an increased utilization of paraprofessionals in school guidance programs.

In view of the increased acceptance of the

paraprofessional in the school guidance program, four major principal relevant to the role and function of paraprofessionals are examined in the paragraphs that follow.

a. Paraprofessionals are employed only ;when their utilization enables the professionals in the program to function more effectively. Most practicing counselors do not have to review the proliferation of articles in the professional journals to know that they are spending a disproportionate amount of their professional ;time and effort on clerical and other repetitive tasks which do not require their professional skills. The employment of paraprofessionals to relieve school counserlors of such routine chores, is a popular and appropriate paraprofessional role. However, when the paraprofessional is viewed as an alternate to the employment of additions professional personnel with the duties, the guidance program suffers both in image and function, as well as in potential service. This suggests that paraprofessionals should only be employed in those activities which are commensurate with their training and experience.

b. Where employed, paraprofessionals should be provided with opportunities for both training and advancement. If the paraprofessional is an asset to school guidance and counseling programs, his or her contributions to; the program can be further enhanced by a planned training program that seeks to provide the paraprofessional; with additional appropriate knowledge and skills and to prepare him or her for increased program responsibility. The latter would also suggest the existence of career ladders that would enable the professional to anticipate and work toward advancement in school system. In some inward advancement in the school system. In some instances, it may be possible for the paraprofessional to complete a counselor training program and thus move from the role of paraprofessional to professional.

Many community colleges around at the country have developed human services training programs which focus on the preparation of paraprofessionals for work in psychological, social; welfare, and educational agencies and institutions. A few community colleges have also initiated programs that are tailored to a given paraprofessional specialty. Zimpfer notes that a community college program will typically lead to an associate degree, which provides a sense of status and achievement to the student. The opportunities for job advancement are greater for this person than for the lesser-trained paraprofessional. Similarly, the opportunity for transfer into four-year and ultimately even into graduate training, if the student has the aptitude and the desire, is also afforded. Horizontal mobility is also an advantage of a community college program. Because of its breadth, the knowledge and skills acquired by the paraprofessional are often generalizable acquired by the paraprofessional are often generalizable to a variety of settings.

c. Individuals who are selected to work as paraprofessionals in school guidance programs should be carefully secreened prior the their employment. As previously stated, school guidance program personnel should demonstrate positive human relationship techniques and understandings. This "modeling" cannot be limited to just the professional staff. Such nonprofessionals as the receptionist, student helpers, secretaries, and paraprofessionals will also be in contact with students and others served by the school guidance program. They, too, are important in the creation of models and perceptions by which others make judgments.

d. Paraprofessionals should function within the ethical guidelines of the professionals they are assisting. Those paraprofessionals who are associated with the school guidance program should be informed of, and expected to function within, those ethical guidelines prescribed for their professional colleagues. This initially means that they must be informed of their guidelines and the resultant expectancies, and that adequate supervision must be provided to ensure their conformity to the guidelines. the objectives of the school guidance program could be thwarted if, for example, paraprofessinals inadvertently broke rules of confidentiality or good human relationship practices.

The Professional helping team for community agencies

Mental health centers

The Community Mental Health Centers Act of 1963 and its subsequent amendments stimulated a nationwide development of community-based agencies that provided services for the prevention and treatment of mental health disorders. The act originally provided for five essential services: inpatient care, outpatient care emergency services, partial hospitalization, and counsultion and education. Later, additional services, prepare and aftercare services, training, research, and evaluation. These services are available in mental health centers to all individuals who reside in the geographical area designated as the center's responsibility. The inability of individuals to pay for these services need not prevent them from being utilized. No minimum period of residence in the service area is required for treatment. Self-referral or referrals by the family of clients is the most popular approach to the services of community mental health centers. Next in popularity are referrals from family physicians, the legal system, schools, and other community agencies.

The professional team for community mental health centers may include psychiatrists, psychologists, social workers, and other mental health personnel, including counselors and psychiatric nurses. In addition to the professional team, administrators and support personnel and even volunteer workers also work in many centers. The responsibilities of the professional staff is dictated by their professional training and background.

Other Social Service Agencies

Small Community-Based Social Service Agencies: During the past fifteen years, thousands of small, nonprofit, community-based social service agencies have been established. Community-based social-service agencies are those whose scope of operation is focused on the immediate community or on specific needs within a caused on the immediate community or on specific needs within a community and whose principal function is to meet a specific social or human-service need. These grass roots organizations are usually effective, because they are able to take risks, adjust to societal changes, and provide opportunities for people willing to engage in one-to-one relationships with clients.

The staffs of these agencies usually consist of a director, an assistant director or project coordinator, a secretary (usually part-time), and a volunteer support system. Volunteers perform highly specialized functions that require experience and skills as will as odd jobs that require no formal training.

The services provided by these small community-based agencies may emphasize or include referral assistance; educational activities such as consumer skills, remedial education, and training for the handicapped; job placement and job training related to placement; and advocacy and outreach functions. The small social service agencies provide assistance to a wide range of individuals; elderly people who have limited financial resources, teenagers "on the run". veterans involved with drug abuse, family members coping with divorce, recently widowed individuals struggling to deal with their loss, and countless others.

The "team" for these small agencies may consist of only one or two full-time professionals, frequently psychologists or sociologists, "backed up" by a variety of volunteers, and, in some settings, by part-time employees as well.

Service Agencies for the Aging: The" graying of America" has led to increased interest in and services for the aged. The largest network of agencies to serve out aging population are those agencies that were established under the 1973 amendments to the Older Americans Act. Approximately 600 agencies nationwide are operative under this act. Each agency is responsible for determining the needs of the elderly in its area and planning a strategy to meet these needs. Roles and activities for which counselors may be particularly well qualified are providing retirement counseling, assisting in adjustments to the deaths of spouses, and providing a vocational and recreational guidance.

Aging agency "teams" are typically headed by the agency program administrator whose staff may include social workers, psychologists, counselors, nurses and nurses aides, and nonprofessional assistants, who are often volunteers.

Rehabilitation Counseling: Rehabilitation counselors work with disabled clients to assist them kin overcoming defects in their skills. In these efforts the counselor is seeking to bring physically, mentally, or emotionally disabled adults, this includes entry into an appropriate career. The rehabilitation counselor's role is a complex one and may include providing fro a broad range of psychological and career-oriented services, coordinated with other community agencies and consultation with families and employers or types of clients such as the deaf, blind, the mentally ill, or the physically handicapped. The majority of rehabilitation counselors work for government agencies oar nonprofit organizations. In these settings, they often work in close cooperation with physicians and/or psychiatrists. With the e implementation of Public Law 94-142, which provides for the integration of handicapped students be increasingly employed by school systems or utilized as resource personnel to consult with school counselors in dealing with the particular problems that handicapped individuals face in the school setting.

9

Vocational Guidance

Introduction

Why single out vocational guidance for separate treatment in a book on counselling? There are several reasons. We have seen that in fact the separation of a man's vocational life from his personal life is a false distinction; then again, it is in his vocation that a man often takes on the stereotypes of his time, and of his society, as William James so graphically described it many years ago. Finally, it is the case that both in Britain and the United States, specialised guidance emerged out of vocational guidance-curiously enough, both systems started at almost the same time, with the publication of Frand Parson's book in 1909 and the rise of his Vocation Bureau at Boston; and in Britain, with the attachment of juvenile departments to some of the Employment Exchanges in the same year. Again, in Eastern Europe, we shall see that the new appearance of specialist counsellors, as they are called, is very largely to help the efficient development of the national economies. Even in Sweden, where pupil-centered systems of thought dominate educational reform, the importance of the Labour Market Board in the formulation of policy about counselling, has been and remains very real.

Man's attitude to something which takes up much, if not most, of his waking hours, has rarely been neutral. Work has been seen as a necessary evil, as one of the virtues that pave the path to heaven, as the most important way in which an individual contributes to his society, and as a major instrument of self-realisation. Butmany discussions about work beg the question of what it is, and this distinction is important. If we define work as 'what you do to earn a living,' then a distinction between work and leisure becomes possible. If we say that work is 'doing anything which you would rather not do' then the distinction becomes a little blurred, since when a man builds a sailing-dingly for pleasure, for example, he may engage in many hours of painful toil in his leisure time to gain a distant goal. Making a rather cautious start, however, let us take this preliminary position about work and its significance: work is the purposeful expenditure of mental or physical effort resulting in fatigue. The purposes may be legion: to propound a doctrine, to build up a stamp collection, to avoid punishment, to play football. This is, after all, implied in the common uses of the word. The labourer straightening his back after a hard spell of digging, the schoolboy closing his books after a nights' homework, the mountaineer lying exhausted above the cliff-face he has just conquered, may all say 'that was hard work.' The concept of fatigue is necessary: we expend a small amount of energy in eating, but this is hardly work; on the other hand work and pleasure may be inextricably mixed; and the very act of love can be an exhausting experience.

One of the most satisfying experiences in human life

is that of creativity; the creative process is essentially that of a search, and this search is inseparable from a process of work as we have so far defined it. It is impossible to avoid the suggestions of sexuality in this: to create is to give birth, whether physically in woman after her labour; or to new ideas after a period of creative disturbance; or to an object after mental and physical labour on it. It is also associated with the release of aggression and even with the concept of war: to gain victory after struggle and after sustaining intermittent defeats in which the individual may have felt not only his self-confidence, but his personal integrity, threatened. A successful outcome to a creative struggle is in fact the outward projection of part of the individual's life force; in the newly born child, the completed boat, the beautiful garden, the individual sees a material assurance of his own identity, and even at times a kind of immortality. Just as work is central to the creative process, so this in turn provides the context within which work takes on its deepest significance. Boris Pasternak once wrote: 'the fabulous is never anything but the commonplace by the hand of genius,' and genius itself has been described as an capacity for taking pains. Even at its highest level, the transformation of the mundane involves a process of work. These thoughts give us the possibility of refining our definition of work: in its most significant from, work is the sustaining of tensions, or risks, and intermittent failures, inseparable from the process of forming new ideas and giving them material reality.

Seen in this light, then, work should always be involved in some way with the realisation of at least some part of the worker's dream: it should express, however imperfectly, some aspect of that world of phantasy that once gladdened his childhood's play; it should symbolise, in part of from time to time, the deeper values of the worker's life. The idea, sometimes heard, that a child passes in adolescence from a phantasy view of the world of work, to a reality view of it, seems to miss the fact that human development is normally a continuous, unfolding pattern in which the past can never be dismissed or neglected. When an individual is required to work for long periods of time, usually out of economic or social necessity, at tasks which afford him to opportunity whatever for any expression of his personality, both the concept of work and the individual are thereby degraded, and the destructive effects are no doubt proportional to the length of time over which such a situation continues.

Much, but not all, of peoples' work takes place in the context of earning a living, or following a career, and for ease of discussion let us call this 'employment'. A man's employment of course includes its social setting: the people he meets in the course of his employment, and the social recognition which his employment affords, both of which are important influences on his attitude towards it.

Employment roles usually require a fairly massive commitment of work, and this is a good point at which to examine some of the broad possible consequences of this. The most satisfying employment is one which presents challenges that we can meet by a deep and creative personal involvement. This is usually seen as a good thing, and we are apt to forget some negative sides of it. Success here, as elsewhere in behaviour patterns generally, is likely to be followed by a deeper involvement. This can usually be justified, if the need arises, but the requirements of 'earning a living' or 'following a career.' If progressive improvements is accompanied by increasing success, the employment may begin to draw in too much available energy, and insidiously to attenuate the private life, which may become correspondingly shallow. Too much work now take place in one setting only-the employment role-and is not sufficiently distributed over the broad spectrum of life. Whether this is seen as a good or a bad thing depends greatly on the social values that are accorded to private life, the family, religion, and so on. These may well vary from one society to another. A friend of mine, who once worked in Africa, found that the attendance of his labour force was rather erratic. One day, when very few men had turned up, he went out and found one of them, a huge negro, lying on the side of the road with his hands behind his head. "Why are you not at work?' He asked. And got the reply: 'for a long time now we have had very hot, wet, unpleasant weather: this is the first good day, and any sensible man will lie on his back in the sun.'

One specific aspect of a deepening involvement with a employment role is, however, worth a special mention: a tendency to use it to compensate for failures in private life, and to evade the need for more effort there. Work-especially creative work-can take the mind off other things, and release the tension generated by frustration elsewhere. Persistent evasions of this sort may well amount to a rejection of life itself, impossible to justify except by rare creative genius in the employment role.

At the other extreme are employments which are potentially creative, but in which the individual has failed in the sense that the cannot involve his deeper life with the work, whose functions he discharges in a mechanical way; and employments which are basically sterile, such as many forms of factory labour. In the first of these we may find the imitator-the individual who conforms over-closely to the style of clothing, the turns of speech, the ways of thought, the patterns of activity appropriate to his employment role, as a compensation for a deeper failure there. 'Action', wrote Canard, 'is consolatory. It is the enemy of thought and the friend of flattering illusions.' This over-identification with the trivia of the employment stereotype may extend into many distant and apparently irrelevant areas of life, so that in extreme cases we may say with the scathing words of Volatire about an acquaintance: 'he was born a man, and died a grocer.'

If, on the other hand, the work offered by the employment role is both demanding and boring, the concept of work itself may be rejected wholesale, leading to the use of non-creative, non-demanding leisure activities upgraded out of all proportion to their value. Harold Entwhistle has emphasised the high likelihood that boring employment leads to the dull and unimaginative use of leisure: a man whose brain has been dulled by eight hours of monotonous toil can hardly be expected to burst into creative leisure activity: in short his ability to work has been damaged. It is perhaps significant that throughout history we see examples of those sections of the population engaged in the dullest, most routine work, putting a high value on non-demanding 'viewing' activities, from the circuses of ancient Rome to the football stadiums of today.

Implications for vocational guidance

How far does vocational guidance, as practised in our schools, stand up to examination from this viewpoint? Nearly everywhere, in the practice of vocational guidance, it is assumed that work means employment, and this is particularly clear in the description of the various offices and activities in this field, such as 'careers officers,' 'careers teachers,' 'careers convention,' 'careers literature,' and 'work experience'. The over-emphasis on this association of work with employment reflects a general failure to think deeply enough about the meaning of work; and implies an acceptance of the popular idea that work and leisure are different things. Perhaps this is partly the price of an empirical approach to guidance generally, with its unwillingness to explore concepts at the abstract level. The idea of a clear distinction between work and leisure certainly needs to be broken down, perhaps by more attention in training programmes and conferences in counselling, to the definition and discussion of goals and assumptions. If it is not, there may be some future danger of the spread of courses and programmes of 'education for leisure', carrying further the artificial distinction already present in the terms we looked at earlier. Where pupils can be encouraged to relate ideas which they find personally exciting, to those which they associate with work, the basis of a new approach exists, meaning, in effect, the marriage of vocational guidance to counselling.

However, the question of how far children should be encouraged to express their creative energies through employment *alone* is very complex, and illustrates the impossibility separating vocational guidance from the need an overall philosophy of life. At one extreme is a certain view of employment as a 'job' void of anything worthwhile; a daily interruption of life; at the other extreme is the obsessively employment-dedicated man to whom nothing but a career matters. Proponents of the first viewpoint sometimes take a 'realistic' or 'tough-minded' approach to the formation of employment-attitudes, and hence to vocational guidance. They argue that at the present time, and in the foreseeable future, many forms of industry will require large reserves of manpower for the dullest and most routine jobs. For such people education should concentrate on the creative use of leisure; and in any case, not encourage a false view of the world of work, among those most likely to fall into routine employments. Such unimaginative attitudes ignore the onrush of automation, the increasing geographical mobility of urbanised societies, and the whole background pattern of change, which we look at in the next two chapters, and which, however materialist its methods and aims, is swiftly changing the approach of many young people towards their vocational futures. The question which adolescents increasingly ask, in Britain and elsewhere, is not how to find a good job, or to make a career, but whether to bother about such things. I have little sympathy with those who dismiss such young people as being simply lazy: their problems seem to me to arise out of a deeply sincere questioning of the worth of modern urban civilization. The spread of cynicism about accepted values, the rejection of the 'establishment,' of authority, seem to me to go wider than the characteristic and temporary rebellion in adolescent development against the older generations; and as we shall see later, even in communist countries there is some evidence of a similar trend, masked by lip-service to stereotype ideals. The drift of this wind through our societies further illustrates the change of separating vocational guidance from counselling.

From job placement to counselling: an evolution of processes and techniques

Why in fact has the development of guidance in semi-specialised from in British schools, been so closely identified in the past with careers work? Why have these simple and essential ideas about the relationship between work, leisure, and personal development not been sufficiently considered to lead guidance away from a narrow pre-occupation with employment, to a wider view of life goals? The answers probably lie in the tendency in British society, which we have looked at, to concentrate on processes rather than on concepts; on immediate problems rather than on long term goals. Thus the earliest government intervention, represented by the Employment Acts of 1909 and 1910, set up juvenile departments in some Employment Exchange to help place boys and girls in jobs, and to allow Local Education Authorities to do this also. To be fair, the wording of the Acts and official memoranda at this time indicate a recognition of the need for guidance on a wider basis; but in practice the provision become one of job-placement, predominantly for the children of the poor. The excessive concentration on job-placement has remained as part of the official attitude towards vocational guidance, in spite of various attempts at improvement, and in spite of being drawn much more closely into the frame work of L.E.A supervision since 1948. Why did the concept not evolve faster? There are several possibilities. One is the fact that guidance structures existed outside and independently of the schools: the contact between Youth Employment Officers and school staff was too fleeting for serious discussion of deeper issues in guidance. The fact that an organised structure existed outside the schools; and school heads, often tending to think of the successful pupil as one who made the ascent into a university or teacher-training college, may, as we have suggested earlier, have thought of an early leaver looking for a job, as an educational failure. Also, for many years, the use of psychological tests was almost totally unknown among teachers, so that no independent pointer to the relationships between personal, educational, and vocational needs of children was available.

But the main reason why for so long the idea of guidance lay at the level of job-placement in Britain is almost certainly to be found in the social stratification of education. The acceptance of new ideas in guidance and the rise in the numbers of careers teachers, and the emergence of the counsellor as a new figure in schools, co-incide closely with the rise of comprehensive secondary schools. We have already emphasised the tendency of grammar and public school heads to judge success in terms of educational attainment. This limited the development of the concept in those areas. In the secondary modern schools which emerged after the 1944 Education Act, a large number were situated in industrial slum areas, where the prospects, career or otherwise, were too grim to think about. Here there was little or no incentive to start thinking along sophisticated lines about guidance. But the comprehensive schools which emerged a few years later were in a different position: they offered a diversity of educational opportunity at the secondary level unknown in the other kinds of school, and extended deep into adolescence the problems of educational, vocational, and personal choice. In such circumstance, especially in the larger schools, sense of uncertainty, even of being lost, can easily emerge, and for the young pupil soon grow to formidable proportions among so many new faces, both of pupils and staff, most of them stranger. In such a situation, the development of an effective guidance system, able to make contact with such pupils is completely necessary if the main aims of the school are to achieved: one can go further and say that it is the presence of such a system, and its efficient functioning, that largely holds the balance between a comprehensive school approaching its ideals, and an 'education processing factory' of the kind described by opponents of the comprehensive school principle.

In fact, the sort os situation we have suggested here has involved fairly specific problems, and their solution has here has involved fairly specific problems, and their solution has encouraged the emergence of *techniques*. The newcomer has to be introduced to the school; at its simplest this means making certain that the pupil understands what opportunities are open to him, and how to use the main lines of communication. Pupil records have to be developed beyond the simple report-card stage, in order to record as much as possible of the kind of information which, in a smaller community, would be casually picked up by teachers in getting to know their pupils. The advantages of using psychological tests as a short-cut to objective information have begun to be recognised, and teachers involved in guidance work in comprehensive schools frequently seek courses at which they can build up their knowledge and experience with such instruments, and so improve the quality of the record system. There has been considerable attention to the formation of guidance teams, and to the use of team work techniques to help overcome the communication problems in big establishments, and to deal with the wide diversity of problems encountered. These developments, as Moore emphasised in his study of five such systems, have taken place response to immediate problems, and, judging by the growing importance attached to them, seem to have met with a good deal of success. As we have already seen, movements of this kind tend to call for role-differentiation, and specialists of the kind or another tend to appear in the teamwork, leading naturally to the question of appointing a personal counsellor, or counsellors, for the pupils. The tradition of guidance, as employment-centered vocational guidance, was of course inadequate to meet this need, and hence the importation wholesale of the American theories and practices of counselling.

But the solutions worked out from the 1950's onwards, and increasingly throughout the 1960's, were in terms of how to develop and integrate *new areas* of guidance to meet the peculiar problems of big schools, and not generally in terms of deeping thinking about the existing concepts-especially, of vocational guidance. The goals were seen in terms of the solution of immediate problems. Thus it happens that we can only say that vocational guidance in Britain has evolved during the last two decades, if by 'evolution' we mean the expansion and refinement of provision, not of concepts. This means that a difficulty is sometimes found in how to relate the specialist in vocational guidance to the specialist in personal counselling, in the organisation of school guidance to the specialist in personal counselling, in the organisation of school guidance teams. In some such patterns the careers teacher actualy appears as an additional specialist *outside* the main guidance team, itself organised around a system of pwesonal counselling. Again, in some schools, counselling is dominated by a concept of vocational guidance crudely centred on helping the adolescent to make a happy 'first-job' choice, which of course means that the emphasis is on the early leavers rather than over the whole school population. Again, some at least of the confusion that exists about the difference between 'counselling' and 'guidance' stems from the fact that there has been a continuous development of provision in this semi-specialist area, but as a result of the failure of the concept to evolve, there is now a spilt between a concept which began in Britain, and a similar one, which evolved in a totally differednt fashion in North America, and was then imported into Britain in its matured form, as counselling, in the 1960's. As an example of this difficulty, an authorative article in *New Era* in 1968 stated that vocational guidance was essentially *informative*, and should be handled by careers teachers, whereas personal guidance was essentially *problem centred*, and constituted the main role of the counsellor in secondary schools. Likewise, vocational guidance is still seen by the Youth Employment Service in terms of employment-guidance. In this however the Service is not to blame, being hamstrung by its terms of reference.

Underlying all these questions about the relationship of vocational guidance to couselling are of course big questions about the relationship between the individual and his society, and about social duties. While we shall touch on some of these issues in the second part of this book, we can immediately turn to look at the institutional framework within which the various guidance functions take place, and by which they are also partly shaped and limited.

10

Counselling for the Physically Disabled

In the popular mind, a handicap is physical in nature. In fact, much that has been written about he difficulties surrounding that implementation of P.L., 93-112 and P.L. 94-142 relates to mobility problems of the physically handicapped. the physically handicapped are highly visible and their problems and successes are readily noticed. As a group they comprise the most heterogeneous group of exceptional children. They may have a wide range of medical diagnoses and greatly varying special education and support services needs. Some will not be classifiable as handicapped for special education purposes. Many will be educationally retarded, usually due to lack of experiences or suitable adaptations. They may have problems of personal, social, and emotional adjustment possibly related to the physical impairment, that is, somatopsychic, although the presence and degree will depend on the makeup of the individual pupil. There are also some myths associated with this heterogeneous subpopulation. One is that they possess special educational gifts to compensate for the physical impairment.

Obviously, such gifts would be a matter of individual pupil. There are also some myths associated with this heterogeneous subpopulation. One is that they possess special educational gifts to compensate for the physical impairment. Obviously, such gifts would be a matter of individual differences related to aptitude, compensation, and availability of time. Another myth is that the physical impairment is accompanied by a mental limitation. It is easy to generalize the handicap because it is so visual and, at times, limiting in terms of participation in school activities.

Classifications

With this subpopulation it is not uncommon to differentiate between a disability and a handicap. The disability is the measurable constant condition and the handicap is a consequence of the disability. This distinction is probably useful for his group in that many do not, or do not want to, qualify for special education programming. As pointed out by Sirvis, want to, qualify to, qualify for special education programming. As pointed out by Sirvis, "it is not the actual physical variation but, rather, the individual's attitude in relation to society's view of physical conditions that determine the extent of the handicap".

All classification systems rely heavily on medical diagnosis and degree of functional defect. P.L. 94-142 yields the following classifications and descriptions.

> "Orthopedically impaired" means a severe orthopedic impairment which adversely affects a child's educational performance. The term includes impairments caused by congenital anomaly and impairments from other causes.

> "Other health impaired" means limited strength, vitality, or alertness, due to chronic or acute health problems such as a heart condition, tuberculosis, rheumatic fever, nephritis, asthma, sickle cell anemia, hemophilia, epilepsy, lead poisoning, leukemia, or diabetes, which adversely affects a child's educational performance.

A more specific breakdown can be made into the broad categories of neurological, orthopedic, infectious disease, and other health impairments. Thee is always a danger in generalizations made from inclusion in broad categories due to overlap, but the technique is useful as a point of departure for purposes of educational planning.

Neurological impairments

Neurological impairments involve the nervous system and generally prove to be more educationally handicapping than other kinds of physical disabilities since the nervous system is the activation of the whole organism. Pupils so impaired present a particular challenge to pupil services staff due to the fact that impairment of learning may compound the physical disability.

1. Cerebral palsy describes a number of neuromuscular disabilities that may range from mild motor incoordination to almost complete helplessness. Prevalence estimates vary according to definition and classification but a reasonable estimate would appear to be three per thousand. In addition to the motor problems there are usually secondary handicaps that impede sensory ad receptive functions. The most prevalent secondary handicaps are speech impairments and mental retardation.

2. Epilepsy is a convulsive disorder that results in some kind of seizure. Brain lesions result in uncontrolled neuron firings in the brain or idiopathic and may be either permanent or temporary, depending on etiology. The seizures are usually described as grand mal, petit mal, and psychomotor. The latter form has been of interest to youth workers because some deviant behaviors, including antisocial behaviour, has been traced to this malady. Epilepsy can be controlled by medication but may have as sequelae some drowsiness, poor concentration and incoordination. Prevalence is about one per hundred.

3. Multiple sclerosis is a disorder of the central nervous system characterized by the hardening of the protective covering on nerve fibers. Symptoms include muscle weakness, unsteady gait, and sensory complications. It is a disease of older adolescents and adults and tends to progressive deterioration. Management of the condition involves interpretation of the condition to the individual, provision of a protective regimen, and appropriate treatment.

Orthopedic impairments

Orthopedic handicaps comprises musculoskeletal conditions that effect the limbs, spine, and joints. These conditions may handicap a pupil in terms of mobility or coordination, either gross or fine. Such conditions may be either congenital or acquired. A partial listing follows.

1. *Scoliosis* is a condition involving curvature of the spine which can cause limited movement. It will most likely require casting ad bracing.

2. *Rheumatoid arthritis* involves inflammation of the joints, tendons, and muscles. Frequently, there is

severe inflammation of the eyes. It represents one of the few conditions where the incidence for girls is higher than for boys. It is more common in children than is generally recognized.

3. *Muscular dystrophy* is a disease characterized by the weakening of the skeletal muscles. In children the form of the disease is called pseudo-hypertrophic or Deschesne. Muscle weakness becomes so pronounced that the pupil becomes confined to a wheelchair. This form of the disease is hereditary and is rarely seen in girls.

4. *Spina bifida* is a term that describes a congenital condition that takes a variety of forms. Basically, the disorder is caused by a failure of closure in the spinal column. This damages the spinal cord and nerve roots in a variety of ways and may result in neurological, sensory, and organ problems. Orthopedic care usually begins at birth and continuing physical therapy is often necessary.

5. *Limb deficiencies* may be congenital or acquired after birth. Successful prothesis and adaptability to normal routines are dependent on the location and severity of the loss. Pupils who are handicapped in this way often make excellent adjustments due to he long-standing nature of the condition.

6. *Miscellaneous crippling conditions* result from accidents, both vehicular and home. Included in this category would be instances of child abuse that results in impairment of function. The latter is a situation that will often involve investigation and intervention by members of the pupil services staff.

Infectious diseases

These are conditions that may be either acute or chronic depending on time of onset and subsequent treatment. Some may be transmitted in the school situation.

1. *Hepatitis* is manifested by a jaundiced appearance which is caused by swelling and soreness of the liver. It has the highest incidence rate, including all diseases, among children of school.
2. *Nephritis* is seen as puffiness about the eyes and other body parts due to disease of the kidneys. It tends to occur most often in young males.
3. *Mononucleosis* is most prevalent among high school and college age youth. The disease is caused by a virus but can be brought on by fatigue and stress.

Other health impairments

1. *Cystic fibrosis* is a hereditary disorder found most often among whites. The condition is characterized by dry coughing and frequent bowel movements. In recent years, medical advances have improved prognosis.
2. Cancer takes the form of leukemia and tumors of the eye, brain, bone, and kidney in children ad youth. The various forms of cancer in children tend to be acute and progress rapidly. Treatment of the disease may result in symptoms like fatigue, weight changes, and nausea. The emotional sequelae may necessitate intervention by pupil services staff.
3. *Asthma* is one of the allergic conditions, often triggered by emotional stress. This illness results in spells of coughing and difficulty in breathing. Although those with mild and moderate involvement

will be able to be mainstreamed, there will often be frequent absences from school.

4. *Rheumatic fever* follows a streptococcus infection and is characterized by chronic infection of the connective tissues. Prolonged attacks may result in heart damage. In the latter instance, the pupil services specialist will want to participate in decisions as to program modifications.

In case involving physical disabilities one often encounters the phenomenon of the multiple handicap. Friedman and MacQueen in the survey of physically handicapped school-aged children found that many had secondary handicaps.

> Multihandicapped means concomitant impairments, the combination of which causes such severe educational problems that they cannot be accommodated in special education programs solely for one of the impairments. The term does not include deaf-blind children.

Unfortunately, pupils who are so characterized often find themselves shunted into special education programming based on the primary presenting school-related handicap. This means that if a neurological impairment causes school assessment and performance results that appear to be at the level of mental retardation, this then becomes to replacement. The challenge to the pupil services administrator and staff is to insure that the total pupil is considered in such placement decisions. The parents who have lived with a diagnosis of cerebral palsy from birth do not want school personnel to inform them that the child is mentally retarded. Physical disabilities will often cause secondary handicaps and this should be recognized. Appropriate diagnostic services will probably reveal that there are a number of variables that impact performance. It is short-sighted and less than humanistic to ascribe a handicapping condition to the result of one test score or series of observations.

The visually impaired

The visually impaired, frequently listed under the sensorihandicapped, are a group that has captured popular interest. A visual impairment is a malfunction of the eye or optic nerve which prevents normal vision. It is standard practice to define visual impairment by degree of visual acuity and field of vision. The term blindness implied sightlessness but the definition refers to severe limitation in visual functioning. The legally blind are those who have central visual acuity of 20/200 or less in the better eye with correction or whose peripheral field is no grater than 20 degrees. The partially sighted have visual acuity between 20/200 and 20/70 in the better eye. Thus, most legally blind people can see some things but they may look dim, blurred, or out of focus. In addition, they may see only part of an object. The blind usually need braille systems while the partially sighted will require large print books.

It is estimated that approximately 0.1 per cent of school age children are visually handicapped. In translation, this means that a school district population of 5, 000 will have only five pupils so designated. They represent a small number of pupils and according to statistics comprise the smallest group of exceptional children. Etiologically, the visually impaired are the result of events that occurred prior to, during, or shortly after birth. Some have cataracts or retrolental fibroplasia. The diagnosis is usually as follows:

1. Refractive disorder: myopia, hyperopia, cataracts, astigmatism.
2. Muscle disorder: strabismus, nystagmus, amblyopia.
3. Receptive disorder: retrolental fibroplasia, optic atrophy.

Instructional provisions

Over the years, instruction for the physically disabled has moved increasingly from the hospital to the school setting. In the school setting, as a result of P.L. 94-142, there is also movement from the self-contained special class to the specially adapted regular classroom. In perhaps no other exceptionalitly is the need for multidisciplinary planning so crucial. The team may frequently involve specialists from social work, psychology, speech therapy, nursing, rehabilitation counseling, and physical and occupational therapy, nursing, rehabilitation counseling, and physical ad occupational therapy as well as recreation. Whereas the other handicapping conditions involve essentially mental and emotional components, the physically disabled subpopulation will often entail these in combination with physical limitations. In many school districts, this range of services may not be readily available; therefore, these services must be rendered on a consultative basis. Providing for the full range of services poses a particular problem for the pupil services administrator. However, once the team is assembled, there should be a focus on four developmental goals.

1. Physical independence, including mastery of daily-living skills.
2. Self-awareness and social maturation.
3. Academic growth.

4. Career education, including constructive leisure activities.

These components should become an integral part of the Individualized Education Program. The team will be assisted by the parents in the development of the IEP, an ingredient that was lacking in the pre-P.L. 94-142 era.

There is probably nothing more important to the physically disabled pupil than physical independence. It has been noted that one of the prime targets for professional personnel is to move the physically disabled person from dependence to independence. Not surprisingly, one of the cornerstones of independence is freedom of physical movement from place to place. If one must depend on others for daily living activities, it is bound to foster dependence or frustration in the best adjusted person. Key personnel in the attainment of physical independence are physical and occupational therapists. The importance of occupational therapy is specified in the 1977 P.L-142 regulations under related services.

Occupational therapy includes

1. Improving, developing, or restoring functions impaired or lost through illness, injury, or deprivation.
2. Improving ability to perform tasks for independent functioning when functions are impaired or lost.
3. Preventing, through early intervention, initial or further impairment or loss of function.

Prior to the advent of P.L. 94-142, these services were rarely seen in the schools. Physical ad occupational therapists have been traditionally hospital-bound personnel and individuals have been referred to these settings for evaluation and treatment. This still obtains for only a limited number of school districts employ physical and occupational therapists. However, more are being hired on a consultative basis to serve the schools. One of the persistent problems for the pupil services administrator is to locate such personnel for employment particularly if the district is removed from metropolitan areas or areas that have comprehensive medical facilities.

In the attainment of physical independence during the school hours, there is need for adaptive physical sites, equipment, and materials. The emphasis in the Rehabilitation Act of 1973, P.L. 93-112, Second 504, has increased sensitivity to barrier-free locations but adaptive equipment ad materials remain the responsibility of educators who wish to implement least restrictive environments. Although not all locations have to be adapted, most existing buildings with heavy concentrations of physically disabled pupils could make modest modifications without exorbitant costs. A partial list of some minor changes is as follows:

1. Ramps as well as steps for wheelchairs and crutches.
2. Handbars by drinking fountains, toilet stalls, and blackboards
3. Removal of desks to make room for a wheelchair.
4. Modification of furniture to provide for the pupil with braces.
5. Rubber mats over slippery floors.
6. Wide doorways.

While only a general statement can be made about the adaptation of equipment and materials, there should be available to the teaching staff a variety of devices to meet individual pupil needs. Each disability, or combination of disabilities, requires its own adaptations. Some of these adaptations are as follows:

1. Availability of pencil-holding devices or other modification of pencils to assist holding.
2. Provision of trays to keep pencil and crayons from falling to the floor.
3. Provision of book holders or mechanical page turns.
4. Modification of electric typewriters with cutouts for keys.
5. Installation of foot rests.

Some of these approaches may seem minor, but sometimes small steps taken toward the achievement of independence can lead to greater self-confidence and a desire for more physical independence.

Social, academic and career development

In terms of *self-awareness and social maturation* nothing is more important than the development of a positive self-concept. The development of a positive self-concept may be difficult because the physical disability can engender feelings of inadequacy and insecurity. In addition, the physically impaired pupil may experience an attitude of rejection from parents and peers. Not only is self-concept derived from interactions with others but from self-image which, in turn, may be influenced by body image. In essence, the physically disabled pupil must be assisted of feel good about himself or herself which can lead to self-awareness and social maturation. Physically disabled pupils will have their share of adjustment problems but there is nothing in the literature to indicate that this subpopulation is automatically maladjusted. Meyerson states that the physically disabled may be more vulnerable to emotional disturbance than the non-disabled for two reasons:

1. Being placed in more "new" situations than their non-disabled counterparts.
2. Being forced to live in overlapping psychological worlds-one for the disabled and the other for the "normal".

Meyerson suggests solutions to these problems (1) lie in increasing frustration tolerance and teaching adaptation skills and (2) reducing pressure that cause one to seek inaccessible and unobtainable goals that tend to exclude. Certainly, the physically disabled must learn more about their potential and limitations so that coping mechanisms can be at their highest level. As part of the self-awareness process, physically disabled pupils must be assisted in the exploration of feelings sot that they can deal with both frustration and criticism.

Academic growth is important because, as previously pointed out, the physically disabled as a group tend to be educationally deficient. If a pupil loses much time for school it may be necessary to offer tutorial instruction. Obviously, comprehensive diagnostic assessment is necessary in order to determine educational and sensory deficits. However, the curricular approach to the physically disabled must be flexible in the realization that some pupils, particularly at the secondary level, must learn survival skills. Individual academic growth will be facilitated by the new electronic technology which will provide support for missing or defective body parts as well as sensory and motor deficits. Individualization of instruction will revolve around the IEP and annual growth will be charted and monitored through this vehicle. The pupil services specialist should be alert to the need for innovative approaches to the instruction of the physically disabled. Beyond this the pupil services specialist should ensure that needs and strategies are introduced at the team meeting. In this endeavor he or she must have the active support of the pupil services administrator for there is apt to be resistance to such suggestions on the grounds of time and costs. Pupil services staff will be reluctant to assume an activist stance in these matters without administrative support.

The area of *career education* received heavy emphasis during the 1970s in the schools with all subpopulations. By the midseventies, there was an awareness that this concept should also be applied to the handicapped. It is particularly relevant for the physically handicapped because over the years they have been systematically excluded from a variety of options in the work place. Related to career education is career education, career development cannot take place. What has hampered the career development of the physically disabled is the presence of stereotypes that the general public, and perhaps, the physically disabled themselves believe. These stereotypes have been summarized by Osipow.

A discussion of stereotypical assumptions about the disabled have also been discussed by Beane and Zachmanoglou and Humes. Stereotypes must be combated because they tend to be internalized by the physically handicapped and result in self-fulfilling prophecies. The starting point for comprehensive career development is a sequential, systematic program of career education. Career education is intended to help the handicapped as well as the nonhandicaped. There are five psychosocial components to career education and they all have relevance for the disabled.

1. Career education assists individuals in becoming aware of the relationship between their maturity and their evolving aspirations, values, and potentialities.
2. Career education assists individuals in developing a sense of worth, purpose, and direction in life.
3. Career education assists the individual in becoming a part of rather than apart from society. This sense of participation leads to direct application of the principles of normalization.
4. Career education provides the individual with the security of legitimation in relation to the norms of achieving adult status.
5. Career education enables individuals to become fully capacitated to perform all of life's role more effectively.

Carrer development in the Nonhandicapped and handicapped

Assumptions About Career Development in the Nonhandicapped	*Assumptions About Career Development in the Handicapped*
1. Career development is systematic.	1. Career development is unsystematic, i.e., the handicapped had better take what it available.
2. Career development is psychologically influenced	2. Career development is not psychological since the handicapped don't have much psychological life.

3. Carrier development is a major force in	3. Career development one's life is not important for the handicapped.
4. The total person is involved in career development.	4. The handicap overrides other characteristics in determining career behaviour.
5. People are multipotential in careers.	5. The career options of the handicapped are very limited.
6. Career behaviour is developmental	6. The career development of the handicapped is arrested or retarded.
7. Career development is stressful at choice	7. The career development of the handicapped is stressful at all points.

At the same time that career education is going on, there is a concurrent growth in career development. Career development of the physically disabled should have as its goal the "preparation for all meaningful ad productive activity, at work or at leisure, whether paid or volunteer, as employee and employer, in private business or in the public sector, or in the family". Career development activities for the physically disabled should have a K-12 emphasis. At the secondary level, a period of exploration should embrace the following elements.

1. Exposure to occupational information via lectures, books, pamphlets, films, and filmstrips, and multimedia kits. Occupationally field trips and resource speakers afford excellent opportunities for the student both to acquire occupational information and to become aware of work opportunities available in the community.

2. Exposure to physically disabled adults representative of a wide variety of semiskilled, skilled and professional occupations.

3. Exposure to job-related equipment and devices that can assist a physically disabled individual in overcoming his/her physical limitations. Ideally the exposure should include opportunities to (a) observe others use these devices and (b) engage in "hands-on" experience in the classroom, vocational or scientific laboratory, or at the work site of a disabled person.

4. Opportunity to acquire knowledge about one's occupational interests, strength, and weaknesses via comprehensive educational-occupational assessment that should include work samples and/or other forms of simulated work experiences.

5. Opportunities to participate in a wide variety of a academic-occupational classroom, laboratory, and work-training experiences. It is especially important that the physically disabled not be arbitrarily excluded from such "nonacademic" subjects as art and music, physical education, laboratory science, and homemaking/industrial education at either the elementary or secondary level. For some of the more severely disabled individuals, specially organized classes or an individualized program in these subjects may be needed. Supervised work experience also is important for the physically disabled since they typically have more difficulty than the able-bodied in obtaining part-time or summer employment.

Characteristic of many of the physically disabled reflect the absence of work-related and social experiences that are part of the every day lives of the nondisabled adolescent. These experience deficits put the physically disabled at a severe disadvantage in relationship to their nondisabled counterparts. Some of the physically disabled have been so sheltered that they do not realize that lower echelon jobs usually precede higher level responsibilities ad that one earns vacation time only after a period of successful employment. Pupil services workers should not take for granted the existence of back-ground and experience that contribute to an understanding of the work world.

The aforementioned goals, while not all-inclusive, should provide a blue-print for pupil services workers and administrators as they approach the delicate task of providing an appropriate educational experience for physically disabled pupils. Developmental goals such as these must be believed and subscribed to by those who promote them. To this extent, pupil services specialists and administrators must examine their own attitudes toward the physically disabled.

Counseling the physically disabled

Counselling strategies with the physically disabled will not be markedly dissimilar from those used with the nondisabled. Client-centered, behavioural, and cognitive-oriented techniques may be equally applicable depending on the pupil, counselor, and setting. It is important that the counselor know something about the nature of physical disabilities ad have some coursework or practical experiences. As an entry point the counselor must be cognizant of some of the characteristics of the physically disabled. They are as follows:

1. Many have had few of the social experiences and as a result may be immature and lacking in self-confidence.

2. Some will have aspirations that are too low, while others may have aspirations that are much too high.
3. Many will be reluctant to trust their own judgment and will be sell inclined to take on a planning role.
4. Much of career planning may be unrealistic or stereotypic.
5. Many will focus on their limitations rather than abilities.
6. Some will feel that educational weaknesses are due to mental limitation rather than lack of opportunity.

The counselor in assisting physically disabled pupils must be oriented to individual coping levels particularly as they affect career and vocational issues. The coping levels must zero in on the areas of work-accessibility, work performance, and work rewards. Various questions must be posed by the counselor both to himself or herself and to the counselee. However, in order to make the counseling process meaningful, the pupil must assume a participatory stance in order to resolve the questions. The physically disabled are so conditioned to having things done to them or for them that it is difficult to reverse this expectation and assume responsibility for their own actions. The ultimate goals is to permit the physically disabled to assume responsibility for their own lives. However, this cannot happen unless all avenues and opportunities have been made available at the appropriate time and place.

Attitudes toward physical disability

One of the problems facing the pupil services administrator and staff deals with attitudes of the nondisabled toward disabled peers. As pointed out by

Siller, most individuals coming into interaction with the physically disabled feel anxiety or even a version. Numerous studies can be quoted to confirm that physically disabled persons are often regarded less favourably than the nondisabled. One can reasonably expect this range of feelings from the regular education staff. If the teaching corps cannot view the disabled in a reasonably positive fashion, one can expect a limited range of interest at the IEP team meetings. Modification of such negative attitudinal components involves the necessity of comprehensive staff development ad in-service efforts. A number of techniques have been used to produce positive attitudinal changes toward the physically disabled. They can be placed in categories as follows:

1. Director or indirect contacts between the disabled and nondisabled.
2. Provision of information about disabilities.
3. Persuasion and exhortation.
4. Analysis of the roots of prejudice.
5. Simulation exercises.
6. Discussion in groups.

Some of the techniques are not effective than others. One of the more successful is actual contact but it works best in structured situations when the participants have equal status. Mere information and persuasion have a limited effect. Any effort to produce attitudinal change should be spearheaded by the pupil services administrator by virtue of his knowledge about the dimensions of the problem. In planning such programs the administrator should remember the following:

1. Attitudinal components toward the physically disabled can be identified and measured.
2. A generalization of attitude components appears to exist across all disabilities.
3. The separate components of attitude within physical disability are positively correlated.
4. Demographic variables are important in the way that attitudes are expressed.
5. Negative attitudinal components are recognized by persons holding to them.

One may expect negative attitudes in some pupil services staff and even in some pupil services administrators When these occur, it will undoubtedly be necessary to provide intensive and well-organized seminars, for the feelings may be deep and not readily retrievable. The pupil services administrator with negative attitudes will have to work especially hard to bring the reasons for the devaluation to awareness.

In dealing with the physically disabled a method of work sampling is crucial if the pupil services worker is to have some direction for training and placement. Work sampling is particularly important when the vocational prospects for the pupil are not clearly evident. Work sampling or assessment can be accomplished in on-job-training or in workshop settings. The objective is to expose the pupil to a variety of work stations where practical job skills can be demonstrated. Work station experiences can include paper-and-pencil tests, commercial exercises, or job simulations with step-by-step instructions. In work sampling experiences in workshop or rehabilitation settings it is customary to use one of a variety of commercially produced work sample packages. Among them are:

1. *Jewish Employment and Vocational Service System:* Measures potential in industrial categories and includes 28 work samples for hands-on assessment of skills, behaviour, and interests. Work activities of assembly/disassembly, binding, clerical, display/printing, electrical, mail handling, structural development, and metal work are included.
2. *Testing, Orientation, and Work Evaluation in Rehabilitation:* Is the oldest and perhaps best-known work sample system for the disabled. Consists of 94 work samples clustered into 14 occupational areas. Work activities include jewelry manufacturing, drafting, drawing, sewing, and electronics assembly. Personality dimensions of work habits, work tolerance, attitudes, speed, and motivation are also assessed.
3. *Social and Prevocational Information Battery:* Developed for use with retarded individuals and includes knowledge areas in employability, economic self-sufficiency, family living, personal habits, and communication.
4. *Singer Vocational Evaluation System:* An audiovisual approach to work activities in areas of bench assembly, electrical wiring, plumbing and pipe-fitting, cooking and baking, and cosmetology.
5. *Valpar Component Work Sample System:* Has 16 individual assessment units which have been standardized for both able bodied workers and the physically disabled. Units measure skills of size discrimination, clerical comprehension and aptitude, independent problem-solving, eye-hand-foot coordination, and money handling.

11

Counselling the Emotionally Handicapped

There is no one group that will need and receive more counseling and support assistance than the emotionally troubled. Assistance will be rendered along the entire spectrum of the handicap and will include those who are designated as emotionally disturbed and eligible for special education. The need for counseling or therapeutic intervention with this subpopulation is greater than for any other. The stakes are not only immediate but life-long. According to Dimick and Huff the lack of intervention with those who have emotional problems will result in more disabilities than all other health conditions in combination. This is most surprising when one considers that success of failure in life is contingent on an individuals' reservoir of adaptive responses.

Counseling activities with the emotionally handicapped may be either indirect or direct. Pupils being treated therapeutically by outside practitioners will usually be seen by a pupil services specialist in only a consultative or liaison role. On the other hand, pupils with mild handicapping conditions may have no other service but other service but the efforts of the school counselor, school psychologist, school social worker, and so forth. Eyde has developed a descriptive figure which relates the level of emotional handicap to degrees of counseling involvement.

1. *Severe disorder*: This is the group of emotionally handicapped pupils who fit the P.L. 94-142 definition of "severely emotionally disturbed". These pupils will, and should be treated by psychiatrists, clinical psychologists, or mental health treatment teams. The pupil services specialist will generally perform a liaison function between the outside clinical service and the school. It is a rule of thumb that counseling within the school will not take place simultaneously with treatment rendered by an outside source.

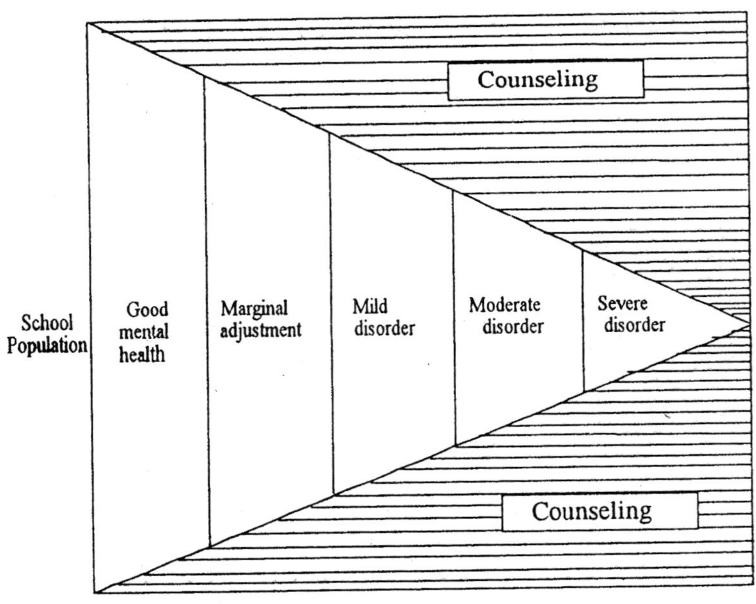

Degree of counseling intervention related to level of emotional handicap

2. *Moderate diorder*: Pupils within this grouping may be in a resource room situation or in regular classes. It is practically certain that these pupils will require counseling from either outside sources or school personnel. If counseling takes place within the confines of the school, there may be need of a counseling IEP. These pupils may manifest conflicts in the areas of affect, anxiety, and impulse control.

3. *Mild diorder*: This relatively large group comprise the group who will remain in the regular classroom. They may not qualify for special educational services but will yet appear emotionally troubled. The pupil services workers' role will be consultant to the teacher in the realm of classroom management. It is likely that most referrals will come from impulse control management. It is likely that most referrals will come from impulse control problems which will be shown through disruptive behavior and aggressive reactions.

4. *Marginal adjustment:* The marginally adjusted pupil is the one who can benefit from preventive measures. The pupil services worker, and specifically the school counselor, serves as a developmental specialist for this group of pupils. The counselor will often alert both the teacher and home about a potential problem that may be avoided through the structuring of learning experiences.

5. *Sound mental health*: The pupil services specialist may focus on the developmental needs of the "normal" population and will function essentially as a mental health educator. The pupil services specialist will endeavor to promote group and individual activities

which will reinforce sound mental health. The pupil services worker will also attempt to develop an ecosystem that will be conducive to sound mental health. With this group the staff member functions as a curricular adviser, teacher trainer, and parent educator.

Along this spectrum of degree of handicap the pupil services administrator may see the opportunity to parcel out areas of responsibility so that territorial concerns are minimal. The school counselor would have prime responsibility for those with sound mental health, marginal adjustment, and mild disorders. The school psychologist and school social worker would have principal responsibility for dealing with those pupils who manifest moderate and severe disorders. Naturally, this division of labor will be dependent on availability of staffing and philosophy of the district.

Indirect and direct services

It is possible to identify three supportive counseling services for the pupil services worker which can be considered indirect services. These are consultation, collaboration, and conceptualization. The consultant attempts to achieve a match between the pupils' developmental needs and the learning environments. In order to serve as an effective consultant to the providers of instructional services to the emotionally handicapped the pupil services workers must deal with issues of lack of information, lack of skills, lack of confidence, and lack of objectivity. As *collaborator* the pupil services specialist will assist in the coordination of IEPs which for the emotionally handicapped pupil will probably involve considerable contact with regular classroom teachers due to the fact that may of these pupils will be mainstreamed.

The pupil services specialist as *conceptulizer* is somewhat more difficult to delineate because it entails observation of the total or "big" picture and reaching some conclusion as to what may be the cause or cure of an individual or institutional problems. If the conceptualizer role does not fall to the pupil services specialist, it may fall to no one. The conceptualizer must determine what areas are impacting the pupil, whether school, home, or community, and how these forces may be modified.

Direct services may include behavioral change counseling, biofeedback training, life-space interviewing, affective education classes, leisure education and therapeutic play, peer counseling, and parent education. The latter is a particularly useful form of counseling to ameliorate the problems of the emotionally handicapped. It has been often observed that part of many emotional disturbance situations is a disordered parent-child relationship. If parents can understand their own adjustment problems, the dynamics of the home situation may change and in so doing the interactions with the pupil may improve. All direct services with emotionally handicapped pupils and their families require special personal qualities and personal commitments. Establishing a relationship and conveying a sense of caring is a must. Typically, the emotionally handicapped pupil and his/her parents have felt frustrated, neglected, isolated, and misunderstood. In order to overcome these feelings of rejection it is necessary to focus on the individual rather than the problem. It is not easy to work with those who experience emotional problems. Those who need the most help often engage in self-defeating behavior in an effort to reinforce feelings of self-rejection and to encourage hostility on the part of those who seek to help. It goes without saying that every pupil services specialist is not equipped to engage in direct services with this subpopulation.

Development and administration problems

Next to learning disabilities the emotionally handicapped represent the newest category. As such it is still in a process of growth and redefinition. While P.L. 94-142 served to delimit the number of pupils who could be so categorized, it remains a fact that the emotionally troubled are still out there. They must be served, either through special education avenues or some modification thereof. It remains the category of most concern to teachers and administrators because of the daily challenged posed by this subpopulation. Some of the issues to be dealt with by a pupil services administrator will be discussed in further detail.

Role of support personnel

An issue of considerable interest to pupil services administrators and staff is the role of support personnel in identification, placement, and follow-up of the emotionally handicapped. The pupil services specialist is usually the first person, after the initial referral, who sees the pupil suspected of being emotionally disturbed. Undoubtedly, the pupil has emotional problems, as perceived by another person, but the task of the pupil services worker is to conduct an initial "screening" to determine whether the pupil is within normal limits in terms of adaptive behavior. Such screening will depend on may situational variables, for example, adequacy and philosophy of the district, competency of the teaching staff, socioeconomic climate of the school, and so forth. Accordingly, it is not as simplistic as many classroom teachers and general administrators would like it to be. The pupil services worker must make a decision either to go forward with diagnostic instrumentation, a costly procedure, or refer back to the teacher. Unfortunately, the initial introduction is judge like in nature, a heavy role indeed. This role will be especially difficult in small schools or districts where the pupil services worker cannot talk with colleagues about prediagnostic impressions. During the placement or IEP process the pupil services specialist who reviewed and prepared the case materials will be expected to make a recommendation based on diagnostic impressions. This will probably be easiest for the school psychologist, due to the availability of test instrumentation, but even here the problem is exacerbated by the fact that test instrumentation is imprecise in terms of diagnosis of emotional disturbance. Once a pupil is placed, there is more need for follow up of the emotional handicapped than for any of the other subpopulations because emotional handicaps are dynamic and reversible. If possible, a pupil service worker should remain in contact with every pupil who has been designated as emotionally handicapped and determined by the IEP team to be in need of special education. If there are staff shortages the pupil services administrator must try to design alternative strategies to make the consultive approach work. Adul education programs might be considered as an alternative.

Diagnosis

Related to the role of support personnel is the question of diagnosis. The federal IEP regulations are quite specific as to who should be classified as "severely emotionally disturbed". Should such a classification be assigned by a group of school professionals, based on demonstrated behavior, or should the designation be reserved for clinic personnel? The answer rests, **in part**, on whether one chooses to follow an educational or medical model. It is possible to mount compelling arguments on both sides. While the education model will tend to move pupils in and out of special education programs more readily, clinical diagnosis is more apt to result in treatment and parental acceptance. If a given district chooses to use a categorical model, it may be expeditious to utilize outside clinical personnel for consensual validation. The designation "emotional disturbance" is a heavy label to assign to any pupil for it may convey more to the parent, community, and society than school staff intend. For example, there is evidence that behavioral disorders have both a sexual and racial bias in that minority males are often overrepresented. Conversely, it has been suggested that the moderately disturbed child is being denied services due to regulatory exclusion.

Negative Stereotypes

While it is debatable as to whether emotional disturbance or mental retardation has the most negative image, there is no doubt that emotional disturbance is a label that few people cover for a pupil. The label suggests disordered and unacceptable behavior that is a threat to others. From a parental point of view, it is usually construed as an indictment of the parent-child relationship. The negative stereotypes associated with this handicap have prevented many pupils from getting needed help. In most districts, IEP teams must either label or describe behavior before goals and objectives can be finalized. In the process such labeling or description of behavior must be interpreted to parents who may have habituated an avoidance mechanism. In recognition of this eventuality, a pupil services specialist may decide not to label or describe the pupils as "seriously emotionally disturbed" for fear that the parents will reject the diagnosis and withdraw support of any treatment and placement considerations. In many districts attempts have been made to devise a short-form of the IEP so that parents will not have to face the narration of the uncomfortable details of a full-blown disturbance. The pupil services administrator must seek ways to make an emotional handicap more respectable and palatable. Such strategies may include parent seminars, teacher in-service programs, and pupil self-awareness.

Juvenile Delinquency

While the P.L. 94-142 regulations exclude the "socially maladjusted" it is a fact that a higher proportion of social offenders show behavioral disorder than nonoffenders. Although it is widely accepted that the phenomenon of juvenile delinquency-that is, minors who have violated the law and have been apprehended-is largely in the eyes of the beholder, the fact remains that young people who are so designated have a wide range of emotional problems. Whether the problems are autoplastic or alloplastic, there is no doubt that this group poses a considerable problem for pupil services staff and administrators. There is mounting evidence that juvenile delinquents have a high incidence of learning disabilities. This finding is remarkable only in that it took so long to establish the linkage. Juvenile offenders are typically school failures and early dropouts. Aside from other socioeconomic factors these youth obviously never found learning to be either relevant or simple. Certainly, the likelihood of school failure can lead to emotional problems and-depending on intrapsychic, family, and community pressures-can precipitate juvenile delinquency. Although juvenile offenders are hardly a homogeneous group, a large measure of hostility may be expressed in socially unacceptable ways. These are the "acting out" pupils who plague the lives of many teachers. Such pupils will be a constant source of referrals to pupil services staff. In order to deal with the phenomenon the pupil services worker will have to assume a change-agent role. That is, there must be a recognition that many of the causes are alloplastic in nature which necessitate going to the community or family for modifications in the environment. The high dropout rate with this subpopulation indicates the need for more intensive effort in the area of primary prevention.

Mainstreaming

It is a truism that most emotionally troubled youth will be served in the regular classroom by regular teachers. A relative handful will be categorized as emotionally disturbed and therefore eligible for special education of some kind. Those who remain in regular classrooms will continue to be troubled or to trouble teaching staffs. Pupils who are not designated as in need of special education will probably received no extra assistance unless pupil service specialists choose to intervene. Such intervention will support the regular class placement and may involve counseling, consultation, community mobilization, and the like. In such situations no team meetings are required nor is an IEP necessary. On the surface, this procedure would seem to make the possibility of service more flexible and less bound to bureaucratic restrictions. However, the pupil service specialist will be under great pressure to serve first those who have an IEP. By virtue of traditional job roles intervention can probably best be carried out by the school counselor. The school counselor, serving the developmental needs of *all* youth, is nor restricted by special education parameters. The fact that the school counselor receives scant mention in the P. L. 94-142 regulations will allow the counselor to provide services to those who do not qualify for special education benefits. The concept of mainstreaming does receive a lot of publicity and was in the forefront of special education thinking even before P. L. 94-142 was enacted. When it has succeeded, it has usually been through the efforts of special education teachers and a selected few regular education teachers. There is evidence that pupil services workers and special education teachers are more in agreement on behavioral objectives for this subpopulation than regular class teachers.

Need for more service

A recent report by the Children's Defense Fund indicates that two-thirds of the nations' seriously emotionally disturbed pupils are not receiving appropriate special education and related services. The researchers for the Fund, an advocacy group, reviewed the statutes and litigation involving emotionally disturbed children and adolescents and reached the following conclusions:

1. Implementation has been hindered by confusion about how severe a disturbance must be to be covered by the regulations;
2. The schools' responsibility for psychotherapy, often a needed adjunct service, remains unclear;
3. Resistance to the obligation to pay for residential treatment, when needed, where documented by the schools inability to provide;
4. School psychologists spend practically all their time testing and do not have enough time left for counseling pupils and consulting with teachers;
5. Emphasis on serving the seriously emotionally disturbed has reduced mental health intervention strategies for early attention;

6. Some school are not referring emotionally disturbed pupils for services;
7. States have been remiss in not encouraging the development of training programs to increase the pool of qualified teachers.

12

Counselling the Learning Disabled

The need for counseling is obvious when one is aware that early recipients of learning disabilities services were found to need supportive ad vocational assistance as adults. Practically all pupil services specialists may become involved in counseling SLD pupils. Counseling has proven effective with this subpopulation. Due to the fact that behavioural and adjustment problems often overlap cognitive deficits, there is a need for the counselor to deal with coping and self-control skills. In dealing with these strategies, the helper may choose to use either a counseling or consultation model. In addition to the student, the counselor will work with the teacher(s) and parent(s).

Students with long standing SLD problems will demonstrate a variety of behavioural symptoms, chief among them will be low self-esteem, anxiety, anger and frustration. Counseling strategies which apply particularly to the adolescent, should:

1. Offer a chance for success, no matter how small.

2. Build an inclination to try by structuring small segments of assigned tasks.
3. Minimize situations where threats, punishment, and strong reactions of adults are prevalent.
4. Keep the student to a reasonable time schedule once he begin to make progress.
5. Ally deep-seated fears that he is somehow mentally subnormal.

Counselors who deal with students who have ambivalence over intelligence may find it useful to use Lloyd Thompson's entitled "Language Disabilities in men of Eminence". In this provocative piece, Thompson uses a psychohistorical approach to illustrate that some great men in history probably had SLD. Among the people described are Thomas Edison, Harvey Cushing, Auguste Rodin, George Patton, Woodrow Wilson, Paul Ehrlich, Albert Einstein and George Washington. Adolescents can identify with these eminent people and realize that all is not necessarily lost because one had a learning problem in school.

Counseling techniques will differ on the basis of specific problem behaviour. However, Edge, Brown, and Brown suggest some that may be generally applicable.

1. For inadequacy, try "strength bombardment" in a group setting.
2. For anxiety, try relaxation training.
3. For anger, try a cognitive approach, perhaps rational-emotive counselling, or "I messages."
4. For frustration or inappropriate interactions try "time out".

There is also need for parent and family counseling. Stress and sibling rivalry are commonly found in families of learning-disabled students "parents feel ambivalence guilt, fear...but... must always subside to the reality that theirs is still a handicapped child who seems normal, but doesn't appear to learn and/or behave normally". This is the essence of the parental frustration, namely, trying to understand how a child who is normal in most ways can fail to learn in school, even with massive amounts of tutoring and family support.

Career preparation and developscareer development. As is true with most mildly handicapped adolescents, the youth who make up this subpopulation will most likely enter the competitive work force after graduation from high school. Of course, some will advance to higher education but it is apparent that an academically delimiting handicap like SLD will dictate circumscribed horizons. Too little attention has been paid heretofore to the postsecondary future of the SLD pupil. Part of the problem is related to the difference between career and vocational education/development. Vocational development has a narrower focus and in terms of special education populations has tended to emphasize a limited clientele. Vocational education programs, albeit sorely limited in some parts of the country, have been targeted primarily at those pupils in some parts of the country, have been targeted primarily at those pupils categorized as educable mentally retarded. This targeting developed, in part, from the belief that the mildly retarded had very few choices. The learning-disabled, however, comprise a heterogeneous group with much broader options. Accordingly, the concepts of career preparation and development are highly applicable If a career is the totality of work or activities over a life time, then a more comprehensive approach is necessary with SLD pupils. However, before strategies are instituted there must be a realization that the SLD pupil required career development assistance.

Due to the fact that the SLD pupil has the given of "normal" intelligence it is often assumed that he or she can move through the secondary school situation in lockstep with nonhandicapped pupils. The implication is that SLD pupils will somehow absorb incidental career information that will be self-utilized upon graduation. While this rationale is difficult, at best, for even the nonhandicapped pupil it is disastrous for the SLD pupil. A SLD pupil is typically exerting every ounce of energy to survive the academic demands of the secondary school. If one accepts this restraint it is easy to see why little attention will be given to incidental types of learning that are part of the repertoire of informal career preparation and development. Bingham has observed that boys with SLD are less mature in their responses on the Carrier Maturity Index and require planned experience to develop vocational maturity. Kendall found that subjects enrolled in vocational-training classes were superior in social maturity and career attitudes.

Another hurdle for school counselors who are concerned with career development is the often unreasonable expectations of the parents. This "hidden handicap" will sometimes lead parents astray and arouse expectations of educational and occupational choices that are far beyond the proven capabilities the SLD pupil. This can be a particular problem for youth who come from college-educated or professional families. Although some youth have internalized these parental expectation, most will feel relieved to be guided toward more realistic choices. An additional variable is the actual range of possibilities that may be available. IT has been pointed out previously that some colleges are now opening their doors to the identified learning-disabled motivated, successfully-coping pupil. However, the range of possibilities between vocation and college education is much less appealing. Technical schools and related occupations have yet to feel the need to adapt to the needs of the learning-disabled.

The pupil services administrator and staff must be alert to the need for career preparation and development for the SLD adolescent at these times. If quantity and quality of academic programming were the issues of the seventies then postsecondary career issues will be the frontier of the eighties. It should be reiterated that P.L. 93-112, the Rehabilitation Act of 1973, does recognize specific learning disabilities as an adult disorder. The SLD person is entitled to the same considerations as others with more visible handicaps. The pupil services staff must forge a linkage with rehabilitation counselors and employers. This is a task that will fall to school counselors, school psychologists, and school social workers.

Development and administration problems

There are a number of issues conforming the pupil service administrator within the domains of both development and management. The problems may differ depending on the maturity of the department, but the problem areas have similarities. An initial development problem centres around the instructional delivery system that is best for the district and the student configuration. For example, is it better to go with a tutoring program as opposed to the resources room concept? Once a procedure has been initiated, it is difficult, but not impossible, to change. The pupil services administrator must examine the nature of the SLD staff/ parental expectations and financial resources and act accordingly. A development or redevelopment should utilize the needs-assessment technique so all parties are in agreement. Another development issue to be faced in the 1980s is when expansion should cease. During the 1970s the objective was to increase services so as to meet the needs of an unserved population. The time will come when not only will it be appropriate to limit expansion but also to reduce services. At a time when general school enrollments are decreasing and regular class teachers are being dismissed, can one in good conscience continue SLD services at the same level? This issue must be resolved through analysis of caseloads and the generation of "hard data" for justification.

Specific management problems may revolve around the maintenance of identification standards, standardization of caseloads, interstaff relationships, least restrictive environment, and evaluation/accountability.

Maintenance of identified standards

As the nationwide concern for specific learning disabilities has increased, it was inevitable that more mild conditions would be included. There are many pupils in school with learning problems and some may have some of the characteristics associated with definitions of SLD. The issue for a pupil services administrator is whether such pupils are eligible for special education. Gearheart recognizes this issue but believes that preventive efforts may be one of the most effective ways to deliver learning disabilities programming. Others would agree that prevention is the best way to approach any emerging disability but might quarrel with the designation of the delivery system. The instruction of mild cases, which may not meet formal identification criteria, might properly belong in the domains of remedial or compensatory education. A pragmatic view would hold that the pupil should receive service wherever it is available, with the recognition that the budget climate of the eighties is not conducive to either the establishment or maintenance of nonspecial education programming. The team, whether by school or district, will decide who is eligible for services and the pupil services administrator must exercise leadership in developing a philosophical point of view as to what constitutes a specific learning disability which, in turn, will influence standards. The problem for the pupil services administrator is no an easy one, for it involves a number of variables differing from district to district. Some of the questions that can be posed are:

1. Will the dilution of standards eventually do more harm than good by resulting in reduction for funding brought on by greater numbers?
2. If some kind of service is provided, even if not condoned by the regulations, will it eventually reduce the prevalence of SLD?
3. Should the broad range of learning problems be served, from whatever source, for the grater good of society?

Standardization of caseloads

A building-oriented approach to specific learning disabilities is becoming standard in many parts of the country due both to the ubiquitous nature of SLD and to the fact that it is often the preferred choice of most general administrators and parents. That there is no threat or stigma to having an SLD center in a given school contributes to its desirability and popularity. As this development occurs, SLD teacher who are completely building-based become increasingly under the jurisdiction of building principals. There is nothing wrong with this traditional supervisory model nit it presents a problem to the pupil services administrator because principals tend to view services from a different perspective. As building managers, principals are under pressures different from those of central office administrators. Principals, unlike most pupil services administrators, have a constituency that is composed of the parents and/or pupils of the entire school. Accordingly, the principal as to meet the demands of the constituency in terms of services. If remedial services in the school are limited or nonexistent, he/she may be inclined to request services from the SLD center even though a pupil may not have yet cleared a team meeting or, at best, is marginally eligible. The motivation in such requests is usually commendable and eminently pupil-centered so the principal cannot be faulted on help-giving grounds. Naturally, such requests are difficult if not impossible to deny for a building-based special education teacher. As a result caseloads in individual schools may vary widely, sometimes from 15-30 pupils per teacher. When such a discrepancy is revealed it causes a furor among special education teachers and parents. It is the responsibility of the pupil services administrator to insure that standard caseloads are observed both for quality of service and staff morale. To his extent, it is advisable to have an approved policy statement on record to indicate minimum and maximum pupil limits. Once these and similar questions are addressed the pupil services administrator may determine if the standards are set, it is certain that they will not be popular with all segments of the administrator's constituency, whether other administrators, teachers, pupil services staff, or parents. Therefore, in trying to modify or maintain standards, the administrator will have to use all the managerial skills at his/her command.

Interstaff relationships

Relationships among SLD teachers, psychologists, speech-language pathologists, and social workers often need improvement. Specifically, the different specialities sometimes are at variance with regard to the identification and instructional needs of those pupils who are described as learning-disabled. This kind of intergroup conflict seems to occur with the SLD population more than with other exceptionalities. It is due, in part, to the nebulous quality of the handicap but, in addition, it reflects the compelling need of all specialists to get involved in program planning. All have a take in the IEP whether by virtue of professional identity, administrative requirements, or parental expectations. Due to "turf" issues interstaff relationships often deteriorate and assume conflict proportions. For a host of reasons, among them being popularity and acceptance, most staff members want to participate in SLD program planning and development. It is probably crucial that IEP meetings be attended by representatives of all the disciplines. This is a good strategy because no one specialty will feel slighted or left out. The essence here is participation and not necessarily decision making. Another potent device is to involve all disciplines in policy-making decisions that affect the SLD subpopulation. Noninvolvement can lead to feelings or rejection, frustration, and hostility. Another technique is to involve all specialities in any efforts at parent education.

With regard to SLD it is expedient to allow each specialty to become identified with SLD in the parents' minds. The parental lobby in specific learning disabilities has been a powerful one and this has not been lost on pupil services staff. The hidden agenda here is that if programs are expanded, usually at the behest of parents, then all specialities should have an opportunity to partake of the largesse.

Least restrictive environment

Nowhere is the debate about the least restrictive environment more intense than in the arena of specific learning disabilities. Support and arguments run the gamut from advocates of total normalization to the need for private school placement. It is possible to make a case for his range of placements as it is for no other exceptionality. Normalization or mainstreaming is not always successful because it is often administratively inspired and a "competency-based assessment" has been suggested. P.L. 94-142 leans a variety of ways. An activist parents of a severely learning-disabled adolescent will often see least restriction being offered in a residential private school pectations of public school personnel. Similarly, a school social worker might see the same pupil as requiring contact with normal environment sot that "them" arrangement. Sometimes, representatives of the "us,"- namely, school personnel-become advocates for the parent posture which presents an interesting loyalty dilemma. The pupil services administrator must deal with this explosive issue, which represents one of the persistent challenges. First, the pupil services administrator must campaign actively for a true continuum of environments within the school district so that parents can perceive that they have a variety of options. Second, the pupil services administrator may convey to all that he or she is a fair person who can see the merits in an opposite point of view when a case is well made and laced with facts. Third, there must be a staff development of team participants so that case materials are reviewed objectively and recommendations made on personal conscience and not because of administrative fiat. When such a climate prevails it should be possible to determine the least restrictive environment for an SLD pupil that will have the approval of most and the acceptance of the rest.

13

The Future of Guidance and Counselling

The conditions that support the need for guidance have been highlighted all through the preceding chapters. It is inconceivable that any of them will fade away; recent events in social, economic, and political life show that problems and needs will become more complex and pressing.

The viability of guidance as a major helping service depends not only on the profusion of societal problems, complexities, and needs; it must be seen as an effective response. The many publics-pupils, parents, legislators, the community at large, and educators-must view guidance as a profession that provides a need service, available from no other source. Two factors determine whether or not this will occur. The first is the sensitivity and perceptiveness of guidance workers in discerning the *real* problems and needs, particularly those of which the general public is only dimly aware. The second is the effectiveness in communicating goals and results to this same public.

Obviously something positive has to happen in the

lives of those who come in contact with guidance. Identifying needs and publicizing results will not alone accomplish the task of ensuring the support of guidance services. But guidance already has the means to ensure that it has a significant impact, and the dynamic nature of the profession, documented throughout this book, practically guarantees that it will enlarge and improve on present approaches and techniques.

Thus, the question needs to be faced, will the guidance professions able to respond effectively to the two major tasks? My position is that it will; the motivation, competency, and imagination of those who will do the job are already plentiful. In fact, a recurring theme in earlier chapters is the inventiveness guidance workers have repeatedly demonstrated not only in dealing with current needs but in anticipating emerging or hidden ones. Failure will come only if enthusiasm falters, and pressures and challenges are allowed to cause a futile search for security through ingratiatingly taking on a myriad of insignificant and irrelevant tasks in the attempt to become indispensable rather than be professional.

Our future and implications for guidance

Predictions are hazardous but necessary. The task is made easier by the post-Bicentennial climate of taking stock and looking to the future. A positive orientation towards the future is essential in the midst of the present confusions and dilemmas:

America is wallowing in a period of disappointment and disillusion. The idea of progress is till alive, but it is not well. There is an emerging 'new pessimism', not only in foreign policy but in domestic affairs. Government is viewed as, inevitably, bumbling and corrupt. Other social institutions are considered obsolete and ineffectual.

But, Elam's view is not one of long-term pessimism. Hopeful signs both of society in general and schools in particular can be drawn from the position that ours is a "self correcting society" and the schools are "a major instrument in shaping the future".

The bases for optimism are substantial. Resources re being depleted, but there are avenues available utilizing selective growth and alternative energy resources that can, if used fully and promptly, head off disaster. The nation's collective ingenuity can find new ways to cope with destructive trends. Scientific and social innovations and breakthroughs have served to improve the quality of life in past years and have the potential for equally or greater success in the future. We are only beginning to use our intellectual potential for progress on all fronts; education, especially, stands to gain enormously from new developments in both the cognitive and affective areas. But we may need to experience a "socioquake" and thus arrive at new ways of viewing man in relation to the environment rather than patching up the old perceptions and practices.

With an assumption of constructive and positive changes, what are major directions for the next several decades? A review of even a handful of the significant themes required a look at political, economic, social, and educational aspects.

There is a continuity in the international political alignments among power blocs, even as new nations strive for status and recognition, and energy resources modify relations among countries. International politics will be based on power balances and energy resources, but there will be a greater recognition and acceptance of the concept of interdependence of nations. The related worldwide problems of growth, crowding, and inadequate resources will be faced; cooperative efforts will be made to slow down the population explosion, increase worldwide food production, and enhance the self-sufficiency of third-world countries.

Economic problems, primarily inflation, and unemployment, will continue to cause hardships for individuals, while increasing both the cost of services and the need for them. Cooperation among nations will be emphasized, while reduced energy resources and needs of undeveloped countries heighten problems in this country.

The trend of a rising median population age will continue, and the effects will be felt in every aspect of life. Not only will there be a shift in the emphasis of guidance and counseling, but retirement policies and benefits, education, housing, medical care, and the world of work will be dramatically affected.

Work and the work setting are changing in ways that will have profound effects in the years ahead. There will be an increased demand for job security as protection against the fluctuations in the economy. At the same time, however, more humane and stimulating working conditions will be sought. The work week and work day will be shortened, and variations such as splitting job and self-selected work hours will be tested. The increasing age of the labor force and the steady trend for more female participation will affect the workplace in many ways not yet known to us.

Changes in education will range from introducing new financing plans to establishing programs for lifelong learning. As the proportion of school-age individuals decreases, the cost of public education rises, and the needs and political power of older persons become more visible, we may see a higher quality of schooling. It seems certain that there will be provisions for lifelong easy entry and exit in educational and training programs. New school models will merge education and life-family, community, and work-in ways that will make education more significant. Writz predicts that "some kind of prevision for enterprising the earning and learning of a living, for interweaving for interspersing the earning and learning of a living, for interweaving employment and self-renewal, is going to have to be recognized as the essential condition for an effective career as worker, citizen, or human being".

A host of trends are encompassed by the need Shane describes as "how to remotivate youth to feel that life is good, that it is worth living, and that it can bring enduring satisfaction". Many of the problems of today stem from the lacks this statement implies; some young people seek solutions in fads, cults, drugs, or deviant life-styles. The educational institution will play a significant part in building new values and purpose, but the next several decades will be marked more by questions and searching than by answers and solutions.

If we translate the societal trends into guidelines for counseling and guidance, a general picture of increased pressure for services emerges. The need to make the most use possible of human and material resources leads to a greater concern for individual awareness of potential and opportunities. Material resources will be carefully used by those who are sensitive to the needs of others and are aware of the importance of sharing rather than thinking only of themselves.

The increasing interdependence among nations could enhance concern for problems that are common to different cultures and bring guidance workers in different countries closer together to pool strategies and techniques. Developing and underdeveloped countries can profit from learning about what is done in other areas if they have the opportunity to adapt principles and strategies for local uses. It would be well to avoid an attitude that what is done in technologically advanced countries is best for others. A cooperative approach to unique needs of each culture would be true implementation of the spirit of guidance.

Many of the cutbacks that appear to be inevitable will very likely cause disruptions in established patterns of travel ,recreation, and day-to-day living. New modes may actually be growth-producing-there may, for example, be less dependence on commercial entertainment-but the changes may call for difficult adaptations.

The changing age of the population has obvious and important implications for guidance. Not only will there be a shift to include expanded services for those in their middle and later years, but new types of help will be needed, e.g., assisting mid-life and older persons with educational and work planning.

The changing world of work offers some of the most direct implications for guidance and counseling of any aspect of life. Even though efforts are being made to adapt work to individuals and to develop new patterns of work hour and sharing jobs, the central problem of finding meaning and fulfillment will demand increased attention. Perhaps a combination of meaningful leisure activities and income-producing work will needed. Whatever the eventual solutions, it seems that some kind of human development services both the workplace and in the community will be needed.

The changing world of work offers some of the most direct implications for guidance and counseling and aspect of life. Even though efforts are being made to adapt work to individuals and to develop new patterns of work hours and sharing jobs, the central problem of finding meaning and fulfillment will demand increased attention. Perhaps a combination of meaningful leisure activities and income-producing work will be needed. Whatever the eventual solutions, it seems that some kind of human development services both in the workplace and in the community will be needed.

The increasing need for accountability and making the most productive use of resources will make education give additional emphasis to helping all pupils understand and utilize their full potential. Questions are being raised about the assumed benefits of large schools, and there is a shift emerging that emphasizes compulsory education, not just compulsory attendance. These and other trends imply that help will needed to make the school a place for learning and development attuned to the needs of the individual and the community.

The task of helping youth to find challenge, meaning, and stimulation in school programs, work, and productive community life is made even more demanding by the changing social and economic conditions. This is a school-community problem that demands the best efforts of practically everyone, but it is one in which guidance personnel have a unique opportunity for effective leadership and service.

A brief and general review of major trends slights a multitude of specific issues, problems and directions of critical significance for guidance workers (e.g. licensure, ethics, preparation, and affirmative action), but it gives the backdrop against which they will be worked out. Moreover, the major trends contain an formation of an increasing need for guidance and counseling for helping all individuals in lifelong growth and development and to give guidelines for dealing with the specific questions and problems.

The need for new approaches

A major point of this book is that new strategies, techniques, and technology are vital of effective delivery of services today. The future will make even greater demands on the creativity and inventiveness of guidance workers. Two factors support this prediction-accountability and financing. From the counselor's point of view, the major reason is to provide better-quality help to more people; improving the quality of life ranks above the demand for hard evidence of effects and adjusting to cope with financial limitations. But the realities of the situation require a consideration of the most effective use of personnel and material resources to achieve desired goals. Tomorrow may usher in strategies that are unknown today.

The past few years have witnessed a proliferating of approaches, technology, and strategies. Some are destined for a brief meteoric life before falling into oblivion. Others are sure to become major styles of guidance in the future. The problem that counselors face is how to tell the difference. There is no quick or easy way; research and evaluation provide the most valid answers. Intuition may seem a trusty guide, but it is often so entangled in personal commitment to an approach or enthusiasm for a cause that its value is doubtful.

Moreover, the attitude that what is new is new is good and what is old is bad leads to a distorted view that inhibits a thoughtful and perceptive selection of the most effective means. This naive position, coupled with a tendency to partially try out and quickly dispose of new approaches, not only creates discontinuous development but often relegates to the scrap heap potentially valuable methods and materials. There is much faddishness in U. S. guidance, abetted by an affluence that permits spending of enormous sums on new developments that are discarded even before rigorous testing can be completed. This luxury is fast disappearing. It will take careful evaluation and use of both the old and new to fashion the guidance of the future.

Productive elements that will gain additional use in the years ahead are reflected in earlier chapters. Consultation is one. Together with psychological education and "giving guidance away", it represents a new taking shape for many years. Paraprofessional and computers also have great potential. The needs survey, a new label for holding guidance close to what the public wants, is obviously here to stay. It has never disappeared since the concept of guidance first surfaced at the turn of the century but since then it has fallen on hard times. Accountability is of course not new; the only surprising things is that it took so long to emerge as a major consideration in the helping services. A number of other strategies have been endorsed in the preceding pages; the movement toward lifelong learning and guidance, and integrating the school with the community and workplace are the most significant. The separate elements are not new, but the synthesis brings into being a strategy of tremendous importance.

One front along which the profession advances does not involve largescale movements nationwide in scope-it is in the day-to-day work of the counselor who may, for example, develop a better way to help a counselee explore goals, make decisions, and carry out plans, or devise a new mode of working with groups of pupils or parents. It could be any of the mutitude of things the counselor does. Shared with colleagues, these activities have a ripple effect that eventually makes a difference in school guidance.

Reflections on programs naturally lead to speculaton about the practice of guidance five, twenty, or thirty years ahead. What will it be like? Is it possible to look into the future with any certainty?

Guidance in the next five years

Some trends appear to be fairly clearly indicated by current developments. One of these is licensure. There almost certainly will be some type of widespread provisions for licensure, which will have an impact on school counselors. Effects will be felt more definitely by those in non-school gettings, however, as it is predicted that employment in an educational institution will enable the counselor to practice regardless of licensure status.

Accountability will be given more attention in all settings. Evidence of positive effects will be needed to ensure the continued existence of school guidance services as well as to maintain support for programs in other settings. Moreover, counselors will be expected to expand services with little additional financial support.

The counselor's role will be more clearly defined, partly because of accountability and partly because of the use of new strategies such as outreach and psychological education, which give the work a visible structure and purpose.

Increasing attention will be given to the needs of special groups, e.t., mid-life and older persons, minorities, the handicapped, and women. Moreover, we will see at least the beginning of the implementation of lifelong learning and school-community cooperative approaches.

Changes in public education, particularly the expanded infusion of career education, will make the school a more dynamic and realistic learning environment. At the same time the "basics" will be increasingly emphasized. All of these changes will offer counselors opportunities to serve in new ways and to build a solid position in education.

More processes and personnel will be utilized to expand the reach of guidance services. Paraprofessionals are one example, particularly peer counselors. After their slow start in the past decade, computers will be used with increasing frequency.

As school budgets are examined, questions will be raised about the necessity for guidance services. The predicted outcome, however, is that there will be an increase in the support for services because the offer ways to deal with the most pressing school and community problems.

Guidance in twenty years

The impact of the social, economic, and political trends described on pp. 342-345 will have a more pronounced effect on guidance and counseling than in the immediate future. It is predicted that more definite patterns of those trends given for the next five years will have emerged, e.g., licensure regulations will be crystallized, career education will be the major mode in public education, and guidance roles will be more clear-cut and more widely understood. Computer technology will be used, and counselors will have much more time to devote to the personal, effective, and decision-making needs of youth.

Lifelong education and school-community cooperation will be realities, and counselors will work with all ages in both school and community. There will be increases in the number of counselors needed; preparation standards will provide for differential staffing, with high levels of technical and human-relations competency for those in supervisory positions. At the same time there will be increased attention to prevention of problems and the provision of easily available community-wide services. School counselors will be regarded as logical persons to coordinate all school-guidance and pupil-personnel services, and will provide leadership for community-wide coordination strategies.

Guidance beyond the year 2000

Disregarding the gloomy projections of those who question the likelihood of civilization lasting into the 21st century-such apprehension would have been equally appropriate in any approach of recorded history-it is not only possible but essential to look ahead to try to discern a reasonably accurate, if tentative, outline of the shape of guidance. Leaders in the field, such as Berdie, Harris, Morgan, and Walz, show a substantial consensus about major developments in the future.

Four characteristics stand out. First, the counselor will go where people are; outreach will be major strategy, and there will be considerable use of support persons. Marple describes a thought provoking fantasy of the future in which "Friendship Centers" alter the lives of people nationally and internationally. But typically, no clear-cut definition of the arrangement of such a center is given; but the implication is that location and type of housing will be of less importance than what happens in the community.

The second major prediction is that services will be available lifelong; the school-age emphasis will have disappeared. Guidance will be provided over the whole range of individuals and groups; no social strata or subculture will be favored over any other. Along with this breadth, helping agencies and institutions will collaborate far more than they do today, and guidance workers will have a more comprehensive knowledge of and better working relationships with, colleagues in other settings.

Much of the counselor's work will emphasize prevention; while crisis help will be provided, the major thrust will be the change agent's task reducing or eliminating destructive features of the environment that generate problems.

The counselor's increased versatility will require a sound background in theory, research, and techniques, the quality of preparation will rise. Facilitating personal development, building effective working relationships, and gaining an in-depth understanding of various cultures will be given higher priority. Preparation programs will utilize input from the school, the community, and the working world, and measure student progress on the basis of competency.

Other aspects of the role in the years ahead involve legal status, ethical practices, professional organizations, and counselor's supply and demand. Prospects are good for increased professional status and the attendant legal and ethical responsibilities. Professional organizations will again the prestige to induce employers to upgrade hiring standards. Some form of licensure will be in operation; counselors will participate in setting qualifications and examining applicants. It is very probable that counselors will be completely in charge of this process.

Expansions in the directions predicted here-lifelong service, and broad applications in life areas-will mean that the demand for counselors will exceed the supply. Notwithstanding changes in support at the federal and state levels, and increased competition for available funds, the need for counselors will be so apparent and the efforts of guidance so well documented, that ample financing will be forthcoming and opportunities for employment will be plentiful.

Index

Notes

Adaptations and Responses of Woody Plants to Environmental Stresses

Adaptations and Responses of Woody Plants to Environmental Stresses

Dr. K.P. Singh

RANDOM PUBLICATIONS
NEW DELHI (INDIA)

Adaptations and Responses of Woody Plants to Environmental Stresses

ISBN 978-93-5111-949-4

Published in 2016 in India by

RANDOM PUBLICATIONS

4376-A/4B, Gali Murari Lal, Ansari Road
New Delhi-110 002
Phone : +9111-43580356, 011-23289044, 011-43142548
e-mail: sales@randompublications.com,
info@randompublications.com, randomexports@gmail.com

Reprinted 2022

Type Setting by : Friends Media, Delhi-110089
Digitally Printed at : Replika Press Pvt. Ltd.

Preface

A woody plant is a plant that produces wood as its structural tissue. Woody plants are usually either trees, shrubs, or lianas. These are usually perennial plants whose stems and larger roots are reinforced with wood produced from secondary xylem. The main stem, larger branches, and roots of these plants are usually covered by a layer of bark. Wood is a structural cellular adaptation that allows woody plants to grow from above ground stems year after year, thus making some woody plants the largest and tallest terrestrial plants.

Wood is primarily composed of xylem cells with cell walls made of cellulose and lignin. Xylem is a vascular tissue which moves water and nutrients from the roots to the leaves. Most woody plants form new layers of woody tissue each year, and so increase their stem diameter from year to year, with new wood deposited on the inner side of a vascular cambium layer located immediately beneath the bark. However, in some monocotyledons such as palms and dracaenas, the wood is formed in bundles scattered through the interior of the trunk.

Woody plants serve a wide variety of important purposes in our landscapes. They can provide a canopy or "ceiling" for our outdoor rooms, provide shelter from winter winds or shade from hot summer sun, create a backdrop for ornamental herbaceous plants, screen undesirable views, visually anchor or balance buildings in the landscape, and help us conserve energy in our homes. They can also provide food and shelter for wildlife, provide edible food for us, create spectacular seasonal interest with flowers, fruit, bark and twigs, and fill the air with fragrance.

This book will appeal to graduate students, instructors, and researchers who specialize in plant stress physiology in botany, agriculture, horticulture, landscape design, or forestry.

– Author

Contents

1

Woody Plant

A woody plant is a plant that produces wood as its structural tissue.Woody plants are usually either trees, shrubs, or lianas. These are usually perennial plants whose stems and larger roots are reinforced with wood produced from secondary xylem. The main stem, larger branches, and roots of these plants are usually covered by a layer of bark. Wood is a structural cellular adaptation that allows woody plants to grow from above ground stems year after year, thus making some woody plants the largest and tallest terrestrial plants.

Wood is primarily composed of xylem cells with cell walls made of cellulose and lignin. Xylem is a vascular tissue which moves water and nutrients from the roots to the leaves. Most woody plants form new layers of woody tissue each year, and so increase their stem diameter from year to year, with new wood deposited on the inner side of a vascular cambium layer located immediately beneath the bark. However, in some monocotyledons such as palms and dracaenas, the wood is formed in bundles scattered through the interior of the trunk.

Fig. A section of rosemary stem, an example of a woody plant, showing a typical wood structure.

Woody herbs are herbaceous plants that develop hard woody stems. They include such plants as Uraria picta and certain species in family Polygonaceae. These herbs are not truly woody but have hard densely packed stem tissue. Other herbaceous plants have woody stems called a caudex, which is a thickened stem base often found in plants that grow in alpine or dry environments.

Under specific conditions, woody plants may decay or may in time become petrified wood. The symbol for a woody plant, based on Species Plantarum by Linnaeus is η, which is also the astronomical symbol for the planet Saturn.

INTRODUCTION TO WOODY PLANTS

Woody plants are plants that live for more than year and make wood, which, as you know, is the stuff furniture is made of. They have one or more stems as well as branches. These grow in diameter every year as additional wood is made.

The mature stem on a tree is called a trunk. Shrubs (bushes) and trees are woody plants. Woody plants are the big players in your home landscape: your shade, your foundation plants, your screens and hedges, and your majestic specimens.

They also serve as backdrops for your seasonal colour, the annuals and perennials. Woody plants all flower, but the flowers may not be showy. Except for crape myrtles, roses and a few other summer bloomers, they have short blooming periods.

When planting trees and shrubs, it's important to consider how big they will get, and how fast they grow. Many a homeowner plants Leyland Cypress as an evergreen screen to either block out the neighbours or hide from the neighbours (or both).

But they may not know that Leylands grow up to three feet a year, and may get 70 feet tall. (They usually don't because they usually don't live that long, but, they can.)

You also need to consider the ultimate height of foundation plants—usually shrubs—planted along the base or foundation of the house. Most folks don't want something that will block the windows, or grow up past the gutters, but frequently, that's what happens. When planting trees and shrubs, consider their seasonal characteristics. In addition to flowers, woody plants often have attractive fall colour, colorful fruits (*e.g.*, berries; not specifically fruit in the edible sense), or attractive bark. And they may or may not be evergreen.

So take the aforementioned crape myrtle: nice flowers—yes, and for a long time. Colorful fruits; no. Fall colour; yes, yellow to orange to red. Nice bark in winter? Yes, cinnamon-colored, peeling bark on older specimens.

Evergreen—no. Also consider native plants (loosely defined as plant species that lived here shortly before European colonization). Natives are good for native wildlife. They provide a food source (leaves) for insects which themselves are food for nesting birds, and if they survive long enough, they might turn into butterflies.

So, a native: winterberry. Its flowers aren't showy. Its fall colour is yellow. Its fruits are very colorful, usually red, and they persist through the winter; good food source for squirrels and birds. Winterberry bark is gray and yes, it loses its leaves in the winter.

Each one, winterberry or crape myrtle, deserves a spot in the garden, and both are important landscape plants. It's up to you (with help) to determine if you have the right growing conditions for them in your garden, and to decide what aspects of the woody plants ornamental characters are the most important to you.

Fig. Winterberry hollies at the National Arboretum in January.

WOODY PLANTS AND PHYTOREMEDIATION

Twenty-five years ago, studies on phytoremediation techniques were rather scarce; now the scientific and social interest on this subject has increased substantially after the increasing pressure of public opinion. The use of plants to decontaminate soils and waters has been developed only recently, the first reports appearing in the eighties, followed by more exhaustive articles during the nineties. Much effort still has to be directed towards an understanding of the basic mechanisms and towards improving knowledge of the applications, but its usefulness has been demonstrated in many sites and this technology is now used by several environmental companies.

Phytoremediation is based on the removal of contaminants from the soil by mechanisms such as phytoextraction, phytodegradation, rhizofiltration, phytostabilization and phytovolatilization, but the mechanisms involved in heavy metal remediation are limited to uptake, adsorption, transport and translocation, sequestration into vacuoles, hyperaccumulation and, in some cases, volatilization. Within this frame, studies on allocation plasticity and plant-metal partitioning can be of great significance. When present at increased concentrations, both essential (copper, iron, manganese, molybdenum, zinc) and non-essential metals (*e.g.*,cadmium, chromium, lead, mercury) are toxic.

Mercury and selenium can also be converted by plants into a volatile form to release and dilute into the atmosphere. Heavy metals cannot be metabolized, therefore the only possible strategy to apply is their extraction from contaminated soil and transfer to the smaller volume of harvestable plants for their disposal; biomass can also be used in producing energy and, if economically profitable, metals can be eventually recovered.

It must be stressed that some processes can limit the efficacy of plants in phytoremediation, such as the availability of the toxic metal ions in the soil for root uptaking, their rate of translocation from roots to shoots and the level of tolerance, the rate of chemical transformation into less toxic compounds. At the basis, we find the mechanisms implicated in plant metal tolerance and homeostasis. Remediation using plants may take longer than other technologies, but the most relevant limitation is that it is most suited to cases where contaminants are present at shallow levels within the root layer.

Phytoremediation technology has been recently extensively reviewed and several species have been classified as hyperaccumulators and extensively investigated. However, on a large scale, metal uptake by trees can be more effective, mainly because of a deeper root system and a greater yield of biomass. High productivity and elevated uptake and translocation of pollutants to the harvestable biomass are the basis for efficient in situ restoration by means of vascular plants. Some woody species can be advantageously used also for phytoremediation of soils and groundwater from organic pollutants and hydrocarbons. The potential in phytoremediation of metal contaminated soils expressed by forest trees has been assessed for several species in recent years. Resistance to metals often appears to be clone- or hybrid-specific rather than species-specific.

Poplars are particularly suitable for remediation purposes, having already been considered for trials on metal tolerance in in vivo and in vitro observations. Salicaceae are also reported to grow even in severe soil conditions and to accumulate heavy metals. Many studies have thus been focused on the use of willows and poplars in phytoextraction. These species can be advantageously exploited in short rotation coppice cultures (SRC), a strategy whose application in phytoremediation presents interesting and economically promising perspectives.

USE OF IN VITRO CULTURES FOR RESEARCH ON PHYTOREMEDIATION

The inherent difficulties of experimenting on very large long-lived organisms such as forest trees, motivates the development of model systems. Besides the exploitation of hydroponic cultures, the in vitro model systems using shoot and cell cultures of plants demonstrated to be a useful tool for investigating efficiency of metal uptake and translocation. Cell and organ culture, in fact, as well as hydroponics, allow very fast accumulation of data in comparison with whole plant experiments under field conditions, and offer the advantage of testing the effects of contaminants under controlled conditions. Hydroponic screening is often used to evaluate tolerance, accumulation and translocation in plants. Watson et al. demonstrated in Salix that results obtained in hydroponics and in field experiments are comparable. It is always advisable, however, to confirm data obtained by hydroponic tests by field performance trials. Using this technique, several studies have concerned, for instance, the response of willows to a metal cocktail and of willows and poplars to the presence of cadmium, the response of a clone of Populus x euramericana to high concentrations of copper, the mechanism of resistance to aluminium of Picea abies, the determination of the role of glutathione reductase metabolism in the defence of poplar (Populus deltoides x P. nigra) against high zinc concentration.

As stated by Golan-Goldhirsh et al., the use of in vitro systems enables dissection of the complex system of plant, soil, and microbial interaction in order to evaluate the effect of stress factors on metabolism, specific enzymes and metabolites involved in plant response to the pollutant. For many woody species, moreover, the application of in vitro propagation techniques, allows for fast plant production and the application of promising genetic engineering prorammes.

High concentration of zinc has been found to negatively affect the photosynthetic machinery in poplar: inhibition of adventitious root formation and leaf chlorosis indicated that the clone used was tolerant to external concentrations less than or equal to 1 mM, while in Eucalyptus globulusmoderate concentrations of this metal were shown to either enhance or have no effect on rooting. Phytoremediation potentials of poplar lines (Populus nigra and transgenic P. canescens) were investigated using in vitro leaf discs cultures and found that $Zinc^{2+}$ was phytotoxic only at high concentrations (10^{-2} to 10^{-1} M) in all P. canescens lines, but P. nigra was more sensitive. Cadmium added to the culture medium was shown to reduce the fresh and dry weights and the shoot length of white birch, while root length was not affected.

Copper at a concentration of 0.05 mM, manganese at 0.80 mM, and zinc at 0.12 mM showed a negative effect on shoot growth (number of shoots per explant and shoot length) in Ailanthus altissima, considered a fast-growing and contamination-resistant species. Zinc was found toxic in aspen (Populus tremula x tremuloides) cultures at 0.5 mM concentration, while lead at the same concentration did not show toxic effects and was accumulated at 3500 ìg per g of biomass. In vitro studies were also developed to investigate the effects of high concentrations of zinc and copper on the biosynthesis and accumulation of polyamine in Populus alba.

On the basis of leaf symptoms, rate of adventitious root formation and ethylene production, it was found that Zn at 0.5-1 mM concentration was transiently toxic, while at 2-4 mM was increasingly toxic. Free and conjugated putrescine and spermidine accumulated proportionally to toxicity; also Cu strongly reduced rooting already at 5 μM and caused severe, dose-dependent toxicity symptoms (shoot chlorosis and necrosis) using concentrations up to 500 μM. In in vitro growing microshoots of Populus alba, the effect of high concentrations of cadmium, copper, zinc, and arsenic was investigated, showing differences in the response of different clones.

Axenic poplar tumor cell cultures were tested for demonstrating the capability of taking up trichloroethylene (TCE) and degrading it to several known metabolic products, while poplar (Populus deltoides×P. nigra) in vitro culture has been used for developing mathematical models to define degradation pathways of nitramine compounds within plant cells. Metal tolerance was detected in a callus culture established fromAcer rubrum seedlings growing in soil contaminated by zinc, cadmium, nickel and arsenic.

A positive linear correlation was found between zinc resistance of callus and total Zn in soil beneath sampled trees, while no significant correlations were evidenced with the other metals. InAcer pseudoplatanus callus culture, Cu-, Zn- and Cd-resistance traits were identified in cell lines originating from trees at a site contaminated by these metals. In vitro screenings were also used to investigate how several heavy metals affect pollen germination and tube elongation inPinus resinosa and to test the tolerance for Zn and Cu in mycorrhyzal isolates collected in an abandoned Cu mines, in view of their inoculation into Pinus sylvestris seedlings.

Combined micropropagation and hydroponic culture were used to study tolerance to copper and zinc in Betula pendula, finding that a seed-derived clone from a Pb/Zn-contaminated site showed more tolerance to Cu and Zn than bud-derived clones from a Cu/Ni-contaminated site or from an uncontaminated area.

ROLE OF ENDOPHYTIC BACTERIA AND MYCHORRHIZAS IN PHYTOREMEDIATION

Bacteria living within plant tissues without causing disease are referred to as endophytes. Some of these have shown the capacity to enhance plant growth and resistance to biotic and abiotic stresses by various mechanisms (*e.g.*, nitrogen fixation, production of phytohormones, solubilisation of minerals, etc.), therefore, recently attention has been focusing on the role of endophytic bacteria in phytoremediation. Endophytes have been inoculated and studied, *e.g.*, in hybrid spruce, lodgepole pine, Douglas-fir, poplar and willow.

Based on their potential for remediation, three Pseudomonas strains were identified and tested in a clone of hybrid cottonwood (Populus trichocarpa x P. deltoides). A large part of the research on this subject has been dealt with the activity of endophytes on hydrocarbons. For instance, in hybrid cottonwood a strain of the endophyte Rhizobium tropici was found active in the degradation of explosives, as well as a Methylobacterium strain isolated from hybrid poplar; poplar endophytic bacteria have been engineered for enhancing thrichloroethylene degradation and observed a horizontal gene transfer of a plasmid conferring toluene degradation.

Concerning specifically heavy metals, it has been observed that heavy metal resistant endophytes are present in various hyperaccumulator plants growing on heavy-metal contaminated soil. Among herbaceous plants, *e.g.*, shoot endophytes of Thlaspi goesingense were found more tolerant to high nickel concentration than the correspondent rhizospheric bacteria, endophytic bacteria of Nicotiana tabacum could reduce cadmium phytotoxicity, recombinant heavy-metal resistant endophytic bacteria were studied in Lolium perenne and Lupinus luteus. Among woody species, some isolates of hybrid cottonwoods have demonstrated tolerance to heavy metals; bacteria associated with Zn/Cd-accumulating Salix caprea have been studied regarding their potential to support heavy metal phytoextraction.

Arbuscular mychorrhizas are also well known to be involved in the metal uptake; their presence in the soil may significantly affect the plant response to metal stress. A vast amount of literature is available on the effects of mycorrhizal colonisation of plants living in heavy metal-polluted soils, on the protective role of mycorrhizas against heavy-metal induced oxidative stress, and on their possible role in remediation. In the hyperaccumulating fern Pteris vittata, for instance, they have been found to increase arsenic uptake.

Adriaensen et al. found that Pinus sylvestris seedlings colonized by a Zn-tolerant isolate of Suillus bovinus grew much better and remained physiologically healthier when exposed to elevated Zn concentration than seedlings not inoculated or colonized by a Zn-sensitive isolate. The response to high copper and zinc concentration was studied on poplar clones inoculated with arbuscular mycorrhizal fungi, while in mycorrhyzed Betula spp. tolerance to zinc and Cu and Pb accumulation were studied.

By X-ray microanalysis of heavy metals, it was found that, in mycorrhized Picea abies seedlings, extracellular complexation of Cd occurred predominantly in the Hartig net hyphae and both extracellular complexation and cytosolic sequestration of Zn occurred in the fungal tissue. The potential benefits of ectomycorrhizal fungi in protecting their host plants from metal contamination were also investigated by Blaudez et al. after testing thirty-nine ectomycorrhizal isolates for their tolerance to cadmium, copper, nickel and zinc. The potential of Salix viminalis and Populus x generosa for the phytoextraction of heavy metals, inoculated or not with the fungus Glomus intraradices, was recently assessed, while in Eucalyptus globulus grown in Zn-contaminated soil, the improving potential of interactions between saprophytic and arbuscular micorrhizal fungi was investigated.

MOLECULAR BIOLOGY AND GENETIC ENGINEERING FOR PHYTOREMEDIATION

Molecular biology and genetic engineering are being increasingly considered as effective tools for better understanding and improving the phytoremediation capability of plants, whose biological functions can now be analyzed in detail and partly modified. The metal resistance systems are better known in microorganisms; in plants only a few systems of metal tolerance and/or sequestration are sufficiently characterized.

In recent years, several key steps have been identified at the molecular level, allowing an increasing application of molecular-genetic technologies and a transgenic approach to a better understanding of mechanisms involved in heavy metal tolerance and accumulation in plants. It has been demonstrated in classic genetic studies that only a few genes are responsible for metal tolerance. Transfer and/or overexpression of genes responsible for metal uptake, translocation and sequestration may allow for the production of plants which, depending on the strategy, can be successfully exploited in phytore mediation. In this case, special attention must be paid to problems related to the introduction of genetically modified trees, particularly concerning their legal and social acceptance. Promotion of growth and biomass production is a correlated task accomplished, for instance, by increased gibberellin biosynthesis.

The improvement of the phytoremediation properties of plants can be achieved by the modification of their primary and secondary metabolism and the introduction of new phenotypic and genotypic characters.

Even if most of the genes involved in metal uptake, transport and sequestration have been studied on the herbaceous model plant Arabidopsis, it must be considered that this species, as well as the most common species defined as hyperaccumulators, have a limited phytoremediation capacity due to their small size or slow growth rate. On the contrary, large, fast-growing plants, like some woody plants, are an important tool for this purpose; on poplars, for instance, reasonable transformation frequencies have been achieved.

Studies on Arabidopsis and other species (hyperaccumulators), however, open the way to a transfer and application to high-biomass plants. Among these, Populus species (poplars, cottonwoods, aspens) and hybrids have become a model system in forest tree biotechnology, due to several useful features: short rotation cycle, rapid growth rate and ease of vegetative propagation and in vitro multiplication. Moreover, the poplar genome has been entirely sequenced. It is always important, however, to take into account the risks associated with the biotechnological applications and carefully evaluate the field performances of transgenic plants.

Hairy roots induction by Agrobacterium rhizogenes is probably the easiest method for enhancing the root biomass and, consequently, improving metal uptake.

This has been demonstrated for some hyperaccumulator plants. Transgenic white poplar has been recently obtained expressing the PsMTa1 gene from Pisum sativum for a metallothionein-like protein. Transformed plants showed enhanced resistance to heavy metal, surviving high concentrations of $CuCl_2$ in in vitro culture, which strongly affected the non-transgenic plants. Rooting capacity of microshoots was maintained in transgenic lines exposed to 0.1 mM $CuCl_2$, while it was totally destroyed in non-transgenic shoots. In the presence of 1 mM ZnSO4, non-transformed shoots rooted abundantly, while different rooting rates were observed in transgenic lines.

Genes encoding enzymes changing the oxidation state of heavy metals can be introduced into plants. For instance, compared to wild type, transgenic Populus deltoides overexpressed mer-A9 and mer-A18 genes, when grown in soil with high mercury concentration, developing higher biomass and higher amount of Hg(0), which evaporates through the cell surface. Increased tolerance to ionic mercury was first obtained in yellow poplar (Lyriodendron tulipifera) transformed with mer-A gene.

For the remediation of Hg, Populus deltoides has been engineered with the bacterial mer-A (mercuric ion reductase) and mer-B (organomercurial lyase); transgenic trees expressing both genes showed tolerance up to 10 μM of phenylmercuric acetate. Significant results on tolerance to mercury and related remediation capacity were obtained also in Oryza sativa and in Spartina alterniflora. In Salix spp. it was proved that the majority of the mercury is accumulated and retained in the cell wall of the roots and only a very small part is transferred to the shoots.

Genetic engineering for arsenate reduction, increased translocation from root to shoot, and volatilisation has been recently illustrated and discussed. Arabidopsis has been transformed in order to better control the mobility and sequestration of arsenic. In Pteris vittata,genes have been identified that encode enzymes with arsenate reductive activity. For selenium, a strategy to protect protein synthesis from the activity of this metal was applied in transformed Arabidopsis by the expression of a mammalian selenocysteine lyase and could be now tested on woody species.

Transgenic poplar, with increased glutathione peroxidase activity, showed increased tolerance to zinc, probably due to an enhanced ability to detoxify the active oxygen species generated by the pollutant. Alterations in photosynthetic parameters and reduction in growth have been reported for a Populus x euramericana clone after treatment with high concentrations of zinc.

Cadmium in the environment derives from industrial processes, urban pollution (heating systems and traffic), fertilizers and mineralization of rocks. Sensitivity to and accumulation of cadmium in some woody species have been recently studied in Sweden. In a relatively new strategy, aimed to compartmentalize the metals, tolerance to lead and cadmium was enhanced in Arabidopsis by the overexpression of the yeast vacuolar transporter protein YCF1, demonstrating the possibility to engineer phytoremediators for increasing their ability to sequester heavy metals. Poplars overexpressing a bacterial glutamylcysteine synthetase in the cytosol reached a 30-fold increase in its foliar activity compared to untransformed controls; this allowed greater tissue cadmium accumulation but had only a marginal effect on cadmium tolerance.

Plant roots are able to release into the rizosphere chelating agents with binding ability for metals. These metal chelators or other molecules within plant cells that have a high affinity for metals can help in the metal sequestering. Plants may also be engineered to enhance the synthesis of metal chelators. Metal chelators include phytochelatins, metallothioneins, organic acids and amino acids. In vitro experiments have shown that cadmium in the form of phytochelatin complex is much better tolerated by plant enzyme than its free radical ion.

In Nicotiana glauca transformed with a gene encoding a phytochelatin synthase, more metals were accumulated when grown in mine soils compared with non-transformed plants. Attempts have been made to increase the formation of phytochelatins by overexpressing genes encoding enzymes stimulating the synthesis of cysteine and glutathione. Metallothioneins, a category of remarkable interest, are defined as low molecular mass cysteine-rich proteins that can bind heavy metals and may play a role in their intracellular sequestration.

In the hybrid poplar genome, they form a multigene family and it has been hypothesised that they participate in the process of metal homeostasis and possibly in the process of tolerance. Advances in understanding the regulation of phytochelatins biosynthesis and metallothioneins gene expression and their possible roles in heavy metal detoxification and homeostasis have been recently reviewed.

PLANTS AND THEIR ENVIRONMENT

Plants are living organisms that contain chlorophyll and use it to manufacture their own food. Their cell walls are more or less rigid and support both the individual cells and the whole structure. Even when plants have reached what we regard as their full, mature size, they continue to expand and develop new leaves, flowers, fruit and shoots.

Unlike animals, plants cannot move when the environment changes. They are at the mercy of the climate and the gardener because they are rooted in place. Even though it appears that many plants, especially larger ones, are quite tolerant of change, they sometimes do not show adverse effects until long after the event. For example, tree roots are often damaged or killed by suffocation during building projects or flooding. An established tree may still have strength to leaf out and may appear to thrive for several years. But in its weakened state, the tree is more likely to blow down, become infested or simply decline. To understand why plants respond as they do to natural influences and to cultivation, gardeners must understand something about their structure and how they grow. This publication provides such an introduction.

WAYS TO GROUP PLANTS

Uses

Gardeners tend to group plants by their horticultural uses: fruits, vegetables, flowers, trees, shrubs, turf and so on. These categories are a convenient way to think and learn about plants.

Life Cycle

The length of each plant's life cycle is another way to categorize plants. Annual, biennial and perennial are terms that describe how long a plant will live and also indicate when it is likely to bloom.

Annual

An annual plant's entire life cycle from seed germination to seed production occurs in one growing season, and then the plant dies. Many flowering plants that we consider to be annuals are not annuals in their native habitats. They would continue to grow and flower if freezing temperatures did not kill them.

Annuals may be further subdivided into summer and winter annuals:

- Winter annuals begin their life cycle in late summer or fall, survive in the vegetative state through winter, and then flower quickly in the spring before dying.

- Summer annuals, on the other hand, begin their life cycle in spring or summer and complete their entire life cycle before fall or winter.

Biennial

A biennial plant starts from seed and produces vegetative structures and food storage organs in its first full season. A rosette of basal leaves persists through winter. During the second season, the plant's life cycle is completed with flowers, fruit and seed. The plant then usually dies. These plants will often reseed. Examples of biennials are carrots, beets, cabbage, celery, onions, hollyhock, Canterbury bells and Sweet William. Sometimes plants that typically develop as biennials may complete their entire cycle of growth from seed germination to seed production in only one growing season. Conditions of drought, unusual variations in temperature or other climatic changes can cause the plant to pass through the physiological equivalent of two full growing seasons in one year.

Perennial

One definition of a perennial is a plant that would have come back year after year in your garden had it not died! Typically, perennials live for several to many years and, after reaching maturity (adult or full size), produce flowers and seeds each year. Examples include flowers such as daylilies, blackeyed-susan and coneflower. Plants often characterized as weeds such as common milkweed and morning glory are also perennials.

Perennials are classified in various ways:

- *Herbaceous:* Plants that die back to the ground each winter and have new stems that grow from the roots each spring.
- *Woody:* Plants where the top persists, such as shrubs or trees.
- *Deciduous:* Plants that shed their leaves and are leafless during a portion of the year.
- *Evergreen:* Plants with leaves that persist throughout the year.
- *Tender:* Plants that do not survive cold winters. Tender perennials are often grown as annuals.
- *Hardy:* Plants that tolerate cold temperatures.

Structure

The structure and appearance of plants' flowers, leaves, fruit and seed play a large part in how we think of them and also provide useful information about their classification. For example, the flowers of a daisy indicate a probable relationship with other plants that have similar flowers. The majority of grasses are easily recognized by their long leaf blades. More than 500,000 different kinds of plants and plantlike organisms exist in the world. Of these, the flowering plants classified as angiosperms are the most abundant and familiar to us. Gymnosperms are the other main group of flowering plants. There are also more primitive plants such as mosses and ferns that reproduce by spores.

Differences in Angiosperm Plant Structure and Function

Monocots:
- One seed leaf
- Xylem and phloem paired in bundles and randomly dispersed throughout stem.
- Parallel-veined leaves
- Floral parts in 3s or in multiples of 3.

Dicots:
- Two seed leaves
- Continuous rings form inside the stem. Phloem is near the bark or external stem cover, becomes part of bark in mature woody stems. Xylem forms inner rings, is sapwood and heartwood of woody plants.
- Net-veined leaves
- Floral parts in 4s or 5s or in multiples of 4 or 5.

Angiosperms

Angiosperms have seeds encased in closed ovaries that become plants' familiar fruits, pods, grains or capsules. They represent virtually all crop plants and those we think of as flowers.

The angiosperms are further classified into two groups according to the number of seed leaves, called cotyledons, that emerge from a germinating seed:
- Monocotyledonous plants (monocots) are those like grasses whose seed first extends a single cotyledon or seed leaf. Lilies and other bulb plants are also monocots.
- Dicotyledonous plants (dicots) have seed that forms a pair of cotyledons; examples are bean, petunia and tomato.

GYMNOSPERMS

Gymnosperms are plants that develop exposed or naked seeds. These include the coniferous plants such as fir, pine and spruce. Ginkgo and the tropical cycads are also gymnosperms.

MODERN PLANT TAXONOMY

Taxonomy

The science of classifying plants and animals according to their morphology (form and structure), and morphological relationships and principles. Modern plant taxonomy is based on a system developed by the Swedish physician Carl von Linné, who is also known as Linneaus. His classification is based on the flowers and reproductive parts of a plant. Because these are the parts of a plant least influenced by environmental changes, this system has been found to be the best. Grouping plants with similar botanical structure helps us to understand how they are related to one another. Close relatives often have similar pest problems. Botanical similarities may also show, for example, how long certain plants can be expected to live and why they react as they do to certain conditions. In addition, their botanical, Latin or "proper" names help to avoid confusion when the same or similar common names exist for different plants.

Binomial Nomenclature

Each plant is assigned two names. The genus or generic name can be likened to a person's last name, as in "Doe." The specific epithet or species name is that person's given name, "Jane" or "John." This combination of two names is the plant's botanical, scientific or Latin name. For example, the botanical name for sugar maple is Acer saccharum (pronounced AY-ser sa-KAH-rum). The genus name Acer is a classical name. The genus name for the Indian bean tree Catalpa is a North American Indian name.

Other botanical names provide descriptions of the flower: for example, Antirrhinum (snapdragon) is from the Greek anti,which means "like, " and rhinos meaning nose or snout. One familiar genus is Narcissus (daffodil) named for the mythological character who was turned into this flower when he drowned attempting to reach the person he saw reflected in a pool of water. Specific epithets may have similar descriptive value, such as rubra for red and major for large or larger. In the sugar maple example, the word saccharum is from the Latin for sugar cane, and it is similar to words we know that mean sweet.

Some species commemorate a botanist or plant explorer. The late 18th century Swedish naturalist Carl Peter Thunberg introduced many Asian plants. He is remembered in plant names, including the species Berberis thunbergii,the Japanese barberry, and a genus of the warm-climate, climbing blackeyed-susan, Thunbergia. Words in many complete Latin names include botanical variety, subspecies and cultivar. These build upon the basic binomial naming system to further separate individuals that differ from one another in, for instance, flower colour or growth habit. They are not so different as to require new specific names.

Botanical Classification

Botanical classification of four plants

	Colorado blue spruce	**Ornamental pear**	**Cauliflower**	**Sweet corn**
Kingdom	Plantae	Plantae	Plantae	Plantae
Division	Tracheophyta	Tracheophyta	Tracheophyta	Tracheophyta
Class	Gymnospermae	Angiospermae	Angiospermae	Angiospermae
Subclass		Dicotyledones	Dicotyledones	Monocotyledones
Order	Coniferales	Rosales	Papaverales	Cyperales
Family	Pinaceae	Rosaceae	Cruciferae	Graminae
Genus	Picea	Pyrus	Brassica	Zea
Species	pungens	calleryana	oleracea	mays
Variety (botanical)	glauca		botrytis	rugosa
Cultivar	'Fat Albert'	'Bradford'	'Snow Crown'	'Silver Queen'

Every living organism — plant, animal, insect and so forth — can be classified into the following categories or taxa:

- Kingdom
- Division
- Class
- Subclass
- Order
- Family
- Genus (plural: genera)
- Species (abbreviated sp. [singular] or spp. [plural])
- Cultivar or variety

For plants, the kingdom is Plantae and division is Tracheophyta. Class is usually either Angiospermae or Gymnospermae, the angiosperms and gymnosperms that make up most of our cultivated plants. At the subclass and order level, further groupings of similar plants are named.

Family

A family of plants shares similar characteristics. For example, the spring-flowering magnolia trees, whose deciduous forms are best known in the north, and the evergreen southern forms are in the same family, not surprisingly called Magnoliaceae. Different magnolia specimens can be "keyed out" using a botanical key. The combination of characteristics that identify this family are enclosed ovules, flowers that are not catkins, flowers with calyces, clear and separate "distinct" carpels (reproductive portion of flower), overlapping or imbricate sepals, and alternate, simple leaves.

In another example, peas belong to a large family of legumes called Leguminosae (recently renamed Fabaceae). The edible pea flower is shaped much like the flower of a tree in the same family commonly referred to as redbud (Cercis canadensis). All legumes have similar flowers and fruiting structures even though they may be vastly different in form. Other legumes include alfalfa, beans, clover, honeylocust, Kentucky coffee tree, Siberian pea shrub and wisteria.

What do roses have in common with apple trees? They are members of the same family — Rosaceae. Their fruits are pomes. Plants in this family share susceptibility to the same diseases. For example, pears and roses are susceptible to fire blight, and both are subject to mildew during humid weather. Other plants in the Rosaceae family include cotoneaster, spirea, juneberry, quince and mountain ash.

Genus

When groups of similar plants are categorized into families, the next lower level of classification is the genus. Plants in the same genus often share similar fruits, flowers, roots, stems, buds and leaves. The genus name is always capitalized and italicized or underlined.

Examples:

- Acer = maple
- Begonia = begonia
- Catharanthus = vinca
- Lycopersicon = tomato
- Quercus = oak

Species

Specific definition comes with the species name, or specific epithet. At this level, marked features that are carried from generation to generation distinguish the group. Specific names are not capitalized, but they are italicized or underlined.

Examples:

- Acer rubrum
- Begonia semperflorens
- Catharanthus roseum
- Lycopersicon esculentum
- Quercus alba

Variety (Botanical), Subspecies, Form

Sometimes the specific name is followed by a botanical variety, subspecific name or form that denotes a fairly consistent, naturally occurring variation within the species. This second specific name is preceded by the abbreviation var., ssp., or forma (f.).

Examples:

- Picea pungens var. glauca (Colorado blue spruce)
- Gleditsia triacanthos var. inermis (thornless honeylocust)

Cultivars

Cultivars, short for cultivated varieties, are variations on plants that originated in cultivation. Cultivar names are even more defining than species names. Some cultivar names are Latinized, and others are not. Cultivars can be confusing because there may be hundreds within one species.

Cultivar (Short for Cultivated Variety)

A cultivar is a group of plants that is clearly distinguished by certain characteristics that may be morphological (structural), physiological (functional), cytological (cellular) or chemical. The differences do not have to be visual for a variation to gain cultivar status — perhaps it is simply more hardy or disease resistant. When a plant is reproduced asexually (by cloning), it retains these distinguishing characteristics. Cultivar names are always capitalized within single quotes or preceded by the abbreviation cv. In the nursery industry, the cultivar name is recognized as a plant's official name.

Examples:

- Acer platanoides 'Crimson King' (Crimson King Norway maple)
- Fraxinus pennsylvanica cv. Marshall's Seedless (Marshall's Seedless green ash)

Along with cultivar designation, recent new cultivars may have other assigned names that are often trademarked (Golden NuggetAA dwarf Japanese barberry, Berberis thunbergii 'Monlers').

More Plant Identification Terms

Several more terms may be used to define particular plants or plant groups:

- *Strain:* A variation within a cultivar. For example, 'Spur Red Delicious' apple is a selected type of Red Delicious, which is a cultivar of apple.
- *Hybrid:* The result of natural or deliberate crossbreeding between two or more dissimilar parents is known as a hybrid. Hybrids are denoted by the multiplication sign "x, " placed correctly without a space before the hybrid name. While we find most hybrids at the specific level within a genus, some are intergeneric (result from the cross-breeding of two genera). For example, the hybrid Forsythia xintermedia is from a cross between two species, Forsythia suspensa and Forsythia viridissima.The intergeneric hybrid xSolidaster (hybrid goldenrod) comes from its parent species, Solidago and Aster.
- *Clone:* An individual or individuals that were started by asexual propagation and are genetically identical to each other.
- *Line:* Plants of uniform appearance grown from seed.
- *F1 hybrid:* A cross between two inbred lines.

PLANT IDENTIFICATION USING PLANT KEYS

Plant "Keys"

For successful use of dichotomous "either-or" plant keys, a working familiarity with plant structure and terminology is essential. Dichotomous plant keys are used to identify plants through a series of choices between pairs of alternatives. Each pair refers to a specific plant characteristic such as arrangement of leaves on the stem, type of leaf margin or type of fruit. By selecting the option that accurately describes the plant, you will be led to the next choices until you determine the genus or species.

If a result is ambiguous, final verification can be made by comparison with a known example of that species. In their detailed comparisons, plant taxonomists often use preserved specimens stored in an herbarium. Reference books for specific types of plants, such as ferns, wildflowers or shrubs, frequently contain their own specialized plant keys. Try to use keys that employ botanical rather than common names. Common names can be confusing for several reasons: one plant may have several common names; the common name for a plant often differs from one region to another; and the same common name can also apply to more than one plant. Botanical names, by contrast, are unique and relatively permanent.

PLANT STRUCTURE

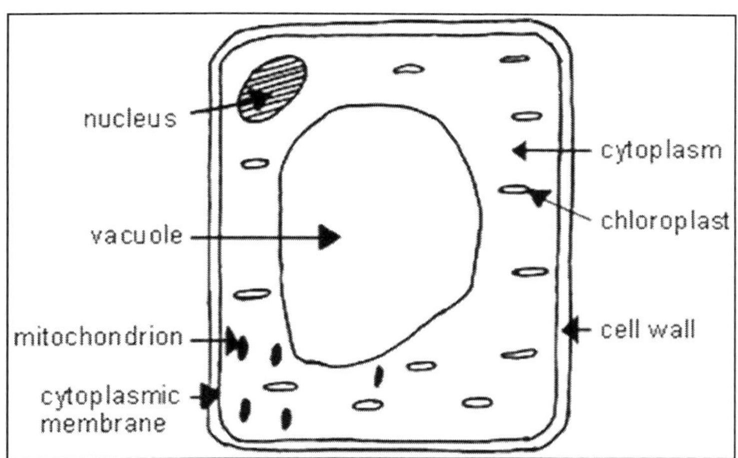

Fig. Plant cell.

The Plant Cell

The plant cell is the basic organizational unit of plants. Each living plant cell contains a nucleus that controls all of the chemical activities in the cell. Within the nucleus, division of the DNA provides the way for the cell to pass on heritable information from one generation of cells to the next. Cytoplasm is the other main part of the living plant cell. It is composed of many cell structures, water, pigments, sugar and various minerals. The cytoplasm is bound by a plasma membrane that regulates the flow of water and nutrients into and out of the cell. The plant's cell wall is one of the fundamental differences between plant and animal cells. The somewhat rigid cell wall is made up of a number of chemical compounds, primarily the carbohydrate cellulose.

The second major difference between plant and animal cells is that many plant cells contain the green pigment chlorophyll. Chlorophyll is contained in chloroplasts, where photosynthesis, the food manufacturing process, takes place. A chloroplast is a type of organelle known as a plastid. There are also plastids that contain pigments other than chlorophyll. Plant cells can have specialized functions, and there are many cell types. Plant cells are largely made up of water held within the vacuole, which exerts a pressure against the rigid cell wall. This pressure, called turgor pressure, gives the plant shape and structure. When insufficient water is available in the plant to maintain this pressure, the plant begins to droop or wilt.

Plant Tissues

Plant tissues are sometimes classified as either vegetative or reproductive. Vegetative tissues (leaves, roots, stems and leaf buds) are not directly involved in seed production.

However, they are often used in asexual or vegetative forms of reproduction such as cuttings. Individual cells work together to form the whole plant. Tissues are organized groups of cells that are similar in appearance and function. An organ is a group of tissues that accomplishes a common function. Plants have two organ systems: roots and shoots. Shoots, in turn, have two main organs: leaves and stems. These organs are made up of various tissues that are called meristematic, which may be dermal or vascular.

Meristematic tissues are sites of cellular activity and division. This is where all of the growing takes place. Meristematic tissues give rise to the other tissue systems and are named for their location. Animal tissues do not have these specific sites of cell division — rather, all animal cells can divide to create new tissues. An apical meristem is located at the apex, or tip, of a shoot or root. The lateral meristems exist in the stems and roots of many plants. They help the plant grow in thickness or diameter. The vascular cambium is a lateral meristem that forms new xylem (water-conducting) cells on the inside and new phloem (food-conducting) cells on the outside. Active cambium cells are exposed when the outer skin or bark is peeled away from a dicot stem (monocots usually have no cambium).

Dermal Tissues:

There are two types of dermal tissues — epidermis and periderm.

- *Epidermis:* This forms the outer covering of the plant and, in most cases, secretes a waxy coating called cutin, which forms the cuticle. This often shiny coating protects the plant from major water loss and protects the underlying cells. Specialized groups of epidermal cells form pores that allow water, carbon dioxide, oxygen and other gases to pass through to and from the underlying tissues. These pores, referred to as stomata (singular: stoma), are made up of two guard cells that open and close to regulate the flow of vapors and gases.
- *Periderm:* The periderm is created by the cambium and forms the bulk of the bark of woody plants. It is a layer of corky cells that, like the epidermis, prevents water loss and protects the cells beneath. The periderm also has pores to allow gas exchange for underlying tissues. These pores, which are visible to the naked eye, are called lenticels.

Vascular Tissues

Vascular tissues make up the water- and food-conducting system of a plant. They consist of the xylem and phloem.

- *Xylem:* The xylem tubes are the water- and mineral-conducting channels and are made up of cells that are shaped into columns that can effectively move water through even a large tree.
- *Phloem:* Phloem tubes move food produced by photosynthesis to other parts of the plant.

PLANT ORGANS

Every plant has a unique form and structure and is made up of several distinct organs. All of these influence a plant's overall health and appearance. Gardeners need to consider all parts of the plant and the effects of the environment on these structures, which include roots, stems, buds, leaves, flowers, seeds and seedlings, and fruits.

ROOTS

Root Functions

The principal functions of roots are to:

- Anchor the plant in the soil
- Absorb nutrients and moisture, serve as food storage organs
- Provide a means of propagation

Healthy roots are vital to the well-being and the continued development of most cultivated plants. Roots' structure and growth habits have pronounced effects on the size and vigour of a plant, its ability to adapt to various soil types, and its responses to cultural practices and irrigation.

In addition, many plants spread through buds that develop on vigorous roots, and portions of root can be used for vegetative reproduction or propagation. Examples are phlox and lilac (Syringa). Roots that store carbohydrates are often used as food for us and for animals. Carrots, beets, sweet potatoes and turnips are examples.

Types of Roots

One or more primary roots originate at the lower end of a seedling or cutting. From here, the root system develops, which is usually characteristic of the plant. Specific soil conditions can cause modifications in roots, however. For example, the taproot of a carrot growing in stony soil will be stunted and branched.

- *Taproot:* A taproot is formed when the primary root continues to elongate downward into the soil to become the dominant and most important feature of the root system. Some trees, such as the sassafras and sugar maple, have long taproots with few laterals or fibrous roots. Such trees are difficult to transplant, and they usually grow only in deep, well-drained soil. If plants that normally develop a taproot are undercut so that the taproot is severed early in the plant's life, the plant will lose its taprooted characteristic and develop a more fibrous root system. In commercial nurseries, this is done so trees that would naturally have taproots will instead develop compact, fibrous root systems. This improves transplanting results, but when the taproot is undercut in this way, nutritional and moisture conditions must be carefully controlled to maintain healthy topgrowth.

- *Lateral roots:* Lateral or secondary roots are side or branch roots that grow from another, larger root.
- *Fibrous roots:* A fibrous root system is one in which the primary root either never existed or ceases to elongate. Numerous smaller or lateral roots develop, branching repeatedly to form the absorptive root system of the plant. Rhododendrons, for example, have shallow, fibrous root systems. By contrast, the tough, vigorous, multiple roots of grasses are capable of penetrating the ground to a depth of several feet. Grasses can, therefore, reach water that is unavailable to the shallower-rooted rhododendron.
- *Root hairs:* These develop on the root just behind the zone of elongation. They perform much of the actual work of water and nutrient absorption.
- *Myccorhizae:* Many plants form a partnership between their root systems and soil fungi called myccorhizae. These myccorhizae, literally "fungus roots, " greatly enhance water absorption and the nutrient-acquiring capacities of the roots. Myccorhizae can be important in plant establishment and survival.

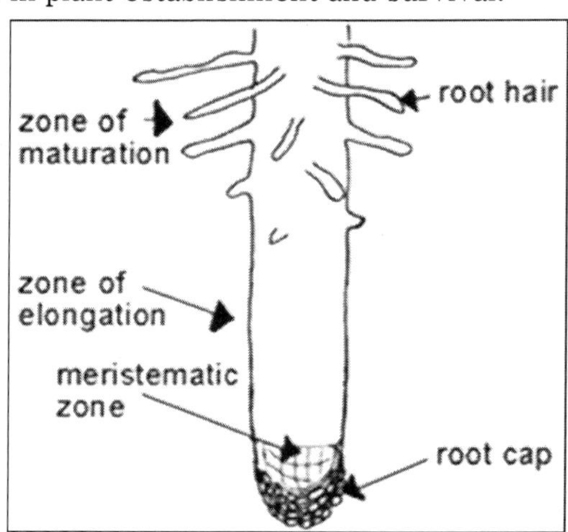

Fig. Longitudinal section of root.

Tuberous Roots

Dahlias and sweet potatoes produce underground storage organs called tuberous roots, which are often confused with bulbs and tubers. However, these are roots, not stems, and have neither nodes nor internodes.

Root Structure

A root has no nodes and never directly bears leaves or flowers. Internally, it has four main parts:

- *Root cap:* The outermost protective tip of the root. It consists of cells that are sloughed off as the root grows through the soil. The meristem, the area of cell division, is located right behind the root cap and is protected by it.
- *Meristem:* The tip where new cells are manufactured. It is an area of cell division and growth and is protected by a root cap.
- *Zone of elongation:* The area immediately behind the tip. Here, cells increase in size through food and water absorption. These enlarging cells push the root through the soil.
- *Zone of maturation:* The region in which the enlarged cells undergo changes to become the specialized tissues of the epidermis, cortex and vascular system.
  - *Epidermis:* This layer of cells surrounding the root is responsible for absorption of water and minerals dissolved in water.
  - *Cortex:* These cells are involved in food storage and the movement of water from the epidermis.
  - *Vascular system:* This system consists of cells located at the core of the root, whose function it is to conduct food and water.

More on Roots

The quantity and distribution of plant roots are important because these two factors have a major influence on the root's ability to absorb moisture and nutrients. The depth and spread of the roots depend on the plant's inherent growth characteristics and on the texture and structure of the soil. Roots will penetrate more deeply into a loose, well-drained soil, where there is adequate soil oxygen, than into a dense, poorly drained soil. A solidly compacted layer in the soil, sometimes called a hardpan, will restrict or terminate root growth.

During early development, a seedling plant absorbs nutrients and moisture from the soil within a few inches of the location of the seed from which the plant grew. As plants become well established, the root system develops laterally and usually extends to several times the spread of the branches. The greatest concentration of fibrous roots occurs in the top 12 inches of soil, but significant numbers of laterals may grow downward from these roots to provide an effective absorption system several feet or more underground.

STEMS

Stem Functions

The distinguishing feature of stems is that they must have buds or leaves. *The principal functions of stems are to:*

- Form the framework that supports leaves, buds, flowers and fruit
- Be a major part of the plant's transport system
- Serve as food storage organs
- Provide a means of propagation

Stems are generally the bulkiest and most obvious part of the plant. They support the leaves, buds, flowers and fruit. Water, nutrients, the products of photosynthesis, and gases pass up and down stems, to and from the roots. Stems function as storage organs for food manufactured through photosynthesis. They may spread out and root, making new plants. Portions of stem, often called cuttings or slips, are used in vegetative reproduction or propagation. Examples are ivy, blackberry and willow (Salix). We commonly use stems as food — examples include asparagus, kohlrabi, broccoli, cauliflower, rhubarb and potatoes.

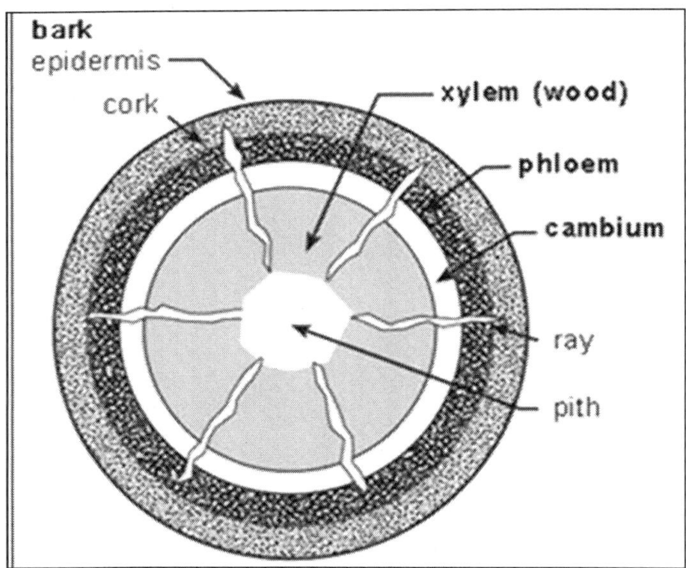

Fig. Cross section of woody plant stem.

Structure of Stems

Bark is the external covering of the stem. Internally, the stem's three major parts are the xylem, phloem and cambium. The xylem tubes are channels that conduct water and dissolved minerals and gases in the stem, while the phloem tissue conducts food products. The cambium is dicotyledonous meristematic tissue with cells that divide and enlarge to force the stem to expand outward.

New xylem is formed on the inner side of the cambium and new phloem on the outside. The cambium is a thin, actively growing layer that is vulnerable to girdling by wires, weed trimmers and even a tree's own roots.

While monocots and dicots both contain xylem and phloem, their vascular systems are arranged differently. In the stem of a monocot, the xylem and phloem are paired into bundles that are dispersed throughout the stem. In herbaceous dicots, those vascular bundles are arranged in a circle in the stem. The vascular system in a woody dicot is said to be continuous because it forms rings inside the stem.

The ring of phloem is near the bark or external covering of the stem. It is part of the bark of mature stems. Xylem forms the inner rings to become sapwood and heartwood of woody stems. Thus, the cross section shown here is of a dicotyledonous plant.

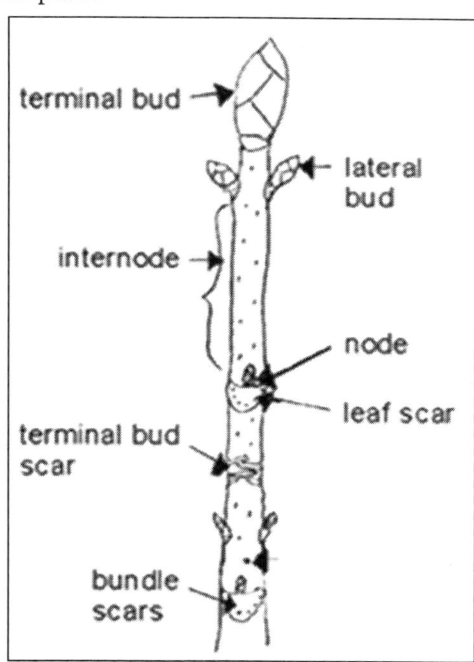

Fig. Typical Woody Stem.

External Features of Stems

Stems grow either above- or belowground. They may be long with large distances between leaves and buds, or they may be compressed with almost no distance between leaves and buds. The location on the stem where a leaf or bud occurs is called a node. It is sometimes difficult to distinguish between stems and roots, but one sure way is to look for nodes. Stems have nodes; roots do not.

The internodes are the regions between nodes. The length of an internode depends on many factors. One of these is genetic — oaks usually have shorter internodes than sycamores. Environment is also a great influence. For example, decreasing fertility will decrease internode length. Early-season growth, which is often the most vigorous, usually results in the greatest internode length. Too little light will cause stems to elongate, resulting in long, spindly growth. Paradoxically, plants that are growing vigorously tend to have longer internodes than weak plants.

Internode length will also be affected by competition from surrounding stems or fruits. If the plant's energy (available water and food) is divided between three or four stems, or if fruits (seeds) are also developing on the stem, less energy is available for any one shoot, and internode length is shortened.

Look at the varying internode lengths in a full season's growth of a deciduous tree, such as an oak or an apple. An interesting exercise for a gardener is to look at a stem and then try to identify the conditions that may have affected growth.

Types of Stems

Typical stems are the trunks and branches of shrubs and trees, and the stalks of non-woody plants. Modified stems can be found both aboveground and belowground.

Parts of aboveground modified stems.

- *Crowns:* Compressed stems having leaves and flowers on short internodes (strawberries, dandelions, African violets).
- *Spurs:* Short, stubby, side stems that arise from the main stem and are common on such fruit trees as pears, apples, and cherries where they may bear fruit. If severe pruning cuts close to fruit-bearing spurs, the spurs can revert to become non-fruiting, long stems.
- *Thorn:* Thorns develop as modified twigs on stems. They may be single (Cockspur hawthorn) or branched (honeylocust). Some thorns are modified leaves (cacti).
- *Stolons:* Horizontal stems that are fleshy or semi-woody that lie along the top of the ground (strawberry runners and spider plants).

Parts of belowground modified stems.

- *Rhizomes:* Similar to stolons, rhizomes generally grow underground rather than above it. Some rhizomes are compressed and fleshy like those of many irises. They can also be slender with elongated internodes, as in quack grass.
- *Tubers:* Thickened, fleshy underground stems. The eyes of a potato are actually the nodes on the stem: each eye contains a cluster of buds. The tuberous stems of tuberous begonia and cyclamen are

shortened, flattened, enlarged and mostly underground. Buds and shoots arise from the top or crown; fibrous roots grow from the bottoms of these tuberous stems.

- *Bulbs:* Tulips, lilies, daffodils, onions and some irises have shortened, compressed, underground stems surrounded by fleshy scales (modified leaves) that envelop a central bud located at the tip of the stem, which is usually buried deeply and protected by the thickened scales.
- *Corms:* Solid, swollen stems with dry, scale-like leaves on the outside, as in a gladiolus. A corm is shaped somewhat like a bulb, but without fleshy scales.

BUDS

A bud is an undeveloped shoot from which leaves or flower parts grow. The buds of deciduous trees and shrubs typically are protected by leathery bud scales or, in the case of some evergreens, a resinous covering. Some buds are termed "naked" because they have no covering. Herbaceous plants have naked buds in which the outer leaves are green and somewhat succulent. Buds may require exposure to a certain number of days below a critical temperature before they will resume growth in the spring.

This time period varies for different plants. During rest, dormant buds can withstand low temperatures, but after the rest period, buds become more susceptible to weather conditions and can be damaged easily by cold temperatures or frost.

A leaf bud is composed of a short stem with embryonic leaves and develops into leafy shoots. Leaf buds are often less plump than flower buds. Flower buds are made up of a short stem with embryonic flower parts. Buds are classified by their location on the stem. Terminal or apical buds are located at the apex or tip of the stem. Lateral or axillary buds are found on the sides of the stem, usually in the leaf axil, the point of leaf attachment to the stem. Adventitious buds arise at other sites, including the internode of the stem, at the edge of a leaf blade, from callus tissue at the cut end of a stem or root, or laterally from the roots of plants.

LEAVES

The principal function of leaves is to absorb sunlight for the manufacture of plant sugars. This process is called photosynthesis. The typical leaf has a flattened surface to present a large area that efficiently absorbs light energy. The leaf is supported by a stemlike appendage called a petiole. The base of the petiole is attached to the stem at the node. The angle formed between the petiole and the stem is called the leaf axil. A bud or cluster of buds is usually located in the axil.

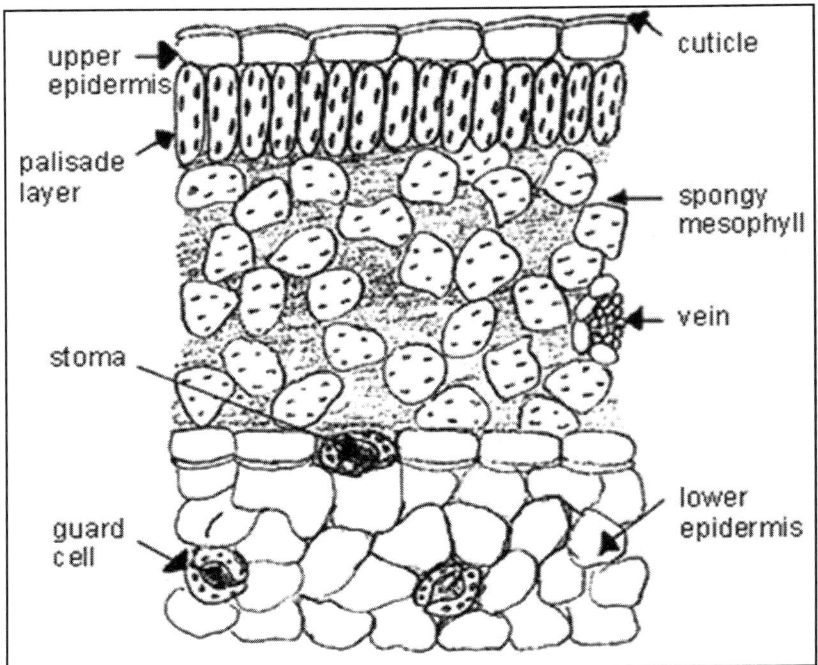

Fig. Cross section of dicot leaf.

Structure of Leaves

The leaf blade is composed of several layers. On the top and bottom is a layer of small, tough epidermal cells. The primary function of the epidermis is to protect leaf tissues. The arrangement of the cells in the epidermis determines the texture of the leaf surface. Hairs that are present on some leaves are extensions of epidermal cells. The thickness of the cuticle (the layer of cutin produced by epidermal cells) is a direct response to sunlight. The stronger the light, the thicker the cuticle. For this reason, plants grown in the shade should be moved into full sunlight gradually over a period of a few weeks to allow the cutin layer to build and to protect the leaves from rapid water loss and sunscald.

Cutin repels water and can shed pesticides if spreader/sticker agents or soaps are not used. This is the reason many pesticide manufacturers include some sort of spray additive to adhere to or penetrate the cutin layer. On the surface of leaves are the stomata.

Some plants have stomata on both surfaces; others have them only on the lower surface. Formed from epidermal guard cells that are capable of opening and closing, the stomata regulate the passage of water, oxygen and carbon dioxide into and out of the leaf. The opening and closing of guard cells is determined by the environment. Conditions that cause large water losses from plants (high temperature, low humidity) stimulate closing, while mild weather conditions leave guard cells open. Guard cells close in the absence of light.

The middle layer of a leaf is known as the mesophyll. This is the location of the chloroplasts that contain the green pigment chlorophyll. Photosynthesis takes place here. In monocot plant leaves, the mesophyll consists of cells and air spaces. In dicot leaves, it is divided into a dense upper layer called the palisade and a lower, spongy layer of cells with air spaces.

Leaf Types

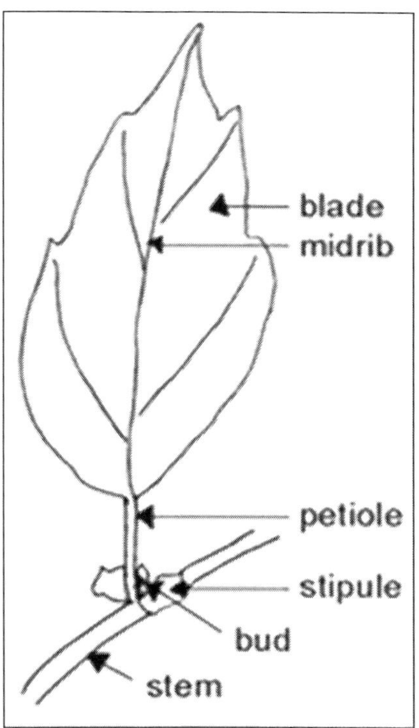

Fig. Simple Leaf Type.

- *Simple:* The parts of a simple leaf are the
  - *Blade:* The expanded thin structure on either side of the midrib. The blade usually is the largest and most conspicuous part of a leaf.
  - *Petiole:* The stalk that supports the leaf blade. It varies in length or may be lacking entirely in cases where the leaf blade is described as sessile or stalkless.
  - *Stipule:* One or more small appendages at the base of the petiole, usually in pairs and soon shed.

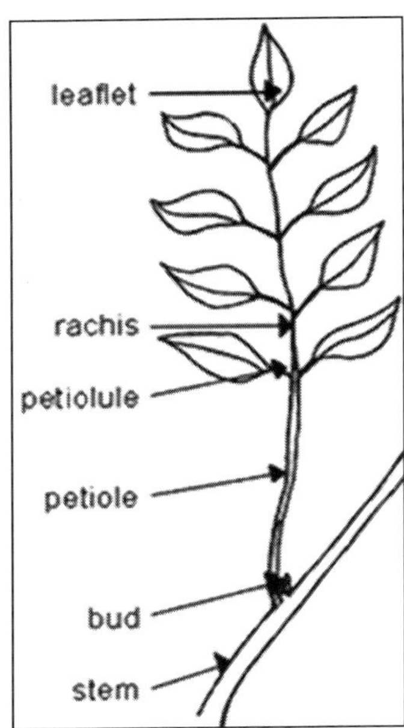

Fig. Compound Leaf Type.

- *Compound:* The parts of a compound leaf are the
  - *Leaflet:* Small leaflike structure; several or many leaflets make up one compound leaf.
  - *Petiole:* The stalk that supports each leaflet. It supports the entire compound leaf. Its length varies as for that of the simple leaf's petiole.
  - *Rachis:* This takes the place of the midrib in a simple leaf.

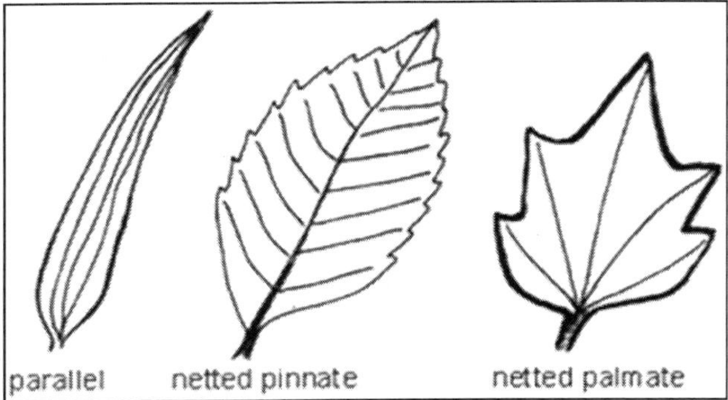

Fig. Leaf Venation.

Leaf Venation

Venation describes the patterns in which the veins are distributed in the blade:

- *Parallel-veined:* Numerous veins that run essentially parallel to each other. Most monocots have parallel venation (corn, tulip, lily).

- *Net-veined or reticulate-veined:* Veins that branch from the main rib or ribs and then subdivide. These venation patterns may be
  - *Pinnate:* A pattern with one main vein or midrib and many lateral veins branching off it (oak and elm).
  - *Palmate:* A pattern with three, five or more major veins originating from one point at the base of the blade. Palmate veins extend outwards like fingers from the palm of a hand (maple, English ivy).

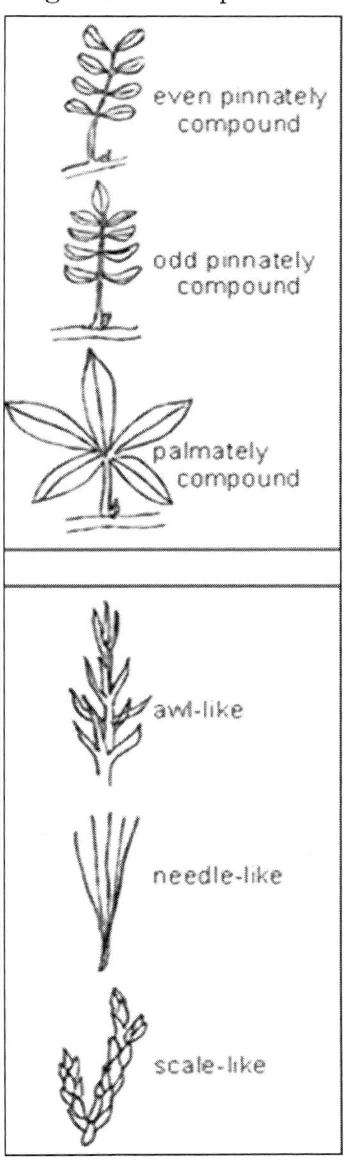

Fig. Leaf shapes, simple, left, compound, above right, and conifers, below right.

Leaf Shapes

The shape of the leaf blade and the type of leaf margin are important characteristics that help identify plants. Leaf blades vary a great deal. They may be simple (apple, oak) or compound (divided into several smaller leaflike segments, as in honeylocust). The smaller segments are called leaflets and are attached to a stalk (rachis) with a petiolule. Leaflets can also be arranged palmately (horse chestnut) or pinnately (ash). Pinnately compound leaves are said to be odd pinnate (ash) when ending in one leaflet and even pinnate when ending in two leaflets (locust). This terminology is important in identifying plants by their leaves.

Leaf Modifications

Leaves have adapted to survive a wide range of environmental conditions. For instance, leaves exposed to strong sunlight are often smaller and have thicker cuticles than leaves of the same plant growing in shade. The reduced surface area and thicker cuticle reduces water loss. Leaves that develop in shade have a larger surface area to absorb light.

Chloroplasts respond to light by exposing as much pigment as possible in low light situations and by exposing less pigment in bright conditions. We see the results: dark green foliage on shade-grown plants and paler green foliage when the same plant grows in a sunnier location. Examples of this include hosta, Norfolk Island pine and weeping fig.

Leaves on plants that grow in dry environments will often be thick or narrow with few intercellular (air) spaces in the mesophyll, while guard cells are sunken below the level of the regular epidermis to minimize water loss. In some desert plants, such as cacti, the foliage leaves may be modified into thorns and photosynthesis occurs in chloroplast-containing cells in the stem. Plants that grow underwater have just a few widely spaced mesophyll cells and big intercellular spaces for holding gases that are harder to acquire underwater.

Many conifers have leaves adapted for windy or low-moisture conditions. Needlelike leaves on pines have little wind resistance, and the flattened or scalelike leaves of junipers are waxy and well protected from the hot sun.

A number of distinct leaf modifications occur on plants. These include

- *Cotyledons:* Also called seed leaves, these are the leaves of the embryonic plant. These commonly serve as storage organs to feed the germinating seedling while true leaves develop.
- *Spines and tendrils:* These specialized, modified leaves protect the plant or assist in supporting the stems.
- *Storage leaves:* Found in bulbous plants and succulents, these serve as food storage organs containing starch and water.
- *Bracts:* These are specialized leaves that are often brightly colored.

The showy structures on dogwoods and poinsettias are bracts, not flower petals.

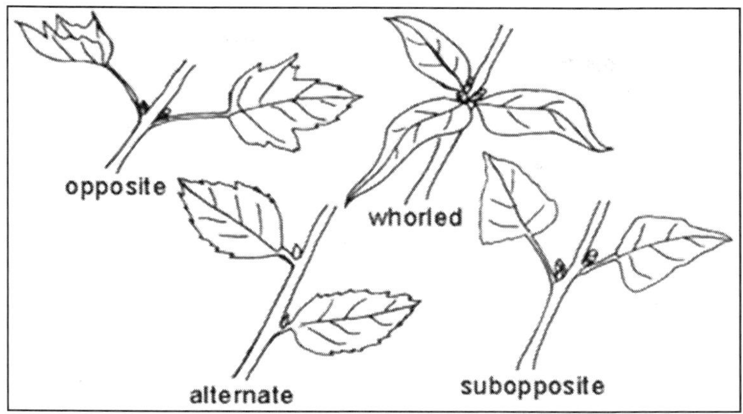

Fig. Leaf Arrangements.

Leaf Arrangement and Attachment

Leaves at the nodes may grow in pairs opposite one another (maple) or alternate (birch) from side to side along the stem. They also may be whorled, with three or more leaves arising from a node, such as hydrangea. Subopposite leaves are slightly offset from one another; these are relatively rare. An example is the katsura tree, Cercidiphyllum japonicum.

FLOWERS

Although there are many different kinds of flowers, they are similar in their organization. The function of flowers is sexual reproduction. Thus, flowers often form the showiest part of the plant. Their colour and fragrance attract pollinators such as insects or birds to assure the continuance of the species. Flowers that are neither showy nor scented rely on other methods for pollination — wind, for example. Yet all have the same basic structures.

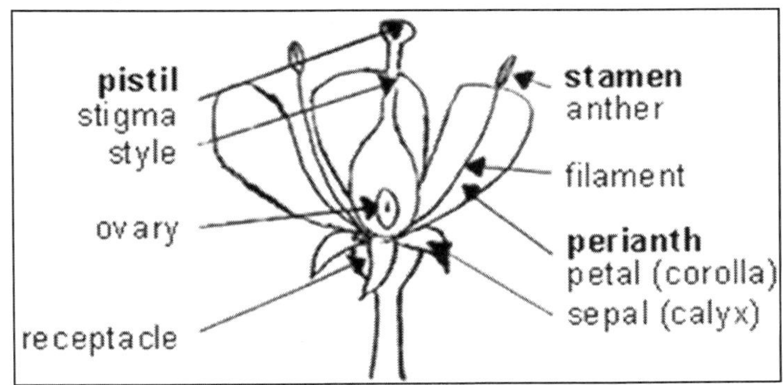

Fig. Parts of a Typical Flower.

How Seeds Form

Pollination is the transfer of pollen from an anther to a stigma. This may occur by wind or by pollinators. Wind-pollinated flowers usually lack showy floral parts and nectar since they don't need to attract a pollinator. Flowers are brightly colored or patterned and contain a fragrance or nectar when they must attract insects, animals or birds as pollinators.

Self-pollinated flowers can be fertilized by their own pollen. Some flowers, like varieties of apple, can rarely be fertilized by their own pollen. In these cases, cross-pollination is necessary. With some fruits such as plums that are capable of bearing a crop without the presence of other varieties, cross-pollination will increase the size and quality of the yield.

The stigma contains a chemical that activates a compatible pollen grain, causing it to grow a long tube down the inside of the style to the ovules inside the ovary.

The sperm is released by the pollen grain and fertilization occurs. Fertilization is the union of the male sperm nucleus from the pollen grain and the female egg located in the ovary. If fertilization is successful, the ovule will develop into a seed.

PARTS OF FLOWERS

Some plants produce solitary flowers like a tulip, while others, such as the garden phlox, have clusters of flowers called inflorescences. Each individual flower consists of a stem portion called a receptacle that supports the rest of the flower parts. As the reproductive part of the plant, the flower contains either the male pollen or the female ovules, or both, plus accessory parts such as petals, sepals and nectar glands.

- *Perianth:* The perianth consists of all the structures that enclose the reproductive organs, the corolla or petals, and the outermost layer, the calyx or sepals.
  - *Sepals:* These are small, leaflike structures at the base of the flower that protect the flower bud. The sepals collectively are called the calyx. Sometimes the sepals are as highly colored and showy as the petals, as in the daylily. These colored sepals are called tepals.
  - *Petals:* The highly colored portions of the flower. They may contain volatile fragrant oils and nectar glands. The number of petals on a flower is often used in the identification of plant families and genera. The petals collectively are called the corolla. The calyx and corolla collectively compose the perianth.
- *Pistil:* The female part of the plant. It is generally shaped like a bowling pin and is located in the center of the flower. It consists of the stigma, style and ovary. The stigma is located at the top and is

connected by the style to the ovary, which contains the eggs in the ovules. After an egg is fertilized, an ovule develops into a seed.

- *Stamen:* The male part of the plant. It consists of a pollen sac called the anther and supporting filament, which holds the anther in position so that pollen from the anther may be disbursed by wind or carried to the stigma by pollinating insects or animals.

Types of Flowers

Complete. A complete flower has stamens, pistils, petals and sepals. If one of these parts is missing, the flower is incomplete.

- *Perfect:* A perfect flower contains functional stamens and pistils. These are considered the essential parts of a flower and are involved in producing seeds. If either of the essential parts is lacking, the flower is imperfect.
- *Pistillate (female):* A flower that possesses a functional pistil or pistils but lack stamens.
- *Staminate:* A flower that contain stamens but no pistils.
- *Dioecious (= two houses):* Male and female flowers on separate plants. Most holly trees and bittersweet vines are either male (staminate) or female (pistillate) plants. To get berries, it is necessary to grow a female plant and have a male plant nearby to provide pollen.
- *Monoecious (= one house):* Male and female flowers on the same plant, either as bisexual flowers or with separate pistillate and staminate blossoms. Some plants bear only male flowers early in the growing season and later develop both sexes, *e.g.*, cucumbers and squash.

SEEDS AND SEEDLINGS

From Embryo to Seedling

An embryo forms after repeated cell divisions of the zygote — the fertilized ovule. While cells are dividing, distinct parts of the seed are forming. These include the

- *Radicle:* Contains the root apical meristem and develops into the root system.
- *Hypocotyl:* Elongates to form the lowest part of the stem.
- *Cotyledons (seed leaves):* Contain food stored for the newly developing plant.
- *Epicotyl:* Contains the shoot apical meristem and develops into the shoot system.

Monocots have one cotyledon and dicots have two cotyledons. As the embryo develops, the outer walls that form the seed coat become a tough, protective layer around the seed.

Seeds

The seed or matured ovule is made up of three parts — the embryo, endosperm and seed coat or testa.

- *Embryo:* This is a miniature plant in an arrested state of development.
- *Endosperm:* The endosperm provides a built-in food supply for the embryo. It can be made up of proteins, carbohydrates or fats
- *Seed coat or testa:* This hard outer covering protects the seed from disease and insects and prevents water from entering the seed and causing germination before the proper time.

Seedlings

Germination is the resumption of active growth of the embryo. Before anything else, the seed must take up water through the seed coat. In addition, the seed must be in the proper environmental conditions — exposed to oxygen, favourable temperatures and for some, correct light; the seed must be ripe or mature; and dormancy must be broken either physically or chemically. Factors that can limit germination include the time of the year seed was harvested, its age and moisture content, and successful fertilization.

FRUITS

Fruits consist of the fertilized and mature ovules called seeds and the ovary wall which may become fleshy as in the apple or dry and hard as in a maple fruit. The only parts of the fruit that contain genetic material from both the male and female flowers are the seeds. The rest of the fruit is actually part of the maternal plant and is, therefore, genetically identical to it.

The fruit is essentially the structure that protects the seeds as they develop. It also functions as a dispersal mechanism, as in the milkweed pod. A fleshy fruit such as an apple keeps the seeds moist until they are ready to germinate. Some seeds are hard and have a thick seed coat to keep the seed from germinating for months or years (for example, Kentucky coffee tree).

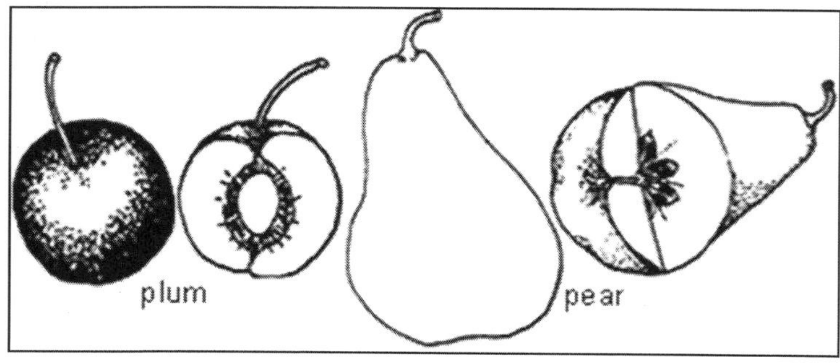

Fig. Simple Fruits.

Types of Fruits

Simple. Simple fruits develop from single ovaries. These include plum, cherry and peach (drupes), pears and apples (pomes), and tomatoes (berries). Tomatoes are a botanical fruit because they develop from a flower, as do squash, cucumbers and eggplant. All of these develop from a single ovary.

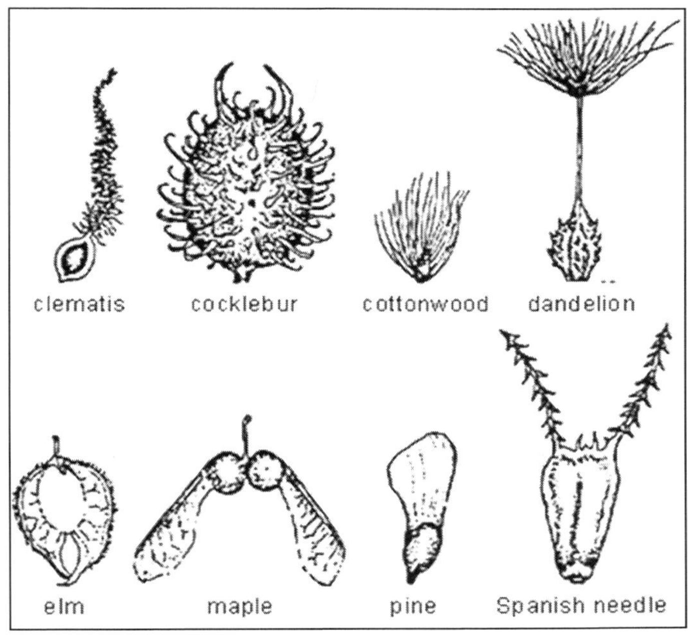

Fig. Dry Fruits.

- *Dry:* Dry fruits are simple fruits in which the fruit wall becomes papery or leathery and hard, as opposed to the fleshy examples above. Examples are peanut (pod), poppy (capsule), maple (samara) and walnut (nut).

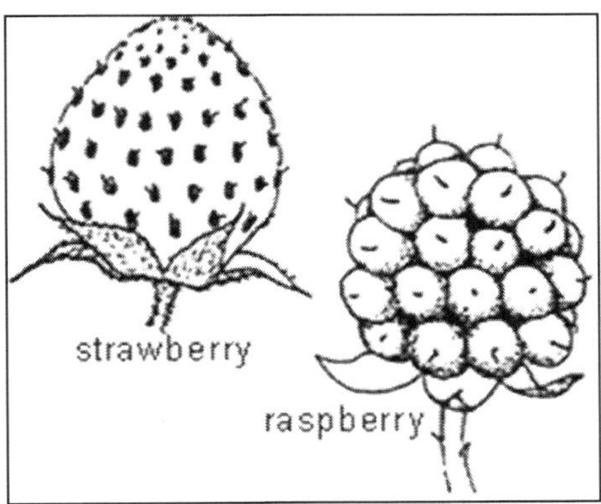

Fig. Aggregate Fruits.

- *Aggregate:* Aggregate fruits come from a single flower that has many ovaries. The flower appears as a simple flower with one corolla, one calyx and one stem but with many pistils or ovaries. Examples are strawberry, raspberry and blackberry. The ovaries are fertilized separately and independently. If ovules are not pollinated successfully, the fruit will be misshapen. In the strawberry, the receptacle becomes bright red and fleshy. The small seeds are actually individual one-seeded fruits called achenes.
- *Multiple:* Multiple fruits originate from a tight cluster of separate, independent flowers borne on a single structure. Each flower will have its own calyx and corolla. Examples of multiple fruits are corn, pineapple and sunflower.

PLANT PROCESSES

In the world of living things, plants are unique. They can make their own food and, except for plants that depend on insects or animals for pollination, they can exist without any other living creature. We, however, cannot exist without plants because in order to survive, we need what plants produce. Because of this, plants are called primary food producers.

In addition, plants maintain an atmospheric balance between carbon dioxide and oxygen, thus providing a vital buffer against rapid global warming. One further benefit plants offer is that of cleansing, of absorbing pollutants from soil, water and air. Sewage lagoons and enclosed spaces — including offices and homes — benefit from plants' ability to filter out unwanted, organic-based chemicals. All living things depend on photosynthesis for survival.

PHOTOSYNTHESIS

Major Plant Functions

To understand how plants are able to manufacture their food and live independently, we need a working knowledge of plant growth processes and development. Three major plant functions are the basis of plant growth and development: photosynthesis, respiration and transpiration. Photosynthesis is the connecting link between solar energy and the energy required for life on earth. To manufacture its own food, a plant requires energy from the sun, carbon dioxide from the air, and water, usually from the soil. If any of these ingredients is lacking, photosynthesis or food production will stop. If any factor is removed for long, the plant will die. Photosynthesis means literally "to put together with light."

The chemical equation below illustrates photosynthesis:

light

$$6CO_2 + 6H_2O = C_6H_{12}O_6 + 6O_2$$

chlorophyll

Differences Between Photosynthesis and Respiration

Photosynthesis:

- Produces food
- Energy is stored
- Occurs in cells' chloroplasts
- Oxygen is released
- Water is used
- Carbon dioxide is used
- Occurs in sunlight

Respiration:

- Uses food for plant energy
- Energy is released
- Occurs in all cells
- Oxygen is used
- Water is producedCarbon dioxide is produced
- Occurs in dark as well as light

During photosynthesis, chlorophyll harnesses light energy and uses this energy to split water molecules into hydrogen and oxygen. In further reactions, the hydrogen from water is added to carbon dioxide in the manufacture of carbohydrates, the plant's source of energy. Only cells containing chloroplasts in the plant's leaves and stems can manufacture this energy. The end product, glucose (a sugar), may be used in cellular respiration to provide energy, or it may be converted into other substances such as sucrose (table sugar), starch or cellulose, amino acids and proteins, fats and other compounds. Oxygen is a byproduct of this process.

Generally, as sunlight increases in intensity, photosynthesis increases. This means greater food production. Many garden crops, such as tomatoes, respond best to maximum sunlight. Tomato production is cut drastically as light intensities drop in the autumn. The same can be said for other high-light species such as corn and beans. The carbon dioxide that is necessary for photosynthesis enters the plant through the stomata. Generally, carbon dioxide is plentiful in the air. However, in a closed greenhouse, plants may use more than can be replenished by outside air movement, and supplemental carbon dioxide can be used to maintain plant growth.

Temperature is also an important factor. In most plants, the optimum range for maximum photosynthetic activity is at temperatures ranging from 65 to 85 degrees F. Higher or lower temperatures may hinder photosynthetic activity. Of the total sunlight energy that falls on the leaf surface, typically only 3 per cent is used for photosynthesis, 15 per cent is reflected and 5 per cent passes through the leaves. The other 70 per cent raises the temperature of the leaf. Cooling the leaf takes place through the plant's process of transpiration (water loss).

RESPIRATION

For Growth

For growth to occur, carbohydrate gains through photosynthesis must be greater than losses through respiration. Carbohydrates made during photosynthesis benefit the plant when they are converted to energy. This energy is used to build new tissues and to help the plant grow. The chemical process by which sugars and starches produced by photosynthesis are converted to energy is called respiration, which is a form of oxidation. The process of respiration is similar to the burning of wood or coal to produce heat. Its byproducts are water and carbon dioxide.

Respiration is essentially the reverse of photosynthesis. Respiration occurs at night as well as during the day. It takes place in all life forms (including animals) and in all living cells. The release of accumulated carbon dioxide and the uptake of oxygen occur at the cellular level. In animals, blood carries both carbon dioxide and oxygen to and from the atmosphere by means of the lungs (or gills in fish). In plants, these gases pass by simple diffusion into the open spaces within the leaf and then through the stomata.

Transpiration

Transpiration is the process by which a plant loses water, primarily through leaf stomata. Transpiration uses about 90 per cent of the water that enters the plant through the roots. The other 10 per cent of the water is needed for chemical reactions and expansion of plant tissues.

Transpiration is necessary to transport dissolved minerals from the soil to other plant parts, to cool leaf and stem tissue through evaporation, to move sugars and plant chemicals, and to maintain the turgidity or firmness of plant tissues. The amount of water the plant loses depends on environmental factors that include temperature, humidity, and wind or air movement. As temperature or air movement increases, transpiration also increases. As humidity decreases, transpiration increases.

These facts relate to the practical activity of watering. Outdoors, we need to water more often in hot, windy and dry weather. Indoors, cool-season heating systems cause drier air than at any other time of year. Even though plants are not growing very fast during short days, they may be using plenty of water.

ENVIRONMENTAL INFLUENCES

Water Stress

When adequate moisture is available to the plant, water flows continuously from the root hairs up to the leaves. If inadequate moisture is available in the soil, or if rate of evaporation from the leaves exceeds the rate at which water can move upward, the plant becomes stressed. The gardener's goal is to reduce the plant's water stress to maintain a quality landscape or a productive garden. This can be done as much through plant selection and placement as by watering.

Plant growth and distribution are influenced by the environment. If any one environmental factor is less than ideal, it will become a limiting factor in plant growth. Such limiting factors are responsible for the geography of plant distribution. For example, only plants adapted to the limited availability of moisture can live in the desert. Most plant problems are associated with one or more environmental factors. The results may be immediate and direct, like wilting or plant death from lack of water. Indirect results are also seen in apparently healthy plants when they become diseased or decline because they were weakened by flood, drought or some other factor.

Water, light, temperature and air are the four main environmental factors that influence plant growth and development. Understanding how each works can help guide selection of the optimum microclimates for setting out plants.

Water

Water plays an important role in all plant functions. First, water is necessary to maintain turgor pressure that gives the plant its rigidity and shape (turgor pressure can be compared to air in an inflated balloon). Water is needed for cell division and expansion. It also provides the internal pressure that pushes growing roots through the soil. Water is used during the biochemical process of photosynthesis. Through respiration, the plant converts carbohydrates back into water and carbon dioxide, releasing stored energy needed for plant growth.

Water also helps in chemical changes that dissolve minerals from the soil — it carries them in solution from the roots to all parts of the plant, where they serve as raw materials in the growth of new plant tissues. During transpiration, moisture is literally pulled through the plant as water evaporates through the leaves and helps stabilize plant temperature.

Water-related Conditions

- *Water stress:* If water is in short supply, the plant shows a series of responses. The most common effect is wilting. However, plants that are water deficient may also show leaf rolling, colour changes from deep green to blue-green, leaf browning and foliage losses such as dropping leaves. During hot, dry summer months, moderate stress can be tolerated by most plants on a daily basis as long as moisture is replenished during the low-stress night period. However, severe or prolonged moisture stress can cause permanent damage to the plant.

- *Drought tolerance:* Plants differ greatly in their ability to extract water from the soil and in the absolute amount of water required for normal plant growth. Some plants are considered drought tolerant because they can function well in dry soil (xerophytic) conditions. Drought tolerance results from one or more of the following factors:
  - Deep and well-developed root systems
  - Waxy leaf surfaces
  - Leaf hairs that minimize water loss from stomata
  - Shiny surfaces that reflect light
  - Leaves that fold up or drop under water stress conditions
  - Small, thick leaves
- Excess moisture: Too much water in the root zone can damage plants because of reduced oxygen in the area around root hairs. The objective of proper irrigation is to supply the right amount of water before harmful stress occurs but to avoid keeping the soil so saturated as to limit oxygen availability to the roots.

LIGHT

Phototropism

Phototropism refers to a plant's ability to lean and grow towards the light. Seedlings are especially sensitive. The principal characteristics of light that affect plant growth are quantity, quality and duration.

Quantity

The intensity or concentration of sunlight varies with the season of the year. Up to a point, the more sunlight a plant receives, the greater its capacity to produce plant food through photosynthesis. However, if light intensity becomes too high, photosynthesis can actually be reduced. This occurs first in low-light plants such as hosta. Light intensity can be reduced in garden or greenhouse by the use of shading materials or by planting in the shade. It can be increased with reflective material around plants, white backgrounds or supplemental lights.

In addition to seasonal variations in light intensity, latitude directly affects how much sunlight reaches us. Light intensity is greatest at and near the equator, diminishing with increasing distance, north or south, from the equator. For example, sunlight in the Bootheel of Missouri is slightly more intense than at locations farther north.

Quality

The colour or wavelength reaching the plant surface affects growth. Sunlight can be broken up by a prism into its rainbow colours of red, orange, yellow, green, blue, indigo and violet. Red and blue light have the greatest effect on plant growth because they are the two wavelengths of light most important to the process of photosynthesis. Red light, when combined with blue light, encourages flowering. Green light has least effect on plants as they absorb less of it — they look green to our eyes because they reflect green light rather than use it for growth processes.

Light quality is important as we consider providing artificial light to plants. Cool white fluorescent lights are high in the blue range of light quality, whereas incandescent lights are high in the red or orange range. They generally produce too much heat to be a valuable light source. "Grow lights" have a mix of red and blue colours that imitate sunlight. A similar balance can be achieved with a mixture of warm-white and cool-white fluorescent tubes.

Light and Flowering

In greenhouses, growers can initiate flowering at any time of the year by regulating light and dark periods. For instance, poinsettias are short-day plants that initiate bloom in response to shorter day lengths.

They can be brought into bloom precisely at Christmas by using black curtains to block out sunlight, thus shortening the photoperiod. Other plants can be artificially lit in greenhouses to initiate flowering when outdoor light levels are low.

Duration

The length of time that a plant is exposed to sunlight or darkness is called the photoperiod. The ability of many plants to flower is controlled by photoperiod. Short-day or long-night plants.

These plants form flowers only when the day length is less than a certain duration. For these plants, it actually is the length of uninterrupted darkness that accompanies a short day that is critical to trigger the flowering response. If even a flash of light interrupts the dark period, plants will fail to flower. Short-day plants include many fall-flowering plants such as chrysanthemum and poinsettia, whose flowers are initiated naturally when days are getting shorter.

Long-day or short-night plants. These plants form flowers only at day lengths longer than a certain number of hours. They include almost all of the summer-flowering plants, as well as many vegetables, including beet, radish, lettuce, spinach and potato. Flowers are initiated as days become longer in spring.

Day-neutral plants. These plants form flowers regardless of day length. Some plants do not really fit into any category but may respond to combinations of day lengths. For example, petunias will flower regardless of day length, but flower earlier and more profusely under long day lengths.

TEMPERATURE

Winter Injury

Winter injury can occur if midwinter temperatures are too low, or if there are unseasonably low temperatures in early fall or late spring. Winter injury may also occur through desiccation or drying out. Plant tissues need water during winter. When soil is frozen, water movement in the plant is severely restricted. On windy winter days, evergreens can become water-deficient in a few minutes; leaves or needles soon turn brown. If temperatures drop too low during the winter, entire trees of some species are killed by the freezing and desiccating of plant cells. On the other hand, unseasonably high winter temperatures can cause premature bud break in some plants; subsequent freezes may kill or severely damage the exposed tissues. Late spring frosts can ruin entire crops.

Temperature affects productivity and growth by affecting the processes carried on in a plant such as photosynthesis and respiration. An individual plant's response depends upon its needs and its adaptability to warm- or cool-season conditions. If temperatures are high and day length is long, cool-season crops such as spinach will flower. Temperatures that are too low for a warm-season crop such as tomato will prevent fruit set. The same problem may be caused by continuous excessive heat. Unfavorable temperatures produce stunted growth and poor quality vegetables. Bitterness in lettuce results from high temperatures. Lupines and delphiniums do not grow well in the lower Midwest because they are not adapted to its hot, humid summers.

Sometimes temperature control is used along with day length to manipulate flowering. The Christmas cactus forms flowers as a result of short days and low temperatures. Temperature alone also influences flowering. Tulips can be forced to flower out of season by putting planted bulbs in cold storage (35 to 45 degrees F) in October. The cold temperatures encourage flower development and stem elongation as the bulb matures.

The thermoperiod is a term that refers to daily temperature changes. Most plants respond to and achieve maximum growth when daytime temperatures are about 10 to 15 degrees higher than nighttime temperatures. They photosynthesize during optimum daytime temperatures, and their respiration rates slow during the cooler nights. Higher temperatures result in increased respiration, sometimes above the rate of photosynthesis, so products of photosynthesis may be used up more rapidly than they are being produced.

Optimum Temperatures

Plants are adaptable and there are both heat- and cold-tolerant choices for plants that grow best in a given environment. Optimum growing temperatures vary. For example, snapdragons grow best with average nighttime temperatures of 55 degrees F and the poinsettia with 62 degrees F. Florists' cyclamen does well in very cool conditions while many summer annual bedding plants, like periwinkle (Catharanthus), prefer higher temperatures.

- *High temperatures:* Above 86 degrees F, photosynthesis in many plants essentially shuts down and, in some, cell protein starts to be damaged. During the long, hot days of summer, plants often rely on stored energy reserves because there is little active photosynthetic activity.
- *Low temperatures:* Low temperatures can also result in poor growth. Photosynthesis slows down when it is cold. Since photosynthesis is slow, growth is slow. For harvest crops, this means lower yields.
- *Dormancy:* In some cases, a certain number of days at low temperature are needed by plants in order to break dormancy and to grow properly. This is especially true of crops that originated in cold regions. Apples are a prime example; most varieties require 1,000 to 1,200 hours below 45 degrees F but above 32 degrees F before they will break their rest period and begin growth. Lilies and daffodils need six weeks of temperatures at 33 degrees F before they will bloom.

Temperature Zones

Plants' range — where they will grow naturally — is affected by temperature and other climatic factors. This information can help gardeners select plants and varieties that are suited to local conditions. USDA Plant Hardiness Zones Map. Whether a plant is considered hardy or non-hardy depends on its ability to withstand cold temperatures. This is the basis of the 11 distinct plant hardiness zones that reflect average minimum winter temperatures for a given area. It does not, however, take into account temperature fluctuations, adaptation to wet or dry soils, humidity or summer temperatures.

In Missouri, the northern two-thirds of the state is mostly in USDA hardiness zone 5 (average winter minimum of -10 to -20 degrees F), although there are a few pockets in zone 4 (-20 to -30 degrees F) or zone 6 (0 to -10 degrees F). The southern third of the state is zone 6, except for the southernmost tip of the Bootheel, which is zone 7 (0 to +10 degrees F).

American Horticultural Society Heat Zone Map. These 12 heat zones are based on the average number of days when temperatures reach or exceed 86 degrees F. Most of Missouri is in heat zone 7, which receives 61 to 90 days per year of temperatures above 86 degrees F. A small portion of southern Missouri is in AHS heat zone 8 (91 to 120 days above 86 degrees F) and the north-central part of the state is heat zone 6 (46 to 60 days above 86 degrees F).

Sunset Garden Climate Zones Map. The 45-region climate zones take into account heat, cold, moisture and altitude for specific geographical areas in the United States.

Air

Air contains nitrogen, oxygen and carbon dioxide, plus water vapor or humidity, and a number of other gaseous compounds. Of the three main components, nitrogen is present in the greatest concentration by volume: 79 per cent. Oxygen is next, at 20 per cent. Carbon dioxide, or CO_2, makes up less than 1 per cent of the air's volume (0.03 per cent). Nevertheless, it has great significance in the biological world as one of the ingredients for photosynthesis and for the manufacture of the carbohydrates that enter the food chain.

Land plants rely almost entirely upon carbon dioxide in the atmosphere. A small part of their photosynthetic need is supplied by carbon dioxide from respiration (which never leaves the plant tissues). The rest must enter the plant through the stomata, most of which are located on the undersides of leaves.

Soil Atmosphere:

Air in the soil usually contains more carbon dioxide than atmospheric air, with concentrations of up to 10 per cent or more in some soils. The higher levels of carbon dioxide result from the respiration of many organisms in the soil, including plant roots. In soil with adequate pore space, the concentration of oxygen rarely becomes too low to support aerobic respiration. In wet or flooded soils, oxygen is often too low to fuel aerobic respiration, and anaerobic organisms and processes take over that exist in conditions with very low or no free oxygen.

Air Pollutants

Many of the gases that get into the air we breathe will affect plants, even in small quantities. For example, tomato plants will respond to small amounts of ethylene with drooping leaves. Continued exposure will cause leaf curling and death. Ethylene is a by-product of the incomplete combustion of fossil fuels such as natural gas and oil. Thus, tomato plants are useful indicators where this type of gas is produced or used. Most ethylene damage to plants occurs in greenhouses equipped with malfunctioning heaters.

Sulfur dioxide and ozone are also damaging to plant tissues. Sulfur dioxide causes dry, dead areas at the leaf margins and between veins. Ozone, which enters leaves through the stomata, destroys plant cells by damaging their membranes so they collapse. As a result, the tissues become marked white to tan.

THE ENVIRONMENTAL AND PHYSIOLOGICAL NATURE OF STRESS

Successful adaptation of a crop species is dependent upon the programming of critical growth stages so that the plant can capitalize on favorable weather periods during the growing season. Plants have evolved a variety of adaptive mechanisms that allow them to optimize growth and development while coping with environmental stresses. These mechanisms include seed and bud dormancy, photoperiod sensitivity, and low-temperature response. Seed dormancy delays germination until after the embryo has gone through an after-ripening period.

The over-winter survival of buds of many temperate zone trees and shrubs is dependent on a dormancy stage that starts in the late summer or early fall and ends after exposure to an extended period of cold or increasing day length in the spring.

In addition to trees, many other dicots and grasses have a photoperiod response that can advance or delay flowering. Vernalization is a requirement for growth at low temperatures before a plant will flower. Most winter annual and biennial plants have a vernalization requirement. Low-temperature acclimation is an ability of plants to cold acclimate when exposed to gradually decreasing temperatures below a specific threshold. This is the most common mechanism that plants have evolved for adapting to low-temperature stress and examples of plants with the capacity to cold harden can be found in most species.

TYPES OF LOW TEMPERATURE INJURY

There are two types of injuries a plant can sustain through exposure to low temperatures. The first is chilling injury that occurs from approximately 20 to 0°C. The resultant injuries may include a variety of physiological disruptions in germination, flower and fruit development, yield, and storage life. Minor chilling stress at non-lethal temperatures is normally reversible. Exposure to gradually decreasing temperatures above the critical range can also result in hardening of plants that may reduce or eliminate injury during subsequent exposure to low temperatures.

The second type of injury is called freezing injury. This type of injury occurs when the external temperature drops below the freezing point of water. Some varieties of plants that are susceptible to chilling injury can be killed by the first touch of frost. At the other extreme, many plants that are native to cold climates can survive extremely low temperatures without injury. Plants may experience intracellular freezing and/or extracellular freezing. Intracellular freezing damages the protoplasmic structure and the ice crystals kill the cell once they grow large enough to be detected microscopically. In extracellular freezing, the protoplasm of the plant becomes dehydrated because a water-vapor deficit is created as cellular water is transferred to ice crystals forming in the intercellular spaces. In some cases, water can remain liquid as low as -47°C without nucleating and forming ice. When nucleation of this supercooled water does occur, intracellular ice forms suddenly resulting in death of the plant.

TYPES OF PLANTS

Plants can be grouped into three different classes according to their low-temperature tolerance. The first group includes frost tender plants that are sensitive to chilling injury and can be killed by short periods of exposure to temperatures just below freezing. They cannot tolerate ice in their tissues and readily exhibit frost injury symptoms that include a water soaked flaccid appearance with loss of turger followed by rapid drying upon exposure to warm temperatures. Beans, corn, rice, and tomatoes are examples of plants in this category.

Low-temperature acclimation of plants in the second group allows them to tolerate the presence of extracellular ice in their tissues. Their frost resistance ranges from the broad-leafed summer annuals, which are killed at temperatures slightly below freezing, to perennial grasses that can survive exposure to -40°C. As temperatures decrease the outward migration of intracellular water to the growing extracellular ice crystal causes dehydration stress that will eventually result in irreversible damage to the plasma membrane, which is the primary site of low-temperature injury. If ice nucleation does not occur at -3 to -5°C, supercooling may result in intracellular freezing and death of individual cells.

The final group is made up of very cold hardy plants that are predominantly temperate woody species. Like the plants in the previous group, their lower limits of cold tolerance are dependent on the stage of acclimation, the rate and degree of temperature decline, and the genetic capability of tissues to accommodate extracellular freezing and the accompanying dehydration stress. Deep supercooling allows certain tissues in plants from this group to survive low temperatures without the formation of extracellular ice. However, the most cold hardy species do not rely on supercooling and can withstand temperatures of -196 °C.

PLANT CHILLING STRESS AND ITS REPERCUSSIONS

Most crops of tropical origin as well as many of subtropical origin are sensitive to chilling temperatures. This limits production areas and causes potential damage during storage if they are exposed to low temperatures. The temperature below which chill injury can occur varies with species and regions of origin, ranging from 0 to 4°C for temperate fruits, 8°C for subtropical fruits, and about 12°C for tropical fruits such as banana (Lyons 1973). Amongst the highest volume world food crops, maize (Zea mays) and rice (Oryza sativa) are sensitive to chilling temperatures. Their growth and development can be adversely effected by temperatures below 10°C resulting in yield loss or crop failure. Christiansen and St. John (1981) estimated annual losses of $60 million to the cotton industry due to chilling temperature immediately following field planting. Chilling during the seedling stage in cotton can reduce plant height, delay flowering and adversely affect yield and lint quality. Seedlings can also suffer water stress and leaf desiccation at chilling temperatures, floral initiation is inhibited at 7°C and seed set is inhibited at 15°C. Other crops suffering stand loss, delayed maturity, and reduced yield as a result of chilling after planting include soybean (Glycine max L.), lima bean (Phaseolus lunatus L.), cucurbits (Cucurbita sp.), tomato (Lycopersicon esculentum Mill.) pepper Capsicum annuum L.), eggplant (Solanum melongena L.), okra (Abelmoschus esculentus L.), and various cereal crops.

Physiological age, seedling development, and pre-harvest climate can also influence chilling sensitivity. Freshly imbibed seeds of chill-sensitive species tend to be very sensitive, as does the pollen development stage. Fruits maturing at high temperature are more susceptible than those maturing at lower temperatures. Post-harvest storage at lower temperatures is commonly used to extend the storage life of fruits and vegetables. Tropical and subtropical plants however are often subject to physiological damage and loss of quality due to chill injury under these storage conditions. The severity of injury to chill-sensitive tissues tends to increase with decreasing temperatures and with length of low-temperature exposure.

Chilling has been found to change the entire metabolic system of the cell with some processes recovering quickly and others only slowly. Chilling affects the entire internal environment of each cell and each molecule within the cells. Enzymatic reactions, substrate diffusion rates, and membrane transport properties are all affected. Chilling injury is therefore likely a direct consequence of these effects.

AMELIORATION OF CHILLING INJURY

Avoidance: To avoid chilling injury, planting dates can be altered though this is often difficult because of its effect on later development of the plant. To overcome this problem, cultivars have been bred for early vigour and maturity. In the case of stored fruits and vegetables, maintenance of appropriate storage temperatures is essential to avoid chilling injury. Investigations have also been undertaken to examine synthetic plant growth regulators for the protection of chilling sensitive crops.

Temperature conditioning: Low-temperature 'hardening' allowing tolerance to chilling temperatures appears to have little effect although some sensitivity to 'slight chilling' can be reduced by exposure to temperatures slightly above the chilling range. It also appears that chilling injury to stored fruits and vegetables can be ameliorated by warm temperatures if they are imposed before tissue degeneration becomes advanced. Other treatments such as waxing, fungicides, hormones, and antioxidants have produced variable results that have been dependent upon the species and treatment conditions.

Duration: Ultrastructural-chilling injury increases with time and with prolonged exposure the injury becomes irreversible. It is therefore important to minimize the time of chilling temperature exposure.

Relative humidity: High (100 per cent) relative humidity has been found to protect chloroplasts from chill injury, an effect that is enhanced by darkness.

THEORIES OF CHILLING INJURY

Early research focused on chilling causing an imbalance in plant physiological processes. Chilling was found to affect O_2 evolution, organic acids, sugars, polyphenols, phospholipids, protein, and ATP. Research indicates that chilling stress in sensitive plants changes most chemical entities. There is evidence of accumulation of toxins such as ethanol and acetaldehyde. Although many altered processes involve key metabolites; it is difficult to separate the critical chilling-sensitive metabolic processes from those that are byproducts of metabolic disruptions or of ultrastructural breakdown. Ion leakage due to membrane permeability changes has often been reported in chill sensitive plants. Phase transition of the lipid portion of the cellular membranes has also received considerable attention as the primary response to chilling temperatures.

Ultrastructural changes: On an ultrastructural level, several changes have been associated with chilling injury. Although there are a number of variables affecting chill injury, the ultrastructural symptoms are very similar across species. Ultrastructural symptoms of chilling injury become evident before obvious physical symptoms are visible. These include changes to chloroplasts, mitochondria and membranes associated with these organelles and the vacuoles (Christiansen and St. John 1981). The symptoms include swelling and disorganization of the chloroplasts and mitochondria, reduced size and number of starch granules, dilation of thylakoids and unstacking of grana, formation of small vesicles of chloroplast peripheral reticulum, lipid droplet accumulation in chloroplasts, and condensation of chromatin in the nucleus.

Chloroplasts are the first and most severely affected organelle. Irradiance during chilling greatly exacerbates the resulting injury. Chilled plants in darkness have been found to remain green and, except for starch depletion, chloroplasts appear normal. In the presence of light, however, chlorophyll becomes bleached, lipid droplets accumulate, and thylakoids degenerate. Mitochondria appear more resistant to chilling temperature but an immediate effect of low temperature on chilling-sensitive species is a suppression of mitochondrial activity. Electron micrographs of chilled sweet potato roots revealed that the mitochondria had a swollen appearance due to the release of phospholipids from the inner and outer membranes during storage at chilling temperatures. The capacity to bind phospholipids was also greatly decreased.

Membrane permeability and phase transition: Measures of solute leakage or ion permeability have provided evidence of increased membrane permeability in response to chilling. The plasma membrane is often considered the primary site of freezing injury and electrolyte leakage. Early work indicated that plants originating in warm climates tend to have more saturated fatty acids in their membrane lipids.

More recent work on mitochondrial membranes has shown that membranes do undergo a physical phase transition from a flexible liquid-crystalline to a solid-gel structure at 10 to 12°C, which coincides with the temperature sensitivity range of species of tropical origin. Fruits of several apple cultivars have been observed to undergo phase transition in the 3 to 10°C range suggesting the same mechanism of chilling injury as found in tropical species. The correlation between fatty acid composition and temperature induced phase transition is, however, not precise. It may be that other membrane components such as sterols also play a role.

It is possible that the phase transition of cellular membranes could account for the entire range of physiological and metabolic changes associated with chilling injury. Increased membrane permeability could lead to an altered ion balance and also to the ion leakage observed from chilling of sensitive tissues. Phase transition could result in conformational changes in membrane bound enzymes and account for the observed discontinuities in the function of many enzyme systems.

This may cause an imbalance between membrane bound and non-membrane bound systems. Over time the cells inability to cope with increased concentrations of metabolites could result in injury. Different tolerances to these metabolites could explain why some cultivars are more resistant to damage while still undergoing phase transition. Imbalances in metabolism, accumulation of toxic compounds, and increased permeability could all be the result of temperature-induced phase transition.

The contribution of unsaturated fatty acids in cell membrane lipids has been discussed for many years in relation to chilling sensitivity. Nishida and Murata (1996) have shown that chilling injury can be manipulated by modulating levels of unsaturation of fatty acids by the action of acyl-lipid desaturases and glycerol-3-phosphate acyltransferase. Lyons (1973) proposed that temperature induced phase transition of membrane lipids may play a primary role in chilling sensitivity of plants. Continued exposure to chilling temperatures would result in phase separated membranes becoming incapable of maintaining ionic gradients resulting in metabolic disruption and eventual cell death. A positive correlation has been found between chilling sensitivity of herbaceous plants and the level of saturated and trans-monounsaturated molecular species of phosphatidylglycerol (also termed high-melting-point molecular species) in thylakoid membranes. However, there is still a question of how directly these high-melting-point molecular species relate to chilling sensitivity in plants. Growth at low temperature generally increases the degree of unsaturation of membrane lipids, which compensates for the decrease in fluidity caused by the lower temperature. This increased unsaturation is also correlated with the sustained activity of membrane-bound enzymes at low temperature. The unsaturation of membrane lipids is therefore considered critical for the functioning of biological membranes and the survival of plant cells at low temperature. However, since low temperature is also known to induce or alter the expression level of a large number of genes it is not clear if the association between membrane lipid unsaturation and chilling tolerance is a cause or effect relationship.

Recently the role of unsaturation of membrane lipids in chilling tolerance and in response to low temperature has been reexamined using mutant and transgenic lines (Nishida and Murata 1996). In this way unsaturated fatty acids can be manipulated independent of temperature so that their individual effects can be evaluated. Tobacco was transformed with squash and Arabidopsis phosphatidylglycerol (PG) species found in thylakoid membranes. Squash has low levels of cis-unsaturated PG while Arabidopsis has relatively high levels of cis-unsaturated PG. It was found that tobacco transformed with squash PG was more chilling sensitive and tobacco transformed with Arabidopsis PG was the most chilling resistant, as measured by photosynthesis at 1°C under strong illumination.

These results indicate that chilling sensitivity can be manipulated by altering the level of unsaturated PG in the chloroplasts. These and other experiments have shown that unsaturation of membrane lipids protect the photosystem II complex from low-temperature photoinhibition by accelerating recovery from the photoinhibited state. However, it is likely that other factors such as accumulation of polyols and amino acids, or their derivatives, contribute to chilling sensitivity in plants. Some specific proteins may also be responsible for chilling tolerance.

Alteration of intracellular pH: Yoshida et al. (1999) noted that intracellular pH was, in part, actively controlled by H^+-transport from the cytoplasm to the vacuole catalyzed by H^+-ATPase located on the vacuolar membrane in mung bean (Vigna radiata L.), which is a very chilling-sensitive species. The vacuolar H^+-ATPase is extremely sensitive to low temperature and is preferentially inactivated upon exposure to chilling temperatures. This inactivation occurs much earlier than the symptoms of cell injury and the decrease in enzyme activity associated with plasma membranes, endoplasmic reticulum, and mitochondria. Cold-induced inactivation of H^+-ATPase also occurs in chilling sensitive rice. Cold-induced suppression of proton transport disrupts cytoplasmic homeostasis and causes a change in the pH. The chilling sensitivity of cultured mung bean cells changed markedly during the growth cycle and a close relationship was found between sensitivity of the cells and of H^+-ATPase to the cold. Cold-induced inactivation of the vacuolar H^+-ATPase was closely linked to acidification of the cytoplasm and the corresponding alkalization of the vacuoles suggesting a passive release of H^+ ions across the vacuolar membrane.

The susceptibility of vacuolar H^+-ATPase to low temperature in vivo was found to be markedly different between chilling-sensitive and chilling-resistant species. In contrast to the H^+-ATPases of chilling-sensitive species like mung bean and kidney bean (Phaseolus vulgaris), the H^+-ATPases of the chilling-tolerant species such as pea (Pisum sativum) and broad bean (Vicea faba) were very stable over long periods of low-temperature exposure. The molecular structures of the 16 kDa proteolipids from the two types of H^+-ATPase appeared to be very different. Low-temperature-induced pH reduction of the cytoplasm caused by inactivation of vacuolar H^+-ATPase may therefore be the cause of extreme chilling-sensitivity.

THE PHYSIOLOGICAL AND AGRONOMIC REPERCUSSIONS OF FREEZING STRESS

LOW-TEMPERATURE RESPONSE MECHANISMS

Plants have adapted two mechanisms to protect themselves from damage due to below freezing temperatures. Supercooling is a low-temperature tolerance mechanism that is usually associated with acclimated xylem parenchyma cells of moderately hardy woody plants. When sources of ice nucleation are absent, pure water can supercool or remain unfrozen to its homogeneous nucleation point of approximately -40°C. The initiation of freezing at the limit of supercooling occurs suddenly and is accompanied by an exotherm that can be detected by thermal analyses of plant tissues. Plant tissues suffer irreversible damage once ice nucleation of supercooled water occurs and the distribution in nature of tree species with the ability to deep supercool is normally restricted to regions where winter temperatures are warmer than -40°C.

The second and most common low-temperature response mechanism is acclimation. Low-temperature acclimation is a gradual process during which there are changes in just about every measurable morphological, physiological, and biochemical characteristic of the plant. These changes are determined by genotype x environment interactions that are quite complex and not clearly understood. They have been studied most extensively in cereals where a wide range in genetic potential and the availability of unique cytogenetic stocks has allowed for novel approaches to investigations at the molecular and whole plant level. Potential gene donors have been evaluated for use in interspecific transfers and the control of alien (donor species) low-temperature gene expression has been studied in a variety of backgrounds. A survey of the published research in these areas has allowed us to construct a field validated winter survival model that successfully simulates the over winter changes in low-temperature tolerance of a wide range of genotypes.Consequently, this review will focus mainly on the genetic systems that winter cereals have evolved for low-temperature adaptation, the regulation of these systems, and their complex interaction with the environment.

LOW-TEMPERATURE ACCLIMATION IN WINTER CEREALS

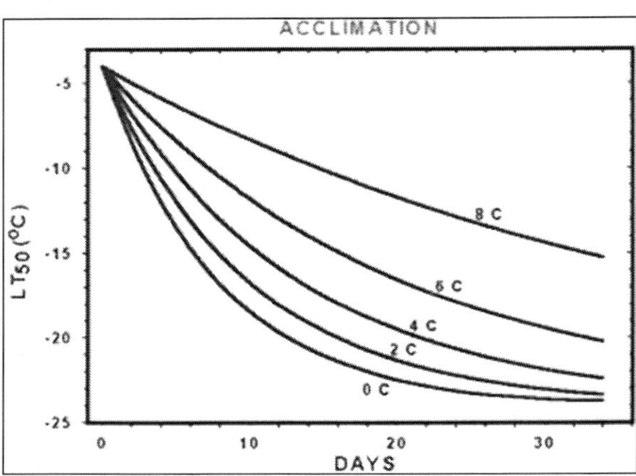

Fig. Relationship between average daily crown temperature (0 to 8oC) and low-temperature tolerance of Norstar winter wheat during acclimation at a constant temperature before vernalization saturation (LT50 for Norstar = - 24oC when fully acclimated).

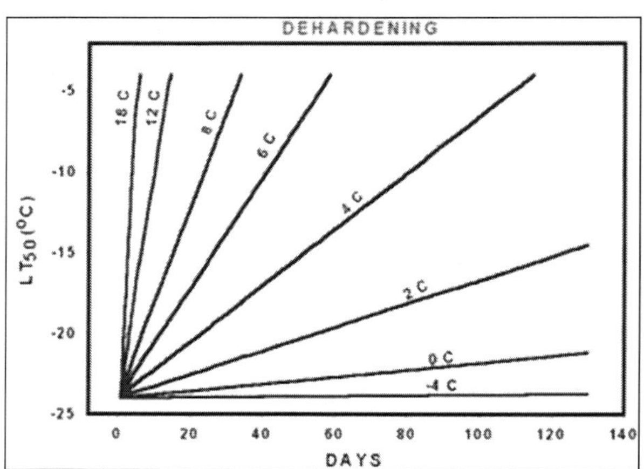

Fig. Relationship between average daily crown temperature (- 4 to 18°C) and low-temperature tolerance of Norstar winter wheat during dehardening at a constant temperature (LT50 for Norstar = - 24°C when fully acclimated = day 0).

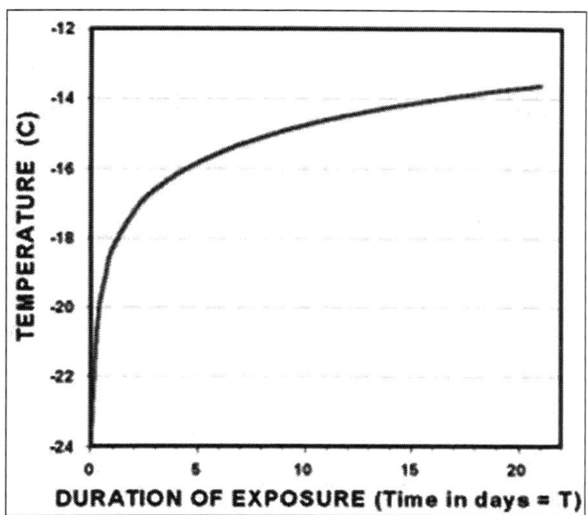

Fig. The effect of exposure to a constant temperature on low-temperature tolerance of Norstar winter wheat (Norstar LT50 = - 24°C when fully acclimated at day 0).

When growth starts in the early fall, winter cereal plants will not survive subfreezing temperatures much better than spring cereal plants. However, winter cereals grown under cool fall temperatures will cold acclimate or 'harden off'. For example, in Saskatchewan (western Canada), the minimum survival temperature for 'Norstar' winter wheat is normally near -3°C at the beginning of September and -19°C or lower by the end of October.

Under field conditions in western Canada, eight to 12 weeks of fall growth is usually required for the full development of cold hardiness in winter cereals. The first four to five weeks is a period of active growth that takes place when average daily soil temperatures at crown depth are above 9°C. Both the cold acclimation process and winter survival require energy and this period of warm temperature allows for the establishment of healthy vigorous plants. Plants with well-developed crowns before freeze-up are in the best position to withstand the rigors of winter and regenerate roots and leaves in the spring. However, plants that enter the winter with two to three leaves are usually not seriously disadvantaged.

Cold acclimation of winter wheat plants begins once fall temperatures drop below approximately 9°C. A translocatable substance that promotes cold acclimation is not produced when winter wheat plants are exposed to acclimating temperatures. Consequently, the cold-hardiness level of different plant parts, such as leaves, crowns and roots, is dependent upon the temperature to which each part has been exposed.

Because the crown contains tissues that are necessary for plant survival, it is the soil temperature at crown depth that determines critical cold-acclimation rates.

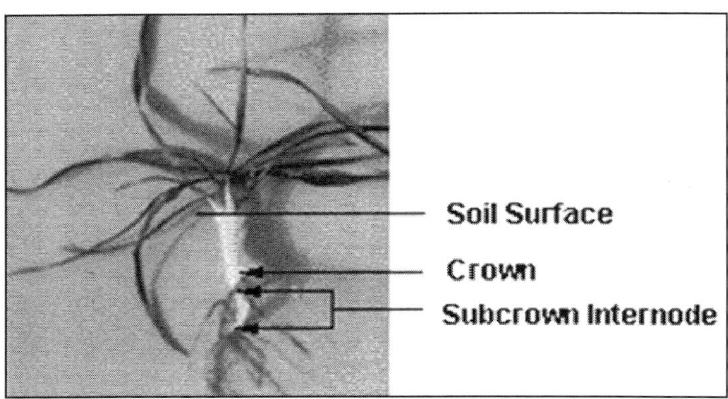

Plant growth slows considerably at temperatures that promote cold acclimation. In the field, soil temperatures gradually decrease as winter approaches and four to seven weeks at temperatures below 9°C is usually required to fully cold-harden plants. Cold acclimation during this period is dependent upon crown temperatures and the rate of acclimation increases dramatically as temperature drop from 9 to 0°C. Exposure of winter wheat crowns to soil temperatures above 9°C during this period results in a rapid loss of cold hardiness. The rate of dehardening is dependent upon the temperature to which the crown is exposed. At this stage, plants that have been exposed to crown temperatures above 9°C will resume cold acclimation once they return to temperatures below 9°C.

Winter wheat normally does not realize its maximum cold hardiness potential until after the soil is frozen in the late fall. In Saskatchewan, full acclimation is usually achieved by the middle to the end of November. Once cold acclimation has been completed, winter wheat can maintain a high level of cold hardiness provided crown temperatures remain below freezing. In the fall, winter wheat will cold acclimate when exposed to crown temperatures colder than 9°C. However, prolonged exposure of acclimated plants to winter temperatures above freezing results in the transition of the plant from the vegetative to the reproductive phase and a gradual loss of cold hardiness. The warmer the crown temperature during the winter, the shorter the period that maximum levels of cold hardiness can be maintained and, once started, the more rapid the rate of decline in cold hardiness.

Death of the crown tissue will result if the soil temperature falls below the plants minimum survival temperature. Exposure of winter cereal plants to crown temperatures that are 2 to 3°C warmer than their minimum survival temperature will cause immediate damage and a reduction in cold hardiness. Longer periods of exposure to temperatures approaching the minimum survival temperature can quickly reduce the plant's ability to tolerate cold stress. The expected LT_{50} for different exposure times (T) to constant temperature can be calculated from Equation 1.

$$LT50_{(T)} = LT50_{(0)} + 5.72 + 1.53 * \ln(T)$$

Where T is the number of days that plants are exposed to a constant low-temperature stress. $LT50_{(0)}$ is determined using a series of test temperatures where the low-temperature stress is removed as soon as the crown samples are exposed to a predetermined minimum temperature. For example, fully acclimated Norstar winter wheat will normally survive to -24.0°C in a controlled-freeze test where plant samples are gradually cooled at a rate of 2 to 6°C hr^{-1} and removed as soon as they reach a predetermined temperature. However, two days exposure to -17.2°C in a controlled environment will reduces the minimum survival temperature of fully hardened Norstar winter wheat from -24.0 to -17.2°C, a cold hardiness loss of 6.8°C.

Once vernalization saturation is complete and the plant enters the reproductive stage, it loses its ability to cold acclimate and it will start to deharden at temperatures warmer than approximately -4°C. This means that winter wheat will eventually completely deharden once plant growth resumes in the spring. Growth rate and rate of dehardening are both temperature dependent and because frozen soils warm slowly in the spring, several weeks of warm air temperatures are required to re-establish and completely deharden winter cereal plants that have survived without serious winter damage.

WOODY BIOMASS PROPERTIES

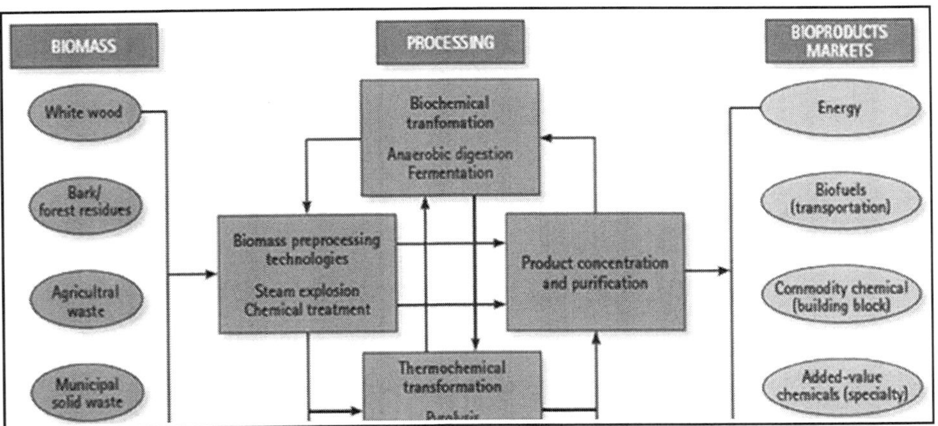

Check out how the properties of woody biomass affects how it may be converted into useful forms of energy (solid, liquid, or gaseous fuels) and products (polymers, bio-plastics, char, pellets, and acids) at a biorefinery.

Woody biomass is converted into useful forms of energy (solid, liquid, or gaseous fuels) as well as useful products (polymers, bio-plastics, char, pellets, and acids) at a biorefinery. A biorefinery is a facility that uses biomass conversion technologies to convert biomass into fuels, power, and value-added chemicals. Each biorefinery process yields different amounts and types of co-products and by-products. Coproducts describe the useful and marketable by-products, other than energy, that are produced simultaneously during biomass conversion. Many of today's co-products may have traditionally been defined as waste or by-products. Biorefinery process technologies include thermochemical (gasification, pyrolysis), biochemical (fermentation), or chemical (chemical synthesis) pathways.

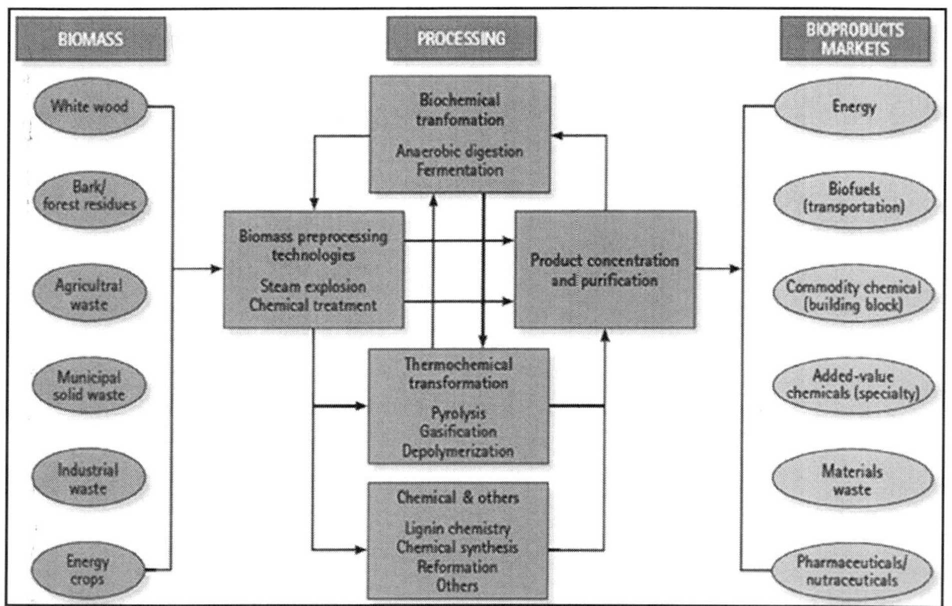

Each route is currently being developed by many different entities. The main challenge is to determine or discover processing technologies that can collect and convert currently under-utilized woody biomass into products with higher value.

Wood is one of the most abundant feedstock resources in the world available for the production of bioenergy and biofuels. It is also a very complex material. Woody plant species are so diverse that they grow in virtually every part of the world and can be harvested to produce solid, liquid or gaseous energy. Wood, in general, is composed of polymers, which are large organic molecules of lignin and carbohydrates (cellulose and hemicellulose) that are physically and chemically bound together. Different species types have varying amounts of cellulose, hemicellulose and lignin.

All tree and woody shrub species that store carbohydrates or oils are suitable for producing liquid and gaseous energy sources. Cellulose, starch, sugar and inulin (Ohta K, Hamada S, Nakamura T. 1993) can be used to produce ethanol, while plant oils can be used to produce bio-oil. Parts of plants containing lignocellulose can provide energy directly as solid fuels or indirectly after conversion.

To learn about a specific plant species and its role in bioenergy and biobased product utilization, you can access Phyllis. Phyllis is an online database sponsored by Shell Global Solutions, Agrotechnology and Food Innovations and is maintained by the Energy Research Center of the Netherlands. This site provides analysis and composition data for over 2000 various biomass and waste materials.

Biomass materials are grouped by untreated and treated wood, grasses, agricultural waste, animal waste, and other organic residues. The system also provides comparisons to fossil fuel sources including peat. Phyllis provides users with information regarding ash and water content, calorific values, and biochemical composition of the material.

COMPOSITION OF WOOD

Wood is composed primarily of cellulose, hemicellulose, lignin, and mineral elements.

- *Cellulose:* Cellulose is the structural component of a green plant's cell walls. It is comprised of carbon, hydrogen, and oxygen in the form of starches, proteins, and sugars and is the most abundant organic material on earth. Cellulose makes up approximately 50 per cent of woody biomass' dry weight. Cellulose from wood is isolated during the pulping process and processed to yield ethanol, cellophane, cardboard, paper, and cellulose ethers such as acetate, rayon, and nitrates.
- *Hemicellulose:* Hemicellulose is another component of a green plant's cell walls. Unlike cellulose, which contains only one sugar (glucose), hemicellulose can include a number of sugar monomers (xylose, hexose, mannose, and galactose, for example). Hemicellulose makes up 25 to 35 per cent of the dry weight of woody biomass.
- *Lignin:* Lignin is a polymer (or glue-like substance) that holds cellulose and hemicellulose together. It makes up approximately 15 to 25 per cent of the dry weight of woody biomass and is what can make the biochemical conversion of woody biomass difficult. Lignin has not yet been used as a raw material for industrial purposes in large quantities.
- *Mineral Elements:* Woody biomass is composed of many elements. Principal elements include carbon, oxygen, and hydrogen. Woody biomass is also composed of mineral elements such as nitrogen, sulfur, chlorine and heavy metals and while these elements do not produce energy during combustion, they do affect the energy content of different types of woody biomass. On average, hardwoods have a higher concentration of mineral elements than softwoods. However, the presence of mineral elements in woody biomass is more

dependent on the site where the particular species of tree is grown rather than the particular species itself.

- Nitrogen is a component of all fuel systems. During the combustion process, it is oxidized into nitrogen oxide (NOx). When emitted from combustion facilities at relatively low levels, NOx may have a useful fertilizing effect on forests. However, as emission levels increase, NOx produces adverse health effects and increases the acidification of water and soils.
- Sulfur emissions from combustion of fuels cause extensive damage to ecosystems and buildings, so fossil fuels are often graded by the amount of sulfur present. As with nitrogen, sulfur is oxidized during combustion to form sulfur oxide (SOx). This compound can have serious environmental effects and causes the acidification of soils and water.
- Most chlorine in trees is found in the foliage as an essential component in chlorophyll. Although only present in trace amounts, its ability to form alkali compounds with potassium and sodium, resulting in oxidation and corrosion, can create serious problems for boiler equipment during combustion2. Eliminating foliage from woody biomass feedstocks can reduce corrosion problems, as can co-firing biomass resources with higher sulfur content fuels such as peat or coal3.
- Heavy metals tend to vaporize during combustion. The remainder contributes to ash formation. Should levels of heavy metals be high, recycling of ash as fertilizer is restricted by environmental legislation, since the metals may leach into groundwater or be absorbed by crops.

MOISTURE CONTENT

The moisture content of biomass material varies greatly and plays a large role in determining the most suitable energy conversion process. Wet conversion processes such as fermentation are often more suited to biomass with a higher moisture content (*e.g.* corn, sugarcane, barley straw). Dry conversion processes such as pyrolysis, gasification, and combustion are more suited to biomass with a lower moisture content (*e.g.* wheat straw, pine, switchgrass, etc). Generally, wet conversion processes are used when the moisture content of the biomass requires excessive energy for drying, compared to the energy content of the end product. Energy yields are often expressed as net caloric values. These values increase as wood moisture content is reduced.

2

Frost Resistance in Alpine Woody Plants

INTRODUCTION

Freezing temperatures are a major environmental stress factor in the alpine life zone and in the treeline ecotone. Woody plants in these areas are frequently exposed to conditions that can result in frost damage. Frost resistance of tree species present at the alpine treeline in temperate climates has been addressed several times in prior reviews.

Less information is available for other woody alpine species that do not grow to the height of trees. Additionally, frost resistance has often been exclusively studied in leaves and detailed seasonal records have been reported. Frost survival of an individual, however, will also depend, if not more so, on the survival of other organs, such as bud and stem tissues. The degree of frost resistance and the underlying frost survival mechanisms of these essential organs are, in many cases, still unknown. The same is true for the effect of frost on reproductive tissues, which can have a dramatic impact on overall reproductive success.

Improvements in imaging methods to study the freezing processes in plants, such as infrared differential thermal analysis, has led to significant advances in our current understanding of ice propagation, ice barriers, and supercooling in plants. IDTA can provide more precise information on tissue-specific mechanisms of frost survival and on the basis of frost damage. Additionally, the development of field portable frost chambers, provides the ability to simulate night frosts and study recovery and recuperation under natural conditions, even though the use of the chambers may not be able to mimic a true radiation frost. These combined approaches can provide results that are more ecologically relevant for the prediction of future scenarios of plant survival and distribution. This may become even more important in view of global warming, as alpine environments are categorized as highly vulnerable ecosystems under climate change projections.

Frost-induced drought and photodamage, typical parameters of winter stress that often occur along with freezing stress, are not addressed in this review, although they may also be critically important for winter survival of woody species. Processes related to cold acclimation have been reviewed by Pearce (1999), Thomashow (1999), and Xin and Browse (2000) are also not the primary focus of this review.

FREEZING TEMPERATURES IN THE TEMPERATE ALPINE ZONE

The temperate alpine life zone extends from treeline at approximately 2000 m (spread over several 100 m of altitude) up to the altitudinal limit of closed vegetation, around 3480 m. The ultimate limit of individual higher plant life in the European Alps was reported to be at 4507 m. Woody species, of course, have a lower upper distribution boundary, which is around 3000 m (Salix herbacea, Landolt, 1992), than herbaceous plants. Freezing temperatures can occur throughout the whole year in the temperate alpine zone and their severity increases significantly with elevation. The seasonal change in monthly minimum air temperatures (2003–2013) of seven meteorological stations in the Austrian Central Alps is shown in comparison to a low land site in order to highlight the characteristics of the alpine life zone with respect to freezing temperatures.

The meteorological stations within the alpine life zone are located along an elevational gradient of approximately 1500 m. While a considerable frost free period is evident (May till September) at the lowland site, a characteristic of the alpine life zone is the lack of a frost free period, as freezing temperature can occur virtually throughout the whole year. At an elevation of 1942 m, freezing temperatures (-4.7°C in June and -1.0°C, July/August) can occur during the summer months, while at 3437 m, temperatures can drop substantially lower (-14.7 June and -10.5°C July/August).

In midwinter, air temperatures can drop to -26.1 (February) at 1942 m and to -31.5°C at 3437 m. The adiabatic lapse rate from these air temperature minima is -0.7 $K \cdot 100\ m^{-1}$. In addition to the increase in frost severity with elevation, the frequency of freezing events also rises significantly with increasing elevation within the alpine life zone.

WOODY PLANTS AND PERENNIALS

Woody trees and shrubs (both fruit and landscape) and many herbaceous perennials (including strawberries) can tolerate very low temperatures if they are allowed to harden off and go dormant in the fall. Hardening off is triggered by the shorter days of late summer and fall, which cause the plant to stop growing. At this time, overwintering buds are matured. These buds are often covered by protective bud scales which protect the bud from water loss and physical damage. The second step for a plant to harden off and become dormant is exposure to low temperatures, at or below freezing, for at least part of the daily cycle. This causes changes in the plant's metabolism, which causes changes in the quantity, location, and make-up of sugars, proteins, moisture, and other plant chemicals. In deciduous plants, this is seen by the change in leaf colour and leaf drop. All of this promotes resistance to freezing to develop. If cold weather occurs before the hardening process is complete, injury can occur.

Many factors can affect a plant's ability to harden off before cold weather. Late summer or early fall nitrogen fertilization can stimulate the production of new growth, which will be too lush and tender to survive. By withholding nitrogen applications in late summer, or reducing the amount applied so that stimulation does not occur, the plant's carbohydrate (sugar) reserves can go into storage, allowing the plant tissues to withstand cold temperatures better (sugars accumulate in the tissues and act like an antifreeze, lowering the temperature needed for the water in the tissues to freeze). Heavy fruit load can deplete these reserves; therefore, it is important to maintain healthy foliage after the crop has been harvested, so that accumulation of carbohydrates in the tree can occur.

Late summer pruning, or a wet fall following a dry summer, can also stimulate new growth, which will not be able to tolerate colder temperatures later. A tree weakened by drought, insect injury (especially girdling caused by borers and defoliation caused by caterpillars and beetles), disease, or mechanical injury to the trunk or roots, will be more susceptible to cold weather. Hardiness can also be affected by the duration and intensity of sunlight, length of growing season, amount and timing of rainfall, soil type and drainage, wind exposure, and cultural practices.

Hardiness is also affected by the return of warm temperatures. A few days of warm weather in mid or late winter can reduce plant cold hardiness significantly. Once cold hardiness is lost from mid or late winter warming, the plant cannot return to the same level of hardiness. If mild winter temperatures prevail, damage is unlikely. However, should severe temperatures occur, the tree will likely be damaged. Different plant tissues have different degrees of hardiness. For example, flower buds are more sensitive to cold than leaf buds. A frost may damage the flower buds of a bulb or fruit tree without harming subsequent foliar growth.

Sunscald and frost cracking are similarly caused problems of trees with thin, dark bark, such as peach or silver maple. They occur when the bark and underlying cambium, usually on the south or southwest side of the tree, heat up on cold, bright days. When the sun sets or is blocked by a cloud, the bark and cambium quickly return to air temperature, which can cause physical and physiological damage. Frost cracks, which are longitudinal splits in the bark, are an example of the physical damage which can occur. The bark and the wood underneath contract at different rates as they cool, causing mechanical stress. Eventually the bark splits, sometimes violently enough to produce a rifle-like noise. The cracks may heal over the following season, but are likely to split again the following winter. In the meantime, wood-decaying organisms and insects have an entry site. Sunscald is an example of the physiological damage caused by extreme temperature fluctuations. The elevated temperature of the trunk causes the cambium to lose its hardiness and become active. The drop in temperature kills the non- hardy cambial tissues. Sometimes physical damage also occurs, and the scalded bark may split, forming an entry point for decay-causing organisms. Many cankers on trees result from sunscald.

Several measures can be taken which will prevent the sun from over-warming the trunk and limbs of trees susceptible to frost cracking and sunscald. Many commercial fruit growers will use white exterior latex paint to reflect the sunlight and keep the bark temperature from rising. The paint does not protect directly against extremely low temperatures; it will, however, reduce the wide fluctuations in temperatures. Do not use oil based paint, as it may kill trees. Apply the paint in late fall or early winter to the entire trunk, from the ground to the main crotch. Paint when the temperature is above 50°F and when dry weather is expected for several days.

Physical barriers can also be used to block the sunlight. These would include plastic or paper tree wraps. These wraps must be removed annually, to prevent girdling of the trunk. Also, insects tend to hide under the wrap, so leaving the trunk exposed during the summer is recommended.

Roots of trees and shrubs are more sensitive to cold injury than the stem tissues. In the landscape or orchard, the roots are not commonly injured because the soil and snow cover protect them from exposure to freezing air temperatures. Containerized plants in nurseries are very susceptible to freezing of the roots, since they are more exposed. Cold hardiness of roots varies with species and rootstocks. Cold injury to roots appears to be greater in sandy soils than in clay, since cold temperatures penetrate deeper into soils with lots of air spaces. For the same reason, injury is more likely in dry soils than in moist.

Another type of winter root injury is caused by "frost heaving." The repeated freezing and thawing of the soil forces plants, especially smaller ones (strawberries, shrubs, young trees), to move upwards in the soil, sometimes pushing them out of the soil altogether. This can break many of the fine feeder roots. Injury or death usually follows if roots are broken or the shoots and exposed roots become dried out. Frost heaving is most common in heavy soils; it is also affected by the soil water content.

Both frost heaving and freezing injury to the roots can be controlled in similar ways. Proper care during the growing season (irrigation, fertilization, and pest control) will promote healthier, hardier plants with deeper, more extensive root systems. Planting trees and shrubs at the proper depth and in well-drained soil will also prevent problems. Snow cover or an organic mulch, such as wood chips or sawdust, will help insulate the soil, preventing rapid fluctuations in temperature. Winter dessication is a serious problem with narrow and broad leaf evergreens, such as pine and rhododendron. Containerized nursery stock, whose small, above ground root balls freeze easily, and newly planted bare root or balled-and-burlapped plants with their reduced root systems, are also very vulnerable.

Winter dessication injury occurs when the absorption of water by the roots cannot keep up with the amount of moisture lost by the foliage (transpiration). This occurs mostly on sunny days, especially when it is windy and when the soil water is frozen and the plant cannot absorb it, or if water is in short supply. Injury appears as brown leaf margins or needle tips at the onset of the first period of warm weather. In severe cases, all of the leaves and buds are killed More commonly, though, the leaves alone are injured or killed, but the buds survive.

Winter dessication can be prevented by making sure the plant is well supplied with water in the fall and early winter. Irrigation of 1/2 to 1 inch of water per week should continue up until the ground freezes. Screens and windbreaks can be used to shelter susceptible evergreens. Antitranspirants, or antidessicants, can also provide some protection by reducing the amount of moisture lost by the plant. Be sure to follow all label directions carefully.

PLANT MINIMUM TEMPERATURES

It is possible for the temperature of plant material to be lower than air temperature. Specifically, the net radiation balance of leaves can become negative during clear, calm nights due to long-wave radiative heat loss (Stefan-Boltzmann-law) which cools the leaves below air temperature. This is the basis for dew or surface ice formation but can also result in the freezing of plant tissues despite an air temperature above 0°C. Leaves of conifers were found to be up to 9.3 K colder than air temperature at treeline (Tranquillini, 1958, 3–8 K: Jordan and Smith, 1994).

Air temperature may exhibit an extreme drop down to -37.4°C (Mt. Sonnblick, 3105 m, 1.1.1905, Austria; Central Institute for Meteorology and Geodynamics, Austria) in alpine areas of Austria during the winter. Winter temperature minima the last ten years (2003–2013) have ranged between -26.1°C (1942 m) and -31.5°C (3437 m). Based on these data, leaf temperatures down to approximately -35 to -46°C may occur in exposed plants during clear and calm winter nights.

Radiative cooling conditions in June may account for leaf temperatures down to approximately -14 to -24°C in July and down to approximately -10 to -20°C in August. In summer, mean leaf temperature minima decrease with increasing elevation at a rate of 0.4 $K.100m^{-1}$(Neuner and Hacker, 2012) which is less than the adiabatic lapse rate of air (0.7 $K.100m^{-1}$). The difference may be explained by the change in growth forms and snow protection of plants during cold spells in summer. Bioclimate temperatures lower than 0°C during the snow free period were found to occur at a frequency of 20 per cent at the treeline (1950 m), while at 3450 m night frost frequency increased to 69 per cent (Larcher and Wagner, 2009).

In addition to the severity and frequency of freezing temperatures, cooling and warming rates also appear to be important for frost survival of woody plants. Natural cooling rates below 0°C in leaves of alpine plants did not exceed $-2 K.h^{-1}$ (mean rate: $-0.3 K.h^{-1}$; Neuner and Buchner, 2012). Exceptionally more rapid cooling rates, however, cannot be fully excluded, as reported by Körner (2012). In northern Sweden, temperature drops below 0°C of up to -15 K within minutes were recorded at the upper border of cold air drained during a temperature inversion. This rapid temperature drop resulted in the mortality of Betula pubescens buds that otherwise would have survived exposure to freezing temperatures down to -70°C under moderate cooling rates.

Snow cover significantly mitigates temperature minima and the rate of temperature change to which plants are exposed. Important factors contributing to of the degree of thermal insulation are the thickness of the snow pack and its consistency. While protective effects of snow cover have long been recognized (Sakai and Larcher, 1987), thermal insulation by snow may also be crucially important for protecting plants from low freezing temperatures during episodes of freezing temperatures in summer (Larcher and Wagner, 2009; Ladinig et al., 2013).

A certain degree of thermal insulation is possible by snow coverage for dwarf shrubs and young trees in the summer months but will be lost at a certain stage of tree development when a specific tree height is reached. The establishment of tree seedlings and young plants may even be favored at growing sites with sufficient snow coverage. On the other hand, being tall as a tree actually reduces the risk of frost injury during summer radiation frosts compared to small statured woody plants because radiative freezing during clear nights is negatively correlated with tree height.

ORGAN-SPECIFIC RISK OF FROST DAMAGE IN WOODY ALPINE PLANTS

In addition to minimum temperatures, the duration of a frost event and the rate of temperature change that can occur at specific parts of the year, play an essential role in determining the potential risk of frost injury to plants and the actual killing temperature of any specific plant species. Frost survival of individual woody plants is difficult to assess as frost resistance can differ greatly in various organs and tissues. For instance, the most frost susceptible organs in woody alpine plants in the summer are reproductive shoots (-4.6°C) followed by developing leaves (-5.0°C), fully expanded leaves (-6.6°C), vegetative buds

(-7.3°C), and then xylem tissue. While hardly any data exist for roots, they are commonly recognized as being the most susceptible to frost injury (Sakai and Larcher, 1987).

A survey of the frost resistance of different organs and tissues of 15 species of woody plants. The selected species comprise four trees, two tall shrubs, and nine dwarf shrubs that all have different vertical distributions in the Central European Alps.

REPRODUCTIVE SHOOTS IN SUMMER

Various strategies have evolved in alpine plants to prevent frost damage to reproductive shoots. To date, the only alpine plant species found to actually exhibit freezing tolerance in its reproductive shoots is the nival herb Ranunculus glacialis.

All other species have been reported to be freezing sensitive, *i.e.* exhibit injury if ice forms in their reproductive shoots. In contrast, fully developed vegetative parts of woody alpine plant species, such as stem, bark, and leaves can tolerate extracellular ice formation down to a species-specific low temperature during the summer months without damage (Taschler and Neuner, 2004). Once ice formation is initiated somewhere inside a vegetative part of a plant, it can propagate rapidly (up to 27 $cm.s^{-1}$) throughout the vascular system in all plant parts colder than 0°C.

Freezing sensitive reproductive shoots of some alpine species have evolved supercooling strategies aided by ice barriers in order to prevent frost injury. The ice barriers prevent the spread of ice from frozen plant parts into the supercooled organs or tissues. In cushion plants, the ice barriers are thermal rather than physical. The spread of ice from one flower stalk to the next is interrupted by the thermal insulation that exists inside the cushion portion of the plant from which the individual flower stalks arise, maintaining the cushion warmer than 0°C during the course of a night frost event. Structural ice barriers have also been found in some species of woody plants. The specific nature of these physical barriers is currently under investigation. It appears that some unique aspect of the anatomical structure in the portion of the stem subtending the reproductive shoot prevents ice propagation into the shoot, allowing it to remain supercooled.

The probability of frost damage to reproductive shoots becomes greater and greater with increasing elevation and has been observed to occur on a recurrent basis in nature. Scarce information exists, however, about the frost resistance of reproductive tissues in woody alpine species. The frost resistance of reproductive tissues of two woody alpine species (Rhododendron ferrugineum and Loiseleuria procumbens) was recently investigated. During anthesis and fruiting in the summer months, the reproductive shoots of these species were freezing sensitive and significantly less frost resistant than their ice tolerant vegetative shoots. Ice propagation into the reproductive shoots of R. ferrugineum via the vegetative shoot is not prevented by any ice barrier and any ice formation in the plant results in frost damage to reproductive tissues (Neuner and Hacker, 2012), which can occur at -3.3°C. In contrast, anatomical ice barriers efficiently prevent ice intrusion into the supercooled reproductive shoots of L. procumbens and other woody species in the summer months.

This allows reproductive shoots to remain in a supercooled state during a night frost and survive completely undamaged despite freezing of the vegetative parts. While vegetative parts froze between -4.7 and -5.7°C, reproductive shoots were able to supercool down to a range of -7.2°C to -18.2°C, and in some cases even below -22°C.

This mechanism of freeze avoidance has been shown to be effective in preventing frost injury during various stages of reproductive development (bud, anthesis, and fruit) throughout the alpine summer. Supercooling was 100 per cent effective in preventing frost damage to reproductive shoots in the woody shrub species Calluna vulgaris and Empetrum hermaphroditum, while the ice barrier failed to prevent ice entrance in L. procumbens in 13 per cent of the total observations. The frost survival mechanism of reproductive shoots in summer months in other alpine woody species is currently unknown.

REPRODUCTIVE OVERWINTERING BUDS

Overwintering reproductive buds of many angiosperm woody plants survive freezing temperatures during the winter months by supercooling (Sakai and Larcher, 1987). Reproductive bud tissues are isolated from acropetally advancing ice in the subtending stem by the presence of ice barriers that restrict ice growth into the meristem. Such a frost survival mechanism has been documented in reproductive buds of R. ferrugineum using IDTA, where single flowers within the floral bud freeze intracellularly at temperatures between -16 and -25°C, while ice formation in the stem and leaves occurs at -4°C (Neuner and Hacker, 2012).

Midwinter air temperatures can drop below the supercooling temperature of overwintering reproductive buds of R. ferrugineum (-16 to -25°C; Larcher and Wagner, 2004) when plants are not insulated by snow cover and causes severe frost damage (personal communication, J. Wagner). Supercooling also appears to be the primary mechanism of frost survival in over-wintering reproductive buds of Vaccinium vitis-idea. The frost survival mechanism of reproductive overwintering buds in most other woody alpine plants has not been examined. While frost damage to reproductive buds is not critical to individual survival, it can strongly influence the reproductive success of a species. In this regard, the deleterious impact of frost injury on sexual plant reproduction has been shown to become significantly greater with increasing elevation, and at higher elevations may even impair successful seed development in most years.

VEGETATIVE BUDS

Primordia within dormant vegetative buds have been reported to survive freezing temperatures by either extra-organ freezing or freezing tolerance (Sakai and Larcher, 1987). In vegetative buds exhibiting extra-organ freezing, ice formation does not occur in the primordial tissue itself. Water within primordial tissues remains supercooled, down to a particular species-specific and developmentally determined temperature. When freezing does occur, however, it is a lethal event. During supercooling, water migrates from the supercooled primordial tissue to specific extracellular locations in the stem and/or bud scales, thus inducing dehydrative conditions in the primordial tissues. This process has been termed extra-organ freezing (Ishikawa and Sakai, 1982).

Three types of extra-organ freezing have been postulated, defined by the mode of freeze dehydration and the dehydration tolerance of bud primordia (Sakai and Larcher, 1987): In Type I, primordia are fully dehydration tolerant, become fully freeze dehydrated, and no freezable water remains. Such primordia can survive immersion in LN_2 (-80 °C). In Type II, primordia experience freeze-induced dehydration due to the migration of water from the primordia to the remote sites of extracellular ice but have a limited level of dehydration tolerance and are thus injured at temperatures in the range of -35 to -50°C. Type III primordia become only partially dehydrated, thus freezable water remains inside the primordial cells and cells are killed when temperatures exceed the extent of supercooling (-25 and -30°C) and the primordia experience intracellular ice formation; which is a lethal event.

For woody alpine species, a paucity of information exists on the frost survival mechanism of dormant buds. Extra-organ freezing was initially reported in conifers for Abies homolepis and A. balsamea and appears to occur in species in the genera Abies, Picea, and Larix.

In contrast, ice seems to form innocuously in Pinus shoot primordia, without any large degree of supercooling, at the same time ice forms in stem tissues; with frost injury occurring at temperatures much lower than when ice formation initially occurs (Ide et al., 1998). Preliminary results on alpine conifers also suggest that similar genus-specific mechanisms of frost survival are present in their dormant vegetative buds. P. cembra and P. mugo tolerate extracellular ice formation in their vegetative buds while P. abies and L. decidua seem to survive by supercooling and extra-organ freezing.

Even less information exists for dormant buds of angiosperm species. Although information on the frost resistance of angiosperm vegetative buds is available (Sakai and Larcher, 1987), the frost survival mechanism of vegetative bud primordia is still little understood. In one study, lateral vegetative buds of Acer japonicum were reported to exhibit Type I extraorgan freezing, *i.e.* primordia become fully dehydrated due to the loss of water to sites of extracellular ice outside of the primordial tissues and the primordia are extremely dehydration tolerant.

Type II extra-organ freezing was suggested to occur in dormant apple buds (Pramsohler and Neuner, 2013). There is also a report that the vegetative buds of the angiosperm, Pyrus syriaca, exhibit Type III extra-organ freezing (Rajashekar and Burke, 1978). Recent observations on dormant vegetative buds of Rhododendron ferrugineum also indicate that they supercool (Zimmermann and Neuner, unpublished). Supercooling, as a mechanism of frost resistance, also seems to be apparent in vegetative buds of V. myrtillus.

Based on data obtained from IDTA images, stems in winter initially froze between -3.2 and -3.5°C during a controlled freezing experiment, while buds appeared to freeze in the range of -18.2 to -22.0°C. Separate freezing events located in the resting buds can be clearly recognized. This is still a higher freezing temperature, however, than the reported midwinter frost resistance of -35°C for V. myrtillus buds (Sakai and Larcher, 1987). Since all of the samples used in the controlled freezing experiments were dug out from under snow, it is presumed that the moderate temperature conditions below the snow are the reason for the lower frost resistance observed in the IDTA.

Winter frost resistance of dormant buds of woody alpine shrubs ranges from -30 to -50°C which is similar to the range found in trees, with the exception of P. cembra whose buds have been shown to acquire an LT_{50} of -63.6°C in midwinter, which is more cold hardy than the leaves (-58.5°C; Buchner and Neuner, 2011). In fact, the frost resistance of resting buds of conifers generally seems to be higher than that of leaves.

In a global survey of maximum winter frost resistance in conifers (Bannister and Neuner, 2001) inhabiting climatic zones 7 and greater, 56 per cent had a level of frost resistance in vegetative buds that was equal to the frost resistance of leaves, and 33 per cent had vegetative buds that were more frost resistant than leaves. Only 11 per cent had leaves that were more cold hardy than buds. No conclusion can be drawn, however, from the scarce data available for angiosperms.

JUVENILE LEAVES AND SHOOTS

Young, developing juvenile leaves and shoots are typically freezing sensitive and exhibit frost damage close to the temperature at which ice formation occurs. Moderate night frosts during the annual period of growth in June have been repeatedly observed to cause severe frost damage to sprouting shoots and leaves of subalpine woody species in the European Alps. It is very clear that current year growth is highly susceptible to frost damage. Initial frost damage (LT_i) can be observed after exposure to -3.4°C (Rhododendron ferrugineum), -4.4°C (Picea abies), -4.8°C (Pinus cembra), -5.5°C (Sorbus aucuparia), and -6.3°C (Larix decidua). These temperatures are likely to occur in the treeline ecotone during the annual periods of growth. Only P. cembra seems capable of escaping natural frost damage due to a later onset of sprouting (late June to July), when potential air temperature minima are much more moderate and insufficient to cause frost injury.

Importantly, after a loss of current year's growth, conifers do not foliate again until the next growing season. While this type of frost injury and subsequent delayed growth did not appear to threaten the survival of trees, it was suggested that it may partly contribute to the distorted growth of small trees in the krummholz belt.

MATURE LEAVES

In contrast to all other plant parts, frost resistance in leaves of woody alpine species has been frequently studied. Unlike developing leaves and shoots, the frost resistance of mature leaves generally appears to exceed environmental demand. Mature leaves of alpine woody species are ice tolerant. The temperature at which initial frost damage (LT_i) occurs in the summer is species-specific but generally occurs in the range of -4.1 to -9.0°C. Evergreen leaves of woody species can attain a midwinter frost resistance of -26.0 to -58.5°C when cold acclimated under natural conditions. A maximum frost resistance in needles of as low as -90°C has been reported for the pine species, P. cembraand P. mugo (LT_0; Sakai and Okada, 1971) which suggests that species that occupy the alpine region in the European Alps may have the capacity to develop a greater level of frost resistance under the proper acclimating conditions.

Seasonal data on frost resistance (LT_{10} monthly means) of leaves of the evergreen shrub Rhododendron ferrugineum and the coniferous trees, Picea abies and Pinus cembra, determined by various authors throughout the 20th century at the same study site. The seasonal amplitude of frost resistance varies in a species-specific manner. Rhododendronshrubs develop a lower level of midwinter freezing resistance than the coniferous trees. The seasonal amplitude of frost resistance of leaves in the evergreen trees P. abies and P. cembra is approximately 40–50 K, but in shrubs it is much less, ranging between 15 and 35 K.

In contrast to trees, smaller statured woody shrubs are usually covered by thermally insulating snow and are thus exposed to more moderate temperature conditions during the winter. Early snowfalls in autumn can interfere with the natural process of cold acclimation, reducing the maximum frost resistance attained in midwinter. Additionally, moderate temperature conditions beneath snow cover in subalpine environments have been shown to be conducive to frost dehardening. The maximum frost resistance of leaves of R. ferrugineum collected in January at the same site but in different years throughout the last century was between -14.0 and -29.5°C (LT_{10}; Neuner et al., 1999b). During mild winters with early snow melt, plants do not frost harden to the same extent as when they remain exposed until midwinter. This variability in frost resistance can also be observed in leaves collected below a thick snow vs. leaves collected from exposed branches on the same sampling date and site.

Differences in frost resistance of up to 13 K could be observed. The most prominent environmental differences affecting exposed vs. snow-covered leaves are the severity of freezing temperatures, the irradiation climate, and plant water status. Woody plants that are exposed experience much lower freezing temperatures under natural irradiation and daylength conditions and quite often are exposed to severe winter drought. In contrast, the insulating properties of snow significantly mitigates freezing temperatures, keeping them close or slightly below 0°C. Additionally, under 15 cm of snow, PPFD can be nearly to completely eliminated and the darkness may protect plants from dehardening in response to long days in May. Additionally, a thick snow pack is the best way to escape winter drought (Sakai and Larcher, 1987). Firstly, water loss is nearly eliminated when plants are covered by a thick layer of snow and secondly, snow cover gets successively wetter during the course of winter allowing to restore water deficits by direct water uptake from the wet snow.

Similarly, frost resistance in leaves of P. abies, which in cold winter periods approaches -45°C at the treeline, was only -30°C during the exceptionally warm winter of 1987/88. Furthermore, plants of the same species cold acclimate to a lesser extent at a lower elevation (P. abies:-10 K, V. vitis-idea:-19 K) compared to plants located at treeline. This corroborates the findings of Gross (1989 cited in Körner, 2012) who reported an increase in the frost resistance of P. abies leaves from -30°C at 950 m to -35°C at timberline in the central Alps.

The risk of frost damage changes significantly with season, which can be derived from the relationship between the temperatures representing frost resistance vs. temperature minima. Leaves of trees at the alpine treeline have a low risk of frost damage at midwinter. This has been previously recognized, as tree-sized woody plants were suggested to exhibit a sufficient level of freezing resistance to avoid freeze damage. Regarding shrubs, given that timely snow falls provide a thermal insulation, the risk of freeze injury must be also considered rather low in winter. This may not be the case, however, if the pattern, duration, and timing of snow cover changes in future.

The overall level of risk for freezing injury in the spring is very different than during midwinter. In general, small statured woody plants have a high risk of frost damage in spring, particularly when these plants have partially deacclimated or never developed full hardiness due to snow cover, and then lose their snow cover in late winter. Severe night frosts can occur in the subalpine environment during this time of the year and the loss of snow cover along with their lower level of frost resistance makes them especially vulnerable to freezing injury.

In such a scenario, the potential risk of frost damage will largely depend on the species-specific ability to rapidly reacclimate. The ability to reacclimate may be reduced in woody plants at this time of year due to changes in the physiology of these plants induced by their exposure to longer photoperiods. Little knowledge exists for most woody plant species with respect to their ability to reacclimate or the rate at which they can reacclimate.

To examine the rate of frost re-hardening (reacclimation) in spring, R. ferrugineum shrubs were exposedin situ to controlled night frosts close to the lowest temperature that did not induce frost damage (LT_0;Neuner et al., 1999b). This experimental protocol was used to determine the potential frost re-hardening response under otherwise completely natural environmental conditions. After a lag period of three days, during which no significant increase in frost resistance was observed, frost resistance suddenly increased by 5.9°C within 24 h. Although a total gain in frost hardiness between 7.8 and 9.2°C was possible, the retarded response appeared too slow to offer sufficient frost protection from a sudden frost event. In a recent study, Wheeler et al. (2014) also reported that earlier snow-melt may increase the risk of a lethal spring freezing event for less frost-resistant alpine dwarf shrubs, such as V. myrtillus andV. uliginosum. This is in line with observations on subarctic heath that readily responds to increased temperatures by frost dehardening (deacclimation; Bokhorst et al., 2010).

Trees may also be at risk of frost damage in the spring. In situ exposure of P. cembra to increased air temperatures in late winter induced rapid deacclimation (Buchner and Neuner, 2011). Similar reports exist for other woody species that also respond to warmer spring temperatures with an untimely reduction in frost resistance. Premature frost dehardening of P. cembra in late winter, induced by artificially increased air or soil temperatures, reduced the frost resistance of buds to -10.2°C (LT_{50}) while the untreated controls still had an LT_{50} of -32.6°C (Buchner and Neuner, 2011). During episodes of low temperature in April at the alpine timberline, air temperature minima can still drop down to -16.3°C (30 years temperature record; ZAMG). This temperature would be sufficiently low enough to cause significant frost damage to P. cembra. Warmer temperatures in late winter will also induce earlier bud burst in P. cembra (Buchner and Neuner, 2011) which must be considered a critical concern for a species that currently escapes frost damage during budbreak and the initial growth of current year shoots by delaying budbreak until the risk of significant frost events is low.

STEMS

The bark tissue of temperate woody plants typically exhibit freezing tolerance, undergoing equilibrium freezing when ice forms in its tissues and the temperature continues to drop (Sakai and Larcher, 1987). In contrast, xylem tissues can exhibit different responses to freezing temperatures. Xylem parenchyma cells (XPC) are the only living cells in the xylem. In some species, XPCs have been shown to survive freezing temperatures by deep supercooling down to -40°C or even lower (Sakai and Larcher, 1987). With the exception of Arctostaphylos uva-ursi, where XPCs were reported to exhibit deep supercooling, the mechanism of frost survival of xylem tissues of European alpine woody plants is not known.

In a survey of woody treeline species in Colorado, the XPCs of some species in genera such as Pinus, Picea, Abies, and Juniperus, exhibited supercooling. This could be indicative for their European counterparts but remains to be elucidated. Freezing of water in the xylem tissue can also have secondary freezing effects that are not discussed in the present review, namely freeze-induced xylem embolism.

Various frost resistance mechanisms have evolved in alpine woody plants. In addition to tolerating the presence of ice in their tissues and the concomitant dehydrative stress, some tissues and organs that rely on freezing avoidance can also be found. In many species, the mechanism by which they survive freezing temperatures is unknown, and thus represents a fertile area for future research.

In freezing sensitive tissues, such as reproductive shoots and buds, and young developing shoots, escape from frost damage is only possible by preventing the initial formation of ice (freeze avoidance). This can be realized in woody plants by a structural ice barrier that prevents ice propagation from other tissues into the freezing sensitive tissues, and the absence or inhibition of ice nucleation active substances in the freezing sensitive tissues or organs which would allow them to supercool. The specific features of structural ice barriers still remain to be elucidated. Outside of a direct role for the absence of mature vascular tissue which would act as a conduit for the spread of ice, the determining factor(s) involved in the prevention of the spread of ice into buds and reproductive shoots is still an open question but may involve specific anatomical and biochemical (cell wall impregnation and porosity, dry tissue regions) adaptations. Additionally, hardly any attention has focused on the presence of metabolites in supercooled tissues which may facilitate their ability to remain in an ice free state.

Woody alpine species can experience frost damage throughout the whole year. In summer, the most frost susceptible organs of woody species are reproductive shoots (-4.6°C); followed by immature leaves (-5.0°C), fully expanded leaves (-6.6°C), vegetative buds (-7.3°C), and xylem tissue (-10.8°C).

These levels of freezing resistance can be insufficient to survive the potential frost events that can occur in June. The severity and frequency of freezing temperatures significantly increases with increasing elevation. Perhaps it is the most frost-susceptible parts with hardly any freezing resistance that define the upper limit of elevation for the distribution of some woody species. Intriguingly, woody species that inhabit the highest elevations bury their stems in the soil, perhaps for a better protection against the impact of summer frost events.

Differences in frost resistance mechanisms and the maximum level of freezing resistance of various plant tissues and organs within the same plant stresses the importance of studying whole plants rather than extrapolating data obtained from plant parts. Most importantly, this emphasizes the need to study plants under conditions that are as close to natural as possible. Field studies that simulate frosts, or even better are conducted under natural frosts, are still rare. This can be partially attributed to the difficulties involved in conducting such studies. Their ecological significance, however, is invaluable as the whole plant; including all tissues, has an impact on the obtained results. Only the ability of plants to survive and recuperate under natural and complex environmental conditions will provide a realistic picture of the potential frost survival of a species at a certain site.

Mean frost resistance in winter is lowest in reproductive buds (-23.4°C), that without snow cover may not escape frost damage in all winters. In contrast, the freezing resistance of all other organs exhibit greater levels of freezing resistance that vary in a species-specific manner (vegetative buds: -30 to -50°C, leaves: -25 to -58.5°C, stem: -30 to -70°C). Seasonal data on frost resistance of leaves of woody alpine species at treeline under natural frost hardening indicate that a sufficiently high level of frost resistance is attained for trees in midwinter to allow them to survive naturally occurring winter freezing temperatures. Leaves of some shrubs, however, may need to rely on the thermal insulation provided by snow cover.

Regarding the risk of frost damage to woody plants, seasonality is a significant factor, particularly given the projected scenarios associated with climate change (Hänninen and Tanino, 2011). The transition period from endo- and ecodormancy in winter and early spring, to the active growing period in summer, is of special concern.

Till now, the dynamics of seasonal and short-term frost hardening has been studied nearly exclusively in evergreen leaves; scarce knowledge exists for other organs and tissues. Phenological data in Europe (1971–2000) has indicated that 78 per cent of all leafing, flowering, and fruiting records have advanced and that the average advance of spring has been 2.5 days decade^{-1}. Alteration in the timing of bud burst may result in a species being less well adapted to the local temperature environment.

This includes an increased probability of spring frost damage. Premature deacclimation (frost dehardening), once photoperiod signals the approach of spring and chilling requirements are fulfilled, is a realistic probability for alpine tree species (P. cembra, Buchner and Neuner, 2011). Woody shrubs, receiving thermal insulation from an early snow fall, harden to a lesser extent, and can occasionally deacclimate below the snow cover. The ability to reacclimate and the speed at which a species can reacclimate in response to unfavorable temperatures is an important parameter that remains virtually unexplored. Generally, the dynamics of the processes that fine-tune the level of frost hardiness to prevailing environmental conditions are only understood to a limited extent. If future scenarios of climate change occur as predicted by Katz and Brown (1992), where in addition to global warming, the frequency of unpredictable extreme temperature events increases, the ability of plants to reacclimate in a timely manner or resist budbreak may be even more critical in the future.

TEMPERATURE: A DRIVING FORCE FOR PLANT GROWTH AND ACCLIMATION

Fighting ice with ice! Alleviating frost damage in a New Zealand orchard with overhead sprinklers. Plant tissues encased in ice that is continuing to form will remain at 0°C, that is, just above the threshold for injury (Photograph courtesy E. W. Hewett)

Habit is hereditary with plants... and this leads me to say a few words on acclimatisation. As it is extremely common for distinct species belonging to the same genus to inhabit hot and cold countries, if it be true that all the species of the same genus are descended from a single parent-form, acclimatisation must be readily affected during a long course of descent. It is notorious that each species is adapted to the climate of its own home: species from an arctic or even from a temperate region cannot endure a tropical climate or conversely...

But whether or not this adaptation is in most cases very close, we have evidence with few plants, of their becoming, to a certain extent, naturally habituated to different temperatures; that is they become acclimatized.

Life on earth is restricted to a narrow thermal band. Within that range, global conditions can still be extreme with air temperatures as low as –70°C in Antarctica and as high as +57°C in North Africa. Remarkably, life can endure those circumstances, and worse. Thermophilic bacteria exist in hot volcanic springs at +94°C and seeds, lichens and mosses may survive down to –260°C as forms of latent life. However, the temperature range for active growth in higher plants is much more modest and generally constrained between about 5°C and 45°C. The minimum temperature for active growth in tropical and subtropical plants that are chilling sensitive is from 10°C to 15°C.

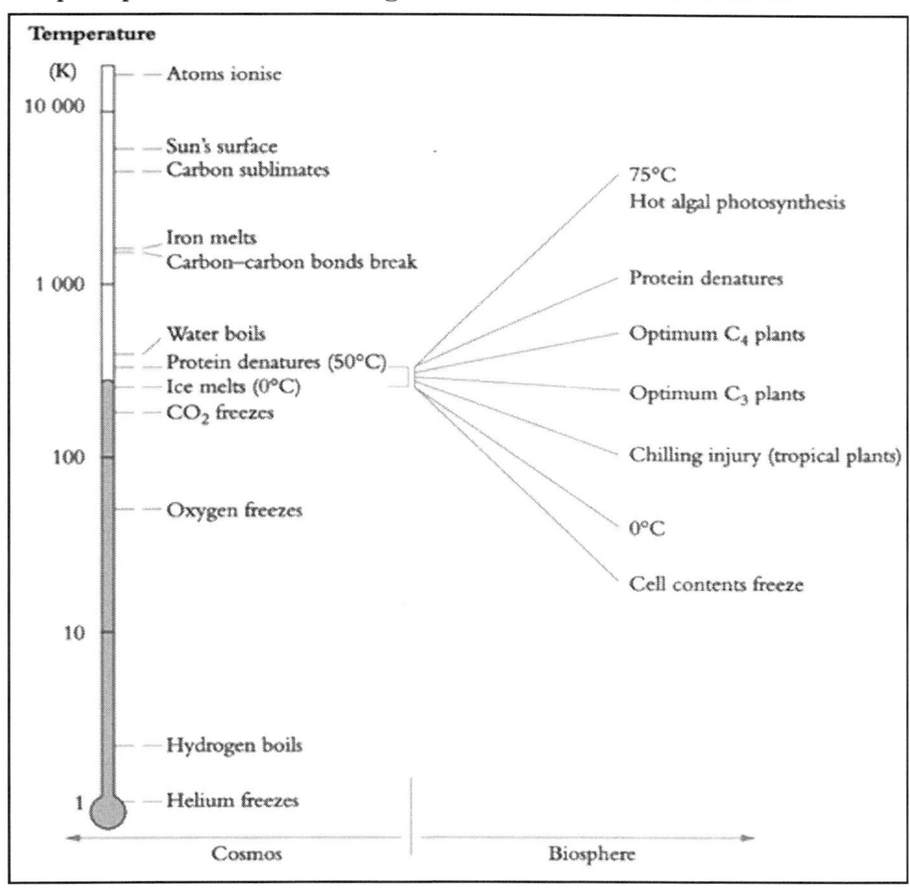

Fig. Plant growth within the earth's biosphere is limited to a narrow range of temperatures compared with the overall cosmic span from absolute zero, where molecular motion ceases, to 10 000 K where atoms are ionised. Taking the life zone as spanning -5 °C to 45 °C vascular plants show remarkable thermal resilience within this range which enables them to colonise a great diversity of habitats.

On a global scale vegetation types have broad mean annual temperature ranges, from the arctic and alpine tundra at the low end of the temperature scale to tropical forests at the high end. Within this classification Australia and New Zealand cover a wide range of temperature conditions with mean annual temperatures varying from 4°C in the alpine areas of Australia and New Zealand to 28°C along the tropical northern coast of Western Australia.

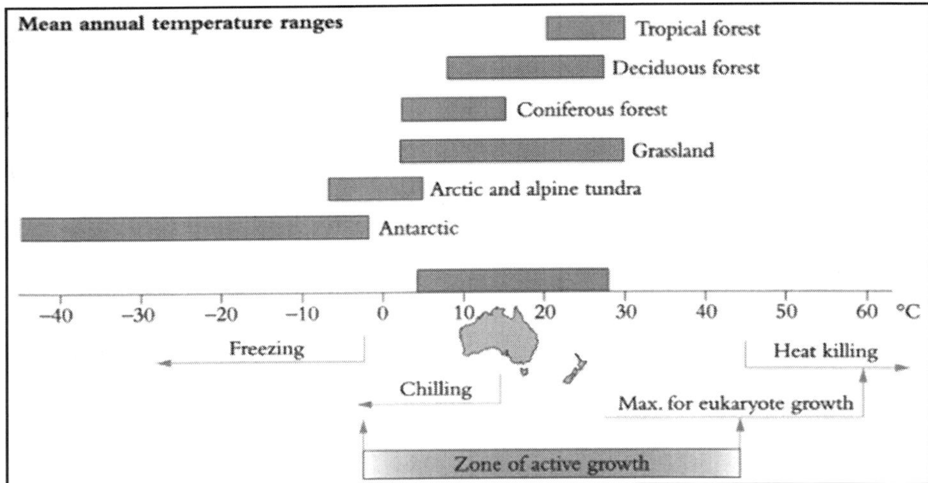

Fig. Mean annual temperatures in Australia and New Zealand range from 28°C in the north (tropical forest zone) to 4°C at higher elevations in the south (arctic and alpine tundra zone). Temperature extremes are an important factor in regulating survival and growth of many species, with periods of heat stress (>45°C) and freezing temperatures (<-2°C) common to some areas. Active growth of higher plants is normally limited to temperatures ranging from 0°C to 40°C, but many subtropical species will be chill damaged by temperatures lower than 10—15°C and many temperate species will not survive long periods of temperatures higher than 30°C.

THERMAL ENVIRONMENT AND PLANT HEAT BUDGETS

Temperatures vary with latitude, altitude, size of land mass (and position within that land mass), atmospheric conditions (cloud cover and air movement) and local topography. Atmospheric temperatures decrease by about 1°C for each 2° increase in latitude, or for each 100 m increase in altitude. Temperatures in high altitudes near the equator can be similar to low-land temperatures further from the equator. The potato, which has its origin in tropical high altitudes, is now grown widely in low-altitude regions of the world where temperature conditions are similar. However, temperature is not the only concern in this expansion of a crop plant to new growing regions, as a change in latitude and altitude may require some adaptation to changing photoperiod and radiation levels.

Seasonal variation in temperature is greatest near the poles, and small near the equator. At high altitudes the increased solar radiation which can result in rapid local heating is balanced by greater night radiation losses. The most stable temperatures occur under oceanic conditions in the tropics.

Survival outside the active growth range of all plants is nevertheless dependent on developmental stage, duration of temperature stress and degree of acclimation. Terrestrial plants have evolved life cycles that match seasonal necessity, which at low temperatures necessitates winter dormancy. Within the dynamic range of plant–temperature relations, where short-term responses are readily reversible, phenology and productivity have been successfully linked with various measures of accumulated heat (thermal time), and predictive models validated.

TEMPERATURE MEANS AND EXTREMES

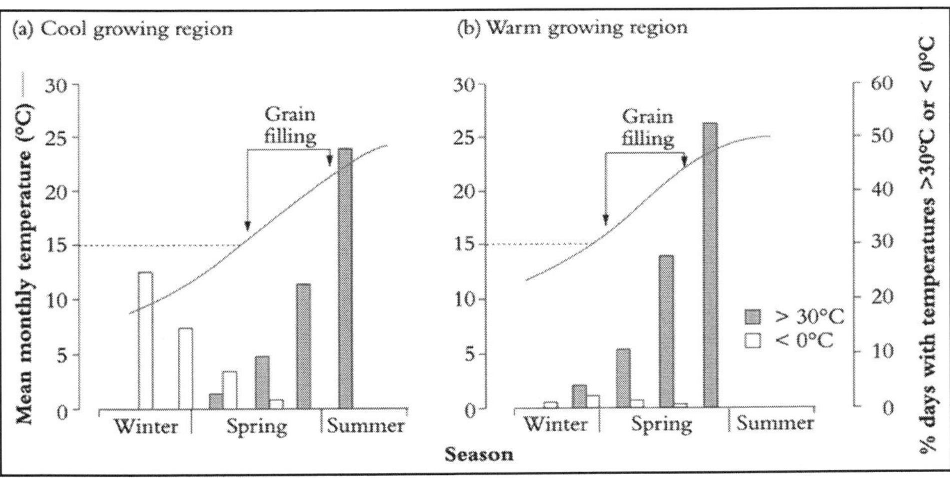

Fig. Wheat-growing areas of Australia have been classified according to the temperature conditions normally prevailing during crop growing seasons (Nix 1975).Temperature increase following heading is common in all regions and plants frequently suffer periods of heat and drought stress during grain filling. Avoiding these late stresses by earlier planting can be difficult, particularly in those regions subject to spring frosts which may damage the developing florets of the inflorescence (ear).

Average monthly temperatures are more relevant to plant growth than mean annual values. Timing cardinal stages in plant development (phenology) can often be predicted from temperature measurements taken during the growing season. This integration of time and temperature is expressed in terms of degree-days. However, when considering the effect of temperature on yield it is necessary to take extreme conditions into account, particularly at sensitive stages of growth.

Although unseasonally warm growing conditions late in winter are not necessarily harmful to fruit trees, this will often result in early bud break and flower development, increasing the possibility that these more sensitive stages of development will be damaged by a late frost.

For annual crops some degree of adjustment is possible to avoid a particular environmental stress by varying the cultivar or time of planting. However, even this increased flexibility may not be adequate to cope with the irregular nature of many stresses.

In the wheat-growing areas of Australia, temperatures increase from the time of heading through to crop maturity so that grain lling often occurs at above-optimum temperatures. Added to this is the possibility of extreme high temperatures (heat shock) or drought.

In warmer growing regions these temperature extremes may be avoided in part by earlier planting, but this approach will depend on suitable temperature conditions and the availability of water for germination and seedling establishment early in the year. In cooler wheat-growing regions earlier planting may expose the developing infloresence to possible frost damage resulting in reduced fertility and grain set.

PLANT TEMPERATURES

Most field studies on the relation between growth (and yield) and temperature are based on meteorological data collected in the vicinity of the crop or ecological area under examination. Although these data have proved to be of considerable value in assessing the response of plants to temperature, actual plant temperatures can differ considerably from air temperature and temperatures can also vary from organ to organ within a plant.

Plant temperatures will be influenced by plant form (erect or prostrate), leaf area, aspect (*e.g.* north- or south-facing slope), irradiance (sun angle, cloud cover and altitude) and air flow (wind). There are also plant characteristics such as reflection from the surface of the leaf, leaf angle and leaf cooling by transpiration which will reduce plant temperature and may minimise the damage associated with above-optimal air temperatures. At the other end of the scale, where there is moisture on leaves, the latent heat produced during external ice formation (a white frost) may provide some initial protection of tissues against frost damage.

Leaf temperatures generally follow the diurnal changes in air temperatures. At sunrise with a clear sky there is a rapid rise in air temperature and leaf temperature, with a slower and lower rise in root and surface soil temperature. This relationship is altered considerably by cloud cover and at night root temperatures will be higher than leaf temperatures. Organ volume (thickness) can also have a marked influence on temperature and this can be seen, for example, in the apple-growing regions around Auckland in New Zealand. On a windless sunny day with an air temperature of 26°C, while leaf temperature in an apple orchard may reach 29°C, the peripheral flesh of the fruit on the sunny side of a tree can reach 45°C.

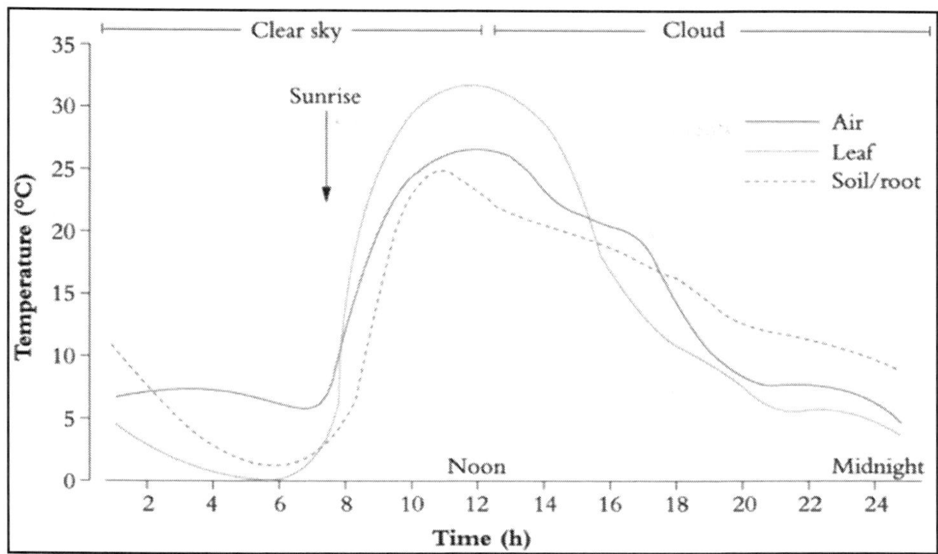

Fig. Plant temperatures generally follow the diurnal pattern of air temperatures, but may be higher (sometimes 10°C or more) due to strong irradiance from full sunlight, or cooler (often by 2-3°C) due to transpirational cooling. Tissues and organs of a plant are not necessarily at a uniform temperature. Root temperatures are generally lower than those of leaves during daytime and higher at night-time, reflecting the differences between air and soil temperatures.

Under normal eld conditions mean day temperatures can commonly be 5°C to 10°C higher than mean night temperatures, with a much greater amplitude between maximum and minimum temperatures. The importance of this day/night differential has received considerable attention in relation to the growth and yield of glasshouse crops where there is the possibility of some degree of temperature control.

However, it is also of interest in eld crops in relation to the development of models for use in predicting the effect of weather conditions on crop development.

Total plant growth would be favoured by low night temperatures as this would reduce respiratory losses at a time when the supply of carbohydrate might become limiting.

However, dry matter production for a wide range of crops grown under constant but optimal temperature is equal to and often greater than dry matter production by the same crops grown under differential day/night temperatures with the same mean value.

Where a day/night temperature differential is imposed, low night temperatures rather than low day temperatures favour growth. The amplitude of the day/night temperature differential is also important and increasing this from 10°C to 20°C can reduce growth.

PLANT ENERGY BUDGETS

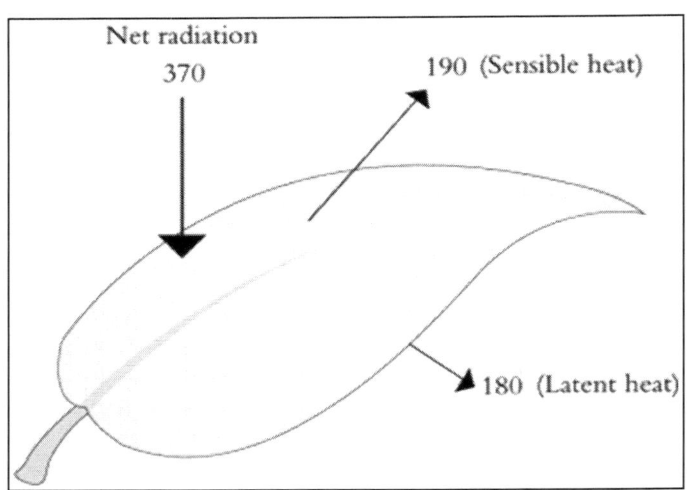

Fig. A notional energy budget for a mesophytic leaf on a well-watered plant. Taking an incident irradiance of 400 J m^{-2} s^{-1} as representative of midday conditions, 30 units are reflected, leaving 370 J m^{-2} s^{-1} absorbed. If air temperature is taken to be 20°C, relative humidity 50 per cent, wind speed 0.8 m s^{-1} and leaf area 0.01 m^2 (*i.e.* 100 cm^2), then transpiration will be about 4 mmol H_20 cm^{-2} s^{-1}, and latent heat exchange will account for about 180 J $m^{-2}s^{-1}$. Sensible heat exchange will account for the remainder (about 190 J m^{-2} s^{-1})

All organisms must balance energy inputs and outputs in order to maintain tissue temperatures within a given range. Plants have evolved a range of adaptations that allow them to balance energy gain and loss and so avoid becoming too hot or too cold. Energy budget equations quantify the energy gained and lost through different processes. More complex energy budget models include leaf and canopy properties that influence the rate of energy transfer.

In a leaf energy budget, energy is gained through radiation absorbed, while energy is dissipated as radiant heat loss by emission of longwave radiation, sensible heat loss by convection, and latent heat loss by transpiration. For a leaf to maintain a constant temperature the energy exchange must be balanced such that:

Radiation absorbed = radiant heat loss + sensible heat loss + latent heat loss

Energy gain comes primarily from the sun in the form of shortwave radiation. Leaves absorb a large proportion of incident solar shortwave radiation, particularly in the visible wavebands. As any object with a temperature above absolute zero emits some radiation, leaves also absorb longwave radiation from their surroundings. A plant can reduce the amount of radiation absorbed by reducing the amount of leaf area exposed to the sun, *e.g.* by changing leaf orientation or leaf dimensions. Leaf properties such as surface wax, hairs and scales will also alter the amount of incident radiation that is reflected and transmitted.

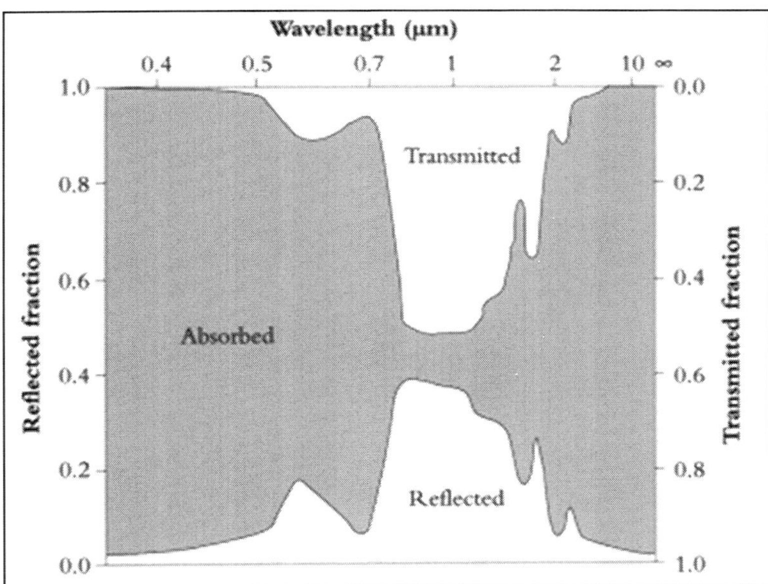

Fig. Solar radiation striking a leaf is either reflected, transmitted or absorbed. Photosynthetically active radiation (0.4 to 0.7 μm) is strongly absorbed, whereas near-infrared radiation which would heat leaves but is useless for photosynthesis (between about 0.8 and 2 μm) is only weakly absorbed. Far-infrared radiation is strongly absorbed, but energy per quantum is greatly diminished at these long wavelengths, so that consequences for leaf heating are greatly diminished.

During the day, thermal energy that is absorbed by a leaf must be dissipated to prevent the leaf from overheating. A large amount of heat is lost through the emission of longwave radiation, but this is normally balanced by inputs of longwave radiation from the surrounding environment. The rate of radiant heat loss is determined by leaf temperature and by leaf emissivity. Emissivity does not vary greatly between leaves; generally darker, smoother leaves have a higher emissivity (as well as a high absorbance). At night time, radiant heat loss can cause leaf temperature to drop well below that of the surrounding air. On long, cloudless nights, when there is little radiant input from the atmosphere, dew can condense on the leaf surface and, in extreme cases, leaves may cool below zero resulting in frost damage.

During the day a leaf typically loses sensible heat to the surrounding air through convection. At night the situation is usually reversed with leaves gaining heat from the surrounding air. The rate at which heat is gained or lost is proportional to the difference in temperature and to the amount of resistance between a leaf and the surrounding air. Characteristics that increase the size of the boundary-layer, *e.g.* large leaf dimensions or presence of leaf hairs, will reduce the rate of heat exchange. Similarly, reduced wind speed will reduce the rate of sensible heat exchange.

For transpiration to occur, water contained in cells within a leaf must change into water vapour and escape through stomatal pores. For the water to move from a cell to the inter-cellular air space it must change from a liquid to a gas (water vapour).

This phase change from liquid to gas consumes a large amount of energy and in doing so cools the leaf. This loss of energy is referred to as latent heat loss. The rate at which transpiration occurs is proportional to the difference in humidity and to the amount of resistance between the inside of the leaf and the surrounding air. As well as wind speed and boundary layer properties, transpiration is strongly influenced by stomatal resistance. When the stomata are closed, heat loss through transpiration is negligible. Although stomatal resistance has a large impact on leaf temperature, it is generally accepted that stomatal opening does not respond directly to changes in temperature. In hot, dry conditions stomata will typically remain closed even when a leaf is overheating.

GROWTH AND DEVELOPMENT RESPONSES TO TEMPERATURE

Plants can be classified in their temperature responses into broad groups. One group is defined by sensitivity to low temperature: 'chilling-sensitive' species are unable to grow, and often suffer visible damage, below 10–15°C and 'chilling-tolerant' species are able to grow down to 0°C and able to survive below this temperature. Within each group, important temperature-sensitive processes are leaf expansion and stem elongation, both of which depend on cell expansion before the cell walls harden.

Another division is based on differences in the pathway of CO_2 fixation during photosynthesis, where species in which initial fixation occurs via Rubisco and the photosynthetic carbon reduction cycle are designated C_3 species and species in which initial fixation occurs via phosphoenolpyruvate (PEP) carboxylase and the four-carbon dicarboxylic acid pathway are designated C_4 species. C_4 species include maize and sorghum and such species have high optimum temperatures (e"30°C) for growth. Most C_4 plants are also chilling sensitive. C_3 species, on the other hand, show considerable variation in their optimum growth temperature, which can range from close to 30°C in rice to less than 10°C in some alpine species, and they also include a wide range of both chilling-sensitive and chilling-tolerant plants.

PLANT VARIATION IN SENSITIVITY TO TEMPERATURE

At any given stage of development, it is possible to define the minimum temperature below which a plant will not grow, suboptimal temperatures where a further increase in temperature will result in increased growth, optimal temperatures when growth is at its maximum, supraoptimal temperatures where a decrease in temperature will result in increased growth and the maximum temperature above which a plant will stop growing. Sustained temperatures beyond this range will be lethal.

Temperature is an important factor in controlling changes in growth and development from germination, through vegetative growth to floral initiation and reproductive growth. Not all stages of development, or different physiological processes, are equally sensitive to temperature. For example, the stage of pollen meiosis during anther development in rice is particularly sensitive to low temperature extremes, whereas in wheat it is less so. Variation in temperature tolerance is also evident within single plants as well as between genotypes.

Young actively growing tissues are generally more sensitive to temperature variation than mature tissues and dormant tissues such as buds and seeds can often survive quite extreme temperatures. Frost tolerance in apple is greatest in the stem and then follows a sequence of decreasing tolerance from the mature leaf to the young leaf and floral parts, with the ovary, style and stigma of flowers being least tolerant of frost.

Variation in temperature sensitivity between tissues and physiological processes is also seen in sorghum, a subtropical C_4 species.

Frost damage occurs to green tissue below –1°C, there is poor seed germination below 6°C, chlorophyll destruction occurs in mature green tissue under high light at 10°C, there is poor pollen development below 13°C and chlorophyll formation in young developing leaves is inhibited at temperatures below 16.5°C.

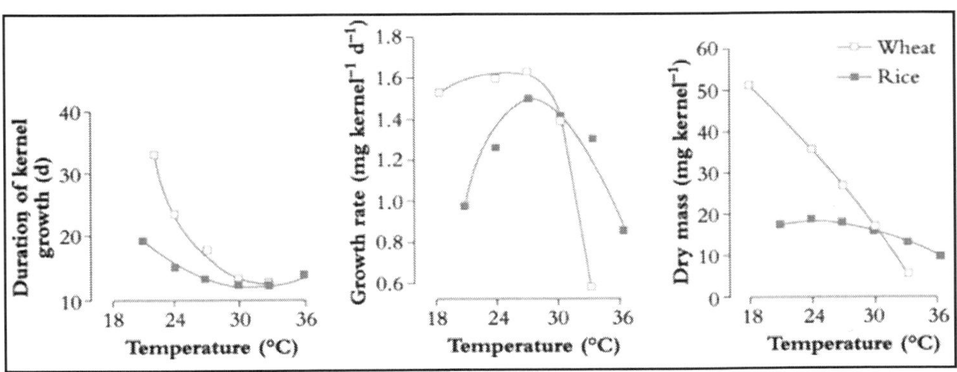

Fig. Temperature effects on growth can be viewed in relation to either rate of organ production or the final size attained. Size results from both rate and duration of growth, and there are many examples where organ size is reduced at high temperature because rate of growth cannot compensate for a reduced duration of growth. This is illustrated for wheat (a temperate cereal) and rice (a subtropical cereal). At low temperature wheat has a much larger grain than rice, but rice has a much more stable grain size than wheat in relation to temperature and at 30°C grain size in the two species is very similar.

Temperature effects on growth can be viewed in terms of rate multiplied by duration of growth where individual components have different temperature optima. As temperature increases within a plant's dynamic range, duration of growth decreases but rate of growth increases. As a consequence, organ size at maturity may change very little in response to temperature despite variation in growth rate. As temperatures are raised further, an increased rate of growth is no longer able to compensate for a reduction in duration, and the final mass (or volume) of a given organ at maturity is reduced. This is providing that soil water can be maintained during this period. This response can be seen in a range of tissues including leaves, stems and fruits (and seeds). A smaller organ size at maturity due to high temperature is usually associated with smaller cells rather than a change in cell number.

THERMAL TIME AND CROP DEVELOPMENT

As already described, the time taken for plants and their organs to develop within their dynamic temperature range decreases as temperature increases. This was first quantified in the eighteenth century when the French physiologist Reaumur showed that grapes growing in different regions and seasons ripened when the accumulated daily temperature, t_i, reached a (fairly) constant value, k, which is known as day degrees, heat units or heatsum. In equation (1) daily temperature is the mean of maximum and minimum temperatures, the subscript i refers to days and the summation was from winter until grape ripening. The units are °C.d.

The system of accumulating temperature in this way is known as thermal time and can be applied to the life cycle of a plant or organ, or a phase of a plant's development such as the seed-filling phase or the expansion of a single leaf. One weakness of this system is that temperature accumulates above 0°C while in reality, for many species, development stops at temperatures well above freezing. Instead of accumulating temperatures above 0°C, thermal time systems now use a base or threshold temperature, $t_{base,}$ which varies with species and is estimated as the value that provides the most constant value of k.

The thermal time system can be simplified providing no daily temperature during a phase falls below t_{base}. An example of the simplified system appears as a graph of duration of a phase, D, versus the mean temperature of the phase, •. This line is defined by the duration of the phase, D, and the mean temperature of the whole phase above the base temperature, •-t_{base}. The product of these variables is the heatsum, k.

The effect of temperature on phase duration from seedling emergence to flowering (anthesis). The curve is a rectangular hyperbola, meaning that the areas of rectangles defined by the graph are constant. For example a duration of 100 days at a mean temperature of 10°C represents a heat sum of 500 °C.d above a base temperature of 5°C *i.e.* 100(10-5) = 500 °C.d. The relationship can be linearised by plotting the inverse of duration 1/D against mean temperature. 1/D is defined as the mean rate of development, with units of day^{-1}, and is equivalent to the proportion of development per day.

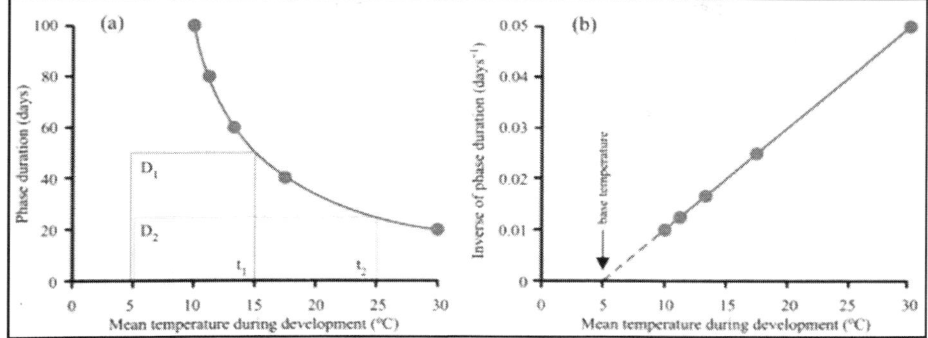

Fig. Duration of a phase in a plant's life cycle, measured as time, decreases as mean temperature increases. For many plants, duration, when measured as thermal units, becomes a constant value. This thermal duration is called a heat sum, heat units or day degrees. It is calculated as the product of time duration and the mean temperature of the phase above a suitable base temperature. The base is 5°C in this graphical example that represents the temperature response of the phase from seedling emergence to flowering (anthesis) of a temperate plant such as wheat. The wheat developmental pattern is shown in (a) as a rectangular hyperbola (purple curve) in which the areas of the rectangles are equal. Expressing the same wheat data as the inverse of time duration against mean temperature (b) produces a straight line. The slope of the straight line is the inverse of the heat sum and the intercept on the x-axis is the base temperature.

Extrapolation of the line to the x-axis provides an estimate of t_{base} and the slope of the line, 1/k, is the heatsum. The advantage of plotting results in this way is that it provides a test of whether the thermal time system works for the data.

According to this example for wheat, a 2°C warming above a mean of 15°C would reduce the number of days to anthesis from 50 to ~42(500 °C.d/ (15°C - 5°C) = 50 days and 500 °C.d/ (17°C - 5°C) = 41.7 days). Reduced duration can mean less crop growth because of fewer days for intercepting solar radiation and photosynthesis.

Rate of development is not always linearly related to mean temperature. At high temperatures the development rate of some plant phases decreases, showing a clear optimum temperature (arrowed). This cardinal temperature along with the base temperature, defines the boundary of the dynamic temperature range for the phase, organ or species. An optimum temperature is more likely to appear when plants are exposed to high temperature when light levels are relatively low. Rate of development is affected by both temperature and photoperiod in photoperiod-sensitive species. So while development responses remain linearly related to temperature the slopes change with photoperiod; a long-day plant develops more rapidly in long days than in short days.

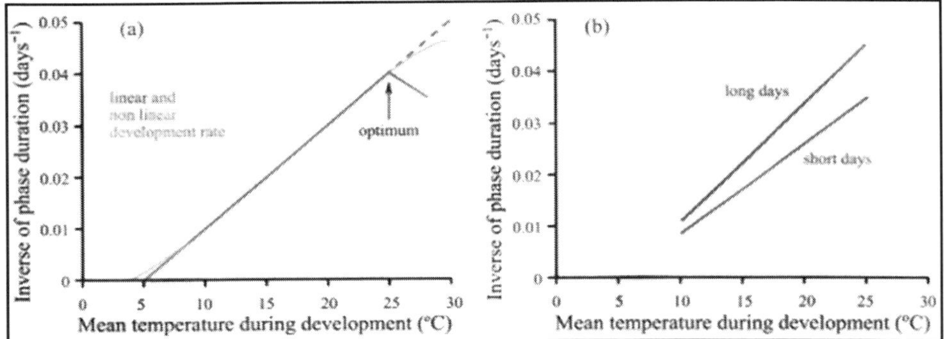

Exceptions to the simple thermal time system. At temperatures close to the base temperature and at high temperatures development may diverge from a linear response of development rate to temperature as the green departures from the purple straight line). In some species and phases there is a reduced development rate with higher temperature, shown in (a) by the purple line declining beyond the optimum). A long-day plant shows more rapid development in long days than short days over a wide range of temperatures (b). Short-day plants show the reverse response.

Thermal time can be used to predict crop development and the stages when herbicides, insecticides and fertilizer should be applied. This is useful for farmers who manage crops over distances of hundreds of kilometres and need to visit them at a particular stage of development. Thermal time can also be used to back-calculate the best sowing date to minimise the risk of frost or excessive heat damage at sensitive stages of development.

G9 =G8+MAX(0,(E9-5))

	A	B	C	D	E	F	G	H	I
1						Heatsum	Heatsum	Heatsum	
2		day	Tmax	Tmin	Tmean	Tbase=0	Tbase=5	Tbase=10	
3		1	20.0	10.0	15.0	15.0	10.0	5.0	
4		2	17.0	7.0	12.0	27.0	17.0	7.0	
5		3	6.0	2.0	4.0	31.0	17.0	7.0	
6		4	10.0	4.0	7.0	38.0	19.0	7.0	
7		5	16.0	2.0	9.0	47.0	23.0	7.0	
8		6	4.0	2.0	3.0	50.0	23.0	7.0	
9		7	16.0	4.0	10.0	60.0	28.0	7.0	
10									

Fig. Spreadsheet to calculate heatsum from daily maximum and minimum temperatures and a base temperature. Daily mean temperatures below the base do not contribute to heatsum, as shown by the equation in cell G9.

The dynamic ranges of temperatures for subtropical and tropical species are much higher than for this example of temperate wheat. Consequently the base temperature will be higher and the heatsum different. Nevertheless the method for calculating thermal time is similar.

It is easy to calculate heatsums from temperature data that you measure yourself or download from the internet. The spreadsheet showing a week's accumulation of heatsums using different base temperatures. When collecting temperature data, remember to shade the thermometer, allow free air circulation and install it at the standard height for your region (1.2 m above ground in Australia). To test the relationship between heatsum and phasic development you can record development of a phase of plant development in several environments by growing plants at different times of year or in different locations. For that, you need to record on your temperature spreadsheet the date of the start of the chosen phase (maybe the sowing date) and the date of the end of the phase (maybe flowering). Work out the thermal time for each day of the phase, and add all sums together to produce the heatsum for the phase. Compare that result with data you collect from other planting dates. Are the heatsums the same despite different temperatures? If you calculate the mean temperature for the phase on your spreadsheet and the number of days from start to finish of the phase you can graph your combined data. If you have enough sowing dates you will be able to work out the real base temperature for that phase of the chosen species.

Some Definitions

Development refers to the changes in form or ontogeny of plants (and animals) rather than growth, which means the increase of mass. While normally growth and development are loosely related, it is possible to have growth without development, for example the continuous growth of vegetative buffalo grass, or to have development uncoupled from growth, for example when the flowering date of stunted drought-affected wheat is similar to the flowering date of well-watered wheat. Phasic development relates to phases in a plant's life cycle. For example the phases in the life cycle of an annual crop are vegetative (between seedling emergence and floral initiation), reproductive (between floral initiation and flowering, called anthesis in wheat) and grain filling (between anthesis and physiological maturity) Phenology is the science of the influence of climate on the occurrence of biological events

PHOTOTHERMAL QUOTIENT (PTQ) PREDICTS POTENTIAL CROP YIELD

PTQ is the ratio of solar radiation to mean temperature during a phase of crop development. Nix (1976) proposed that PTQ could be used to predict potential crop yield, *i.e.* the yield when crop management overcomes the limitations of water deficit or surplus, nutrient deficiency, pests and diseases. Solar radiation is the numerator because it drives photosynthesis. Temperature is the denominator because increased temperature leads to faster development and so reduces the time available for photosynthesis. It is more correct to refer to 'short-wave global radiation' than solar radiation because 'global' here refers to radiation from the whole sky, including diffuse radiation, but excludes the long waves that have no effect on photosynthesis.

The units of PTQ are MJ m^{-2} d^{-1} $°C^{-1}$. In the case of wheat a base temperature of 0°C is acceptable. For warm season crops such as maize, a base temperature of 10°C should be used. Evidence for the accuracy of PTQ comes from three examples of wheat.

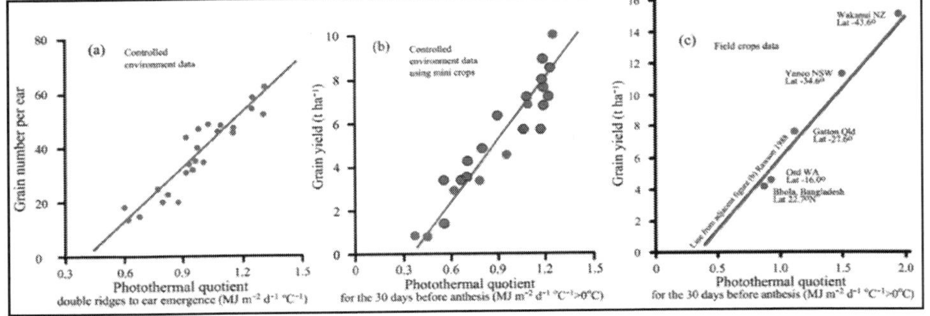

Fig. (a) Grain numbers per ear in wheat are set by temperature and radiation during the period from floral initiation to flag leaf expansion as shown by transferring plants amongst temperatures throughout the period. Numbers were closely correlated with PTQ (accumulated radiation divided by thermal time for each of the 24 treatments): After Rawson and Bagga 1979. (b) The relation between PTQ and wheat yield in 23 mini-canopies in controlled environments, compiled by Rawson (1988). The correlation between PTQ and grain number in (a) translated to a close correlation between PTQ and yield in (b) because weight per grain is relatively stable in wheat. (c) The same linear relationship from (b), see equation 5 below, closely predicts potential grain yield at field scales at locations ranging over many degrees of latitude: southern hemisphere data from Peake and Angus (2009). This suggests that basic meteorological data of temperature and radiation is all that is needed to provide first order estimates of potential crop yields at new locations.

The plants grown in naturally-lit temperature-controlled glasshouses and batches transferred every four days between different temperatures during the phases prior to ear emergence. The number of grains per ear changed with temperature but was better correlated with PTQ than with thermal time alone or radiation alone. Since mean kernel weight is stable for a wheat variety when water and nutrition are adequate, a reasonable hypothesis is that grain yield (grain number x kernel weight) would also be related to PTQ. All that is required to estimate likely potential yield for a location would be local radiation and temperature data. A test of the grain yield – PTQ relationship with data from temperature-controlled glasshouses and growth chambers using mini-crops of wheat grown in different temperature and radiation environments.

The close relationship between the prediction and the data suggests that PTQ can predict potential wheat yield from tropical to cool temperate zones. PTQ therefore provides farmers with a benchmark to assess the yield of their crops. If their yields are well below the benchmark there is scope for improved crop management or genetics.

RESPONSES OF ENZYMES, PHOTOSYNTHESIS AND ASSIMILATE TRANSPORT

Enzyme activity is very responsive to temperature, as is enzyme synthesis, activation and stability. However the response of plant growth to temperature is the result of a number of complex processes involving many enzyme systems, and most likely governed by the response of the enzymes involved in CO_2 fixation.

The different temperature responses of C_3 versus C_4 photosynthesis are described next, along with temperature effects on assimilate transport and on the basic concepts of enzyme activity including the Q_{10}: the increase in rate of respiration for a 10°C rise in temperature.

PHOTOSYNTHESIS

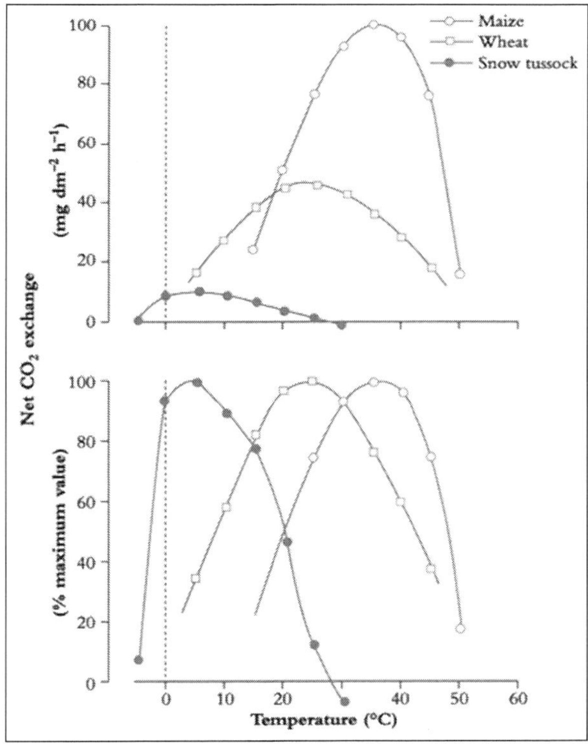

Fig. Plant species show characteristic variation in the way photosynthetic tissue responds to temperature. Maize (a subtropical C_4 species) has a high maximum rate of CO_2 assimilation with a high optimum temperature, while wheat (a temperate C_3 species) has a lower maximum rate and a lower optimum temperature. (a) Absolute values; (b) shows those same data normalised to 100 per cent at optimum temperature. Alpine plants (C_3 species) have an even lower optimum temperature and may show CO_2 assimilation below 0 °C, but their maximum rates of photosynthesis are often low compared with warmer climate species. Based on I F Wardlaw (1979).

CO_2 assimilation underpins plant productivity and is therefore central to any analysis of the response of plants to a change in temperature. In photosynthetic terms, plants can be divided broadly into the groups discussed earlier.

Some C_3 species such as snow tussocks have an optimum temperature for CO_2 assimilation as low as 5°C, but it is important to note that absolute rates at this temperature may be relatively low. Most temperate grasses and cereals as well as many woody species have temperature optima in the range from 15°C to 25°C and within this range many C_3 species show only small changes in CO_2uptake. In contrast to temperate C_3 species, CO_2 assimilation by C_4 species increases considerably with a rise in temperature from 15°C to 30°C and optimum temperatures may be greater than this. Rice, a subtropical C_3 species, has a higher temperature optimum for CO_2 assimilation than temperate C_3 species. Under high light, C_4 species have a characteristically greater photosynthetic rate than the C_3 species, but these differences disappear and may be reversed at low temperature. Growth temperatures may also influence the optimum temperature for net photosynthesis, which may therefore vary with season or location. However, modifications leading to an improvement in photosynthesis at high temperatures can result in decreased performance at low temperatures and vice versa.

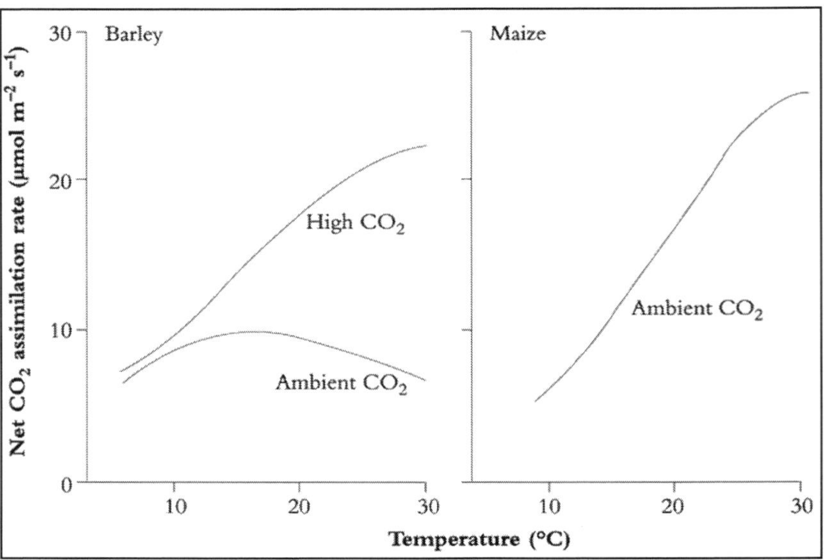

Fig. Maize (a subtropical C_4 species) has a high optimum temperature (~30 °C) for CO_2 assimilation, while barley (a temperate C_3 species) has a lower, but less distinct optimum (~15 °C). Doubling CO_2 has little effect on CO_2 assimilation rate by maize, but greatly increases the absolute rate and optimum temperature for barley by suppressing photorespiration. This O_2-dependent loss of carbon increases with temperature and is largely responsible for the low optimum temperature of photosynthesis in many C_3 species.

A combination of at least two factors may be associated with the failure of C_3 species to respond more favourably to high temperature in terms of CO_2 assimilation. One is the limit placed on photosynthesis by ambient CO_2, and a second is the concurrent rise with increasing temperature of light-stimulated photorespiration, which is effectively absent from C_4 species. Increased atmospheric CO_2 inhibits photo-respiration and results in a much greater uptake of CO_2 in response to increased temperature in C_3 species.

While net photosynthesis is the resulting balance between gross photosynthesis and respiration, low or even negative net photosynthetic rates can have a significant effect on productivity. An example of this would be photosynthesis by the green pod of many legumes where the net uptake of CO_2 is low because of a high rate of pod and seed respiration. A rise in temperature will result in greater respiratory losses from the pod and a reduction in net uptake of CO_2, but this does not diminish the importance of pod photosynthesis.

Variation in stomatal resistance could be another factor associated with temperature effects on net assimilation of CO_2. Adaptation to high temperature can be related to photosystem II electron transfer, the stability of chloroplast membrane-bound enzyme activities and the stability of the photosynthetic carbon metabolism enzymes that require light for activation. For example, enhanced assimilation of CO_2 by rice at high temperature, in comparison with the more temperate C_3 species, is associated with a greater response of ribulose-1,5-bisphosphate carboxylase in rice to increasing temperature.

In chilling-sensitive species such as maize, sorghum and mung bean, chlorophyll formation and chlorophyll destruction both occur in light at low temperatures. However, once greening has occurred quite low temperatures (but not usually freezing) can be tolerated as long as these occur during darkness. Low-temperature tolerance is also associated with a high level of strategic enzymes such as Rubisco, protein stability and membrane lipid composition.

Consideration must also be given to possible indirect effects of temperature on photosynthesis. For example, a change in root growth due to a change in temperature could alter the supply of nutrients or growth regulators, such as cytokinins, to the shoots. It is common to find a build up of non-structural carbohydrates in many parts of a plant under low-temperature conditions, a response indicating that growth is more sensitive to low temperature than photosynthesis.

However, feedback inhibition of photosynthesis associated with this excess carbohydrate accumulation under low-temperature conditions occurs in a number of species. In summary, it is important to take into account the possibility of indirect effects of temperature on photosynthetic tissue when looking for genetic differences in photosynthetic responses to temperature.

ASSIMILATE TRANSPORT

There are three components of nutrient and photosynthate transfer in plants that might respond to temperature in different ways: (1) transfer of metabolites across cell membranes, including the exchange between apoplasm (space external to cell membranes) and the symplasm (space contained by cell membranes); (2) cell to cell transfer (within the symplasm) via plasmodesmal connections, and (3) movement of metabolites over long distances through phloem sieve elements.

Selective transfer of metabolites across a membrane against a concentration gradient is an energy-requiring step involving respiratory activity and membrane-bound ATPase. This metabolically active process is responsive to temperature. Membrane transfer is associated with many physiological functions including movement of metabolites and photoassimilate loading within source leaves, exchange with storage tissues along the path of transport and photoassimilate loading into sinks. The response of long-distance photoassimilate translocation to low temperature varies widely between species.

In many temperate Gramineae (including wheat) a drop in temperature along the path of transport to 1°C has no measurable effect on the translocation of photosynthate, but at this temperature in chilling-sensitive species such as bean and sorghum there is a marked reduction in the translocation of photosynthate. In some chilling-tolerant species such as sugar beet, there is an initial rapid decline in translocation following application of low temperature along the path of transport, but this inhibition is transient in nature, with translocation returning to normal in a number of hours.

In species that are more sensitive to chilling such as squash there is some adjustment to low temperature, resulting in partial recovery. Such adjust-ments vary between ecotypes within the one species, for example in Canada thistle where behaviour is related to altitude and thus temperature in natural surroundings.

Lowering the temperature of the transport pathway also reduces the lateral transfer of carbon into adjacent tissues, or alternatively the remobilisation of stored carbohydrate back into the transport system. By contrast, translocation can be relatively insensitive to temperatures up to 40°C, but will be inhibited by prolonged periods of temperature >40°C. Prolonging a high-temperature treatment, unlike the low end of the scale, does not result in recovery; rather, blockage intensifies.

The exact nature of the inhibition of long-distance transport at temperature extremes is still uncertain. Inhibition appears not to be energy related in a metabolic sense, but low-temperature effects may be due to a displacement of proteinacious material. This would lead to transient responses that reverse in time. More sustained responses under either low- or high-temperature treatments are likely to be due to a build up of callose (a β-1,3 glucan) in sieve-plate pores.

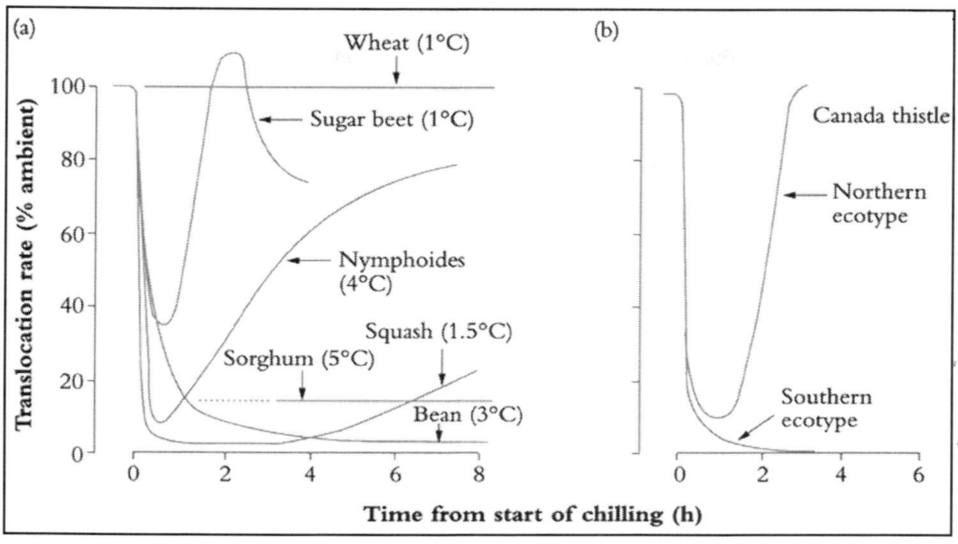

Fig. Effects of low temperature on translocation of photoassimilate through phloem has frequently been measured by changing pathway temperature between a source and a sink and following variation in the rate of movement of radioactively labelled photosynthate. (a) Translocation in some species such as wheat is especially tolerant of low temperature, but greatly reduced in others such as bean. Again, in other species such as Nymphoides and sugar beet there is an initial retardation of translocation immediately after a low-temperature block is imposed, but translocation subsequently improves even though the low-temperature is retained. (b) Canada thistle has both attributes with the northern (colder) ecotype showing rapid recovery of translocation at low temperature and the southern (warmer) ecotype showing very little recovery over the first 3 h.

Whether reduced translocation is the cause of poor growth at extreme temperatures is often difficult to assess. This is partly because of the transient nature of the temperature response in many species and partly because the response of the transport system to temperature has been examined in isolation from other processes. In sorghum, where temperatures below 20°C effectively reduce translocation, this reduction is minor in comparison with the direct effect of the same temperature on growth. Current findings suggest that long-distance transport in the phloem does not have a direct role in regulating whole-plant responses to temperature.

BIOCHEMISTRY AND BASIC CONCEPTS

Enzymes play a major role in regulating the way in which plants respond to temperature. The effect of temperature on enzyme activity is expressed through the maximum rate (V_{max}) and the enzyme–substrate affinity (K_m) and this in turn is related to the effect of temperature on enzyme synthesis, activation and stability.

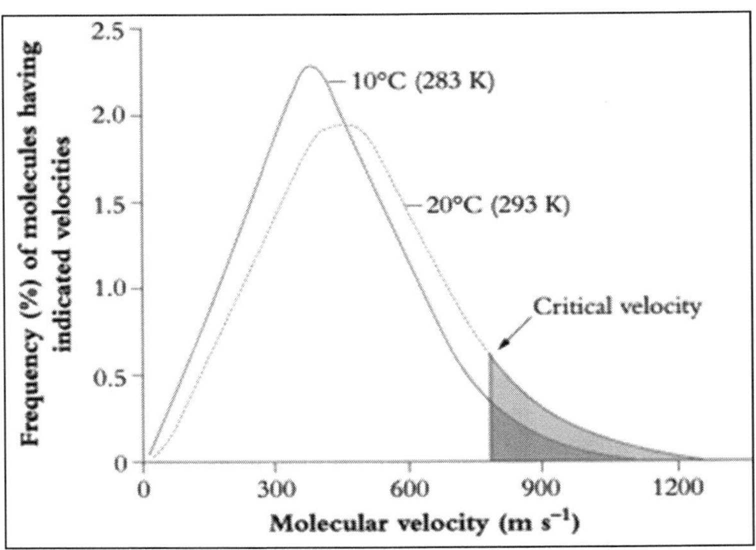

Fig. Molecules must collide for a chemical reaction to occur, but from the expected number of collisions in a given solution it is clear that only a small number of these collisions actually result in a reaction. For a reaction to occur not only must molecules collide but they must do so above a critical velocity or minimum energy (activation energy).This explains an apparent anomoly where kinetic theory predicts that a 10 K (Kelvin) increase in absolute temperature (K = °C + 273) would be expected to increase the number of collisions by about 2 per cent. However, above a critical value the rate of a reaction can increase two- to three-fold (200-300 per cent) per 10°C rise because the number of collisions increases considerably more than average behaviour would predict. This change in the rate of a reaction with a rise in temperature of 10°C is known as the Q10 value and is around 2 to 3 for many chemical (enzyme) reactions which are operating within their dynamic range (Based on various sources, courtesy I.F. Wardlaw)

Basic metabolic rates tend to increase exponentially within their dynamic range (10–30°C) so that a rise in temperature of 10°C will at least double reaction rate, that is, 'Q_{10}' = 2. Q_{10}represents the net outcome of increased activity of an enzyme system with increased temperature, offset by any deactivation of the enzyme associated with this increase. Q_{10} values for metabolic processes are generally in the range of 2–3 and values below this imply that the reaction is at least partly governed by physical rather than metabolic processes. Q_{10} values for physical processes are commonly around 1.3. Physical limitation occurs when there are barriers to the transfer of substrate to reaction sites in a cell. Reaction rates of whole organisms or even organs often increase approximately linearly with temperature. Respiration is a case in point. This departure from an exponential increase results from a progressive shift in the reaction rates of component processes which first increase exponentially with temperature but then become modified by physical constraints such as substrate availability.

Enzymes can adjust to changes in the temperature environment, such that rates in acclimated plants are not as divergent as would be anticipated from the immediate response to temperature change. Acclimation can take a number of forms which may involve changes in isozymes or enzyme concentration, modification of an enzyme by substrate and effectors, or changes in metabolic regulation.

The concept of Q_{10} values has been extended to complex cellular and even whole-plant functions and has been used to provide some insight into the nature of the factors limiting the response of plants to temperature.

The 'thermal kinetic window' is a concept that relates enzyme activity and optimal plant metabolism to the temperature characteristics of the Michaelis–Menten constant (K_m) of substrates and cofactors. Thermal kinetic windows define the temperature range outside which plants experience thermal stress. Many enzymes operate under non-saturating substrate concentrations and substrate binding (K_m) may at times be of greater importance than maximum velocity (V_{max}) for the characterisation of enzyme function under physiological conditions.

The thermal kinetic window for a specific enzyme in a particular species (often spanning 8–15°C) is generally narrower than the plant temperatures experienced on a seasonal or daily basis, and temperature extremes that induce heat shock and chilling injury are not required for plants to experience some degree of thermal stress.

In the event of a sustained change in temperature conditions of plant growth, temperature:K_m relationships for key enzyme reactions can adjust towards a temperature optimisation for metabolism and hence growth under those conditions, an out-come referred to above as acclimation and amenable to analysis via an Arrhenius plot to reveal underlying bioenergetics.

Plotting log k as a function of 1/T yields a linear relationship in the dynamic temperature range where the organism shows readily reversible responses to temperature, and can live indefinitely. Slope indicates the 'energy of activation' (Ea) which is the minimal energy required for the reaction to occur. A change in slope of this line indicates a change in sensitivity. A steeper slope at low temperature indicates that the energy of activation has increased and has therefore become more limiting to maximum velocity (V_{max}) of the overall reaction.

Considerable use has been made of Arrhenius plots in attempts to determine critical temperatures for key enzymatic reactions in plant cells. Membrane lipids may undergo a phase change from the mobile to the solid state with a fall in temperature and this will vary with the nature of the lipids in the membrane, particularly the degree of unsaturation (double bonds). Any change in lipid properties would be expected to modify the activity of membrane-bound enzymes. Because of the complex nature of membranes, such change will often be a gradual rather than an abrupt change at a precise temperature.

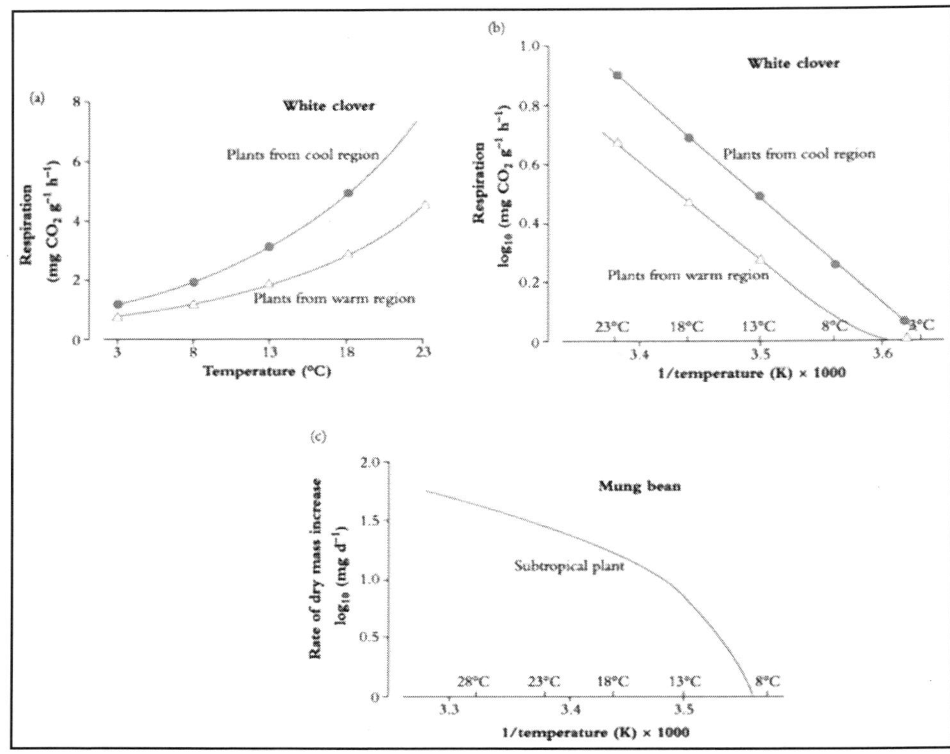

Fig. (a) Dark respiration of white clover leaves (dry mass basis) increases with temperature. However, respiration rate depends on the conditions under which plants have grown and is greater for leaves grown under cool conditions. (b) An Arrhenius plot provides a useful basis for comparing the temperature response of two sets of leaves. Respiration (reaction) rate (log transformed) is plotted as a function of the reciprocal of absolute (Kelvin) temperature (1/temperature (K)). An Arrhenius plot is also used in analysing many chemical transformations and processes in which absolute rates are exponentially related to temperature and thus yield a straight-line relationship as illustrated here. Arrhenius equations have been applied to a whole range of plant functions from photosynthesis to changes in dry mass. Slope is characteristic of a particular reaction and varies between species, but in this example using clover there is little difference between warm and cool region leaves, indicating that the basic activation energies are similar. (c) Many subtropical species, such as mung bean, are chilling sensitive, growing poorly at temperatures well above freezing. An Arrhenius plot of growth (or a more specific biochemical reaction) is no longer linear throughout the whole temperature range. A steeper slope at low temperature implies that the energy of activation has increased and has become more limiting to plant function compared with values above that chilling threshold. At high temperatures the slope of the line is again reversed as enzymes are inactivated. Actual values will vary from one reaction to another and between species.

Arrhenius plots have also been used to analyse the response to temperature of individual organs and whole plants in order to determine critical temperatures for growth. In chilling-sensitive species, the slope of the Arrhenius plot becomes steeper at low temperature, indicating a change in enzyme–temperature relationships. Plant taxa which experience broader ranges of temperature during growth in their native habitats can have smaller Arrhenius temperature coefficients.

Membranes and their associated enzymes are likely to provide a key to many temperature responses in plants and this can be extended to frost damage where membrane destabilisation resulting from freeze-induced dehydration is a major factor in freezing injury.

CHILLING INJURY

Plants may develop physiological disorders when exposed to low but non-freezing temperatures. The German plant physiologist Molisch suggested the term 'chilling injury' as long ago as 1897 to describe this phenomenon. Symptoms of chilling injury can differ widely between species, but usually develop rapidly in plants native to tropical and subtropical climates and almost imperceptibly slowly in plants originating in cool temperate climates. Within the range of chilling temperatures, that is, from the temperature of the freezing point of the plant tissue up to about 13°C, the rate at which chilling injury develops intensifies with decreasing temperature and increasing duration.

Throughout history, people around the world have collected plants on their travels and taken them to other countries and continents. When tropical and subtropical plants collected from low altitudes have been taken to temperate climates they have had to be housed in protective structures for all or part of the year. In the case of Citrus species introduced into northern Europe in the sixteenth and seventeenth centuries from warmer southern climates, summer temperatures in countries such as France and Germany were mild enough to allow these trees to be grown outside in the summer.

At other times of the year, however, potted trees were moved into buildings known as orangeries for protection against the low temperatures. Similarly, during the late seventeenth century, a time when a great number of exotic chilling-sensitive palms, trees and foliage plants were introduced into temperate countries by plant collectors operating in the tropics and subtropics, these plants had to be protected from exposure to low temperatures at all times. Chilling-sensitive foliage plants such as Episcia spp., which are native to the Amazon basin, are killed within 30 min of being exposed to 1°C. Survival of such highly sensitive plants necessitated year-round protection from cold. This requirement was met by the invention of the heated glasshouse in the 1880s.

In modern agriculture, many species are cultivated outside their original microclimate. For example, avocado (Persea americana Mill.) was taken from tropical highlands in Mexico and is now grown in the temperate North Island of New Zealand and in inland Australia where nights are cold. When the new location has temperature minima below those of the region in which the plant evolved, problems of chilling injury can arise.

SYMPTOMS OF CHILLING INJURY

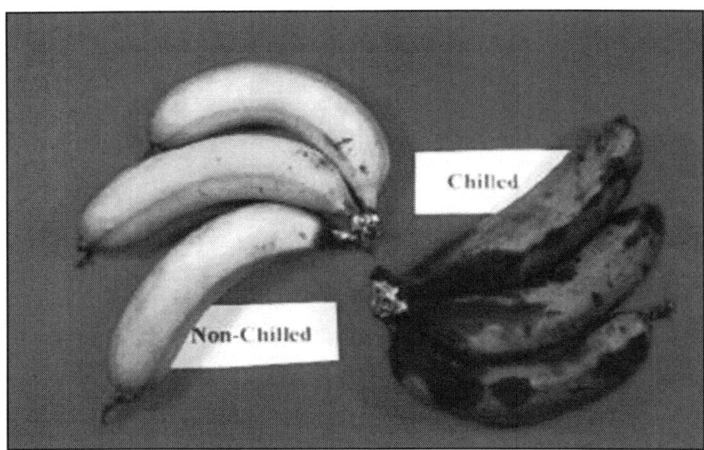

Fig. Cavendish Williams bananas harvested at the hard green stage from the same banana hand were either stored at 22°C for 11 d (non-chilled) or placed at 4°C for 7 d (chilled) before transfer to 22°C for 4 d. Compared to the non-chilled bananas, which gradually turned from green to yellow as they ripened, the chilled bananas failed to yellow and instead developed extensive peel blackening due to cell death. Slight peel blackening was evident when the bananas were removed from the 4°C treatment but greatly intensified at 22°C. To maintain the postharvest quality of Williams bananas, a crop which is worth approximately $180 million per annum to the Queensland economy, marketing authorities stipulate that the produce must not be cooled below 13°C during fruit storage, and for optimal fruit condition it should be kept in the temperature range 14–21°C. During the ripening of green bananas in the commercial ripening rooms at the Brisbane fresh produce market, the lowest temperature the fruit is allowed to equilibrate to is 14.5°C.

With annual crops, the time of greatest risk is likely to be early in a growth season, and especially during seedling establishment. Chilling injury to seedlings can show up as necrotic lesions on the young roots and shoots, with slowed growth and increased susceptibility to disease attack, and even death. Crops adversely affected by low temperatures during the establishment period take longer to mature and this in turn may mean that they are at risk to chilling temperatures towards the end of the growing season.

Not only does chilling exposure retard the growth and maturation of crops, but chilling damage to fresh produce during postharvest storage is also of economic importance. Chilling injury is a particular problem with fresh fruit, vegetables and flowers, because storage at temperatures low enough to retard tissue respiration is still the most effective postharvest method for extending the shelf life of produce. Even in produce-handling industries, there is often insufficient appreciation of requirements and behaviour of individual crops or even specific cultivars, and losses ensue. The time taken for symptoms to develop varies greatly and is influenced by a number of factors including genotype, cultivar, stage of maturity and preharvest growth conditions.

For example, with fruit stored at 1–2°C, it takes several months for chilling injury to develop in apples as a brown discolouration of the cortex, several weeks for the flesh of peaches to become mealy in texture, a number of days for avocados to show areas of grey discolouration in the flesh, and only a few hours for cucumbers to display tissue breakdown in the mesocarp. Obviously storage at 0–2°C is an excellent method for extending the storage life of apples, is moderately useful for peaches, but disastrous for cucumbers. Avocados are better kept at a higher storage temperature; the recommendation for extended storage of avocados is 6°C. Even this temperature is too low for tomato, another sub-tropical species susceptible to chilling injury. Ripe tomatoes should be stored cool, at 12°C or above, and not at refrigerator temperature.

Chilling injury becomes apparent in a variety of ways that vary with species and tissue. Visible symptoms are outcomes of physiological disorders, and may develop slowly during the actual chilling period, to be expressed more rapidly once the tissue is returned to warmer, non-chilling conditions. In defining the physiological basis of chilling injury, loss of membrane integrity emerges as a major symptom and much research has been directed to elucidating the chemical and physical nature of lipoprotein membranes of species having different climatic origins. Dr John Raison and other scientists at the former CSIRO Division of Food Research in Sydney provided evidence that physical changes occur in membranes of chilling-susceptible plants during low-temperature exposure. They suggested that the molecular ordering of membrane lipids is altered in the temperature range where chilling effects become apparent. In particular, lipid composition appears to determine how membranes respond to low temperatures.

Table. Common Symptoms of Chilling.

Leaves - visible symptoms	Wilting Chlorophyll loss and dead patches Increased susceptibility to pathogens
Fruit and vegetables – visible symptoms	Surface pitting and discolouration Internal tissue breakdown and browning Inhibition of ripening Increased attack by pathogens
Physiological symptoms	Decrease in photosynthesis Inhibited chlorophyll synthesis Inhibited development of flavour components in fruit Inhibited starch to sugar conversion in fruit Abnormal increases in some metabolites (ethanol, acetaldehyde, keto acids, alanine) Loss of membrane integrity and leakage of ions Post-chilling increases in respiration rate Abnormal patterns of ethylene production in fruit

Tropical species tend to have lipids with a higher proportion of saturated fatty acids (these are fatty acids such as palmitic acid which lack double bonds in their structure and therefore have higher melting points), while cool-climate plants tend to have more unsaturated fatty acids such as oleic acid. However, a consistent pattern of differences in lipid membrane composition between chilling-susceptible and chilling-resistant plants has yet to emerge and additional factors are likely to be involved. The physical nature of cell membranes remains an important point for research into chilling injury, but as yet no single physiological factor has been linked with plant susceptibility to chilling injury.

QUANTIFYING CHILLING INJURY

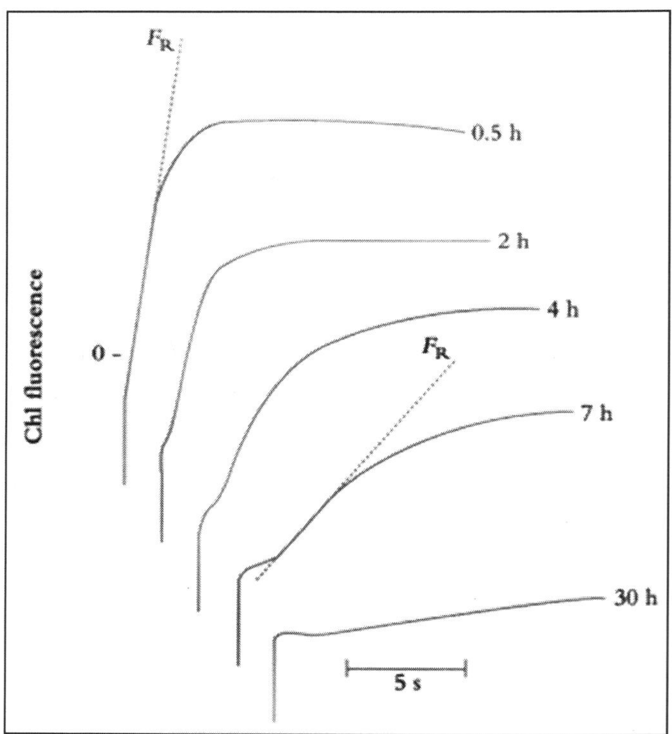

Fig. Changes with time in in vivo chlorophyll a fluorescence induction kinetics in response to chilling. In chilling studies, chlorophyll fluorescence has commonly been measured as the rate of rise in fluorescence yield induced by illuminating dark-adapted tissue (the F_R value). In isolated chloroplasts, a decrease in photosystem II activity is correlated with a decrease in F_R. This figure shows the progressive decline in F_R in a trifoliate bean (Phaseolus vulgaris L. cv. Canadian Wonder) leaflet chilled at 0°C in darkness. The first measurement of F_R was made after allowing 30 min at 0°C for temperature equilibration of the leaflet. The measurement was repeated on the same area of the leaflet at the times indicated on the figure. The longer the time of' chilling, the greater the degree of chilling injury, and the slower the rate of rise of F_R. The greater the chilling sensitivity of a cultivar, the shorter the time taken for a 50 per cent decrease in F_R.

One chilling response is a loss of membrane integrity. This loss has been measured by the extent of electrolyte leakage from cut pieces of chilled tissue. Other physiological methods used to quantify chilling injury include determinations of chlorophyll in seedlings kept at different temperatures, uptake of amino acids into pieces of chilled tissue, comparisons of fruit ripening rates and post-chilling measurements of plant growth and survival.

Pollen development is particularly sensitive to chilling temperatures, and assessments of pollen quality and anther length have been used to select specific genotypes of rice, tomato and other plants showing improved flower fertility under chilling conditions. However, though improved flower resistance to cold conditions is a desirable end-product in its own right, pollen resistance does not appear to be genetically linked with resistance of vegetative tissue to chilling stress. A particularly versatile physiological method for following chilling stress in photosynthetic tissues makes use of in vivo chlorophyll a fluorescence. When plants become chill injured, fluorescence yield decreases in response to effects of chilling on the photosynthetic system. The time taken for a 50 per cent decrease in fluorescence has been used to compare the relative chilling tolerances of different species and cultivars. Using chilled maize seedlings the extent of the decrease in fluorescence has been positively correlated with physiological and visual symptoms of chilling injury (Hetherington and Öquist 1988).

RANGES OF CHILLING TOLERANCE

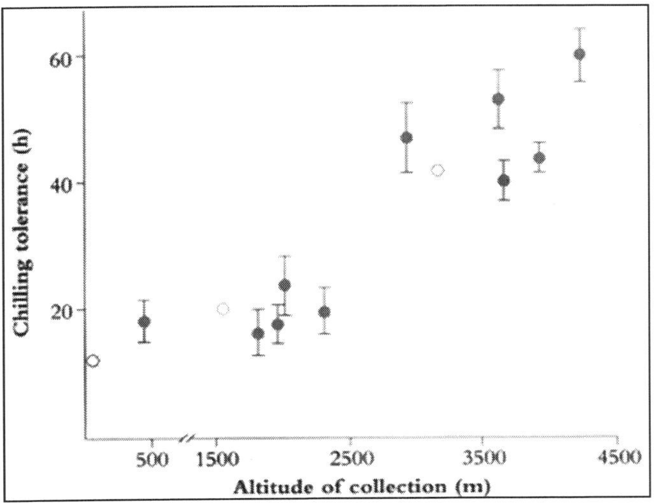

Fig. Increasing chilling tolerance of wild species of potato and tomato with increasing altitude implies an adaptation to that location. Each point represents a different species of Solanum (•), or variant of Lycopersicum hirsutum (O), originally collected at the altitude indicated in the graph and grown under similar field conditions at sea level. Chilling tolerance determined by the chlorophyll fluorescence method.

Plants are commonly reported in scientific literature as being either chilling sensitive or chilling tolerant. This can be a misleading simplification, because in practice when a range of plants are compared for chilling tolerance there is an almost continuous gradient of tolerance between the two extremes. Tolerance of an individual species is likely to be related to the lowest prevailing temperature in the original habitat of that particular species.

Progressive changes in chilling tolerance have also been documented in closely related plants naturally distributed over latitudinal or altitudinal clines. Growth at high altitudes and also at high latitudes represents a selection pressure for cold tolerance. Wild species of potato restricted to ecological niches within narrow spans of altitude in the Andean mountains of Peru and Ecuador provide a good example of how chilling tolerance changes along an altitudinal cline. Variants of wild tomato (Lycopersicum hirsutum L.) collected in the same regions as the potatoes behaved similarly, with chilling tolerance increasing with altitude.

Table. Plnats Exhibit a Wide Range of Chiling Tolerances.

Plant	Climatic adaptation	Chilling tolerance at 0°C (hours)*
Cucumber	Tropical annual	4.3
Maize	Tropical annual	8.4
Guava	Tropical perennial	23
Custard apple	Tropical perennial	31
Lime	Tropical perennial	74
Barley	Cool temperate annual	290
Pea	Cool temperate annual	385
Cumquat	Temperate perennial	620

Note:

* Time (h) for chlorophyll fluorescence (F_R) of leaves to decrease by 50 per cent at 0°C (Based on Smillie and Hetherington, 1990).

CHILL HARDENING

Differences between species imply a genetic basis to variation in chilling tolerance, and this adaptive response includes a further element, namely acclimation. Tolerance shown by individuals of a particular species can be increased by exposing plants to progressively lower but only marginally chilling temperatures. This process is variously called ‘acclimation’, ‘hardening’ or 'conditioning'. Chill hardening of plants appears to bring about changes in their metabolism, including an increase in unsaturation of membrane lipids, and allows plants to withstand subsequent and more severe stress. Such enhanced tolerance is generally lost within a few days of returning to warmer regimes, a process called 'dehardening'.

Fig. The ability to survive chilling stress is increased in chill-hardened maize seedlings. Unhardened, hardened and dehardened seedlings were chilled at 1°C for 3 d and then placed at 20/15°C for 3 d to allow symptoms of chilling injury to develop.

Maize seedlings provide an example of this reversible process. Hardening has a dramatic effect on survival of seedlings subsequently exposed to a chilling stress of 1°C for 3 d. Seedlings were first hardened for 4 d in a 15°C day, 5°C night regime. Dehardening was achieved by returning the hardened plants to the original growth regime (20°C day, 15°C for 2 d). Chilling tolerance monitored by chlorophyll fluorescence measurements increased three-fold as a result of this hardening process.

In conclusion, chilling injury can occur in the field and in postharvest storage, especially when crop or horticultural species have been introduced from warmer climates. Produce losses due to chilling injury are frequently overlooked because symptom expression often takes several days to develop after the produce is returned to a non-chilling environment. A combination of better management and introduction of chilling-tolerant genotypes can reduce postharvest losses.

PLANT RESPONSES TO COLD

Over 95 per cent of the Earth's surface experiences low temperatures below 5°C each year. Exposure to cold slows critical metabolic processes of biosynthesis and cellular maintenance, with low temperatures being important in determining the growth, productivity and distribution of plants. Most plants are capable of rapidly responding to cold. These responses can be fast acting, with rapid metabolic changes in existing tissues. The responses can also be longer-term, resulting from the accumulation of information by the plant over days or weeks, leading to developmental changes such as promotion of flowering, breaking of bud dormancy and formation of new leaves that are thicker and display less leaf area per unit leaf mass than their warm-grown counterparts. Biomass allocation is also sensitive to sustained cold, with long-term exposure to cold resulting in plants exhibiting reduced investment in shoots. These diverse responses to temperature demonstrate that a wide range of processes in plants, leading to diverse changes in whole plant metabolism and wide-ranging changes in gene expression and proteome composition, are controlled by thermal perception.

In following sections, responses of plants to low, non-freezing temperatures are discussed, with the focus being placed on how plants sense and respond to cold. Emphasis is placed on the mechanisms underpinning cold acclimation, defined as modifications of anatomy, physiology and metabolism in response to below optimum temperatures, which minimise irreversible freeze-damage and improves the fitness of the plant. Cold acclimation often results in plants exhibiting greater metabolic capacities than their warm-grown counterparts; as a result, in situ rates of metabolism can be similar in plants experiencing contrasting growth temperatures, when measured at their respective growth temperatures. Importantly, we focus on the recent advances in our understanding of how cold-tolerant plants acclimate to low, non-freezing temperatures.

COLD SENSING AND SIGNAL TRANSDUCTION

All living organisms perceive and process information from the environment at the cellular level through different kinds of receptors, which transfer the signal inside the cell and activate downstream signalling cascades. For example, in humans, 'thermoTRP' proteins are involved in thermosensing and are activated by the cool temperatures (10-23°C) and by compounds that cause a sensation of coolness, such as menthol or eucalyptol. However, to date no cold sensor has been found in any higher plant. Furthermore, it has been shown that cold-responsive gene expression in plants increases in response to gradual decreases in temperature, as well as to sudden shifts to cold temperatures, indicating that plants can sense and respond both to the magnitude and the rate of the temperature change, making it probable that there are multiple mechanisms present to detect and mediate plant thermal responses.

One of the more favoured candidates for sensing low temperature is a change in membrane fluidity (*i.e.* viscosity of the lipid bilayer of cell membranes). This reflects the fact that the structure and fluidity of lipid membranes is dependent on their composition and temperature. Low temperatures decrease the fluidity of lipid membranes as the hydrogen bonding between adjacent fatty acids is increased.

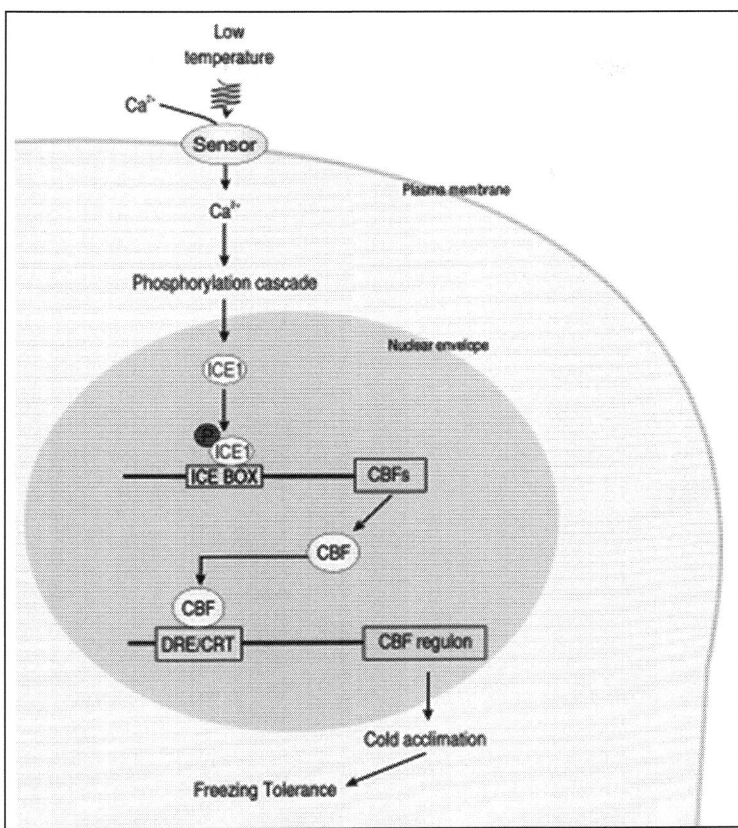

Fig. Simplified model illustrating cold sensing and the induction of stress gene expression during the early alarm stage of cold hardening in Arabidopsis. ICE1 is a constitutive, nuclear localized, transcription factor that is activated by phosphorylation and controls the expression of a range of secondary transcription factors, such as the CBF family of cold-induced transcription factors, that regulate the expression of the functional, delayed response genes. These delayed response genes, in turn, play important roles in cold acclimation and the acquisition of freezing tolerance in both herbaceous and woody perennial species.

The temperature at which membranes undergo a conversion from a fluid state (that exists at warm-moderate temperatures) to a gel-like state (that exists in membranes at low temperatures) is defined as the 'transition temperature' (T_m). T_m values as high as 15–20°C have been reported for some species, with increases in the unsaturated fatty acid content of membranes decreasing the T_m. Below the T_m, the function of membrane-bound enzymes and transport of substrates is often reduced owing to the gel-like state of the membrane.

The mechanism via which the decreases in membrane fluidity are linked to subsequent downstream responses is still unclear, but it is likely that fluidity-mediated increases in cytosolic concentrations of calcium ([Ca^{2+}]cyt) play a role. This is because decreases in fluidity are often associated with a fast, cold-induced increase in [Ca^{2+}]cyt, mainly as a result of Ca^{2+} transfer across the plasma membrane from the extracellular spaces. Ca^{2+} is integral to normal cell function and its signalling network is extensive.

Increases in [Ca^{2+}]cyt are thought play a role in the cold acclimation process, with [Ca^{2+}]cyt acting as a secondary messenger. The increase of [Ca^{2+}]cyt results from the activation of calcium channels primarily located in plasma membranes, and it has been suggested that the Ca^{2+} channels may either directly respond to cold or in some way sense changes in the plasma membrane or the cytoskeleton, triggering the molecular response to the change in temperature. The Ca^{2+} signal is decoded in plants by calmodulins (Ca^{2+}-binding messenger proteins) and Ca^{2+}-dependent protein kinases. Mitogen-associated protein kinase (MAPK) cascades participate in the signalling pathways of an array of abiotic stress responses and act as downstream transducers of the cold stress-induced Ca^{2+} signal. Cold Ca^{2+} signalling is affected by the circadian rhythm and depends partly on cell type and sub-cellular location, potentially allowing specific responses from this generic signal.

While Ca^{2+} is known to regulate the activity of many signalling components, including phospholipases and protein kinases, and lead to the induction of cold-induced gene expression or repression, many questions remain. For example, the identity of the Ca^{2+}-dependent protein kinases and the genes whose expression they control are generally unknown. Finally, while this represents one of the more intensively investigated options to explain thermal sensing and signal transduction, it is important to note that Ca^{2+}-signalling is not the only sensing mechanism, with Ca^{2+}-signalling often exhibiting extensive cross-talk with other signalling systems, including that of reactive oxygen species (ROS).

For example, an increase in [Ca^{2+}]cyt activates mitochondrial external NAD(P)H dehydrogenases, thus lowering the reductive power of the inter-membrane space and potentially reducing ROS formation. Such a combination of signalling networks most likely allows generic stress responses to occur in response to a variety of stimuli, leading to cross tolerance. Finally, Ca^{2+}-signalling events may take place at different locations within the cell (*e.g.* within the different organelles), will have different physiological causes (*e.g.* production of ROS in the chloroplast or mitochondria) and, as a result, will occur at different specific times following exposure to a chilling stress event.

CHANGES IN GENE EXPRESSION UNDERPINNING COLD ACCLIMATION

Once the change to cold temperatures is perceived and the signal transduced to the nucleus, there follows a substantial reprogramming of the transcriptome, proteome and metabolome of the plant cell (*i.e.* cold acclimation). The cold acclimation response is best understood in herbaceous annuals such as Arabidopsis thaliana where members of the C-repeat binding factor (CBF or DREB1) family of transcriptional activators, which bind the cis-element known as the C-repeat (CRT)/dehydration-responsive element (DRE), have been shown to control the transcription of a suite of genes that play important roles in the development of freezing tolerance.

Subsequent to their discovery in Arabidopsis, many CBF homologues have been found in both monocots and dicots, including perennial species such as aspen, birch and Eucalyptus. The CBF/DREB transcription factors are inducible by stress events but are not normally expressed under non-stress conditions. The plants response to stress therefore requires that there are components within the signal transduction pathway that are constitutively present but only active following the perception of the stress signal. For plant cold responses, a MYC-type bHLH (basic Helix-Loop-Helix) transcription factor, ICE1 (inducer of CBF expression 1), serves as an upstream activator of CBF expression.

Transcriptional profiling of the ice1 mutant showed impaired expression of 40 per cent of cold-regulated genes, suggesting ICE1 is one of the main regulators in the cold stress response, but also that it is not the only regulator. ICE1 is constitutively localized to the nucleus and induces CBF expression in a cold-dependent fashion. The ability of ICE1 to activate gene transcription in response to cold may be dependent on protein phosphorylation, making ICE1 a likely target of the MAPK cascades activated by the transient increase in $[Ca^{2+}]$cyt, although the signalling components responsible for this activation are yet to be discovered.

The accumulation of CBF transcripts and the activity of the CRT regulatory motif in Arabidopsis is also modulated by the presence and quality of light during cold stress, and it also appears to be mediated by the circadian gate; with extent to which CBF transcripts accumulate in response to low temperatures being dependent on the time of day plants are exposed to low temperatures. Temperatures are typically at their lowest point in the diurnal cycle at night, and the ability to anticipate this day-night rhythm may give plants the ability to anticipate night frosts and thus confer an adaptive advantage.

Entrainment of the circadian clock has been shown to be affected by temperature as well as by light and it appeared that this entrainment might be linked to the regulation of the cold stress response. Plants in temperate regions are also able to anticipate the onset of winter by detecting the shortening photoperiod. This light signalling, or measurement of the critical day-length, is mediated by the phytochromes and it is not surprising that sensing and signalling mechanisms controlling developmental processes such as bud set, seasonal senescence, growth cessation and dormancy overlap with cold acclimation. This potential for overlap is consistent with the observation that cold acclimation can be modified by the red and far-red light (R/FR) ratio. A decrease in R/FR ratio at the end of the day promotes cold acclimation, including increasing the expression of CBF genes; conversely, exposure to red pulses of light can undo this effect and a high R/FR reduces the accumulation of CBF-regulated gene expression.

Finally, it is clear that there are ICE/CBF-independent pathways that participate in cold acclimation (*e.g.* expressions of ZAT, HOS and ESK); however, evidence pointing to the identity of the components in these pathways is scarce. Furthermore, in field or natural conditions it is likely that the transcriptomic, proteomic and metabolomic changes in response to alterations in the plants thermal regime will be more complex than those revealed by controlled laboratory experiments. Responses to additional stressors such as light and drought will overlap and will introduce different signalling pathways, particularly those involving ABA, but also brassinosteriods and jasmonic acid. As result, constructing a spatiotemporal network linking these different components in order to understand how these factors come together to limiting plant growth, productivity and distribution, is going to be an enormous challenge.

COLD-INDUCED CHANGES IN MEMBRANE CHARACTERISTICS AND METABOLIC PROFILES

One of the most characteristic changes associated with cold acclimation are increases in the degree of saturation of membrane fatty acids, leading to greater membrane fluidity and an increase the functionality of membrane-bound substrate transporters and membrane-bound proteins at low temperatures. Moreover, cold-induced modifications in gene expression, subsequent changes in the abundance and activity of proteins, and alterations in other processes such as source-sink relationships and accumulation of metabolic intermediates, collectively lead to increases in the concentration of many metabolites. Thus, sustained exposure to cold leads to major modifications to the metabolome of plants.

Enhanced concentrations of soluble sugars are foremost amongst these, the most studied being the monosaccharides glucose and fructose, the disaccharide sucrose, and the trisaccharide raffinose; levels of each rise within a few hours of the onset of a cold treatment. Starch also accumulates in cold-exposed leaves. The increase in sucrose is particularly rapid, despite the fact that cold often has strong inhibitory effect on one of the enzymes (sucrose phosphate synthase, SPS) responsible for its synthesis. Levels of sucrose continue to rise during the first few days of cold acclimation, aided by a long-term increase in the abundance and activity of SPS. Moreover, overall sugar levels generally remain elevated in plants exposed to sustained cold; this accumulation reflects shifts in source:sink relationships, underpinned by changes in the balance between carbon uptake by photosynthesis, carbon use by catabolic processes (*e.g.* respiration) and carbon export to other parts of the plant. In some plants, increased concentrations of sugars may convey cryoprotective properties, reducing the incidence of membrane lesions and increasing survival during freezing.

Cold treatment also leads to the accumulation of a range of other metabolites, including compatible solutes (*i.e.* small, highly soluble molecules that are non-toxic at high concentrations). The most studied of these is proline, which accumulates dramatically following cold exposure. Proline appears to act as a cryoprotectant, as evidenced by the fact that freezing tolerant mutants of Arabidopsis accumulate proline to very high levels, even in the absence of a cold stimulus.

COLD RESPONSES OF PHOTOSYNTHESIS

Cold is known to markedly inhibit rates of photosynthesis, via both its kinetic effects on protein activity and membrane fluidity. Rapid increases in soluble sugars also contribute to an inhibition of photosynthesis through feedback inhibition and down-regulation of nuclear-encoded photosynthetic gene expression. Extended cold-treatment of pre-existing leaves can also result in photodamage; low temperature slows the consumption of ATP and NADPH by the Calvin cycle and the resulting over-reduction of the photosynthetic electron transport chain may cause oxidative damage to the light-harvesting machinery. A further (and important) limitation is the exhaustion of chloroplastic orthophosphate (Pi) required for ATP regeneration and maintenance of the thylakoid membrane proton gradient, which in turn drives the chloroplastic electron transport chain. Calvin cycle turnover also decreases (explaining the observed decline in carbon assimilation) as this relies on ATP to drive the regeneration of ribulose-1,5-bisphosphate (RuBP) reduction.

Recovery of photosynthesis occurs during cold acclimation via an increase in the export of chloroplastic triose phosphates across an antiporter that exchanges these Calvin cycle intermediates for cytosolic Pi. As Pi is produced in the cytosol during sucrose synthesis, the recovery of sucrose metabolism via increases in the abundance and activity of SPS and cytosolic fructose 1,6 bisphosphatase (cFBPase) is an important step in the restoration of photosynthetic function during cold acclimation, and has also been suggested to be partly responsible for the decrease in sensitivity to photoinhibition that occurs following cold acclimation. Also contributing to the recovery of photosynthesis is the increase in the abundance and activity of several proteins directly involved in photosynthesis.

The photosynthetic phenotype of cold-developed leaves has been suggested to be distinct from that of pre-existing leaves. Cold-developed leaves exhibit marked physical changes compared to warm-grown leaves. Leaves developed in the cold tend to be thicker, with a higher leaf mass per area and higher nitrogen and protein concentrations than leaves developed at warmer temperatures.

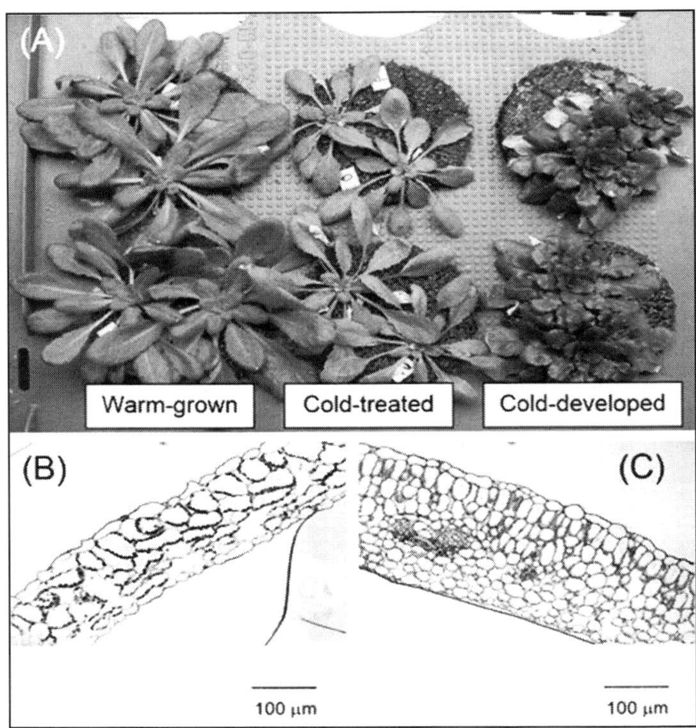

Fig. (A). Warm-grown (left), 10-day cold-treated (centre) and cold-developed (right) shoot phenotypes of Arabidopsis thaliana. Warm-grown plants experienced 25/20°C day/night temperatures, whereas cold-treated and cold-developed plants were exposed to constant 5°C. (B) and (C) show transverse sections of representative warm-grown and cold-developed leaves, respectively.

Cold developed leaves can accumulate soluble sugars without the suppression of carbon assimilation typically associated with an abundance of photosynthates, and the transcript and protein abundance of most of the Calvin cycle enzymes have been found to be greatly increased in these leaves. The abundance of ribulose-1,5-bisphosphate carboxylase oxygenase (Rubisco) increases, whereas the other Calvin cycle enzymes tend to decline with cold acclimation relative to Rubisco. Further recovery of sucrose synthesis in cold developed leaves assists in the recovery from cold stress and photoinhibition; SPS transcript abundance, protein and the activity of the enzyme increases relative to the Calvin cycle and starch synthesis during acclimation.

Associated with the increase in photosynthetic capacity in cold developed leaves is a change in electron transport capacity relative to carboxylation capacity, and an alleviation of triose phosphate utilization (TPU) limitation.

Alleviation of TPU limitation during acclimation to low temperatures has been ascribed to increasing activity and transcription of SPS and cFBPase, and the redistribution of inorganic phosphate between cellular compartments. The net result of these changes is an increase in photosynthetic capacity in newly developed, relative to pre-existing, leaves. This phenomenon may therefore optimise the function of these new leaves to their environment.

INCREASED RESPIRATORY CAPACITY IN COLD ACCLIMATED PLANTS

For over a century, it has been known that short-term exposure to cold in measurements lasting minutes to a few hours results in reduced rates of respiratory CO_2 release and O_2 uptake. When measured over a range of moderate temperatures (*e.g.* 15-25°C), the relationship between respiration and temperature is near exponential, with respiration exhibiting short-term Q_{10} values near 2.0 (*i.e.* respiration increases two-fold for every 10°C increase in temperature). However, when viewed over a wider range of temperatures, the shape of the temperature response tends to be more dynamic, reflecting the fact that the functional form of the short-term temperature response curve of respiration departs significantly from a simple exponential. As a result, short-term Q_{10} values typically increase with short-term decreases in measuring, commonly reaching values >3.0 at temperatures in the 0-10°C range.

Theory and empirical evidence suggests that the increasing temperature-sensitivity of respiration as measurement temperatures decrease is linked to shifts in the control exerted by substrate limitations at moderate-high temperature to maximum enzyme activity at low temperature. This is either because of the inhibitor effect of cold on potential enzyme activity per se (both in soluble and membrane-bound compartments) and/or limitations on the function of enzymes embedded in membranes at temperatures below the T_m.

At moderately high temperatures (*e.g.* 25°C), respiratory flux is less limited by enzymatic capacity because of increases in the V_{max} [*i.e.* maximal flux through the respiratory system as a whole, or parts thereof, in the absence of other limiting factors (*e.g.* substrate supply and adenylates)] of enzymes in soluble and membrane-bound compartments; here, respiration is likely to be limited by substrate availability and/or adenylates (in particular the ratio of ATP to ADP and the concentration of ADP per se, which are in turn influenced by the demand for respiratory energy by growth and cellular maintenance processes). Increased leakiness of membranes at temperatures above the T_m (particularly at high temperatures) could further contribute to substrate limitations. Changes in growth temperature that last several days can also alter the short-term Q_{10}, with Q_{10} values also varying seasonally in some ecosystems.

A further factor that could contribute to variability in the sensitivity of respiration to low temperatures is the extent to which cold differentially suppresses activity by the two terminal pathways via which electrons are transferred to oxygen in the inner mitochondrial membrane [*i.e.* the phosphorylating cytochrome oxidase pathway (COP) versus the non-phosphorylating alternative oxidase pathway (AOP)].

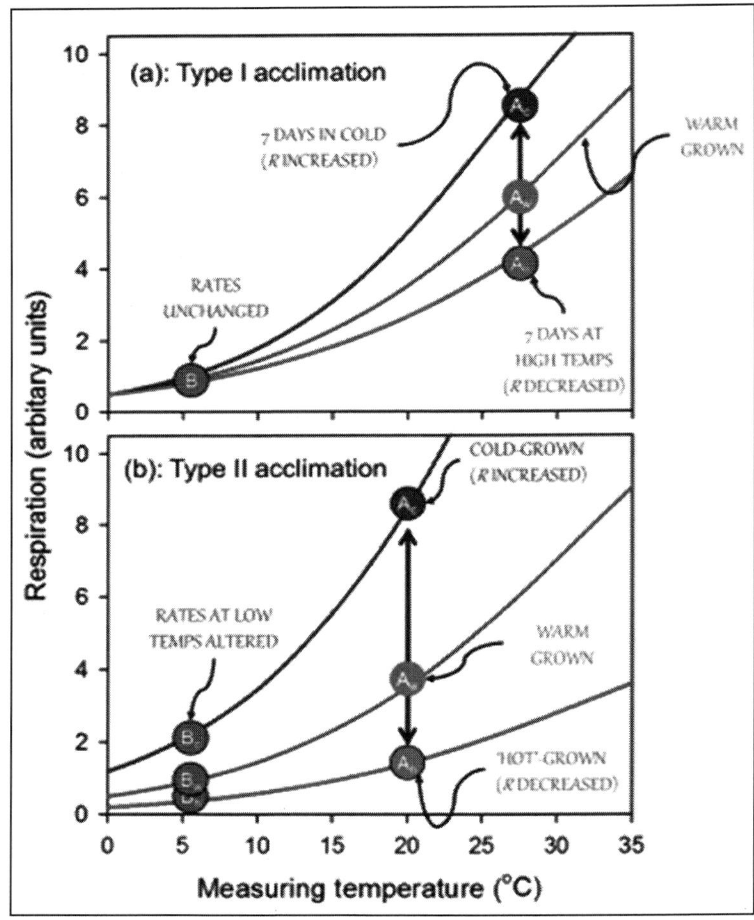

Fig. Theoretical examples of two types of respiratory thermal acclimation: (a) Type I and (b) Type II. (a) in Type I acclimation, changes in growth temperature result in changes in the Q_{10} of respiration with no change in the value of respiration at low temperatures ('B') (*i.e.* the intercept remains unchanged). Rather, changes in respiration are only observed at moderate to high temperatures ('A_c'>'A_w'>'A_h'). Shifting to low growth temperatures for an extended period typically results in an increase in the Q_{10}, whereas the Q_{10} decreases following shift to high growth temperatures. (b) Type II acclimation results in changes in respiration at both low and high temperatures (*i.e.* the overall elevation of the temperature response curve is affected). No changes in the Q_{10} of respiration are necessary for Type II acclimation. Type II acclimation will result in a greater degree of homeostasis of respiration than Type I acclimation.

To date, results from studies with intact tissues and isolated mitochondria from a range of plant species and organs have yielded conflicting conclusions, with some studies suggesting that the AOP might be less sensitive to cold that the COP, while others have reported the opposite or little difference between the temperature sensitivity of the two pathways. Thus, at this stage it is unclear to what extent differential temperature sensitivities of the AOP and COP play a role in influencing variations in the short-term Q_{10} of plant respiration.

With sustained exposure to cold, respiratory rates (when measured at a low temperature) start to recover quickly (within hours), and continue to increase as the plant acclimates. Often, the capacity for respiratory enhancement is relatively low in pre-existing tissues; here, acclimation is associated with a change in the rate of respiration primarily at moderate to high measuring temperatures, with little or no change in respiration at low measuring temperatures (*i.e.* Type I acclimation; reflecting a change in the availability of respiratory substrate and/or degree of adenylate restriction of respiration.

Changes in gene expression may also occur, but are not essential for the overall change in respiratory flux. In other cases, acclimation is associated with an increase in the rate of respiration over a wide range of measurement temperatures ('Type II acclimation'). Type II acclimation is likely associated with temperature-mediated changes in respiratory capacity that can be maximally realized through growth of new tissues with altered morphology and biochemistry. Increases in respiratory capacity in the cold appears to be altered as a result of increases in the density of mitochondria mitochondrial number per unit volume of tissue and/or amount of total protein invested in the respiratory chain.

The observation that mitochondrial density is higher in in situ alpine than lowland plants further supports the notion that an increase in mitochondrial number is a driving force behind increased respiratory rate in cold-acclimated leaves. Intermediate cases of acclimation (*i.e.* between Types I and II) are likely, particularly in individual plants that experience long-term changes in temperature depending on the extent to which respiratory capacity is altered in pre-existing and newly formed leaves and roots. Another characteristic of acclimation (particularly Type II acclimation) is that it can result in respiratory homeostasis [*i.e.* identical rates of R in plants grown and measured in contrasting temperatures.

Previous work examining the impact of sustained exposure to cold on respiration has suggested that the AOP might play a critical role in the cold acclimation response. In some studies, alternative oxidase transcript abundance, protein abundance, and capacity have all been shown to increase following growth in the cold. In addition, there are examples where in vivo partitioning of electrons to the AOP has been shown to increase following sustained exposure to cold. Such studies have led to the proposal that cold induced increases in AOP activity function to prevent the over-reduction of the mitochondrial electron transport chain, and thus the accumulation of ROS, at low temperatures.

However, in reality the response of the AOP to cold may be more complex. For example, in some cases, the recovery of AOP activity in cold acclimated plants is transient (*e.g.* reaching a maximum after few days of sustained cold treatment), while others have reported that re-establishment of respiratory flux in the cold is associated not with an increase in AOP capacity, but rather with an increase in energy-conserving COP capacity. Such variability in the AOP response suggests that different plant species employ different strategies for coping with cold.

Finally, consideration should be given to the fact that plant mitochondria possess two additional non-phosphorylating bypasses of the mitochondrial electron transport chain: the alternative NAD(P)H dehydrogenases (NDHs) and the uncoupling proteins (UCPs). Both of these proteins function to reduce the extent to which mitochondrial electron transport is coupled to the production of ATP.

The NDHs oxidize matrix and cytosolic NAD(P)H, but do not contribute to proton pumping, while the UCPs facilitate proton flux back through the inner mitochondrial membrane, thereby partially dissipating the proton gradient across this membrane. Both the NDHs and the UCPs are thought to play a role in preventing oxidative stress, with sustained cold treatment increasing transcripts for both types of proteins. Moreover, there is growing evidence that transcript levels of these alternative respiratory bypasses exhibit coordinated increases in abundance following sustained cold treatments. Collectively, the above suite of modifications in metabolic processes contribute to the ability of many plants to cope with sustained exposure to low temperatures.

FROST AND FREEZING INJURY

Ice melts at 0°C, and an equilibrium mixture of ice and water has traditionally provided a temperature reference for thermocouples. Ice thawing in pure water will maintain a temperature of 0°C, but if instead of allowing ice to thaw, heat is extracted steadily from a body of water, then ice does not reform at 0°C. Instead, the water will remain liquid, and will supercool until some nucleation event occurs. A tiny particle of ice, or even vibration in the presence of dust particles, is usually sufficient to trigger ice formation together with an abrupt release of heat (latent heat of fusion). $T_F - T_N$ represents supercooling, and the degree to which T_F is less than zero (freezing-point depression) relates to the amount of solute present in solution. Osmotic pressure, vapour-pressure depression and elevation of boiling point are similarly related to the amount of solute present (referred to collectively as colligative properties of solutions).

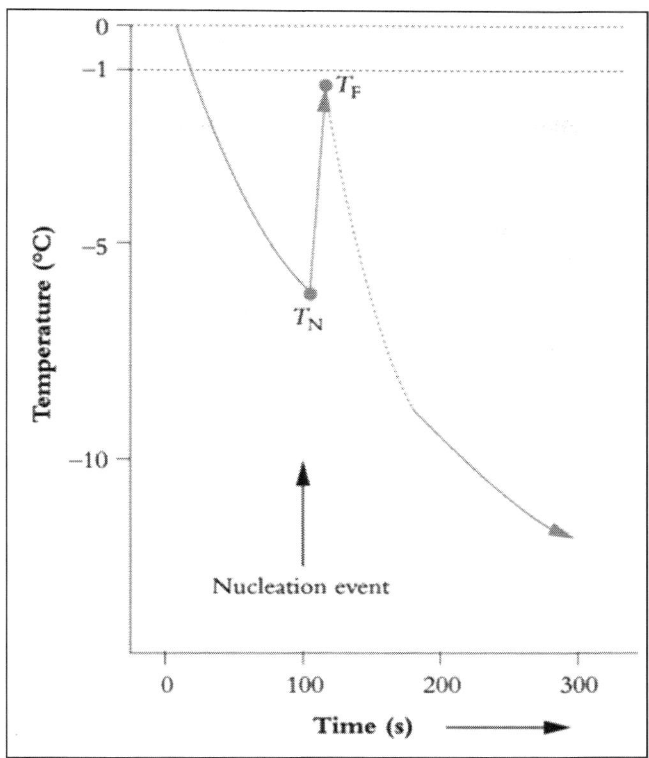

Fig. A notional cooling curve for an aqueous solution. As heat is extracted steadily, solution temperature falls below 0 °C, and water molecules, now in an unstable state, supercool to around -5 °C. A nucleating event occurs at temperature T_N, and heat is released as ice forms (latent heat of fusion), resulting in a sudden increase in temperature to T_F. The extent of freezing-point depression (0 – T_N °C) also serves as a measure of osmotic pressure.

Highly purified water can be supercooled to about –40°C, and ice will form spontaneously, but such conditions do not apply in plants because water is not absolutely pure. Instead tissue water is in contact with cell surfaces and invariably holds solutes in solution and colloids in suspension. This aids ice nucleation.

PHYSICS AND PHYSIOLOGY

During a frost episode in nature, plants experience a sequence of events similar to that summarised. Tissue water supercools, and cell sap freezing point is depressed by osmotically active material. Moreover, plants are also equipped with ice nucleating agents that can be of either plant or bacterial origin (*e.g.* Pseudomonas syringae). As with solutions, formation of ice in plants is accompanied by a release of heat. This exothermic response can be detected by sensitive infrared thermography, and has been used to trace ice propagation during a freezing event in leaves and shoots.

When plants experience a frost, ice initially forms within intercellular spaces (apoplasm) where solute concentration is least. Water potential in that region is immediately lowered and water molecules migrate from symplasm to apoplasm across plasmalemma membranes and towards regions of ice crystallisation. Water potential in the apoplasm will decrease by about 1.2 MPa per degree below 0°C, so that an apoplasm at –4°C will have a water potential of around –4.8 MPa (*i.e.* equivalent to an osmotic pressure twice that of seawater), which will dehydrate the symplasm. As one positive trade-off of the high solute concentration, the symplasm is less likely to freeze. In addition, plasmalemma membranes discourage entry of ice crystals that might otherwise seed ice crystal formation within the symplasm. Nevertheless, partial dehydration does perturb cell biochemistry due to concentration of metabolites, and the accompanying shrinkage of cells and organelles generates structural tensions.

In frost-sensitive material, cell disruption follows the course outlined above, which unfolds over about 3°C on a cooling curve. Membrane integrity might be lost at around –4°C as apoplasm ice formation ruptures membranes. Intracellular freezing ensues at around –7°C and is inevitably lethal due to the combined effects of membrane injury, symplasm dehydration and protein denaturation.

Tissue damage following freezing can be demonstrated by a loss of membrane integrity, metabolite leakage and failure to achieve either plasmolysis or deplasmolysis. Solutions bathing frozen/thawed tissue thus show a sudden increase in electrical conductivity according to freezing damage, and that value then serves as a reliable assay for comparative frost tolerance. For example, population screening based on metabolite leakage has enabled breeding for improved frost tolerance in Eucalyptus nitens for plantation forestry.

Leaves on temperate plants often need to accommodate ice formation, and Rhododendron provides such an example. Frozen leaves appear wilted, but regain their normal turgid appearance following thawing. Camellia leaves behave similarly. They take on a semi-transparent appearance when frozen, but recover without damage when thawed. In both cases, their altered physical appearance at low temperature is due to formation of a frostblaze, that is, a lens of ice crystals that forms between layers of tissue that are readily cleaved. Ice localised in this way is rendered harmless, and is lost easily on thawing.

Frost hardiness is a dynamic and composite property of plant cells involving cell size, wall thickness, osmotic pressure of cell sap and membrane properties, all of which can feature in either delaying onset or diminishing adverse consequences of ice formation. In any plant, organs that are growing rapidly are frost sensitive, and this is especially the case with early spring growth. Frost hardiness is thus least during the growing season, but increases during autumn and reaches a peak in winter with acclimation to low temperatures. This is an adaptive feature of perennial plants that is attuned to seasonal necessity. Moreover, the extent of this hardening process is heritable, and requires low temperature for onset and maintenance.

Return to milder conditions can lead to dehardening with disastrous consequences for horticulture when an early spring temperature increase is followed by an unseasonal period of cold nights. Frost prevention then becomes crucial for reducing damage to buds, flowers or fruitlets. Susceptibility to low temperatures is dependent on stage of morphological development of plant organs. As spring temperatures increase, fruit develop into buds, flowers then fruitlets with a concomitant increase in susceptibility to cold temperatures. In many fruit trees, buds emerging from dormancy can tolerate temperatures as low as -16 to -17°C, while at full bloom critical temperatures for 10 per cent kill of buds after 30 minutes of exposure -2 to -3°C are -1.5 to 3.0°C. To prevent frost damage, growers generally commence frost protection measures at least 1°C above the 10 per cent critical temperature

ALLEVIATING FROST DAMAGE IN HORTICULTURE

Radiation frosts are common in some horticultural regions of Australasia caused by high radiation losses from earth to sky on still calm nights. The air at ground level becomes chilled by contact with radiating surfaces and drains downslope to low lying areas to form 'frost pockets' or 'frost lakes' that are commonly 5°C colder than the surrounding countryside. One related outcome, especially on calm mornings, is formation of a temperature inversion.

Upper layers of air (30–50 m above ground) remain warmer (5–15°C) than the air at ground and tree level. Under these conditions, static wind machines can be used to drive the warmer air down into the crop and over the soil surface, displacing the cold air and countering radiation heat losses. Given a consistent layer of warm air within reach of these fans, one wind machine every 5–7 ha will protect an orchard against temperatures down to about –3°C. A combination of clean burning oil heaters plus wind machines is even more effective. Helicopters are often used as mobile wind machines that move constantly to zones of low temperatures.

An alternative but remarkably effective method of alleviating frost damage relies upon the latent heat of freezing. Stored irrigation water, either from wells or ponds, is typically around 10°C, and as it cools on irrigated surfaces each gram of water will release about 10 calories of heat. On top of that, the latent heat of fusion adds a further 80 calories. In effect, a thousand litres of water supplies as much heat by this means as complete combustion of 12 L of oil.

The photograph shows both water and ice phases present on trees. While ice is continuing to form, plant tissues so encased will remain at 0°C, just above freezing point for plant tissues. This is above the threshold temperature for frost damage to sensitive buds, blossom and fruitlets. Overhead sprinklers are thus used with good effect to prevent frost damage, but application rate has to be closely controlled. Too little water and plants freeze, too much water and orchards become waterlogged, thereby exchanging one damaging condition for another. Application rates between 3 and 8 mm h^{-1} will generally suffice to prevent freezing damage to crops at air temperatures down to –6-8°C. Overhead sprinkling is not so effective in strong advective frost conditions, where cold winds cause evaporative cooling, thus reducing sprinkler efficacy.

COLD-INDUCED PHOTOINHIBITION AND TREE REGENERATION

Fig. Snow gums (Eucalyptus pauciflora) in the Gudgenby Valley (sub-alpine region of southeastern Australia) are subject to frost for about 200 d each year. Exposed juvenile trees have to endure low temperature and the strong sunlight of early morning to survive.

Re-establishment of eucalypts in open pastures of the New South Wales tablelands is problematic, with up to 80 per cent of young trees failing to survive beyond three years.

An urgent need for landscape restoration following deforestatation and overgrazing of these areas has become widely recognised, and a successful strategy for tree establishment is crucial to that process. Photoinhibition of young trees at low temperature was soon recognised as a factor in those early losses (Ball et al. 1991). The first clue that sunlight × temperature was an issue came from two chance observations of unusual patterns in seedling establishment.

The first observation concerns mountain beech (Nothofagus solandri). This is a dominant canopy tree in subalpine forests of New Zealand, and patterns of seedling regeneration around isolated trees on the Waimakariri floodplain are highly characteristic. While 95 per cent of young seedlings occur beneath the canopy of a parent tree, they are not distributed randomly. Rather, they tend to cluster on the western side, and 65 per cent occur in a narrow sector between 165°S and 285°S. Wind effects on seed dispersal are not responsible because prevailing winds blow in the opposite direction; however, seedlings on the south to western sides of parent trees are protected from direct sunlight all day throughout winter, and from morning sun in spring and early summer. The second observation concerns a similar asymmetric pattern of regenerating seedlings the occurs under isolated trees of snow gum (Eucalyptus pauciflora) growing along the Orroral Valley in southeastern Australia. In this case, tiny seedlings probably establish randomly around a parent tree during favourable seasons, but are subsequently culled by adverse conditions to produce this now familiar pattern of seedling regeneration.

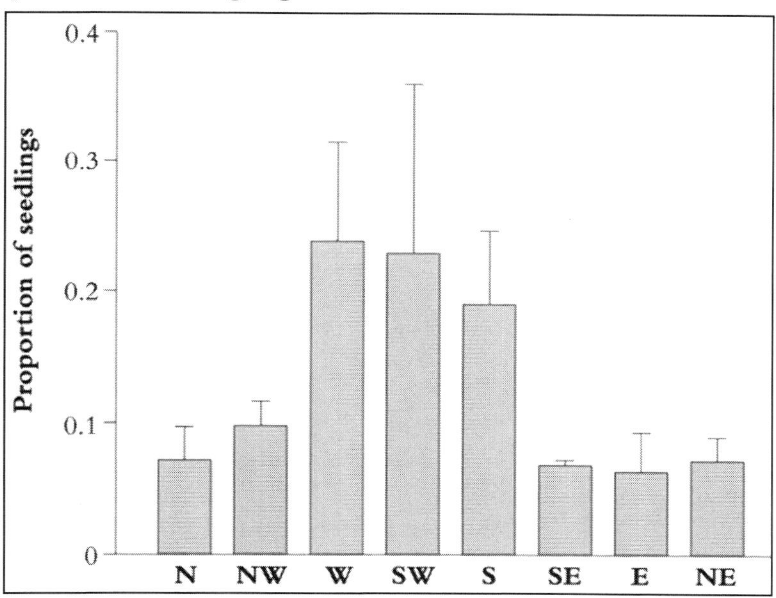

Fig. Relative distribution of seedlings in relation to geographical bearing around adult trees of mountain beech on the Waimakariri floodplain.

In both cases, the combination of intense cold and strong sunlight seemed to be proving adverse to seedling survival because the asymmetry in seedling establishment roughly coincided with morning shadows cast by parent trees. Chris Holly tested this idea with artifical shelters on Eucalyptus polyanthemos seedlings in an open pasture. Seedlings were planted either on open ground or in individual shelters consisting of open-topped cylinders made from one of three types of shadecloth transmitting 30 per cent, 50 per cent or 70 per cent sunlight. Air temperatures inside and outside of these shelters differed by less than 2°C so that irradiance was the major factor that differed between treatments. During winter, leaves became photoinhibited as indicated by a loss in variable fluorescence (F_v/F_m fromin vivo chlorophyll a fluorescence measured in situ). The extent of this loss in variable fluorescence (measured pre-dawn) was in direct proportion to treatment irradiance. Seedlings grew only slowly during winter, and most severely photoinhibited plants grew the slowest. Correlations between growth and photoinhibition as measured during winter persisted into spring even though pre-dawn F_v/F_m made a substantial recovery in all plants.

Spring growth of Eucalyptus polyanthemos appears to be adversely affected by cold-induced photoinhibition over winter. A loss in photosynthetic effectiveness reduces carbon gain during spring, and recovery presumably extends over many weeks, hence a persistence of slower growth despite recovery in F_v/F_m.

In practical terms, establishment of eucalypt seedlings in frost-prone areas benefits from a reduction in irradiance over winter. By analogy, cold-induced photoinhibition could also be responsible for patterns of seedling establishment under parent trees as noted originally.

HIGH TEMPERATURE STRESS

Exposure to excessive temperatures during development limits the yield of many of the world's major crops, especially in the tropics. Increasing global temperatures over the last three decades have resulted in significantly reduced yields in many crops. In addition to the general warming, a predicted increase in the occurrence of heatwaves is likely to result in further yield losses (Long and Ort 2010). Increasing global temperatures and increasingly frequent heatwaves are likely to have similarly negative effects on natural systems in the tropics and subtropics.

In daylight hours leaf temperatures are often higher than that of the surrounding air, as the canopy absorbs incident solar radiation. Overheating occurs when heat dissipation from the canopy is unable to keep pace with the thermal energy absorbed. This typically occurs when incident radiation is high and transpirational cooling is low. Even at temperate latitudes, such conditions often develop at midday when solar radiation peaks and soil water reserves are depleted. In warm, dry environments heat stress can persist for prolonged periods. As heat stress is frequently encountered in combination with water deficit and excess irradiance, it can be difficult to disentangle the effects of the three factors. Nonetheless, there is a distinct set of injuries and plant responses that are associated with heat stress.

The effect of heat stress on staple crops like wheat can be severe. The impact varies depending on the developmental stage of the plants, with the most vulnerable stage being flowering. High temperatures shorten the duration of growth of both the leaves and the grains, accelerating their development and thus limiting the ability of the plant to accumulate the carbohydrate necessary for grain growth. In addidtion, heat stress before flowering can cause floret sterility, causing yield losses due to reduced grain number. This effect is most acute when heat occurs at or just after pollen meiosis, when carbohydrate supply to the developing pollen grains appears most critical. Grain size in heat stressed plants can be severely reduced, predominately from a reduction in starch, which makes up most of the mass of the grain.

Wheat (a temperate C_3 species) produces its most grain at temperatures below 26°C; and its yield is reduced at higher temperatures. Yet in most grain-growing areas in the southern hemisphere, and in Meditteranean climates in the northern hemisphere, temperatures increase steadily during the growing season, and brief periods above 30 °C often occur during the grain-filling period. In many arid countries mean day temperatures can easily exceed wheat's high temperature threshold during much of the growing season and so heat stress can significantly reduce crop yield by accelerating plant senescence, diminishing seed number and final seed weight. Where vegetation is sparse, maximum daytime temperatures occur at the soil surface where exposed soil absorbs solar radiation and quickly warms above ambient. Under such conditions soil temperatures can exceed 50°C. Exposed soil is a particular problem when planting crops in warm regions where the dark, moist soil surface can reach high temperatures and severely inhibit germination and seedling emergence

PLANT RESPONSE TO HIGH TEMPERATURE

Plants have developed a range of mechanisms to keep tissues from overheating (heat avoidance) or to prevent inhibition and injury where high temperatures occur (heat tolerance). A key aspect of tolerance to heat stress is the degree to which a tissue exposed to moderately high temperatures can acclimate in a way that improves its ability to function at higher temperatures (hardening or acquired thermotolerance).

Table. The optimal, maximum and lethal temperature for a range of important physiological process in wheat (a temperate C_3 species) and maize (a subtropical C_4 species). Data from nuerous authors cited in porter and gawith, 1999; stone, 2001; bewley et al. 2006. See Larcher (2003) for a comparison of lethal temperatures across a range of ecosystems.

	Wheat			Maize		
	Optimal	Maximum	Lethal	Optimal	Maximum	Lethal
Germination	15-25	< 35		30	>40	
Seedling growth	20	<37	47	25	>40	52
Net photosynthesis	15-30	<40		30-40	>40	
Fertilisation (pollen viability)	20	<30	30	28	<35	35
Grain Filling (kernel mass)	20	<35		20-35	>40	

The optimum, maximum and lethal temperature for a range of processes in wheat and maize. Optimum temperatures for plant metabolism vary between species, reflecting the thermal range found in the environment in which they evolved or were selected. Metabolic processes in plants typically have an optimum below 30°C and temperatures above 40°C are considered a stress.

The degree of damage from heat stress is mediated by the intensity, duration and rate of change in temperature as well as by the plant's developmental stage and growing conditions prior to exposure. For most species, actively growing tissue is damaged by brief exposure to temperatures above 45°C, while prolonged exposure can result in fatal injury. Temperatures between 30-40°C can be termed moderately high temperatures and result in reversible inhibition of metabolism (moderate heat stress). Temperatures above 40°C can be termed very high temperatures as they result in irreversible or prolonged inhibition of metabolism.

The effect of heat stress is often measured by exposing tissue to high temperatures for a short period (typically 0.5-1 hour) and measuring the response.

This can be termed high temperature shock (heat shock). In addition to identifying the maximum threshold temperature above which metabolic activity ceases, heat shock experiments can determine the lethal temperature above which irreversible injury occurs. Although lethal temperatures rarely occur when plants are grown within their native range, determining the lethal temperature is a useful method for assessing a species tolerance to high temperature in general. Species adapted and/or acclimated to high temperature environments can withstand temperatures well above 40°C. Extreme examples of tolerance to high temperature are found in the desert succulents, such as the prickly pear cacti (Opuntia spp.) which can survive short term exposure to 70°C.

HEAT AVOIDANCE

Plants can avoid overheating by regulating the components of their energy budget. The amount of solar radiation intercepted can be reduced using specialised leaf and canopy arrangements.

The vertical leaves and canopy architecture of many eucalyptus trees are arranged to minimise the area of the canopy exposed to direct sun (as a consequence they cast a relatively small shadow). Other species, such as dragon trees (Dracaena spp.) and some acacia trees, adopt an umbrella-like form to raise the canopy above the warm ground and shade the trunk. Some species employ leaf movements, rolling their leaves or changing leaf orientation so that the surfaces are never parallel to the sun. Leaf movements are particularly common in legumes (Fabaceae).

Fig. Thermal images showing midday leaf surface temperature of two savanna sedges, Lagenocarpus guianensis (left) and Lagenocarpus rigidus (right), growing in close proximity at a forest edge. The accompanying photograph indicates the areas used for the thermal images. The white areas in the thermal image represent dead leaves which are above the maximum temperature range. Replicated measurements showed the midday leaf surface temperatures were significantly different ($P < 0.001$) between the two species. The greater potential for 'canopy temperature depression' allows L. rigidus to grow in the open savanna, while L. guianensis finds its range restricted to the shaded savanna edges where heat and light are less overbearing.

The amount of incident radiation absorbed by a leaf can be reduced by increasing the reflectance of the leaf surface. Leaf hairs and scales scatter the incident radiation such that the leaf appears silvery white, *e.g.* the sagebrush (Artemisia tridentata) and the brittlebush (Encelia farinosa) common in many arid areas of North America. Pubescence is common in hot, dry environments, where as well as reflecting solar radiation, leaf hairs form a thick boundary layer reducing water loss (although this also reduces the potential for transpirational cooling). Such adaptations are so common among plants of warm arid and high altitude regions that these habitats can be seen to form a 'silvery landscape'. Waxes deposited on the epidermis perform a similar function, preventing water loss and forming an irregular surface to increase reflectance.

The amount of heat lost can also be regulated by favouring small or divided leaves that reduce the boundary layer allowing for greater convective cooling as well as more effective transpiration. Tropical savanna plants with smaller leaves are better able to keep cool in the full glare of the equatorial sun, while species with larger leaves are restricted to areas shaded by tree canopies. Small leaves are also a distinguishing feature of desert shrubs and trees.

An increase in air temperature reduces the relative humidity (increases the vapour pressure deficit), which increases the evaporative demand and the transpiration rate. Where water supply is restricted the stomata will close causing transpiration rate to fall, resulting in an increase in leaf temperature. Where water supply is not limiting, transpirational cooling is an effective form of heat avoidance. Transpirational cooling often reduces leaf temperatures to 5°C below ambient, while temperatures can be reduced by 15°C in extreme cases.

This contrasts with plants growing in arid conditions where leaf temperatures may be 15°C or more above ambient. In agricultural environments, where high temperatures are not necessarily combined with water deficit, cultivars showing high stomatal conductance have been shown to be more resistant to heat stress. In fact, stomatal conductance measurements along with direct measurements of 'canopy temperature depression' are among the most valuable parameters for selecting cultivars for growth in warm environments. The recent application of infrared thermometers to examine canopy temperatures has provided a valuable method for directly measuring heat avoidance.

HEAT INJURY AND INHIBITION

Heat stress affects plants through three principle mechanisms: excessive membrane fluidity; disruption of protein function and turnover; and metabolic imbalances. Metabolic imbalances can be due to differences in the activation energy of the component reactions, or to the effect of the other two mechanisms on the thermal response of each reaction. The inhibition of metabolism from these three mechanisms also results in the accumulation of toxic compounds and reactive oxygen species (ROS), the removal of which is also inhibited by heat stress.

Whole Plant Effects

Generally, inhibition of photosynthesis is seen as a critical factor in heat stress. Net photosynthesis is typically the first process to be inhibited at high temperatures (Berry and Bjorkman 1980; Allakhverdiev et al. 2008). As temperature rises above optimum, gross photosynthesis is inhibited while respiration and photorespiration increase. The combined effect of these three processes is a marked reduction in net photosynthesis during moderate heat stress.

C_4 plants do not suffer from the increase in photorespiration and so can maintain a higher photosynthetic optimum; however, the maximum temperature does not vary to the same extent. The imbalance between photosynthesis and respiration is itself damaging, as carbohydrate reserves can become depleted. As temperature rises further, membrane transport and respiration become inhibited, eventually leading to cell death. Both the light reactions and the Calvin cycle are highly sensitive to moderate heat stress. Injury following severe heat stress is perhaps most acute for the light reactions, with even brief exposure resulting in long-term inhibition of photosystem II (PSII). As the activity of PSII is highly temperature sensitive it can be used as an indicator of heat stress and heat injury; measurements of chlorophyll fluorescence have been widely used for this purpose.

For many years, the inhibition of gross photosynthesis was thought to occur at temperatures too low to be explained by the thermal deactivation of photosynthetic enzymes. Experiments comparing the thermal response of many steps in the photosynthetic apparatus, suggested the initial inhibition was due to the sensitivity of the thylakoid membrane to high temperatures (Berry and Bjorkman 1980).

However, this view has been questioned recently with the observation that at moderately high temperatures photosynthetic inhibition coincides with a reversible reduction in the activity of certain Calvin cycle enzymes. Severe heat stress is still thought to be due to injury of PSII, through direct cleavage of the D1 protein and a range of other mechanisms. Although the thermal sensitivity of PSII is not solely due to the thermal sensitivity of cell membranes, membrane properties are a major regulator of both inhibition and injury of PSII.

The thermal sensitivity of reproductive processes can be a limiting factor for plant productivity and it is often the critical factor for crop production in areas prone to heat stress. Heat stress can reduce the duration of reproductive development and severely inhibits floral development, fertilization and post fertilization processes in many species. Pollen viability is particularly vulnerable to heat damage. Severe heat stress inhibits both the photosynthetic source and the reproductive sink, resulting in a significant reduction in the number and size of seeds and/or fruit. This is a particular problem in fruit and grain crops such as tomato, cowpea, wheat, and maize.

At high temperatures dry matter production is often more limited by photosynthesis than by cell expansion (while at low temperatures dry matter production is more limited by cell expansion than by photosynthesis). Generally, the inhibition of photosynthesis and other growth maintaining processes during moderate or short-term heat stress results in a comparatively small reduction in the rate of dry matter production (relative growth rate). As temperature increases within a plant's thermal range, the duration of growth decreases but the rate of growth increases, as shown earlier in this chapter. As a consequence, organ size at maturity may change very little in response to temperature, despite variation in growth rate. As temperatures are raised further, an increased rate of growth is no longer able to compensate for a reduction in the duration of development, and the final mass of any given organ at maturity is reduced.

This response can be seen in a range of tissues including leaves, stems and fruit. A smaller organ size at maturity due to high temperature is associated with smaller cells rather than a change in cell number. This implies that cell enlargement is more sensitive to temperature than is cell division. The reduced duration of development can also limit the number of organs that are produced, *e.g.* grain number in wheat is reduced when plants are grown at moderately high temperatures. Under certain conditions plants grown under moderate heat stress accumulate sugars in their leaves, indicating that translocation can be more limiting than photosynthesis, but this is not thought to be a general limitation.

Membrane Properties

The structure and fluidity of lipid membranes is dependent on their composition and on temperature. An increase in temperature will result in an increase in the fluidity of lipid membranes as the hydrogen bonding between adjacent fatty acids become weak. This increase in fluidity is associated with an uncontrolled increase in membrane permeability as the activity of membrane bound proteins is disrupted. Indeed, this uncontrolled membrane permeability is used as an assay to test for damage due to heat stress.

Membrane-associated processes, such as photosynthesis and membrane transport, are typically the first to be inhibited during exposure to high temperature (Berry and Bjorkman 1980; Allakhverdiev et al.2008). The high temperature sensitivity of PSII is thought to be due, at least in part, to its close association with the thylakoid membrane. In addition to these direct effects on metabolic function the changes in membrane fluidity during heat stress act as a signal to initiate other stress responses in the cell.

Protein Function and Turnover

For most metabolic reactions, the optimum and maximum temperatures are determined by the thermal response of key enzymes. Enzymes act to lower the activation energy and increase the rate of reactions at any given temperature. However, as temperature increases the catalytic properties of most enzymes are lost and they begin to denature (*i.e.* enzymes are thermolabile). The synthesis of replacement enzymes and other cell proteins is also impaired, resulting in an overall limitation due to reduced protein turnover. Under prolonged severe heat stress many enzymes will become denatured. This, combined with the loss of membrane function will result in cell death.

For some reactions, the thermal response of a particular enzyme can be rate limiting. The inhibition of photosynthesis during moderate heat stress has been associated with a reduction in the catalytic activity of Rubisco (Ribulose 1:5 bisphosphate carboxylase/oxygenase), due in part to the thermal sensitivity of Rubisco activase. In some species, production of heat stable forms of Rubisco activase has been shown to play role in acclimation to high temperature. There have been attempts to engineer less temperature sensitive forms of Rubisco activase in order to increase the thermal range of crop species, but it remains to be seen if altering a single component of the photosynthetic system will improve overall heat tolerance.

Metabolic Imbalances

When a plant is grown outside of its optimum thermal range, metabolic imbalances occur. Imbalances may result in a short-fall of essential metabolites or intermediaries, or in a build-up of substances that becomes toxic (*e.g.* aggregated proteins). Such imbalances cause further inhibition of processes such as photosynthesis and respiration. The imbalances can be due to differences in the thermal response of particular reactions. For instance, the enzymes used in photosynthesis are deactivated at a lower temperature than those used in respiration. This has the result that as temperatures increase, the rate of carbon fixation falls while the rate of carbon use may rise.

The point at which the plant is using more carbon than it is assimilating is termed the 'temperature compensation point'. Beyond the temperature compensation point, the plant begins to use up carbohydrate reserves, *e.g.* in many legumes the net uptake of CO_2 by the green pod is low due to the high rate of pod and seed respiration, at high temperatures net uptake can become negative. As plants acclimate to high temperatures the rate of respiration falls lessening the impact on net photosynthesis.

Imbalances can also occur due to the effect of temperature on physical processes, *e.g.* as temperature rises, the solubility of oxygen increases more than that of carbon dioxide, so oxygen becomes more concentrated in the cell solution compared to carbon dioxide. This imbalance contributes to the increase in the oxygenation of RuBP at high temperatures (*i.e.* an increased rate of photorespiration).

The high temperature sensitivity of reproductive development can be viewed as an imbalance. Detailed studies have found that the yield of certain cowpea varieties was limited at high temperatures due to reduced seed set. This limitation was mitigated by increasing sink demand through breeding with more heat tolerant varieties. The fact that seed set can be limited by the demand for assimilates at high temperature shows that the thermal sensitivity of the reproductive sink can be out of balance with than that of the photosynthetic source. A similar sink restriction is found in cereals grown at high temperatures, where grain development is restricted by its ability to convert the available assimilates into starch.

HEAT TOLERANCE

Where overheating cannot be avoided, plants have developed a range of mechanisms to tolerate high temperatures and to resist the stresses outlined above. Many of these mechanisms have been harnessed by plant breeders to develop more heat resistant crops. Each species has a different capacity to respond to heat stress. The degree of heat tolerance tends to follow the species' native thermal range, with plants irreversibly damaged by temperatures between 30-40 °C termed 'heat sensitive' and those only damaged above 40 °C designated as 'heat resistant'. A key aspect of tolerance to heat stress is the ability to acclimate and the mechanisms described below are typically up-regulated when plants are exposed to moderate heat stress.

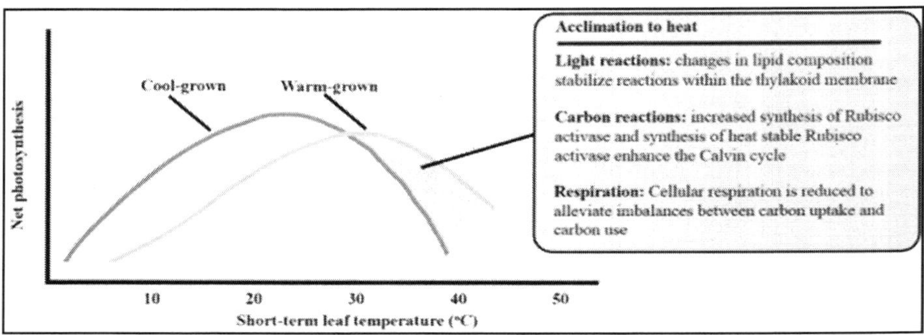

Fig. In heat tolerant plants, growth at warm temperatures results in acclimation of photosynthesis. Adjustments in membrane composition, protein synthesis, and metabolic regulation alleviate some of the effects of high temperature. Acclimation is mediated, in part, by an increase in expression of heat shock proteins.

Membrane State, Structure and Composition

In order to tolerate high temperatures, plants must maintain membrane fluidity within a biologically functional range (membrane thermostability). The degree to which membrane fluidity increases with temperature is dependent on membrane composition. Lipids that have unsaturated fatty acid chains, short fatty acid chains or a low sterol content generally form membranes that are more fluid and less stable at high temperatures. The sensitivity of membranes to heat stress can be reduced by increasing the proportion of saturated lipids or by altering the composition of specific lipids. Early work by Jim Lyons and John Raison at the CSIRO Division of Food Research highlighted the fact that tropical species tend to have a higher proportion of saturated lipids than temperate species, but found that the full role of lipid composition in regulating membrane fluidity was complex.

Changes in lipid composition during acclimation to high temperature, including increases in the proportion of saturated lipids, have been described in cyanobacteria and a number of plants from both warm and cool regions. Some of the changes in the physical properties of membranes are regulated by the activity of heat shock proteins, but others are not.

Alteration of lipid composition through gene manipulation has been shown to increase heat tolerance in Arabidopsis, soybean and tobacco. Murakami et al.(2000) produced transgenic tobacco plants with a reduced proportion of trienoic fatty acids (unsaturated lipids with three cis double bonds) in the chloroplast membranes. Exposure of the plants to 45°C for 5 minutes reduced photosynthesis by 50 per cent in the wildtype while the transgenic plants were unaffected (all plants showed complete inhibition of photosynthesis after exposure to 50°C for 5 minutes).

Heat Shock Proteins

Within minutes of temperature rising above the optimum, the expression of most genes used for general metabolism is inhibited, however, a sub-set of specialised stress response genes are actively up-regulated. The best characterised of these genes are a multi-family group known as heat shock proteins (HSP). HSP occur in all organisms. In plants, they show differential expression in many tissues and many cell compartments. HSP utilise a novel transcription factor to respond directly to heat, and their levels have been shown to rise along with temperature until the lethal threshold temperature is reached. On exposure to high temperature HSP expression typically peaks after 1-2 hours and diminishes after 6-8 hours, after which the cell environment is modified enough for the transcription and translation of other genes to resume.

Many HSP are thought to act as chaperone proteins, protecting other proteins from denaturation by reducing misfolding, unfolding, and aggregation. Chaperone activity also helps maintain the translocation of proteins across cell membranes. The up-regulation of HSP has been shown to improve tolerance to and recover from heat stress in several systems, *e.g.* addition of purified HSP of isolated tomato chloroplasts significantly improved their heat tolerance by protecting PSII electron transport (Allakhverdiev et al. 2008). This chaperone role can offer protection from stresses aside from heat, and HSP have been shown to be up-regulated by a variety of stresses that escalate protein denaturation.

Larkindale et al. (2005), describe five classes of HSP the names indicating the molecular weight:

- HSP60 and HSP70 have been shown to act as chaperone proteins in plants and other organisms, and some also function to stabilise membranes preventing the loss of permeability.
- HSP90 are less well characterised in plants, they are thought to interact with signal transduction proteins that form part to the overall heat stress response.
- HSP100 act as chaperone proteins in conjunction with HSP60 and

HSP70 and may perform other roles. Plants lacking HSP 100 can grow normal at optimum temperatures but are unable to acclimate during heat stress.

- Small HSP are particularly important in plants but are less well characterised than HSP60 and HSP70. Small HSP are a diverse group including several gene families that are targeted to different cellular compartments, including the cytosol, chloroplast and mitochondria. The function of many of the Small HSP is still unknown. Some may be involved in chaperone protein activity and some are involved in maintaining membrane stability including the protection of membranes essential for the functioning of PSII.

Certain HSP also act to clean up the cell, removing denatured proteins by increasing the proteolysis activity of ubiquitin. The removal of potentially toxic protein aggregations is thought to be a key part of acclimation to heat stress. Indeed, heat stress also stimulates the up-regulation of ubiquitin itself.

Reactive Oxygen Species (ROS)

The impairment of metabolic function during heat stress results in increased production of ROS, which in turn causes secondary damage to proteins and membranes. Accumulation of ROS during heat stress has been associated with both the light reactions and the Calvin cycle reactions. The reaction centre of PSII is particularly vulnerable, producing superoxide radicals, hydroxyl radicals and hydrogen peroxide under heat stress.

Antioxidant enzymes and non-enzyme systems serve to limit the formation of the most damaging ROS, such as singlet oxygen, and to detoxify the cells through ROS-scavenging. Although some antioxidant systems are impaired at high temperatures, others are up-regulated and can be considered part of the heat stress response.

Heat Stress Response: Other Mechanisms

Although HSP form a critical part of the heat stress response, they still account for a small minority of the transcripts that are up-regulated during heat acclimation. Several groups are currently working to elucidate the role of other changes in the transcriptome, proteome, metabolome and lipidome in regulating signal transduction and response to heat stress. Among the metabolites associated with heat acclimation perhaps the best characterised are the compatible solutes (which also play a crucial role during water stress and salinity stress. In the case of heat stress, their primary role is thought to be similar to that of the chaperone proteins, *i.e.* the protection of protein and membrane function. There is also increasing interest in the role of isoprene in heat tolerance. Isoprene is a small hydrocarbon sometimes released from plants in large quantities.

It is particularly associated with certain tree species, such as eucalyptus. Indeed, it is isoprene that is responsible for the distinctive blue haze that characterises Australia's 'blue mountains'. Although the full purpose of isoprene has not been established, there is good evidence that it is involved in the development of heat tolerance. In particular, the production of isoprene has been shown to reduce the inhibition of photosynthesis during moderate heat stress, perhaps by associating with the thylakoid membrane to increase hydrophobic interactions and protect membrane function.

3

Ice Nucleation, Propagation, and Deep Supercooling in Woody Plants

ANATOMICAL PARAMETER OF ICE NUCLEATION AND CAVITATION HELPS TREES TO STAY ALIVE COLD AND DROUGHT PRESSURE

In a changing climate, plants will meet new environmental conditions such as different regional temperature and precipitation patterns. These changes will affect the probability of freezing and cavitation 1, *i.e.* phase change of liquid water to ice or gas, respectively, in the xylem of pants. Freezing and cavitation form a risk for tree function and survival because water conductance inside trees scales with photosynthesis and growth 2, but water conductance is only possible in liquid form. Cavitation has been recognized as one of the key factors leading to reduced plant productivity and mortality during drought 3, and factors influencing the vulnerability of the xylem to cavitation have been studied extensively4. It is known that there is a relation between the critical pressure causing cavitation during drought and anatomical plant characteristics, although the causality has not been satisfactory shown. However, the critical temperature causing ice nucleation in the water transport system has not been given much consideration.

Liquid water is vulnerable to phase change into ice at sub-zero temperatures, similarly as it is into vapour at liquid pressures below its saturation vapour pressure. The ecological significance of the freezing temperature of the xylem to plant productivity and survival worldwide is likely less important in comparison to that of cavitation. However, the factors influencing freezing could be important for plant function and survival in colder environments. Ice nucleation temperature in xylem conduits, the dead cells responsible for transporting water from the roots to the foliage, determines the frozen time period and the number of freeze-thaw cycles a tree experience during winter. Short frozen period and low number of freeze-thaw cycles have a positive effect on tree function and survival because as long as water in the xylem is not frozen, there is no risk for typical freezing damages that are especially enhanced by continuous freeze-thaw cycles. Typical freezing damages in trees adapted to colder environments include bubble formation during freezing and thawing causing winter cavitation and further blockages in water transport, and dehydration of unfrozen living cells due to low water potential of extracellular ice as water potential over ice decreases approximately 1.2MPa per 1°C decrease in ice temperature.

Low ice nucleation temperature also makes it possible for an evergreen tree to photosynthesize on sunny days even when the ambient temperature is below zero which will make them effective carbon sinks and aerosol sources. In milder regions, high freezing temperature of xylem water can be beneficial for trees as it protects the living cells by providing temporary cold protection with released heat of fusion. Also in colder regions, too low ice nucleation temperature could be harmful for trees. Lower freezing temperature increases the risk of intracellular freezing of the living cells as dehydration of the living cells due to the extracellular ice increases their osmotic concentration and may allow them to tolerate very low freezing temperatures.

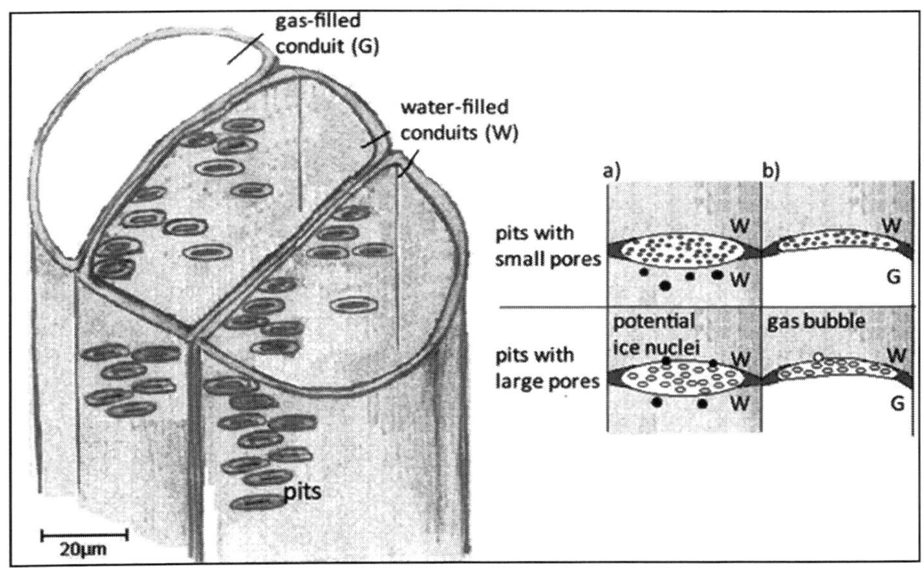

Fig. Schematic presentation of conduits of a deciduous tree species and inter-conduit pits (a) between two water-filled conduits and (b) between a gas-filled and a water-filled conduit.

Liquid water is transported in xylem conduits under negative pressures according to the cohesion-tension mechanism allowed by strong inter-molecular attraction. Negative pressure, *i.e.* large water tension, is created as evaporation at the leaf surfaces pulls water columns, held together by cohesive forces, upwards from the soil through the xylem. Water tension inside the xylem increases with decreasing soil water availability and increasing transpiration rate. At sub-zero temperatures, liquid water is also prone to freezing as the vapour pressure over ice is lower than that over liquid water. In these conditions, water inside the xylem is in a unique thermodynamic state in the sense that it is metastable to two directions: it is simultaneously supercooled, *i.e.* temperature of liquid water is below the equilibrium ice nucleation temperature and under tension, *i.e.* pressure of liquid water is below the saturation vapour pressure.

In (a), impurities and other solid particles can enter a conduit through a pit membrane in the case of large enough pores, and become potential ice nuclei. In (b), gas penetrates from a gas-filled conduit to adjacent water-filled conduit through a pit membrane in the case of large enough pores, and induces cavitation.

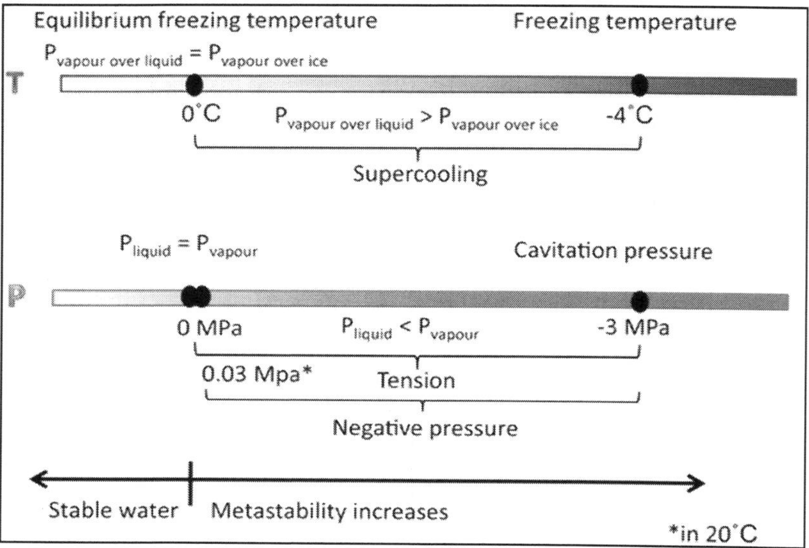

Fig. Schematic presentation of the used terminology related to temperature (T) and pressure (P).

Freezing temperature and cavitation pressure refer to heterogeneous nucleation; homogeneous freezing takes place at approximately "40°C and homogeneous cavitation at approximately "140MPa.

Water can remain in its metastable liquid state as long as there are no solid impurities or gas phases (bubbles or menisci) of large enough size present to act as nuclei and catalyse the formation of a new phase, *i.e.* ice or gas. Homogeneous ice nucleation of water takes place at approximately "40°C and homogeneous cavitation of water at approximately "100MPa, which is far below the pressures found in any plants.

Heterogeneous ice nucleation at warmer temperatures or cavitation at higher pressures requires the presence of nuclei of sufficient surface properties, geometry and size. Here we investigate how an important characteristic of xylem anatomy, its conduit diameter, regulates the sizes of nuclei catalysing freezing inside trees, and how this regulation determines the environmental conditions critical for the phase transition into ice. We then compare the sensitivity of ice nucleation temperature on xylem conduit diameter to the previously well-known relationship of cavitation pressure sensitivity on xylem conduit diameter.

RESULTS

We found that the ice nucleation temperature of water in the xylem increased with increasing conduit size regardless of the species or tree part. There is no known direct causality that would explain the found relationship. We thus hypothesize that the relationship between ice nucleation temperature and conduit radius can be explained from the basis of the classical nucleation theory and the scaling relations between conduit, pore and nucleus radius.

Our theoretical calculation using the classical nucleation theory demonstrated that the maximum supercooling temperature, *i.e.* the reciprocal of ice nucleation temperature, is inversely proportional to the size of a nucleus at the temperature range in which ice nucleation occurs in trees. The size of the nuclei present in the xylem sap is determined by the inter conduit pit pores that act as filters allowing water and dissolved nutrients to enter the conduits, but constrict the spreading of gas bubbles and solid impurities in excess of few nanometres.

It has been empirically confirmed that pore sizes in the pit restrict the size of particles which can enter the conduits, so we further obtain an inverse relation between maximum supercooling temperature and pit pore size. Finally, there are two prevailing hypothesis on the linkage between the pit pore size and conduit size: the pit-resistance hypothesis of nearly linear scaling between average pore size and conduit size, and the rear pit hypothesis of nearly linear scaling between the maximum pore size and conduit size. Thus we concluded that the maximum supercooling temperature is approximately inversely proportional to conduit size, because the size of the largest particles that are able to penetrate through the pit pores determines the ice nucleation temperature in the xylem.

A striking similarity of the relation of ice nucleation temperature to conduit size to the previously known relation of cavitation pressure to conduit size. Both relations are strongly supported by empirical evidence; for ice nucleation from our own results as shown above, and for cavitation from earlier studies. In our theoretical analysis, we linked the susceptibility to freezing and cavitation with plant anatomical characteristics based on the relation between nucleus size (impurity or gas phase) and the ability to penetrate into the metastable region of temperature or pressure, which are both proportional to the inverse of pit pore size.

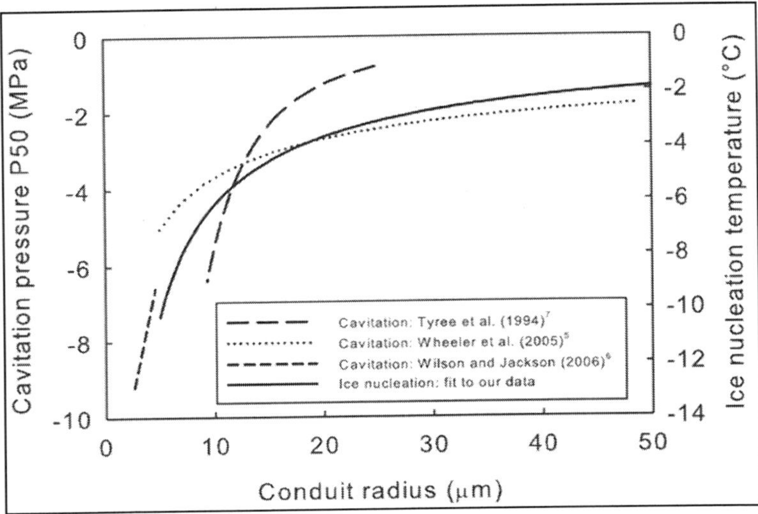

Fig. Empirical results concerning the relationship between drought cavitation pressure and conduit radius are compared with the theoretical relationship between ice nucleation temperature and conduit radius that is also supported by the empirical data ($R^2 = 0.35$, $P < 0.0001$).

Drought cavitation is described with the pressure reducing 50 per cent of the hydraulic conductivity (P_{50}). The linear regression line of Wilson and Jackson was drawn visually from the original figure. The definition of conduit radius was different in different studies: mean conduit radius, hydraulically weighted mean radius ($\Sigma r^5/\Sigma r^4$) and mean radius of conduits responsible for 95 per cent of water flow were used. In this study we used maximum conduit radius.

To get a better understanding of the potential significance of ice nucleation temperature in xylem for tree functioning, we made some calculations from weather data measured in Southern Finland (SMEAR II station 61°51′N, 24°17′E). Within a 15-years follow-up period, the time that the xylem was frozen was half shorter and the number of freeze-thaw cycles was only 15 per cent for a tree with ice nucleation temperature of "10°C compared to a tree with ice nucleation temperature of "1°C.

To confirm that the found relationship between conduit radius and ice nucleation temperature was not an artefact caused by the varying sample size and cooling rate, we tested the effect of these variables together with conduit radius. Conduit radius increased the freezing temperature highly significantly ($p<0.0001$), sample volume barely significantly ($p=0.036$), but there was no effect of cooling rate ($p=0.269$) on ice nucleation temperature. There was some dependency between conduit radius and sample volume ($R = 0.29$). This dependency results from the general trend between conduit size and branch/stem diameter.

However, the multicollinearity was not severe and allowed separation of the studied effects in the statistical analysis.

We further modified the surface energy of the water-ice nuclei by adding a surfactant to the xylem sap. The addition of the surfactant to water decreased the surface energy of the nuclei and increased the average ice nucleation temperature from the average of – 4.3°C (N = 3, s.d. = 0.9) and – 4.2°C (N = 3, s.d. = 0.5) to – 2.1°C (N = 3, s.d. = 0.5) and – 2.5°C (N = 3, s.d. = 0.1) in Pinus sylvestris and Betula pendula,respectively. This result, along with the sharp exotherms associated with the freezing events and thawing occurring always at the equilibrium ice nucleation temperature around 0°C, demonstrate that the freezing of the xylem sap was not an equilibrium freezing but the xylem sap was supercooled.

DISCUSSION

We showed that the temperature at which the xylem of a plant freezes is dependent on its anatomical characteristics as conduit size determines the size of the largest particles that are able to penetrate through the pit pores and catalyse ice nucleation. The theoretical size range of solid particles catalysing ice nucleation in the empirically measured temperature range coincides with empirical findings of particle sizes being able to penetrate through pits into conduits in trees.

Different sized organic and inorganic nuclei, of either external origin or synthesized by the plant itself, are commonly found in plants and their presence has been shown to affect ice nucleation; the ice-like structures of nuclei catalyse the organization of water molecules into an ice crystal lattice. It has also been suggested that conduit walls would act as ice nuclei, and that the properties of conduit walls would correlate with conduit size. It seems that in the absence of impurities in xylem water, conduit walls can act as ice nuclei but only at considerably lower temperature compared to the ice nucleation temperatures typically found from plants in nature.

The surfaces of the conduit walls do not have the sufficient surface properties to induce ice nucleation at such high temperatures as found in the experiments. It is thus much more probable that nuclei catalysing ice nucleation in conduits have similar nature as aerosols in atmospheric ice nucleation in clouds. Also gas bubbles created by cavitation have been found to be potential ice nucleation sites.

We further suggest that conduit size links together ice nucleation and drought cavitation via pit pore size. Drought cavitation most commonly develops in trees by spreading of the gas phase from one conduit to another through heterogeneous nucleation. It has been suggested that the rare largest pit pore in a conduit determines the water tension in which the gas phase enters the conduit from adjacent conduit through inter-conduit pits. This indicates that similar xylem anatomy secures safety in plants growing in either cold or dry environments. There is one difference in the spreading of the gaseous or ice phase following nucleation: inter conduit pit pore size determines spreading of the gaseous phase separately for each conduit, whereas freezing propagates from one conduit to another within a plant organ rather freely following a single ice nucleation event8. However, it has been shown that the extent of supercooling varies between organs within a tree as there can be ice barriers between tree organs.

Running a surfactant through samples of Pinus sylvestris and Betula pendula branches before freezing decreased the degree of supercooling by approximately 40–50 per cent in both species. Similarly to our results, lowering the surface tension has been found to increase the pressure required for cavitation in both conifers and angiosperms.

As ice nucleation is a stochastic phenomenon, both sample volume and exposure time to a given temperature affect ice nucleation probability. In our experiments, we settled for varying sample volume and exposure time as the probability for nucleation will in practice increase from values very close to zero to values approaching one in a narrow temperature range. This was also shown empirically as sample volume had a barely significant effect and exposure time had no effect on the ice nucleation temperature. We also used single measurements instead of averages of several measurements despite of the stochastic nature of nucleation, because theoretical calculations showed that the nucleation probability increases from zero to one in a very narrow range of the nucleus particle diameter, meaning that the largest impurity is practically always expected to act as nucleus for phase transition.

Our results offer better understanding of the anatomical similarities of adaption of plants to cold and drought stress as in global climatic distribution of species, mean conduit diameter has been found to decrease with the probability of both sub-zero temperatures and drought. In cold climates, trees with small conduits have been shown to suffer less from low temperatures and to have superior productivity compared to trees with larger conduits. Large conduits enable efficient water transport, whereas small conduits are reliable in water transport, *i.e.* safe from phase transition from liquid to gas or liquid to solid ice. Efficient and safe water transport is essential for plants because the exchange of water and carbon needed for photosynthesis takes place through the same stomata openings on leaf surface; the rate of water transport scales with metabolism rate on whole plant level.

We conclude that the linkage between ice nucleation temperature and drought cavitation is significant from an evolutionary point of view. Besides the already widely accepted trade-off at the whole tree level between efficient water transport and safety from cavitation through conduit size, there also seems to be a trade-off between efficient water transport and low ice nucleation temperature. The role of conduit anatomy in determining the length of the frozen period and the number of freeze-thaw cycles a tree encounters each winter, offers new insights into the ability of trees to adapt to the changing climate. Boreal trees with low ice nucleation temperature are effective also in climate change point of view decreasing the global warming by being carbon sinks and aerosol sources also during winter.

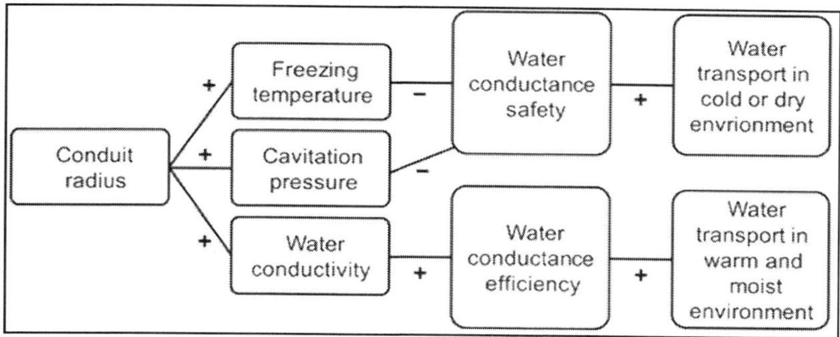

Fig. Schematic presentation of the relationship between conduit anatomy and the trade-off between water transport safety and efficiency at whole tree level.

Conduit size scales with the degree of metastability the tree can experience before spreading of cavitation or freezing. Different sized conduits are favoured in different environmental conditions.

METHODS

Experimental Work

We collected 70 samples during March and April from winter acclimated woody species in Southern Finland near Helsinki. The samples represented 9 deciduous species and 5 conifer species. Different tree parts including roots, stems and branches were covered among the sample set and sample size thus varied from 0.03 to 1 178cm^3.

The freezing experiments were conducted in a climate chamber (Weiss Umwelttechnik WK11 "340/40) directly after cutting the samples using cooling rates between 0.06 and 2.9°C Min"^{1}. Temperature of the samples was detected at a measuring interval of 10 seconds with thermocouples inserted a few mm inside the sapwood. Ice nucleation releases heat seen as a freezing exotherm.

After the freezing experiment, 100-ìm-thick cross-cuts were cut from the samples with a sliding microtome, stained with safranin, rinsed with water and dehydrated in alcohol. In the case of stem samples, a random cut was taken from the two outermost growth rings that typically have the largest cells. The maximum conduit lumen area of each sample cross-cut was measured with imaging software, and the conduit radius calculated assuming the conduits to be circular.

Because of the stochastic nature of ice nucleation, large sample size and long exposure time can be expected to increase the probability of a nucleation event and thus increase the ice nucleation temperature. Increasing sample size may increase the ice nucleation temperature also because the likelihood of having an efficient ice nucleator present increases with sample size. To confirm that the found relationship between conduit radius and ice nucleation temperature was not an artefact, we tested the effect of conduit radius on ice nucleation temperature in a multivariate analysis together with the effects of cooling rate and sample volume (measured over bark). The used method was generalized linear modelling (PROC GENMOD, SAS 9.2, SAS Institute Inc.), so the explanatory variables conduit radius and sample volume were transformed with natural logarithm to obtain a linear relationship with ice nucleation temperature.

We made few additional freezing experiments, where we artificially lowered the surface tensions in the xylem sap using a surfactant (Tween 80) and compared the results with control samples in order to see the effect of nuclei surface energy to the ice nucleation temperature. We ran the surfactant solution (0.5 per cent v/v), which decreases the surface tension of water to $36Nm^{-1}$, through threePinus sylvestris branch samples and three Betula pendula branch samples for an hour. The sample was connected to a plastic tube and soap solution was poured into the tube from 1.5 meters height in order to create pressure difference large enough to ensure fluent water conduction.

THEORETICAL ANALYSES

Effect of Particle Size on Ice Nucleation According to Classical Nucleation Theory

The equilibrium ice nucleation temperature is 0°C at atmospheric pressure for pure bulk water, and slightly (typically only a few tenths of a degree) lower for the water in the conduits of trees due to dissolved solutes. Below the equilibrium ice nucleation temperature, phase change to ice would allow the water in conduits to fall to a lower, more favourable energy state. However, before the phase change can occur, new surfaces between the new ice phase and liquid phase need to be constructed which requires energy. Change in the free energy (ΔG) of a spherical ice crystal in a phase change from liquid to ice is

$$G=-\frac{4}{3}\pi r_{ice}{}^{3}\frac{L\Delta T}{T_E}+4\pi r_{ice}{}^{2}\sigma_{LI}$$

where r_{ice} is radius of the spherical ice crystal, L is latent heat of fusion ($333.55*10^6 Jm^{-3}$ for a temperature of 273.15K), T_E is equilibrium ice nucleation temperature (273.15 K), ΔT is supercooling temperature, *i.e.* the temperature minus the equilibrium ice nucleation temperature, and σ_{LI} is surface energy between the two phases ($0.030Nm^{-1}$). The first term on the right side is the bulk energy term, and the second is the surface energy term. Phase change to ice will occur only if ΔG is positive. The sign of (ΔG) at a given temperature is dependent on the radius of the ice crystal. Differentiating equation (1) with respect to r_{ice} and solving for ΔG = 0 gives the critical radius of the ice crystal $r_{ice}{}^*$

$$r_{ice}{}^* = \frac{2\sigma_{LI} T_E}{L\Delta T}$$

Ice crystals smaller than this are crushed by surface forces, while ice crystals larger than this are able to grow indefinitely. Ice crystals of radius above the critical size are created by thermodynamic fluctuations which have the energy of the order of kT, where k is the Bolzmann constant ($k = 1.38 \times 10^{-23} JK^{-1}$). The rate (homogeneous nucleation rate, J_{hom}) at which these ice crystals are created can be predicted by the classical nucleation theory to be

$$J_{hom} = J_0 \exp\left(\frac{-\Delta G(r_{ice}{}^*)}{kT}\right)$$

where J_0 is a kinetic pre-factor which has been estimated in the following way

$$J_0 = \frac{NkT}{h} \exp\left(\frac{-Q_D}{kT}\right)$$

where N is the molecular density of water (3.35 $*10^{22}$ (molecules cm$^{”3}$), h is the Planck's constant (6.626×10^{-34}Js), and Q_D is the activation energy for diffusion in the liquid (2.8$*10^{-23}$J per molecule. In practice, this equation will give a nucleation rate larger than zero only when temperature approaches the homogeneous ice nucleation temperature of water, which is almost –40°C. Ice nucleation in conduits must therefore occur by heterogeneous nucleation

$$J_{het} = J_0 \frac{a}{N^{1/3}} \exp\left(\frac{-\Delta G(r_{ice}{}^*)(1-f)}{kT}\right)$$

where a is the surface area available for heterogeneous nucleation per unit bulk volume of liquid. For a spherical ice crystal on a convex surface, the geometrical correction factor f to obtained formation energy of critical cluster in the case of heterogeneous nucleation

$$f = \frac{1}{2}\left[1 - \left(\frac{1+Xm}{g}\right)^3 - X^3\left(2 - 3\left(\frac{X+m}{g}\right) + \left(\frac{X+m}{g}\right)^3\right) + 3mX^2\left(\frac{X+m}{g} - 1\right)\right]$$

Where X is the ratio of the radius of the ice nucleus ($r_{particle}$) to the critical ice crystal radius (r_{ice}*).

$$X \equiv \frac{r_{particle}}{r_{ice}{}^*} \quad m \equiv \cos\theta = \frac{(\sigma_{L,particle} - \sigma_{I,praticle})}{\sigma_{LI}} \quad g = \sqrt{1 - X^2 - 2Xm}$$

where $\sigma_{L, particle}$ is surface energy between liquid and solid particle, and $\sigma_{I, particle}$ is surface energy between ice and solid particle.

Nucleation is a stochastic process, so that a nucleation will only have a given probability to occur for given conditions. In other words, a nucleation temperature cannot strictly be defined. The probability that heterogeneous nucleation will occur in a wood volume of V within a time of exposure (t) to a certain temperature is

$$P_{nucl} = 1 \exp(-J_{het} Vt)$$

shows the nucleation probability as a function of temperature for varying exposure times to a given temperature. As the figure demonstrates, the probability for nucleation will in practice increase from values very close to zero to values approaching one in a narrow temperature range (similarly to the case for cavitation by heterogeneous nucleation). However, experimental evidence points out to a slightly wider spread in nucleation temperatures. Re-arranging equation (4), the temperature at which the nucleation (freezing) occurs can be written

$$\Delta T = \left(\frac{16\pi(1-f)\sigma LI3T_E 2}{3k\, TL^2 \text{In}\left(\frac{JaN^{-1/3}}{J_{req}} \right)} \right)$$

J_{req} is the nucleation rate which is required for nucleation to occur, here P = 0.5. J_{req} can be explicitly written by substituting J_{req} for J_{het} in equation and rearranging

$$J_{req} = \frac{\text{In}(I-p)}{Vt}$$

In the calculation of the ice nucleation temperature a value of 0.003m^3 (corresponding to a cylinder of 1cm in radius and 1cm in height) is used for the volume (V), 60s is used for the time (t), and 0.5 is used for the nucleation probability (*i.e.* nucleation has a 50 per cent probably of occurring). However, the values chosen for the parameters in calculating J_{req} in equation above influenced the predicted ice nucleation temperature only marginally due to the dominating effect of other terms in equation previous. A value of 10^{-5}m^2 was used for a in equation previous. The value used for a affected the results so marginally that its value could be changed by many orders of magnitude in either direction without a noticeable effect on the result.

PLANT PROPAGATION BY STEM CUTTINGS: INSTRUCTIONS FOR THE HOME GARDENER

Propagation by stem cuttings is the most commonly used method to propagate many woody ornamental plants. Stem cuttings of many favorite shrubs are quite easy to root. Typically, stem cuttings of tree species are more difficult to root. However, cuttings from trees such as crape myrtles, some elms, and birches can be rooted. A greenhouse is not necessary for successful propagation by stem cuttings; however, maintaining high humidity around the cutting is critical. If rooting only a few cuttings, you can use a flower pot. Maintain high humidity by covering the pot with a bottomless milk jug or by placing the pot into a clear plastic bag. Cuttings can also be placed in plastic trays covered with clear plastic stretched over a wire frame. Trays must have holes in the bottoms for drainage. The plastic will help keep the humidity high and reduce water loss from the cuttings. If you need more elaborate facilities, you can construct a small hoop frame and/or use an intermittent mist system. HIL-404, Low Investment Propagation/ Winter Protection Structure, and HIL-405, A Simple Intermittent Mist System For Propagation, describe how this can be accomplished. Another publication that may be helpful is AG-426, A Small Backyard Greenhouse for the Home Gardener.

Fig. Flowering Pot.

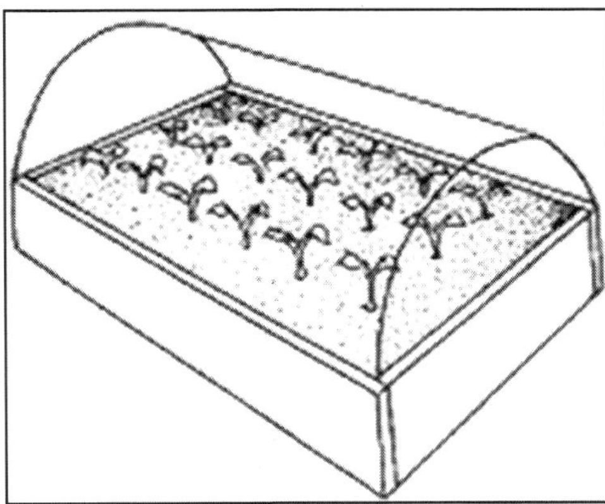

Fig. Plastic trays covered with clear plastic stretched over a wire frame.

TYPES OF STEM CUTTINGS

The four main types of stem cuttings are herbaceous, softwood, semi-hardwood, and hardwood. These terms reflect the growth stage of the stock plant, which is one of the most important factors influencing whether or not cuttings will root. Calendar dates are useful only as guidelines. The best time to root stem cuttings of particular ornamental plants.

Table. Optimum stage of tissue (wood) maturity for rooting stem cuttings of selected woody ornamentals.

Scientific Name	Common Name	Type of Cutting (SW = softwood, SH = emi-hardwood, HW = hardwood)
Evergreen Plants		
Abelia	Abelia spp.	SH, HW
Arborvitae, American	Thuja occidentalis	SH, HW
Arborvitae, Oriental	Platycladus orientalis	SW
Azalea (evergreen and semi-evergreen)	Rhododendron spp.	SH
Barberry, Mentor	Berberis x mentorensis	SH
Barberry, Japanese	Berberis thunbergii	SH, HW
Barberry, wintergreen	Berberis julianae	SH
Boxwood, littleleaf	Buxus microphylla	SH, HW
Boxwood, common	Buxus sempervirens	SH, HW
Camelia	Camelia spp.	SW, SH, HW
Ceanothus	Ceanothus spp.	SW, SH, HW
Cedar	Cedrus spp.	SH, HW
Chamaecyparis; False cypress	Chamaecyparis spp.	SH, HW
Cotoneaster	Cotoneaster spp.	SW, SH
Cryptomeria, Japanese	Cryptomeria japonica	SH
Daphne	Daphne spp.	SH
Elaeagnus, thorny	Elaeagnus pungens	SH
English ivy	Hedera helix	SH, HW
Euonymus	Euonymus spp.	SH
Fir	Abies spp.	SW, HW
Gardenia; Cape jasmine	Gardenia jasminoides	SW, SH
Heath	Erica spp.	SW, SH
Hemlock	Tsuga spp.	SW, SH, HW
Holly, Chinese	Ilex cornuta	SH, HW
Holly, Foster's	Ilex x attenuata 'Fosteri'	SH
Holly, American	Ilex opaca	SH
Holly, Yaupon	Ilex vomitoria	SH, HW
Holly, English	Ilex aquifolium	SH
Holly, Japanese	Ilex crenata	SH, HW
Jasmine	Jasminum spp.	SH
Juniper, creeping	Juniperus horizontalis	SH, HW
Juniper, Chinese	Juniperus Chinensis	SH, HW
Juniper, shore	Juniperus conferta	SH, HW

Leyland cypress	x Cupressocyparis leylandii	SH, HW
Magnolia	Mahonia spp.	SH
Oleander	Nerium oleander	SH
Osmanthus, holly	Osmanthus heterophyllus	Sh, HW
Photinia	Photinia spp.	SH, HW
Pine, Mugo	Pinus mugo	SH
Pine, Eastern white	Pinus strobus	HW
Pittosporum	Pittosporum spp.	SH
Podocarpus	Podocarpus spp.	SH
Privet	Ligustrunum spp.	SW, SH, HW
Pyracantha; Firethorn	Pyracantha spp.	SH
Rhododendron	Rhododendron spp.	SH, HW
Spruce	Picea spp.	SW, HW
Viburnum	Viburnum spp.	SW, HW
Yew	Taxus spp.	SH, HW
Deciduous Trees		
Azalea (deciduous)	Rhododendron spp.	SW
Basswood; American linden	Tilia americana	SW
Birch	Betula spp.	SW
Bittersweet	Celastrus spp.	SW, SH, HW
Blueberry	Vaccinium spp.	SW, HW
Broom	Cytisus spp.	SW, HW
Callery pear	Pyrus calleryana	SH
Catalpa	Catalpa spp.	SW
Clematis	Clematis spp.	SW, SH
Crabapple	Malus app.	SW, SH
Crape myrtle	Lagerstroemia indica	SH
Cherry, flowering	Prunus spp.	SW, SH
Dawn redwood	Metasequoia glyptostroboides	SW, SH
Deutzia	Deutzia spp.	SW, HW
Dogwood	Cornus spp.	SW, SH
Elderberry	Sambucus spp.	SW
Elm	Ulmus spp.	SW
Euonymus	Euonymus spp.	HW
Forsythia	Forsythia spp.	SW, SH, HW
Fringe tree	Chioanthus spp.	SW
Ginkgo, Maidenhair tree	Ginkgo biloba	SW
Goldenrain tree	Koelreuteria spp.	SW
Hibiscus, Chinese	Hibiscus rosa-sinensis	SW, SH
Honey locust	Gleditsia triacanthos	HW
Honeysuckle	Lonicera spp.	SW, HW
Hydrangea	Hydrangea spp.	SW, HW
Ivy, Boston	Parthenocussus tricuspidata	SW, HW
Larch	Larix spp.	SW
Lilac	Syringa spp.	SW
Maple	Acer spp.	SW, SH
Mock orange	Philadelphus spp.	SW, HW
Mulberry	Morus spp.	SW

Poplar; Aspen; Cottonwood	Populus spp.	SW, HW
Poplar, Yellow; Tulip tree; Tulip poplar	Liriodendron tulipfera	SH
Quince, flowering	Chaenomeles spp.	SH
Redbud	Cercis spp.	SW
Rose of Sharon; Shrub-althea	Hibiscus syriacus	SW, HW
Rose	Rosa spp.	SW, SH, HW
Russian olive	Elaeagnus angustifolia	HW
Serviceberry	Amelanchier spp.	SW
Smoke tree	Cotinus coggygria	SW
Spirea	Spiraea spp.	SW
St. Johnswort	Hypericum spp.	SW
Sumac	Rhus spp.	SW
Sweet gum	Liquidambar styraciflua	SW
Trumpet creeper	Campsis spp.	SW, SH, HW
Virginia creeper	Parthenocissus quinquefolia	SW, HW
Weigela	Weigela spp.	SW, HW
Willow	Salix app.	SW, SH, HW
Wisteria	Wisteria spp.	SW

Herbaceous cuttings are made from non-woody, herbaceous plants such as coleus, chrysanthemums, and dahlia. A 3- to 5-inch piece of stem is cut from the parent plant. The leaves on the lower one-third to one-half of the stem are removed. A high percentage of the cuttings root, and they do so quickly.

Softwood cuttings are prepared from soft, succulent, new growth of woody plants, just as it begins to harden (mature). Shoots are suitable for making softwood cuttings when they can be snapped easily when bent and when they still have a gradation of leaf size (oldest leaves are mature while newest leaves are still small). For most woody plants, this stage occurs in May, June, or July. The soft shoots are quite tender, and extra care must be taken to keep them from drying out. The extra effort pays off, because they root quickly.

Semi-hardwood cuttings are usually prepared from partially mature wood of the current season's growth, just after a flush of growth. This type of cutting normally is made from mid-July to early fall. The wood is reasonably firm and the leaves of mature size. Many broadleaf evergreen shrubs and some conifers are propagated by this method.

Hardwood cuttings are taken from dormant, mature stems in late fall, winter, or early spring. Plants generally are fully dormant with no obvious signs of active growth. The wood is firm and does not bend easily. Hardwood cuttings are used most often for deciduous shrubs but can be used for many evergreens. Examples of plants propagated at the hardwood stage include forsythia, privet, fig, grape, and spirea.

The three types of hardwood cuttings are straight, mallet, and heel. A straight cutting is the most commonly used stem cutting. Mallet and heel cuttings are used for plants that might otherwise be more difficult to root. For the heel cutting, a small section of older wood is included at the base of the cutting. For the mallet cutting, an entire section of older stem wood is included.

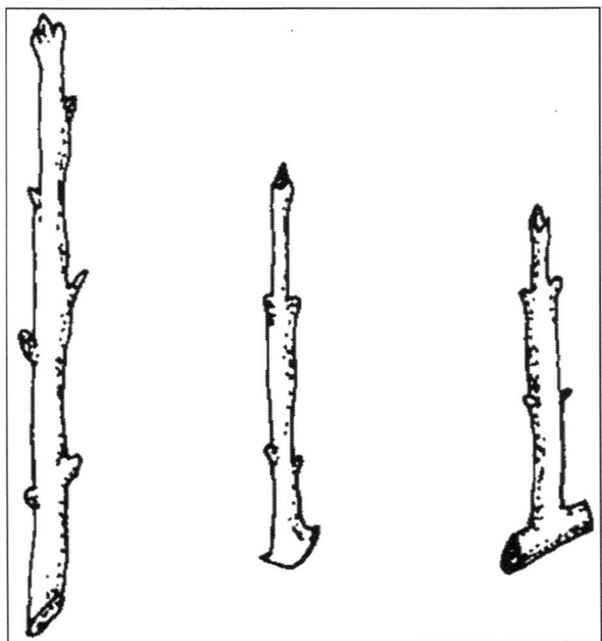

Fig. The three types of hardwood cuttings are straight, mallet, and heel.

PROCEDURES FOR ROOTING STEM CUTTINGS

Cuttings should generally consist of the current or past season's growth. Avoid material with flower buds if possible. Remove any flowers and flower buds when preparing cuttings so the cutting's energy can be used in producing new roots rather than flowers. Take cuttings from healthy, disease-free plants, preferably from the upper part of the plant.

The fertility status of the stock (parent) plant can influence rooting. Avoid taking cuttings from plants that show symptoms of mineral nutrient deficiency. Conversely, plants that have been fertilized heavily, particularly with nitrogen, may not root well. The stock plant should not be under moisture stress. In general, cuttings taken from young plants root in higher percentages than cuttings taken from older, more mature plants. Cuttings from lateral shoots often root better than cuttings from terminal shoots.

Early morning is the best time to take cuttings, because the plant is fully turgid. It is important to keep the cuttings cool and moist until they are stuck. An ice chest or dark plastic bag with wet paper towels may be used to store cuttings. If there will be a delay in sticking cuttings, store them in a plastic bag in a refrigerator. While terminal parts of the stem are best, a long shoot can be divided into several cuttings. Cuttings are generally 4 to 6 inches long. Use a sharp, thin-bladed pocket knife or sharp pruning shears. If necessary, dip the cutting tool in rubbing alcohol or a mixture of 1 part bleach to 9 parts water to prevent transmitting diseases from infected plant parts to healthy ones.

Remove the leaves from the lower one-third to one-half of the cutting. On large-leafed plants, the remaining leaves may be cut in half to reduce water loss and conserve space. Species difficult to root should be wounded. Treating cuttings with root-promoting compounds can be a valuable tool in stimulating rooting of some plants that might otherwise be difficult to root. Prevent possible contamination of the entire supply of rooting hormone by putting some in a separate container before treating cuttings. Any material that remains after treatment should be discarded and not returned to the original container. Be sure to tap the cuttings to remove excess hormone when using a powder formulation.

The rooting medium should be sterile, low in fertility, and well-drained to provide sufficient aeration. It should also retain enough moisture so that watering does not have to be done too frequently. Materials commonly used are coarse sand, a mixture of one part peat and one part perlite (by volume), or one part peat and one part sand (by volume). Vermiculite by itself is not recommended, because it compacts and tends to hold too much moisture. Media should be watered while being used.

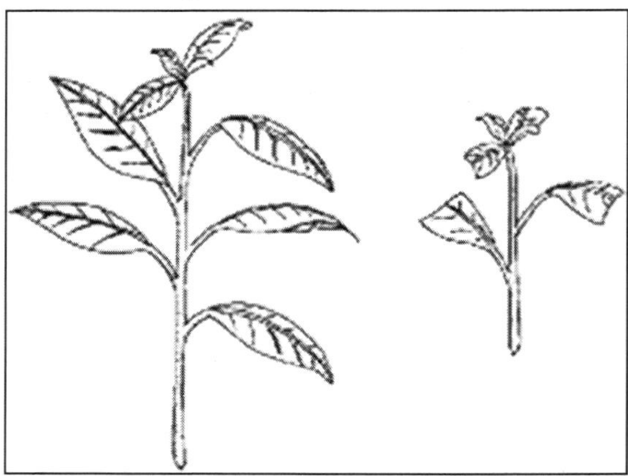

Fig. Remove the leaves from the lower one-third to one-half of the cutting.

Insert the cuttings one-third to one-half their length into the medium. Maintain the vertical orientation of the stem (do not insert the cuttings upside down). Make sure the buds are pointed up. Space cuttings just far enough apart to allow all leaves to receive sunlight. Water again after inserting the cuttings if the containers or frames are 3 or more inches in depth. Cover the cuttings with plastic and place in indirect light. Avoid direct sun. Keep the medium moist until the cuttings have rooted. Rooting will be improved if the cuttings are misted on a regular basis.

Rooting time varies with the type of cutting, the species being rooted, and environmental conditions. Conifers require more time than broadleaf plants. Late fall or early winter is a good time to root conifers. Once rooted, they may be left in the rooting structure until spring.

Newly rooted cuttings should not be transplanted directly into the landscape. Instead, transplant them into containers or into a bed. Growing them to a larger size before transplanting to a permanent location will increase the chances for survival.

HOME PROPAGATION OF GARDEN AND LANDSCAPE PLANTS

Plant pieces severed from a parent plant and rooted to form new plants are called cuttings. New plants formed from cuttings have the same characteristics as the parent plant. The process of rooting cuttings is simple and inexpensive and requires little labour and equipment.

TYPES OF CUTTINGS

Cuttings of landscape plants are usually made from shoots or stems, but a few may be made from roots. Types of stem cuttings generally used for propagating woody plants are softwood, semi-hardwood and hardwood.

Softwood

Softwood cuttings are used for propagating deciduous shrubs such as forsythia and lilac. Softwood cuttings are generally the easiest to root and don't require special handling. They are taken from new growth of the current season, while stems are succulent and not yet woody, but mature enough to break when bent sharply. Avoid young, tender shoots. The best months to take softwood cuttings of shrubs are June and July, though some may be taken in August.

Semi-Hardwood

Semi-hardwood cuttings are used to propagate broad-leaved evergreens such as holly, euonymus and azalea. The term semi-hardwood is also sometimes applied to partially matured cuttings of deciduous plants. These cuttings are taken during late summer but made from the current season's growth that has partially matured and is becoming woody.

Hardwood

Hardwood cuttings may be taken from deciduous plants and narrow-leaved evergreens. Cuttings from these plants are taken during the late fall or early winter after a hard frost when the plants have become dormant.

Deciduous Plants

Privet, willow, poplar, honeysuckle, grape and spirea are examples of suitable plants for hardwood cuttings. The length of these cuttings may range from 4 to 24 inches, though most are 8 to 10 inches long. Diameter varies from ¼ to 1 inch, depending on the type of material to be propagated.

Narrow-Leaved Evergreens

Most narrow-leaved evergreens are propagated using hardwood cuttings. These plants include junipers and yews. The cuttings should be taken from terminal shoots of the previous season's growth and should contain a small portion of year-old wood at the base.

PLANTS SUITABLE FOR PROPAGATING BY CUTTINGS

Many plant species can be propagated by cuttings. Some of these plants and indicates the type of cuttings generally used for each.

How to Take Cuttings

Select cuttings from vigorous, healthy wood, preferably from the upper part of the plant. Avoid excessively vigorous shoots and weak, spindly growth. Take softwood and semi-hardwood cuttings during cool parts of the day. Cuttings should be 4 to 6 inches long. For best results, make a slanting cut slightly below a node using a sharp, clean knife. Immediately place cuttings in a plastic bag to avoid excessive wilting.

Remove leaves from the lower half of softwood and semi-hardwood cuttings. Dip the base of the cuttings in a rooting hormone for faster and better rooting. Rooting stimulants are generally available in garden supply stores. Follow the label directions when using these products.

Rooting Media

The medium used for rooting cuttings must be clean and sterile. Diseases are a frequent cause of poor rooting and may be contracted from containers, tools, workbenches or rooting media that have not been sterilized. The rooting medium should not contain fertilizer. Begin fertilizing after cuttings are rooted and have been transplanted to a growing medium.

Clean, coarse construction-grade sand may be used for rooting cuttings. Avoid very fine sand because it has poor aeration, which hampers root formation. A mixture of half sand and half peat moss is a better rooting medium. Vermiculite, a lightweight expanded mica product, is suitable for rooting cuttings. The horticultural grade, grade 2, is the best size to use and may be used separately or mixed with an equal volume of sand.

Perlite is another excellent propagating material. It is lightweight and provides good aeration to the cutting. Perlite gives best results if mixed with an equal volume of peat moss or vermiculite. Compressed peat pellets that expand when water is added make a convenient propagation medium and container.

Heavy soils should not be used for rooting. They tend to pack tightly, which results in poor aeration and little or no root formation. They also must be thoroughly sterilized to prevent disease development.

Inserting the Cutting

Allow as little time as possible between the time the cuttings are taken and when they are inserted into the medium. Stick each prepared cutting into the medium up to the remaining leaves. Water thoroughly to settle the medium around the base of the cutting.

Care of Cuttings

Do not let the propagation medium dry out during rooting, but avoid excessive watering, which results in poor aeration and death of new roots. High humidity is necessary because cuttings don't have a root system. Low humidity allows wilting, scorch, leaf drop or death.

Enclosures help maintain high humidity. If only a few cuttings are to be rooted, use a miniature greenhouse or place individual pots in large plastic bags. Monitor the plastic bags for condensate, and water the medium when condensate disappears. Never place plastic-enclosed containers in direct sunlight because excessive heat will build up. For rooting large numbers of cuttings, use cold frames, hotbeds or greenhouses.

Care of Rooted Cuttings

The time necessary to form roots differs greatly between plants. Most woody cuttings, such as forsythia, root in several weeks, but hard-to-root cuttings, such as rhododendron, may take three to four months. Check cuttings occasionally by carefully removing a few from the medium. After cuttings have produced some roots at least 1 inch long, they are ready to be transplanted into a growing medium.

The move from high humidity and moist rooting medium to low humidity and drier soil is crucial. Do it carefully. Watch these new plants closely during the first weeks after the move. If only a few cuttings have been rooted, pot them in individual containers. Larger quantities should be placed in a well-prepared but protected bed or cold frame outdoors where they can be given special care for two growing seasons.

Some plants, such as azaleas and rhododendrons, require special acid soil, but for most plants a mixture of equal parts good topsoil, sand and peat moss makes a good growing medium. Add about 1 cup of an all-purpose garden fertilizer, such as 12-12-12, and two cups of ground limestone to each bushel of mix. Thoroughly mix these into the medium before filling the containers. When no other soil is available, potting soils for houseplants may be used for potting cuttings.

Table. Propagation techniques for common garden plants.

Plant	Cutting			Layering		
	Softwood	Semi-hardwood	Hardwood	Simple	Air	Compound
Abelia	X	X		X		
Althea (Rose of Sharon)	X		X			
Arborvitae		X	X			
Azalea		X		X	X	
Barberry	X		X	X		
Birch				X		
Bittersweet	X		X	X		
Boxwood		X				
Butterfly bush	X		X	X		
Clematis	X			X		X
Cotoneaster	X		X	X		
Crape myrtle	X					
Deutzia	X		X	X		
Dogwood	X					
Euonymus	X	X	X	X		X
Forsythia	X		X	X		
Hawthorn	X		X			
Holly		X		X	X	
Honeysuckle (bush)	X		X	X		
Honeysuckle (vining)	X		X	X		X
Hydrangea	X					
Juniper			X	X		
Kerria	X		X			
Lilac	X			X		
Magnolia	X		X	X	X	
Mahonia (grape holly)		X				
Mock orange	X		X			
Poplars			X			
Privet	X		X	X		
Pyracantha		X		X		
Rhododendron		X	X		X	
Rose	X		X	X		
Spirea	X		X			
Sweetshrub	X		X	X		X
Viburnum	X		X	X		
Weigela	X			X		
Willows			X			
Wisteria			X	X		X
Yew			X			

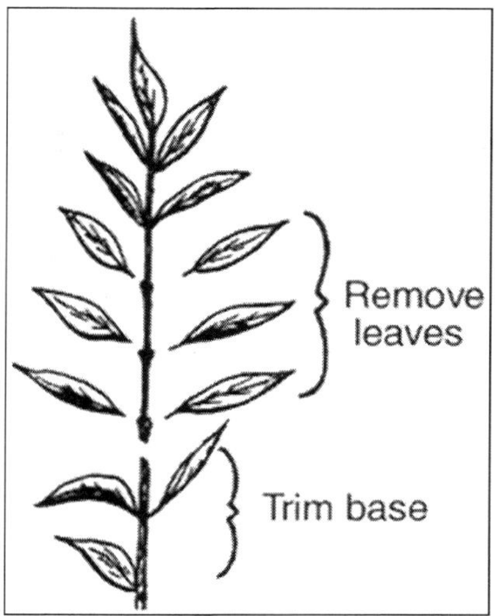

Fig. Trim cuttings and remove leaves from lower half of each cutting.

Fig. Miniature greenhouse constructed over a large flower pot for rooting a few cuttings.

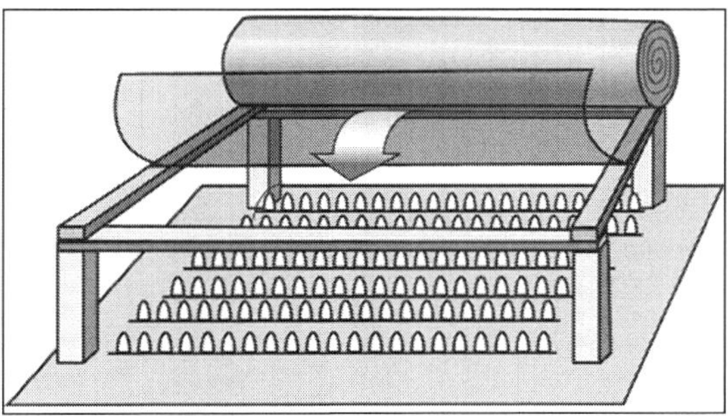

Fig. Place a shade screen over newly rooted cuttings outdoors.

If you use a nursery bed, thoroughly pulverize the soil, and work in 3 to 4 inches of compost, peat moss or leaf mold. Add fertilizer and lime as directed by a soil test. Install some shade over cuttings during the first growing season. A shade screen can be made from burlap, snow fencing or laths. Provide protection for young, rooted cuttings during the first winter season. Either mulch them with straw or construct a cold frame around them. Cold frames may be made from concrete blocks or scrap lumber covered with clear plastic, burlap or cheesecloth. If you use plastic, remove it during warm days or cover it with straw to prevent heat buildup. After two growing seasons in a nursery bed or container, the young plants should be ready to move to permanent locations.

LAYERING

Layering is a method of propagating new plants when seeding, cutting, grafting and other methods are impractical or ineffective. It is the rooting of a new plant while the stem is still attached to the parent plant.

Because an entire branch of the parent plant is often needed to form a single new plant, this method is useful for propagating only a few plants from each parent. For this reason, layering does not lend itself to large-scale commercial production. For home propagation, however, it is a useful and desirable method. Layering is easy and can be done in the house or garden without any special equipment or structures.

METHODS OF LAYERING

This section describes four layering methods: simple, air, tip and compound.

Simple

Simple layering is easiest for the home gardener and may be done whenever a plant has a branch low enough to be pulled down to the ground. Bury the branch several inches deep in the soil, making sure the shoot tip protrudes from the soil. Many plants root when a branch is bent sharply upward. However, making a wound or cut on the stem at the point where it curves upward is generally beneficial. To do this, make a slanting cut about 2 inches long either above or below the bend and about 12 inches from the tip. Dust the wound with a rooting stimulant.

Place the prepared branch or stem into the hole or trench 3 to 4 inches deep, and fasten it down near the point of wounding with a wooden peg or wire wicket. After the branch has been pinned down, bend the tip upward. If the cut was made on the top side, give the branch a half twist to open the wound. A second peg may be necessary to hold the twisted branch in position.

If the branch is stiff, insert a stake next to the shoot to hold the tip in an upright position. Fill the hole or trench with soil. Mound the soil slightly so the wounded portion of the stem is 4 to 6 inches below the soil surface, then firm the soil. This type of layering should be done in early spring on dormant 1-year-old shoots. Choose flexible branches that can be bent easily. For some broad-leaved evergreens — such as rhododendron, holly or southern magnolia — layering can be done later in the season after current season's growth has hardened.

Keep the soil around the layer moist at all times, and mulch with straw, leaves or sawdust. The layer may form roots during the first season but should not be cut from the parent plant until the following spring. Some hard-to-root types may take two years to produce roots. In spring, after the layer is well-rooted, cut off the branch where it enters the soil. Don't disturb the roots of the layer for two to three weeks after the branch has been severed to give the new plant time to recover. Then transplant it to a convenient protected spot or container where it can be tended carefully for one year before being moved to a permanent location.

Air

Air layering is one of the most useful methods of propagation for many houseplants, as well as some garden plants. Air layering is used in situations where the stem of a plant cannot be bent to the soil. Houseplants such as rubber tree are commonly air layered. Air layering is also useful for many tree and shrub species. This technique involves removing a cylinder of bark, treating the cut surface with rooting powder, and covering the wounded section with moist sphagnum moss enclosed in plastic or foil. The moss should be checked regularly for moisture and the layer removed from the mother plant when roots are evident.

Rather than covering with moss, another approach is to cut a pot in half and reattach the two halves around the wounded stem segment before filling with a rooting mixture. Plants air layered in the spring that have formed roots during the summer should not be removed until they become dormant. These layers should be placed in a container or cold frame where they will get good winter protection.

Tip

Tip layering is generally limited to raspberries and blackberries. It consists of rooting tips of the current season's growth. To stimulate more tips, pinch out the top 3 to 4 inches of a cane when it reaches about 2 feet in height. By late August or early September, the new growth will arch down, touch the soil and turn upward. These branches often root without assistance at the point of the curve where they touch the soil.

Rooting can be stimulated in late summer as the drooping canes develop an elongated appearance and leaves become smaller. Pull the tip of such shoots, and insert them in holes 3 to 4 inches deep. Rooting generally happens quickly, and the plants may be transplanted later in the same season. Plants are more likely to survive, however, when transplanting is delayed until just before growth starts in spring.

Compound

Compound layering is suitable for long vines such as honeysuckle, clematis or wisteria. It requires that the shoot be alternately covered and exposed. The technique is simple layering in multiple, with wounds made on the lower portion of each curve. Cut the branch into segments after rooting has taken place.

Care after rooting

The root systems of newly rooted layers are small relative to the tops. As soon as the newly rooted layers are removed from the parent plant and set in the garden or container, prune them so the leaf area is reduced to about one-third. Plants outdoors should be shaded lightly during the first season. Suitable shade screens may be made from burlap, lath or snow fencing. After the first winter, the screens can be removed. Enough roots should be developed so that the plants can be moved to a permanent location.

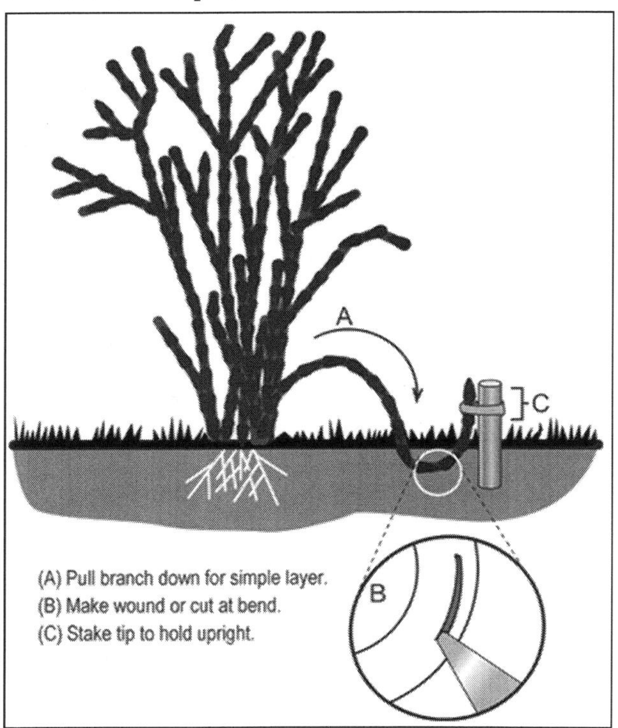

Fig. (A) Pull branch down for simple layer., (B) Make wound or cut at bend.. (C) Stake tip to hold upright.

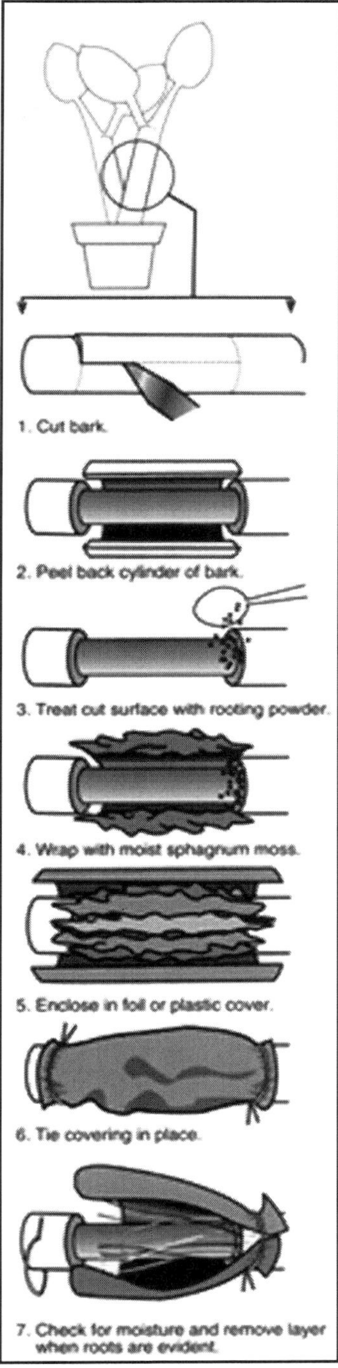

Fig. Steps for air layering a plant.

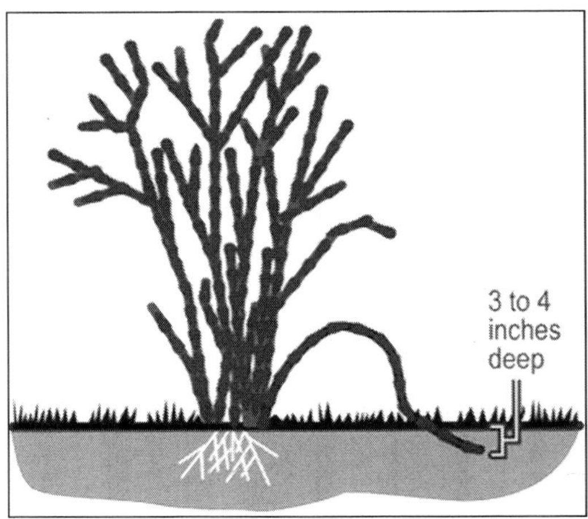

Fig. Tip layers are easy to make on raspberries and blackberries.

Fig. Compound layers are suitable for plants with long stems or vines.

Table: Common garden perennials suitable for division and the best time for division

Common garden perennials suitable for division and the best time for division

- Aster (hardy) Spring
- Baptisia (false indigo) Spring or fall
- Bleeding heart Late summer, early spring
- Chrysanthemum Spring
- Columbine March

- Coneflower (echinacea) Spring or fall
- Coreopsis Spring
- Day lily Late summer, spring
- Delphinium Early spring
- Ferns Early spring
- Hosta (plantain lily) Spring or fall
- Iris, bulbous (Dutch) Late summer, fall
- Iris, rhizomatous (German) July, August
- Iris, fibrous (Japanese) Spring
- Lily Fall
- Lily of the valley Fall
- Loosestrife (lythrum) Spring
- Oriental poppy July, August
- Pampas grass Spring
- Peony Early fall
- Phlox Spring
- Primula Summer
- Red-hot poker (kniphofia) Spring
- Rudbeckia Spring or fall
- Sedum (stonecrop) Spring, July, August
- Sempervivum (houseleek) Spring, summer
- Shasta daisy Spring
- Vinca (myrtle) Early spring
- Yarrow (achillea) Late summer, spring
- Yucca Spring or fall

DIVISION

One of the most important methods for propagating plants at home is crown division. Herbaceous plants such as chrysanthemum, day lily, peony and iris can be divided using this method. The common plants suitable for division. Some woody shrubs that branch or sucker from the base can also be reproduced using this simple and reliable method.

Plants that flower in spring and early summer should be divided in late summer or fall. Those that flower in summer and fall should be divided in early spring before new growth begins.

For crown division, carefully lift plant clumps and remove some soil from the roots. Then cut the crown into sections with a knife. Individual shoots that contain roots may be used to form new plants, or for a larger plant, several shoots may be left together.

For the best chance of success in dividing large old crowns, discard the older center portions, and replant the vigorous young shoots that have developed on the edges of the clump.

Shrubs may be divided in the same manner, but only when plants are dormant. Because shrubs are often woody, they may need to be separated with a shovel or hatchet. Before planting, trim back the shoots and cut off damaged roots. Shrubs that may be divided include red osier dogwood, summersweet clethra, deutzia, euonymus, hydrangea, kerria, spirea and snowberry.

PLANTS AT LOW TEMPERATURES

CHILLING INJURY

Plant chilling injury refers to an injury that is caused by a temperature drop to below 15°C but above the freezing point. The symptoms of chilling injury are usually a rapid wilting of the leaves and the development of water soaked patches that go on to form sunken pits due to cell collapse. Warming will lead to these damaged areas becoming brown and necrotic while continued chilling will eventually lead to the death of the plant.

Plants that live in regions where chilling is common undergo a period of hardening in the autumn that prepares them for chilling. Hardened plants do not suffer chilling injury therefore analyzing the differences between hardened and non-hardened members of the same species can yield clues to the nature of the injury. Comparison of tropical plants, which generally are incapable of hardening, to those that are chill-resistant also provides information of a similar type.

The most common site implicated for chilling injury is the plasma membrane. Many hypotheses concerning phase changes or phase separations have been offered, with the consequences of this change leading to cell leakage or disruption.

Changes in membrane permeability are often invoked as a cause of the loss of cell turgor but the kinetics of the process suggest that altered permeability is not the cause. The activation energy of membrane-bound enzymes has also been studied extensively, with much work going towards looking for discontinuities in the linearity of Arrhenius plots.

The primary cause of chilling injury in some plants has been found to be the opening (and locking) of the leaf stomata when the permeability of the roots to water is low. Thus the leaves lose water faster than it can be replaced and they become dehydrated. Cold hardening alters the behaviour of the stomata so that they close under the same conditions; the root permeability is also increased. Interestingly, drought hardening conditions the stomata similarly but the root permeability is significantly decreased, yet the plant is still able to survive chilling without leaf injury.

In other plants, the stomata behave properly at chilling temperatures and the injury is thought to be metabolic. A decrease in respiration, photosynthesis and fatty acid synthesis may all contribute to the chill-starvation of some plants.

Cold hardening affects the lipid content of cell membranes and has been found to lower the optimum temperature for photosynthesis and respiration.

FREEZING INJURY

Freezing injury in plants can be from two sources: 1. Freezing of soil water, and; 2. Freezing of the fluids within the plant. The soil water that is available to plants is found in the porous regions between soil particles. It freezes at about -2°C, depriving the plant of its source of water. Freezing of water within the plant is a more serious threat, as it can cause disruption of structure and function of cells and tissues.

COLD ADAPTATION

For plants that live in Arctic or temperate regions where temperatures are likely to fall as low as -40°C during the winter, any vegetative structures that are subjected to these temperatures must deal with the potential for internal freezing. They will also have to survive the extended drought that is imposed by soil freezing. The small flowering plants are able to solve both problems by spending the winter as seeds. The vegetative growth renews itself annually and dies off in the autumn. The seeds have a low water content and are able to avoid extremes in temperature by laying on the ground under the insulated snow-cover.

Deciduous trees lose their leaves in the fall, thereby stopping transpiration for the winter so that they are not affected by the freeze-induced drought. The leaves are also the most susceptible regions of the tree to freeze-injury. Environmental freezing in plants is usually extracellular. As there are no efficient nucleators within most plants, ice is usually transferred through the epidermis from frost that forms on the outer surface. Bacteria with ice nucleating proteins in their cell walls are often the sites of frost growth on the plants. Once ice growth occurs within the plant, the normal osmotic and chemical effects will result in cellular injury.

Freeze Avoidance

One strategy for avoiding ice formation within the plant is to exist in a supercooled state. This is not an overwintering strategy for most small plants as they can only supercool to about 4-6°C below the freezing point, sufficient only to avoid a few early frosts. In woody plants, the cells of the xylem tissue remain supercooled throughout the winter although extracellular freezing occurs in other tissues. There is a waterproof barrier that prevents ice growth into the xylem rays (and also prevent ice-driven dehydration of the xylem). Several apocryphal accounts of exploding trees exist, initiated by an axe cut at very low temperatures (below -40°C). In some conifers, the vegetative buds also supercool.

Freeze Tolerance

Plants that have a freeze tolerance will harden as winter approaches, undergoing changes that are necessary for surviving ice growth within the tissues. These changes must occur before the temperature gets too low so that the metabolic demands of tissue remodeling can be met. The alterations that commonly occur consist of an increase in cytoplasmic solutes both to act as a cryoprotectant as well as to buffer any freeze- concentration of other solutes that could be toxic in high concentrations, as well as membrane alterations that increase the fluidity of membranes at low temperatures and increase the stability of the membranes to low water contents.

4

Molecular Biology of Woody Plants

APPLICATIONS OF GENE SILENCING IN WOODY PLANTS

Yield of woody plants is a result of growth that depends on several aspects of the physiological machinery. GS is a powerful tool in an attempt to better understand the organization of this machinery, specially regarding biochemical pathways and gene function. Woody plants have great economic importance in agriculture and economy of several countries in the world. Wood, celulose, fruit, resins, rubber, oils and nuts are some of the products derived from woody plants. In order to guarantee the sustainability of woody crops, it is necessary to keep the high quality and yield levels.

For these purposes, conventional breeding prorammes have been extensively conducted. However, these prorammes have not been enough to supply short-termed solutions for these crops. Woody plants normally have slower growth rates than herbaceous plants as well as longer juvenile periods. These characteristics speeds down breeding projects in this area. Similar problems occur in woody fruit crop breeding as well as others such as highly heterozygous material, polyploidy, nucellar polyembryony, pollen and ovule sterility, and sexual incompatibility, which have limited progress towards the production of new cultivars through conventional breeding prorammes.

The introduction of biotechniques in breeding prorammes for woody plants was motivated by the search for pest and disease resistance and to fulfill the demands of the consumer market. Transgenesis is an important alternative for engineering traits into forest trees and developing basic research in gene function. In this scenario, genetic transformation came into context and, consequently, the aplication of GS technology.

After the genetic transformation of the first model plant (tobacco) (Herrera-Estrella et al., 1983) as well as other rapid growing species, the next step was to obtain transgenic woody plants. This has proven to be a though challenge since woody plants are harder to transform and require a long evaluation process. More than 16 species of woody plants were transformed between 1988 and 2000. These transformations were focused on several traits such as herbicide resistance, insect resistance, virus resistance, lignin biosynthesis, marker genes, and self-sterility suppression. Some of these traits are obtained by specific transgene expression into proteins. However, others are achieved by silencing of transgenes or endogenous genes.

GENE SILENCING AND PLANT DISEASE RESISTANCE

Woody crops are particularly susceptible to systemic virus diseases because of their long-term life span. Once infected by viruses, these plants must be rouged. Virus disease resistance in plants may be achieved by several approaches, including coat protein mediated protection, antisense RNA, replicase mediated protection, PTGS (Lindbo and Dougherty, 1992), RNAi, and pathogen derived resistance (PDR) (Sanford and Johnston, 1985). The concept of PDR suggests that the resistance to a determined pathogen could be obtained from its own genetic material.

The quest for virus resistant plants led researchers to accidentally discover the PTGS phenomenon (Angell and Baulcombe, 1997) and aid the establishment of RNAi models. Currently, RNAi is the major strategy in plant transformation for virus resistance. Citrus tristeza virus(CTV) - resistant citrus plants, expressing the coat protein of the virus has been obtained (Domínguez et al., 2000; Domínguez et al., 2002a). In this work, virus resistance was related to the accumulation of the transgenic viral protein in the plant tissue. The mechanism proposed was pathogen derived resistance.

Scorza et al. (2001) demonstrated for the first time that PTGS (RNAi) functions as a mechanism for virus resistance in a woody perennial species. They obtained resistant transgenic plums containing the silenced Plum pox virus (PPV) coat protein gene. Signs of PTGS could be observed within the resistant plants such as high level of transgene transcription in the nucleus, low levels of transgene mRNA in the cytoplasm, a complex multicopy transgene insertion with aberrant copies, and methylation of the silenced PPV-CP transgene.

Other strategies such as the expression of PPV-specific hairpins in plums have also been effective (Di Nicola-Negri et al., 2005; Zhang et al., 2006). In another case, transgenic viral protein accumulation was negatively correlated to resistance. Silenced transgenic citrus lines for the p23 CTV - silencing suppressor were resistant to CTV. PTGS seems to be the best explanation for these results since resistant citrus plants had multiple copies of the transgene, low levels of the corresponding mRNA, methylation of the silenced transgene, and accumulation of the p23-specific small interfering RNAs (siRNAs).

Despite of the potential application of GS as a viral defence system, there is a drawback. Viruses have developed RNAi suppression strategies during co-evolution with plants. The main strategy used by both RNA and DNA viruses is the incorporation of silencing suppressor proteins into their genomes

(Moissiard and Voinnet, 2004). It is suggested that dsRNA binding is one of the main strategies used by viral silencing suppressors. The model proposes the sequestering of long and/or short dsRNA molecules preventing the proper functioning of the RNA silencing pathways.

CTV, for instance, is known to contain at least three distinct suppressors of RNAi. Proteins p20, p23, and the coat protein act in different stages of RNAi, affecting both intercellular (p20 and coat protein) and intracellular silencing. RNAi suppressor proteins can alter the pattern of gene expression in virus hosts, since they affect both miRNA and siRNA pathways, leading to developmental abnormalities and possibly viral symptoms. Ectopic expression of the CTV p23 gene in Mexican limes (Citrus aurantifolia (Christ.) Swing.) caused aberrations resembling viral leaf symptoms. In order to obtain virus resistant plants through GS techniques it is important to understand all of the viral counter defence strategies.

Silencing has also been applied in an effort to protect plants against the crown gall disease, caused byAgrobacterium tumefaciens. This disease is economically important in fruit and nut orchards, vineyards, and nurseries. A protection technique based on the silencing of two conserved Agrobacterium genes – tryptophan monooxygenase (iaaM) and isopentenyl transferase (ipt) – have been developed (Escobar et al., 2001; 2002). Inducers of PTGS (self complementary transgenes) homologous toiaaM and ipt were expressed in Juglans regia L., resulting in degradation of oncogene mRNA in planta and functional resistance. Crown gall resistant apple tree roots were obtained by transformation with transgenes designed to express double-stranded RNA from the iaaM and ipt genes.

GENE SILENCING AND WOOD QUALITY, FRUIT QUALITY AND OTHER TRAITS

During chemical pulping of wood, one of the most expensive and environmentally hazardous processes is to separate lignin from cellulose and hemicellulose. The production of plant material with lower contents of lignin would mean a significant reduction of cost and pollution to the paper industry. One of the approaches to obtain reduced lignin forest trees has been the down regulation of lignin biosynthesis pathways.

The main genes involved with genetic transformation targeting lignin reduction are 4-coumarate: coenzyme A ligase (Pt4CL1), cynnamyl alcohol deshydrogenase (CAD - the final enzyme in the biosynthesis of lignin monomers) and caffeate/5-hydroxyferulate O-methyltransferase (COMT - enzyme involved in syringyl lignin synthesis).

The downregulation of the Pt4CL1 gene in Populus tremuloides Michx., produced trees with a 45 per cent reduction of the lignin content compensated by a 15 per cent increase in the cellulose content. In the transgenic lines obtained plant growth was substantially enhanced, and structural integrity maintained both at the cellular and whole-plant levels.

Silencing was also registered when trying to boost up the expression of the caffeic acid O-methyltransferase (COMT) in Populus tremula X Populus alba. On some transgenic lines, silencing of the transgene was observed, and the down regulation of COMT reduced the lignin levels in 6-month-old Populus tremula X Populus alba. This was the first report of lignin reduction in COMT down regulated plants.

Cad GS by transgenic inverted repeats has been reported in Pinus radiata. The authors also suggested that there are similar mechanisms of GS for angiosperms and gymnosperms species. In order to become rate limiting in lignin biosynthesis, CAD levels must be significantly reduced in Pinus radiata and conifers. In Eucalyptus camaldulensis the reduction of CAD activity by using antisense transgenes did not result in lignin reduction in transformed plants.

In some woody plants, self-incompatibility stands as a major problem in fruit set and breeding prorammes. Broothaerts et al. (2004), reported the production of transgenic apple trees able to self pollinate and develop fruit. This break through was achieved by silencing of the S-gene responsible for self-incompatibility. The self-compatible transgenic plants lacked the pistil S-RNase protein, which is the product of the S-gene.

Fruit quality has also been addressed by silencing experiments. Several characteristics are involved in fruit quality. Transgenic apple fruits silencing key enzymes involved in autocatalytic ethylene production were significantly firmer and displayed an increased shelf-life. Apples containing reduced amounts of the Mal d 1 allergen were obtained by the expression of an intron spliced hairpin RNA containing Mal d 1-specific inverted repeat sequences. According to these reports, it is possible to produce transgenic hypoallergenic apples using RNAi.

Research on leaf sorbitol silencing suggests that sorbitol distribution affects fruit quality such as starch accumulation and sugar-acid balance (Teo et al., 2006). In Citrus,the down regulation of putative thermostable pectin methylesterase genes is projected as a possible solution for the undesirable separation of juice into clear serum and particulate phase. In this case, RNAi could be used to achieve this goal.

MECHANISMS OF GENE SILENCING

Some early findings regarding GS occurred when a team of researchers tried to obtain transgenic petunias with greater amounts of anthocyanin pigments, by amplifying the gene activity of chalcone synthase. Instead of obtaining deeper purples in the petals, white or chimeric flowers were produced. Apparently, the transgene was not expressed, and ended up silencing a homologue endogenous gene. The phenomenon, named "co-suppression", was unstably transmitted within generations leading to the hypothesis that it was mediated by a nucleic acid, presumably RNA.

Similar phenomena were named "quelling" in fungi (Romano and Macino, 1992; Cogoni and Macino, 1997) and "RNA interference" (RNAi) in Caenorhabditis elegans (Fire et al., 1998). The research indicated that the presence of double stranded RNA (dsRNA), a non-occurring form in normal cells, was related to the silencing of sequence homologue genes. The fact that the phenomenon seemed to be triggered by the presence of doubled stranded RNA (dsRNA) suggested that this could be originally a defence mechanism against viruses and transposable elements, since these originate dsRNA (Waterhouse et al., 2001).

Most of the GS phenomena are related to RNA activity within the cell. Therefore, the term RNA silencing is often used to describe GS and comprise all mechanisms by which RNA sequences regulate gene expression, except those sequences characterized as mRNAs, tRNAs, or ribosomal RNAs. Genetic and biochemical studies have confirmed that the mechanisms of RNAi, co-suppression, and virus-induced gene silencing are similar. Moreover, the biological pathways underlying dsRNA-induced GS exist in many, if not most, eukaryotic organisms.

The study of similar phenomena in different organisms (Caenorhabditis elegans, Neurospora crassa, Drosophila melanogaster, Arabidopsis thaliana and Petunia x hybrida) allowed the proposal of models for different but interacting forms of silencing.

RNA INTERFERENCE

According to the present model, the RNA interference pathway starts with the presence of dsRNA in the cytoplasm that vary in length and origin (Waterhouse et al., 1998; Meister and Tuschl, 2004; Lodish et al., 2005). The basic pathway for RNAi. This particular molecule is recognized by the Dicer enzyme, a member of the RNase III family of nucleases that specifically cleave double-stranded RNAs, and is evolutionarily conserved in worms, flies, plants, fungi, and mammals. This enzyme cleaves the dsRNA into shorter RNA duplexes of 21 to 28 nucleotides, which have 5' phosphate and 2-nucleotide 3' overhangs (Hamilton and Baulcombe, 1999; Bernstein et al., 2001; Elbashir et al., 2001; Meister and Tuschl, 2004). These short RNA duplexes are known as short interfering RNA (siRNA).

Several organisms contain more than one Dicer gene, with each Dicer preferentially processing dsRNAs that come from specific source (Meister and Tuschl, 2004; Margis et al., 2006). In Arabidopsis, for instance, DCL2 and DCL3 Dicer-like proteins seem to process long dsRNA such as transcripts containing inverted repeats or intermediates formed during RNA virus replication. DCL2, DCL3, and DCL4 have similar functions in Arabidopsis, acting in siRNA processing and establishing and maintaining DNA methylation. On the other hand, DCL1 processes miRNAs precursors exported from the nucleus.

After Dicer processes the dsRNA, the siRNAs are subsequently rearranged into the RNA-induced silencing complex (RISC) (Hammond et al., 2000; Nykänen et al., 2001). The RISC complex was originally identified through fractionation of sequence specific nuclease activity from D. melanogaster extracts. The characterization of RISC includes the presence of an Argonaute protein family member and a guide strand (antisense to the target RNA) of a small RNA (Tolia and Joshua-Tor, 2006). The RISC complex is responsible for the targeting and cleavage of sequence specific mRNA within the cell (Martinez and Tuschl, 2004). RISC acts by cleaving the target mRNA in the middle of the complementary region, ten nucleotides upstream of the nucleotide paired with the 5' end of the guide siRNA.

At least one protein from the Argonaute family, present in the RISC complex, probably acts as endonuclease, cleaving the target mRNAs (often referred to as the Slicer function). This cleavage leads to silencing of the target mRNA by preventing read-through of the message by the translational machinery, resulting in mRNA destruction (Tolia and Joshua-Tor, 2006). Normally there is a bias towards the loading of the antisense strand of the RNA short duplex produced by Dicer into the RISC complex. The antisense 5' end is less stable than the sense end of the duplex, favoring the antisense loading into the RISC complex after helicase processing. However, loading may occur by both ends into the RISC complex.

GS has an additional characteristic in plants: The silencing signal has the ability to spread systemically. The nature of the systemic signal in plants was not yet determined. However, it may be concluded that these phenomena requires firstly a system to pass a signal from cell to cell, and secondly a strategy to amplify the signal. Apparently, it seems that the short dsRNA formed by DICER might be the answer. Some evidence suggests other hypotheses.

For instance, the initial long dsRNA strands could be amplified and transported with the help of movement proteins (Waterhouse et al., 2001). It has been demonstrated that plants have RNA dependent RNA polimerases (RdRP) – like enzymes that probably work amplifying the initial dsRNA thus transmitting the silencing signal. RdRP proteins could possibly mediate primer-dependent (using siRNA) and primer-independent mechanisms of RNA silencing. The production of dsRNA from single stranded template (ssRNA) is probably linked to the primer-independent process, so that silencing can be initiated in virus-infected plants or with transgenic RNAs. The differentiation mechanism between the viral and the transgenic RNAs targeted for silencing from the non-silenced endogenous RNAs is not clear, perhaps the ssRNA targeted for silencing presents aberrant features, which the enzyme is able to recognize.

Recent models classify different siRNA in primary and secondary types. Primary siRNA are generated from the activity of the Dicer enzyme, while secondary siRNA would be generated from a different pathway having the mandatory involvement of a RNA-dependent RNA Polymerase. Secondary siRNA is likely to regulate gene expression in cases where amplification of the silencing signal is important, they would also be important in cases where the original trigger for RNAi is absent. The common reports of GS resulting from plant transformation were proposed to be caused by the integration of multiple transgenes as inverted repeats leading to the formation of dsRNA (Waterhouse et al., 1998). This would initiate the RNAi pathway as previously discussed.

TRANSCRIPTIONAL GENE SILENCING

DNA methylation and chromatin remodeling play a major role in transcriptional gene silencing (TGS), blocking gene expression (Waterhouse et al., 2001). In TGS, silenced transgenes coding regions and promoters are densely methylated. It is also proposed that the increase in DNA methylation possibly induces formation of heterochromatin, which is associated to TGS (Ye et al., 1996; Wassenegger and Pélissier, 1998; Wassenegger, 2000). DNA methylation promotes protein binding that recognizes methylated cytosine, leading to chromatin remodeling, thus avoiding the binding of transcription factors. In Pinus radiata, the extent of DNA methylation increases in mature meristematic regions when compared to juvenile regions, suggesting that methylation is involved in developmental control and aging processes.

Heterochromatin can be defined as condensate chromosomal regions, which are densely stained and known for genetic inactivity. Methylation, acetylation, phosphorilation and ubiquitination of core histones H2A, H2B, H3 and H4 are implicated in gene regulation (Lippman and Martienssen, 2004). These chemical modifications within histones alter the packing state of DNA between euchromatin (active DNA) and heterochromatin (inactive DNA). Histone acetylation is one factor that can destabilize chromatin structure by altering the charge composition within chromatin.

Chemical alterations within histone tails may function as signals for chromatin remodeling complexes, which are responsible for regulating the accessibility of the cells transcriptional machinery to the DNA. At least in plants there is a direct link between DNA methylation and histone methylation suggesting that they play a common role in transcriptional gene silencing (Lippman and Martienssen, 2004).

Early research suggested that TGS and PTGS (RNAi) were independent phenomena. However, it was later discovered that viruses and transgenes originating dsRNA induced both TGS and PTGS (RNAi), suggesting that these could be alternative, but not exclusive routes of regulation (Vaucheret and Fagard, 2001). RNA silencing has also been associated to de novo DNA methylation in plants. The fact that almost all DNA and histone methylation events are confined to transposons and repeats suggests a role for RNAi as a targeting mechanism for specific sequence chromatin remodeling or TGS (Lippman and Martienssen, 2004). Research carried out on Schizosaccharomyces pombe and Arabidopsis indicates that the RNA-directed DNA methylation (RdDM) signal transmitted from the cytoplasm to the nucleus is most likely siRNA. Additionally, chromatin-based silencing guided by siRNAs may act as a genomic defence system to suppress mobile genetic elements or invasive DNA.

On the other hand, RNAi effector complex termed RITS (RNA-induced Initiation of Transcriptional gene Silencing) has been described, and it seems to be required for heterochromatin assembly in fission yeast (Schizosaccharomyces pombe). This same work suggests a mechanism for the role of the RNAi machinery and small RNAs in targeting of heterochromatin complexes and epigenetic gene silencing at specific chromosomal loci. The present model suggests similarities between the RISC and the RITS complex. The RITS complex would target DNA sequences and/or nascent RNA transcripts initiating heterochromatin formation and consequently TGS. It is possible that similar phenomenon occurs in plants since at least ten members of the Argonaute protein family that occur in Arabidopsis thaliana resemble proteins present in RITS (Baulcombe, 2004; Verdel et al., 2004).

MICRO RNA

MicroRNAs (miRNAs) are ~22 nt endogenous RNAs that can play important regulatory roles in animals and plants by cleavage or translational repression of mRNA (Bartel, 2004; Duan et al., 2006). These molecules comprise one of the more abundant classes of gene regulatory molecules in multicellular organisms. Micro RNAs were firstly reported in Caenorhabditis elegans by the discovery that the lin-4 gene coded a pair of small RNAs instead of a protein. Further evidence showed that these small RNA products had antisense complementarity and were responsible for the translational regulation of another gene, the lin-14. Lin-14 mRNAs levels were not altered but the protein output of the gene was reduced.

In plants, miRNAs are involved in the control of leaf and flower development (Aukerman and Sakai, 2003; Emery et al., 2003; Palatnik et al., 2003; Chen, 2004). It appears that a substantial fraction of the gene regulatory molecules in plants could be RNA rather than protein transcription factors. Plant ~22 nt long miRNAs are endogenously expressed and potentially processed from one arm foldback precursors.

These molecules are also generally conserved in evolution and come from regions of the genome distinct from previously annotated genes. Recent data demonstrates that miRNAs are also involved in other mechanisms such as stress and environmental change response.

MicroRNAs and siRNAs have a shared central biogenesis and can perform interchangeable biochemical functions. Therefore, these two classes of silencing RNAs cannot be distinguished by either their chemical composition or mechanism of action. However, some distinction can be made regarding origin, evolutionary conservation and types of genes they silence: (i) miRNAs derive from genomic loci distinct from other recognized genes, whereas siRNA often derive from mRNAs, transposons, viruses, or heterochromatic DNA; (ii) miRNAs are processed from transcripts that can form local RNA hairpin structures, whereas siRNAs are processed from long bimolecular RNA duplexes or extended hairpins; (iii) a single stranded mature miRNA is generated from each miRNA hairpin precursor molecule, whereas a multitude of siRNA duplexes are generated from each siRNA precursor molecule, leading to many different siRNA accumulating from both strands of this extended dsRNA; (iv) miRNA sequences are nearly always conserved in related organisms, whereas endogenous siRNA sequences are rarely conserved.

MicroRNAs in plants are probably processed by DCL1 (Dicer) in the nucleus, and its molecular pathway is exclusively linked to a dsRNA binding protein (HYL1). Mature miRNA can be loaded into RISC or microRNA effector complex (miRNP), the first directs mRNA cleavage and the second is responsible for translational repression. Preferentially plant miRNA use RNA target cleavage instead of translational suppression and are nearly perfectly paired to their targets.

Recently, it has been demonstrated that the modification of plant endogenous miRNA precursors to interfere with viral mRNA sequences can confer virus resistance in Arabidopsis thaliana. These modified miRNA are termed artificial miRNA and this technique will open new perspectives for engineering viral resistant plants.

VIRUS INDUCED GENE SILENCING (VIGS)

Virus induced gene silencing is a technique designed to suppress gene expression and study gene function in plants. VIGS can be defined as the silencing of endogenous plant genes initiated by recombinant viral vectors. The model includes viral dependent initiation and viral independent maintenance of VIGS. The approach consists of cloning and inserting plant endogenous gene sequences in recombinant viral vectors, which are then inoculated in plants, triggering PTGS/ RNAi. This ends up silencing plant genes with homologous sequences to those contained in the viral vectors (Burch-Smith et al., 2004).

In early approaches on VIGS studies, gene sequences were individually subcloned into viral genomes, and plants were physically inoculated using viral RNA produced by in-vitro transcriptional reactions. The previously described technique is time consuming and produces variable results, only being used when dealing with limited number of genes. An easier method for plant infection would be the use of agroinfiltration of viral cloned vectors. VIGS protocols can be optimized by the insertion of viral RNA genomes in binary vectors for agroinfiltration.

This technique uses Agrobacterium tissue infiltration for T-DNA transfer of encoded genes that will be transferred into the cells of the infiltrated region, and transcribed into the viral cDNAs, these transcripts would then serve as inocula to initiate systemic infection of the plant. The use of this form of viral inoculation has the advantage of not having to produce in-vitro viral transcripts.

VIGS is a powerful tool due to its fast initiation of silencing in intact wild-type or transgenic plants. VIGS has been utilized to investigate individual gene and gene family functions. Phenotypic variations attributed to gene suppression by VIGS can be obtained in a relatively short period of time. It is possible to silence genes in mature plants using this technique. Therefore, no plant transformation is necessary since the silencing is induced by the viral infection. The limitation of this approach resides in the viral host range, pattern of viral spreading, and symptoms caused by the infection.

TISSUE CULTURE OF WOODY PLANTS

Much has been written and more has been said about the applications of plant tissue culture to the nursery industry. The subject is still poorly understood by a majority of plant propagators. Tissue culture is often looked upon as being practical only for propagation of those plants which are difficult to propagate by conventional methods. This notion is quickly being laid to rest. An industry is emerging in various areas throughout the country which is taking advantage of technological advances in the realm of tissue culture of woody plants. This technology suggests that propagation by tissue culture is indeed applicable to the "difficult to propagate" species, and equally as important, it may offer economic advantages for some species which are considered relatively "easy to propagate".

The intent of this communication is to briefly describe the contemporary techniques of tissue culture of woody plants, and to review the advantages and limitations of tissue culture as a propagation method.

THE METHODOLOGY OF TISSUE CULTURE

The variety of techniques which can be used to get plant development in vitro (that is, by techniques such as tissue culture) is considerable and completely dependent upon the species in question. Single cells of leaf tissue can regenerate whole plants, as can shoot tips, leaf pieces, root pieces, lateral buds, or stem sections. Not all of these methods are applicable to woody plants, and indeed, not all have been applied to a commercial level to any plants.

Shoot tip culture is the method in widest use for the mass propagation of woody species. An actively growing shoot tip is surface sterilized and placed on a defined culture medium under sterile conditions. The culture medium contains inorganic and organic salts (macronutrients, micronutrients and vitamins) as well as an energy source (sucrose or table sugar), growth regulators, and agar)to gel the medium). If the growth regulators are appropriately balanced, the shoot tip elongates, lateral buds break and begin growth, and adventitious shoots are also produced on the stem piece. This rapid proliferation of shoots results in masses of shoots being produced from a single shoot tip. Up to a hundred shoots may be produced in as little as eight to twelve weeks from a single tip.

The number of shoots produced and the rapidity of shoot proliferation varies between species, and in some cases, between cultivars of a single species. Shoots are removed from the cultures at regular intervals and a portion of the mass is replaced on fresh media to continue proliferation. The small shoots which are removed are then rooted in a separate medium, either a sterile gelled medium or a peat-perlite medium (in much the same fashion as conventional woody cuttings).

Shoots produced through tissue culture are generally easy to root, even though the same cultivar may be difficult to root by cutting propagation. The resulting rooted shoot is referred to as a "plantlet" because of its miniature size, but these can generally be grown in the greenhouse at a rapid rate and with a high degree of survival.

Techniques for rooting tissue cultured shoots are currently receiving a great deal of research attention as are methods for establishing these shoots into the greenhouse environment.

THE TISSUE CULTURE LABORATORY

Most propagators would probably list the expense of setting up a tissue culture laboratory among the reasons for not getting involved with this technology. A lab does cost more than a mist bed! A more severe limitation is without doubt the absence of personnel skilled in the techniques of tissue culture. An individual who has had prior experience with tissue culture methodology can successfully operate a laboratory with a bare minimum of equipment. An autoclave or sterilizer, an accurate means of weighing chemicals, a small inventory of glassware, and chemical stocks or prepackaged media are all that is required to initiate cultures. The laboratory can be enlarged, more equipment added, and additional personnel hired as the need for such arises. The most critical factors are the ingenuity and experience of the laboratory manager.

As a tissue culture laboratory becomes operational, procedures other than the actual culturing process become critical. Maintenance of disease and insect free stock plants with a low titer of bacterial and fungal contamination is critical. Also important is the care and handling of the thousands of plantlets prior to their transfer to the field or containers. The ability to grow off the plantlets ultimately will limit production, rather than any limitation due to the propagation phase.

TISSUE CULTURE PROPAGATION OF WOODY SPECIES

Major advances in the mass propagation of woody plants have been made over the past ten years. Because of the somewhat variable response of species and cultivars to the in vitro environment, much research was (and still is) needed to define the cultural conditions required by ornamental species. As an example of the variability encountered, we have observed that seedling shoot tip cultures of crabapple produce as few as one or as many as sixty-four shoots per explant after three months in tissue culture. Similar variations in the tendency for multiple shoot production have also been noted with adult clonal material of different apple cultivars. The number of woody plant species which have been clonally propagated through tissue culture is increasing at a rapid rate, and in fact, most commercially important ornamental species have been studied. Perhaps the best publicized of the early research on woody plants involved apples, Douglas fir, and rhododendrons. An extensive commercial scale production proramme for apple scion cultivars and rootstocks has developed in England and in several European countries.

Using the successes of the apple, rhododendron, and maple prorammes as a basis, many recent advances have been made which will facilitate the mass propagation of other woody species. While it is true that cultivar differences account for lack of success with some plants, a growing body of evidence suggests that taxonomic families behave somewhat alike in tissue culture. A large number of deciduous and evergreen Rhododendron species share common cultural requirements, the most notable of which is the requirement for the same cytokinin for adventitious shoot formation. A similar relationship exists between the trees and shrubs of the Rosaceae (including crabapples, pears, plums, and hawthorns). Most rosaceous species will likely be mass propagated on media very similar to that found to be optimal for apples.

The anomalies alluded to by the crabapple seedling responses to tissue culture and the emerging similarities between the requirements of rosaceous trees and shrubs demonstrate that much research is needed to define the conditions necessary for commercial scale tissue culture production prorammes. As is often found to be the case with propagation systems, those systems described as optimal in the laboratory would likely need modification to be considered economical by the industry.

IMPACT OF THE TISSUE CULTURE INDUSTRY

As is always the case for any emerging technology, the strongest supporters for the adoption of that technology are likely those involved in its development.

Having acknowledged these biases, one must now consider the advantages and limitations of tissue culture propagation, and what its economic impact on the nursery industry will be.

Not every nursery will OPERATE a tissue culture laboratory. The trend towards specialization of nursery operations as either "propagators" or "producers" is likely to continue in the future. Operation and management of a tissue culture facility requires personnel and physical facilities which are quite different from those required by a container or field production nursery. Previously in this report where the establishment of the laboratory was considered, the relatively small initial investment in physical facilities and equipment was discussed. It should be reemphasized at this point, that the training and quality of the laboratory manager is more important than the laboratory itself, and that this expertise is not currently available among contemporary nursery propagators.

MOLECULAR STUDIES OF SECONDARY CELL WALL FORMATION

Wood properties are known to vary among species and among genotypes within species. This variability is heritable and thus presents an opportunity to select for improved wood properties, *i.e.* superior product quality. Such selection is currently hampered by costly traditional chemical and technological assays and the necessity to wait until the trees are nearly mature to evaluate wood properties. Application of modern genomic sciences to identify the genes controlling these properties, should increase selection efficiency and/or reduce the time and costs associated with measuring such properties, by providing early selection criteria and tools to alter cell wall properties in transgenic trees. As a highly specialized developmental process that is likely to involve a unique set of genes, it is obvious that the first place to study the molecular mechanisms of wood formation in woody perennials is trees.

As the secondary xylem of softwoods and hardwoods is different in many aspects, both gymnosperm and angiosperm species should be studied to fully understand the process of wood formation. Populus spp. and Eucalyptus spp. are evident candidates among the hardwood species, because of their ease of vegetative propagation, their suitability for genetic transformation, their small genome size (5×10^8 and 6×10^8 bp respectively, *i.e.* only a little larger than that of Arabidopsis) and the availability of genetic maps. With regard to the conifer model, and considering the high conservation of chromosome number and gene sequences in conifer species as well as the homogeneous cellular components of the wood, it is likely that the results gathered in the few studied species will be of benefit to research on other conifers.

The formation of the secondary cell wall is driven by the coordinated expression of numerous genes specifically involved in the biosynthesis, assembly, and deposition of polysaccharides, lignins, pectins, and cell wall protein. The use of molecular techniques in wood research has allowed the identification and characterization of a rather small proportion of the key molecular players involved in this process, such as those involved in lignification and cellulose synthesis, but also hemicelluloses, cell wall-associated proteins, and pectins. This lack of information is illustrated by the fact that from the several hundred genes presumably required for polysaccharide biosynthesis and deposition, only a handful have been characterized. Even if the main structural pathways are known to a certain extent, virtually nothing is known about their specific regulation.

It is likely that some unknown fraction of wood quality variability will derive from structural or regulatory genes that have not yet been identified and sequenced. Therefore, much more information at the gene and protein expression level is needed in order to understand the profound basic pathways characteristic for wood physiology and to create tools which could be targets for biotechnological approaches leading to the introduction of desired wood properties.

Large scale cDNA sequencing efforts to identify genes that are related to wood formation are being developed for tree species. Based on the determination of putative gene function by sequence homology, a wealth of genes of known function and that are active during the formation of woody tissues were isolated, providing a pool of candidate genes (CGs) for genetic manipulation of the wood forming processes. A significant proportion of the genes were also classified as orphan. We can speculate that some of these unknown genes could be specific regulators involved in wood formation. Transcript profiling using cDNA microarrays is being used in concert with proteomics for tracking the genes/proteins of interest and to achieve a comprehensive understanding of the molecular process of wood formation. In poplar, the expression patterns of 2,995 genes were analyzed during the successive stages in the differentiation process leading to mature xylem cells. This author also showed that many structural and potential regulatory genes of xylogenesis were under a strict developmental stage-specific regulation.

Of particular interest are those genes/proteins that underlie the anatomical, structural, and chemical differences observed between TW or CW versus NW, EW versus LW, and JW versus MW. The identification and characterization of gene products differentially expressed in developing xylem, associated with a range of wood characteristics, pinpoint important genes controlling chemical composition and architecture of cell walls and cell shape, therefore determining wood and end-use properties.

Proteins accumulating abundantly in young differentiating xylem of pine and poplar also provide us with essential knowledge of secondary cell wall formation. It is remarkable that S-adenosyl-l-Met synthases, one of the most highly expressed genes in poplar and pine developing-xylem expressed sequence tag libraries, were also strongly expressed at the proteome level in both species. The presence of severalS-adenosyl-l-Met synthases points out the importance of methyl transfer reactions and the complexity of gene regulation for methyl-group donation during xylogenesis.

The identification of genes specifically expressed in the highly specialized vascular cambium or differentiating xylem tissues may also give us substantial information with respect to the molecular processes involved in xylogenesis. Such genes are thought to play critical roles in the genetic engineering of wood properties, because genetic manipulation will require precise spatial regulation of introduced sequences.

All of these studies are powerful strategies to the identification of CGs potentially involved in wood formation and in controlling the chemical and mechanical properties of wood. Whether these CGs are involved in the genetic control of wood quality traits still needs to be tested by using (a) reverse genetics experiments in trees or model organisms or (b) forward genetics experiments: colocation study between CGs and wood quality quantitative trait loci or linkage disequilibrium mapping in natural populations. Mapping such CG is already under way in eucalyptus, pine and poplar, for which quantitative trait loci for wood and end-uses properties have been localized on genetic linkage maps.

PROSPECTS

Non-Woody Systems Shed New Light on the Cell Biology of Xylogenesis....

It is obvious that for the study of wood formation, woody models are desirable. However, a deeper understanding of the molecular mechanisms involved in cell wall biosynthesis and assembly can also arise from model plant systems such as Arabidopsis and zinnia (Zinnia elegans). Crucial to the use of such wood-forming models is the degree of similarity of xylem formation in these plants to that in the tree. More and more evidence supports the view that the vast majority of the biochemical, metabolic, cellular, and developmental processes is conserved throughout the plant kingdom.

This theory also applies to secondary xylem formation. Indeed, even if wood properties can be highly specific for a given species, it is reasonable to assume that the differences in wood properties are the result of natural variation in expression patterns or biochemical properties of proteins, and are also part of the biochemical, metabolic, cellular, and developmental pathways conserved by the evolution processes. Some of these conserved pathways have already been identified. They include for example, the synthesis, deposition, and orientation of cellulose MFs. The formation of reaction wood, although highly specific to trees, also involves conserved signaling pathways including thigmomorphogenesis, ethylene, and auxin signaling pathways. Arabidopsis undergoes secondary substantial thickening in the hypocotyl under appropriate growth conditions, and can therefore be viewed as a miniature tree. This species is the most advanced model system used in plant biology, with the complete genome sequence already available. With respect to wood formation, screening for Arabidopsis mutants has already yielded interesting results concerning structural and regulatory genes (*e.g.* homeobox genes). A gene playing a crucial role in the control of the orientation of microtubules in Arabidopsis has been identified and is very likely to play a similar role in other plant species including tree species. An alternative use of Arabidopsis in research in xylogenesis would be to reveal the function of CGs identified in tree genomics projects by reverse genetics or identification of knock-out mutants.

Certain aspects of wood development are also being studied in the ornamental garden plant, zinnia. In zinnia, mesophyll cells can be induced to redifferentiate synchronously, into tracheary elements, hence, proteins and genes can be identified at different stages of xylem formation.

But Trees Will Remain the Main Model for Field Testing

The limited amount of cambium and secondary xylem and the small size of these non-woody models make it difficult to isolate large amounts of tissue for investigations into the molecular biology and biochemistry of wood formation. In contrast, during the active growth of trees, kilograms of maturing xylem may be readily collected by simply peeling away the bark, thus providing highly enriched material for molecular studies. Given also the heterogeneous structure and complex functioning (*i.e.* seasonal cycle of cambial dormancy-activity, wood maturation, and production of HW) of wood, trees will remain the main model to investigate the whole dimension of the "making" of wood.

For a long time, the understanding of the process by which the vascular cambium produces wood has progressed very slowly. There has been an extensive descriptive literature addressing wood anatomy, chemistry and physical properties.

The understanding of the molecular and physiological mechanisms of cambial activity and wood formation is now considered as the main research area which must draw upon diverse disciplines, including genomics as well as the more traditional biochemical and wood sciences.

WOOD BIOSYNTHESIS

Wood (secondary xylem) is manufactured by a succession of five major steps, including cell division, cell expansion (elongation and radial enlargement), cell wall thickening (involving cellulose, hemicellulose, cell wall proteins, and lignin biosynthesis and deposition), programmed cell death, and HW formation.

WOOD CELLS ORIGINATE FROM VASCULAR CAMBIUM ACTIVITY

The vascular cambium is a secondary meristem derived from the procambium, which in turn develops from the apical meristem. The cambium plays a major role in the diametral growth of gymnosperm and angiosperm shoots and roots and is of great significance, particularly in respect to the wood that is produced. Cambial activity ensures the perennial life of trees through the regular renewing of functional xylem and phloem. The cambial zone includes the cambium sensu stricto made up of only one layer of juvenile cells, called initials, and the phloem and xylem mother cells, which are both produced by the dividing cambial initials.

Xylem mother cells always divide more compared with phloem mother cells, which explains the considerable disproportion existing between phloem and xylem tissues. The cambial zone consists of a few layers of narrow, elongated, thin-walled cells and comprises two types of highly vacuolated cells. Short radial initials give rise to rays that are essential to the translocation of nutrients between phloem and xylem. Elongated fusiform initials divide lengthwise and produce secondary vascular tissues through periclinal divisions (tangential plane) in a position-dependent manner: on the inner side, wood elements (mostly tracheids in gymnosperms, but also vessel elements, vessel-associated cells, axial parenchyma and fibres in dicotyledons) and, on the outer side, phloem cells (sieve tubes, and, in dicotyledons, companion cells, axial parenchyma, and fibres).

Anticlinal (radial) divisions of the fusiform initials also produce daughter cells similar to mother cells and ensure the harmonious increase in circumference of the cambium. New ray initials are formed by subsequent anticlinal divisions of fusiform initials.

THE DIFFERENTIATION OF XYLEM CELLS INVOLVES FOUR MAJOR STEPS

The daughter cells, produced by the cambial initials, give rise to a wide variety of wood cells, whose unique characteristics and three-dimensional associations define the intrinsic structure of wood. We will focus on the maturation process engaged by the xylem cells: tracheids, vessels, and fibres involved in water transport and mechanical support of the entire tree. The differentiation of these cells involves four major steps: cell expansion, followed by the ordered deposition of a thick multilayered secondary cell wall, lignification, and cell death.

Derivative cells expand longitudinally and radially to reach their final size during the formation of the primary wall. Xyloglucan endotransglycosylases, endoglucanases, expansins, pectin methyl esterases, and pectinases are among the primary determinants of this process. Once expansion is completed, the formation of the secondary cell wall begins, driven by the coordinated expression of numerous genes specifically involved in the biosynthesis and assembly of four major compounds: polysaccharides (cellulose, hemicelluloses), lignins, cell wall proteins and other minor soluble (stilbenes, flavonoids, tannins, and terpenoids), and insoluble (pectins and cell wall proteins) compounds in a neutral solvent.

Between 40 per cent and 50 per cent of wood consists of cellulose. The fundamental structure units are the microfibrils (MFs), which are the result of a strong association of inter- and intrachain hydrogen bonds between the different chains of β-linked Glc residues in a manner so precise that microfibrillar cellulose is largely crystalline. Until recently, not even one single enzyme involved in cellulose biosynthesis and deposition was purified or cloned. A first breakthrough had been the identification of genes encoding the catalytic subunit of the cellulose synthase (Ces) complex.

In Arabidopsis, at least six genes encode putative catalytic subunits of Ces. In addition, a large gene family of over 20 more distantly related genes, so-called Ces-like (Csl) genes, exists, whose gene products most likely are involved in the synthesis of other polysaccharides. In higher plants, the substrate for Ces (UDP-D-Glc) is provided by Suc synthase. The complex Ces/Suc synthase is thought to have a cytoplasmic localization and the growing cellulose chain may be secreted through the membrane via a pore. Cortical microtubules (mainly composed of α- and β-tubulin) may determine the wall pattern by defining the position and orientation of cellulose MFs during the differentiation of conducting elements, probably by guiding the movement of the cellulose-synthesizing complex in the plasma membrane. However, although in many cases co-orientation of microtubules and MFs were observed, mathematical models (that remain to be tested in wood-forming tissue) relying on the geometry of the cell, have been proposed to challenge this dogma.

The water-insoluble cellulose MFs are associated with mixtures of soluble non-cellulosic polysaccharides, the hemicelluloses, which account for about 25 per cent of the dry weight of wood. They generally occur as heteropolymer such as glucomannan, galactoglucomannan, arabinogalactan, and glucuronoxylan, or as a homopolymer like galactan, arabinan, and β-1,3-glucan. The biosynthesis of these polysaccharides occurs in the Golgi apparatus by a process that can be divided into two main steps: the synthesis of the backbone by polysaccharide synthases, and the addition of side chain residues in reactions catalyzed by a variety of glycosyltransferases.

The third major component of wood (25 per cent–35 per cent) is lignin, a phenolic polymer derived from three hydroxycinnamyl alcohols (monolignols):p-coumaryl alcohol, coniferyl alcohol, and sinapyl alcohol, giving rise to H, G, and S units, which differ from each other only by their degree of methoxylation. Lignin embeds the polysaccharide matrix giving rigidity and cohesiveness to the wood tissue as a whole, and providing the hydrophobic surface needed for the transport of water. Lignin content and monomeric composition vary widely among different taxa, individuals, tissues, cell types, and cell wall layers. As an example, no S units are detected in gymnosperms compared with angiosperms. Lignin biosynthesis has been the most studied pathway, resulting in the cloning of several structural genes. However, it is somewhat surprising that recent attempts at engineering lignin biosynthesis have demonstrated that our current models of the pathway are incomplete.

Cell wall proteins and pectins are among the other minor compounds of the cell wall. Although different proteins are present in the cell wall at different times during development, the amount of protein remaining in the wood is small. Nevertheless, such proteins could play important roles determining the composition and morphology of xylem cell walls. Abundant cell wall associated proteins have been found in many plants and have traditionally been classified into four main groups: Gly-rich proteins, Pro-rich proteins, arabinogalactan proteins, and Hyp-rich glycoproteins (or extensins). These proteins are cross-linked into the cell wall and probably have structural functions. Pectins are thought to play a fundamental role in the regulation of cell wall extensibility. They are also thought to be exported from the Golgi apparatus as highly esterified galacturonan and then de-esterified in muro by cell wall-bound pectin methylesterases, thus allowing the formation of intermolecular bonds through calcium ions.

When lignification is completed, conducting xylem elements undergo programmed cell death, involving cell-autonomous, active, and ordered suicide, in which specific hydrolases (Cys and Ser proteases, nucleases, and RNase) are recruited. Several factors (auxins, cytokinins, and Suc) prepare the cell to die by determining the profile of hydrolases synthesized by the cell. These hydrolases are inactive in the vacuole. By a signal that remains unknown, a calcium flux provokes the vacuoles to collapse with the release of hydrolases that degrade all of the cellular content but not the secondary cell wall.

REGULATION OF WOOD BIOSYNTHESIS

The role of phytohormones in procambium initiation, cambial cell division, primary cell wall expansion, and secondary wall formation has been reviewed by Sundberg et al. (2000) and Mellerowicz et al. (2001). Recent findings have demonstrated the existence of an auxin (indole-3-acetic acid [IAA]) gradient across the developing vascular tissues of pine and poplar.

This IAA concentration gradient seems to have a function in positional signaling, *i.e.* cambial derivatives develop according to their position along the gradient, and neighbouring cell files receive the same dose to develop in a synchronized manner. A Suc gradient has been observed as well and may provide additional positional information for xylem and phloem differentiation.

Other hormones than auxins have been shown to be involved in xylogenesis by interacting with IAA in a synergetic (gibberellins, cytokinins, and ethylene) or inhibitory (abscisic acid) manner.

Knowledge of the molecular events that determine the differentiation pathway of a cambial derivative is embryonic. Even if the intervening signal transduction steps remain mysterious, we can assume that these signaling inputs result in altered patterns of gene transcription, which in turn requires the activity of specific transcription factors. In particular, considerable progress has been made in understanding the roles of transcription factors in controlling lignification. The analysis of lignification genes have also shown the presence in the promoter of conserved motifs that have been demonstrated to be important in xylem localized gene expression. Proteins that can bind this motif and activate the transcription, belong to the MYB family. Two MYB genes preferentially expressed inPinus taeda xylem were proposed to be involved in regulating transcription during xylogenesis.

WOOD CELL WALLS ARE HIGHLY STRUCTURED

The cell wall is composed of several layers that are fabricated at different periods during cell differentiation. The first layer to be developed after cell division is called the middle lamella, which is found between the wood cells, and ensures the adhesion of a cell with its neighbours. The middle lamella is only 0.5 to 1.5 µm thick and is made up of pectic substances to which lignin may be added during the differentiation period. At the beginning of cell differentiation, the primary cell wall forms. This new, highly elastic layer is attached to the middle lamella and is approximately 0.1 µm thick. The primary cell wall is made up of several layers of MFs, which are arranged randomly within this wall. Pectic substances, lignin, and hemicelluloses can be found between these MFs.

As the developing cell reaches its definitive size, a new layer is formed inside the primary cell wall, which is the most important layer for the cell, in terms of mechanical strength. This new secondary cell wall is divided into three different layers, S_1, S_2, and S_3. Each of these layers is composed of cellulose MFs, aligned in an ordered, parallel arrangement, which differs from S layer to S layer. Hemicelluloses and lignin are also present in each of these layers. These three S layers can be modified during cell maturation, which lasts for several days after the birth of the wood cell, *e.g.* the amount of lignin and cellulose laid down in the secondary cell wall may be influenced by abiotic factors such as mechanical stress, *i.e.* wind and stem lean.

The S_1 layer is the thinnest of the S layers, being only 0.1 to 0.35 µm thick, and representing just 5 per cent to 10 per cent of the total thickness of the cell wall. This layer is considered as an intermediate between the primary cell wall and the S_2 and S_3layers. The MF angle with regard to the cell axis is

60° to 80°. The S_2 layer is the thickest layer in the secondary cell wall, and is the most important, with regard to mechanical support. The thickness of the S_2 layer varies between 1 and 10 μm, and accounts for 75 per cent to 85 per cent of the total thickness of the cell wall.

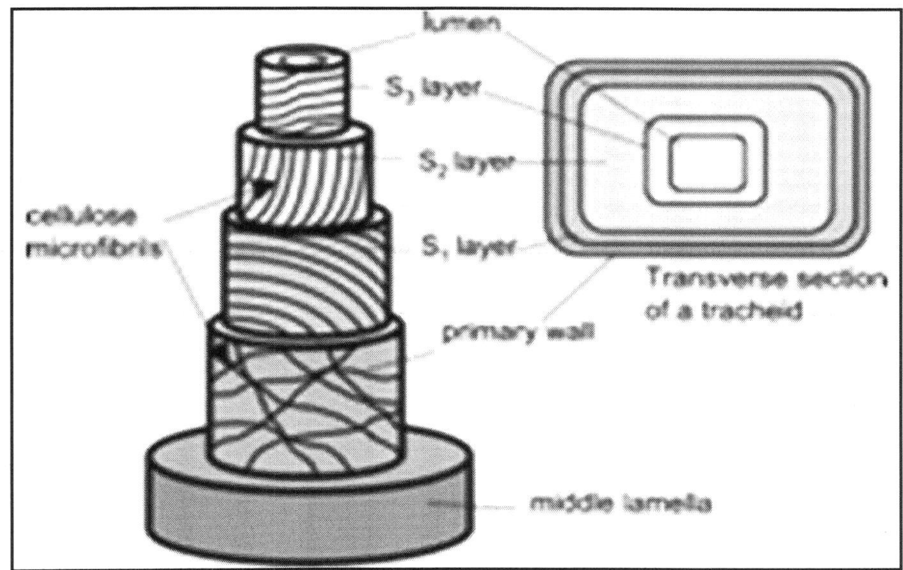

Fig. Three-dimensional structure of the secondary cell wall of a tracheid (xylem cell). The cell wall is divided into different layers, each layer having its own particular arrangement of cellulose MFs, which determine the mechanical and physical properties of the wood in that cell. These MFs may be aligned irregularly (as in the primary cell wall), or at a particular angle to the cell axis (as in layer S1, S2, and S3). The middle lamella ensures the adhesion between cells.

The MF angle in this layer is 5° to 30° to the cell axis, and can be even higher, depending on external mechanical stress. The angle of the cellulose MFs in the S_2 layer can influence greatly the physical and mechanical properties of the cell and even stem wood as a whole. As the MF angle increases, with regard to the cell axis, wood becomes less rigid, and the longitudinal modulus of elasticity decreases, as in the case of juvenile and compression wood (CW). The innermost layer of the secondary cell wall, the S_3 layer, is relatively thin, being only 0.5 to 1.10 μm thick. The MFs are ordered in a parallel arrangement, but less strictly than in the S_2 layer, and the MF angle is 60° to 90° with regard to the cell axis.

NEWLY DEVELOPED WOOD IS STRETCHED LONGITUDINALLY AND COMPRESSED TANGENTIALLY

Immediately after cell birth, the newly developed cells undergo a several day long "maturation" period, in which two mechanisms take place in the cell wall: (a) as lignin is deposited, the amorphic cellulose matrix swells transversely, and (b) when cellulose crystallization occurs, MFs shrink longitudinally. The combined effect of these two mechanisms results in a longitudinal shrinking of the cell. However, as the maturing wood cells are attached to older, already lignified cells, they cannot shrink completely.

Hence, these maturing cells are held in a state of tensile stress, and it is only on cutting the wood, that these "maturation stresses" can be released in the form of residual strains along the longitudinal axis. The wood cells at the surface of a tree are therefore stretched longitudinally and compressed tangentially and can be said to be held in tension. However, as more and more wood is added to the tree surface, the wood cells inside the trunk are slowly compressed, until they are completely held in compression, towards the center of the trunk. This gradient of mechanical stress in a trunk, whereby the outside is held in tension, and the center in compression, is called growth stress, and can be highly detrimental to wood quality, resulting in warping and twisting of boards and planks.

HW: The Final Transformation of Xylem Cells

On cutting a mature tree, several different colored zones may be observed, a lighter colored external zone: the sapwood (SW), and often a darker colored wood: the HW situated at the center of the tree. A third zone, often intermediate in colour—the transition zone, TZ—may exist between the two. SW is known as the functional part of the tree and is sometimes termed the "living" part of the tree. Although SW contains living cells, most of its mass is comprised of terminally differentiated non-living tracheids or libriform fibres. Soon after their birth in the cambium, wood cells die, except for the longitudinal and radial parenchyma cells, which remain alive and functional until several years later, when they too die.

It is when these parenchyma cells become dysfunctional, that HW forms. A specific role for HW has not yet been determined, although it has been suggested that it forms to provide long-term resistance to pathogens or even provides a mechanical role in tree support. Recent research suggests that HW forms as a response to a hydraulic stimulus and that HW may even develop irregularly, both radially and longitudinally in the trunk, to maintain a constant and optimal proportion of SW in the tree stem. As yet, there is no clear explanation as to why or how HW forms, although a theory has been put forward by Higuchi (1997), which is supported by recent research. Higuchi (1997) proposed that endogenous factors trigger expression of genes involved in phenolics biosynthesis in parenchyma cells bordering the TZ. As the parenchyma cells die, these phenolics are released and diffused into the neighbouring cell walls and lumens.

Possible candidates that may trigger the molecular signal include an increase in ethylene, which is needed for polyphenol production, or a rapid change in water content near the TZ resulting in bordered pit aspiration, and even external mechanical stress, *i.e.* wind loading or stem lean, as trees which have been subjected to such a stress, show greater HW formation near the zone of mechanical loading. However, HW formation is also under species-specific genetic control as some species exist which do not even produce HW, even at a very advanced age. Once genes in the TZ have been activated by a molecular signal, a cascade of events occurs resulting in eventual cell death.

Very little work has been carried out on the identification of the genes involved in this process. However, recent research has shown that in black walnut (Juglans nigra), flavanol biosynthesis was up-regulated in the TZ. Flavonoids are highly soluble polyphenols and in black walnut, the flavanol production was found to be highly correlated with the transcript levels of genes encoding the enzymes chalcone synthase (CHS), flavanone 3-hydroxylase (F3H), and dihydroflavonol 4-reductase (DFR), all of which are implicated in the flavonoid pathway (Beritognolo et al., 2001). At the same time that these genes are being expressed in the TZ, carbohydrate content decreases drastically in this zone. Magel et al. (1994) found that in black locust (Robinia pseudoacacia) non-structural storage carbohydrates (Glc, Fru, Suc, and starch) decrease from the outer to the inner SW, with only trace amounts present in the TZ, thereby suggesting that these sugars and starch are necessary for polyphenol synthesis.

To elucidate the mechanism by which HW forms, future research should concentrate on the genes expressed in the TZ of different species, as well as the factors, endogenous or exogenous, inducing molecular activity in this zone.

WOOD IS A HIGHLY VARIABLE RAW MATERIAL

Wood differs among trees. Use of the terms "softwood" for gymnosperms and "hardwood" for dicotyledon angiosperms is a crude acknowledgment of this difference. This variability is due to the heterogeneity of the cell types that make up the different woods and the structure of the individual cells. Anatomical, chemical, and physical differences in wood characteristics within a single tree are also a common feature. These include: (a) variation within the annual ring in temperate zones, *i.e.* early versus late wood, (b) variation due to juvenile wood (JW) with extremely variable properties, ranging from the pith to the bark, particularly in the early years of cambium activity, and (c) variation between normal and reaction wood. Wood can also be modified by damage from pathogens and by wounding.

WOOD FORMATION VARIES DURING THE GROWING SEASON

In temperate regions, the annual course of cambial activity (dormancy and activation) is induced by temperature and/or photoperiod. In temperate zones, EW is formed early in the growing season when temperature and photoperiod are favorable for active growth. EW has shorter cells and a lower density resulting from thin-walled tracheids or fibres of large radial diameter. LW is formed in the late summer or autumn when cambial cell division and expansion declines. LW has high density resulting from the small tracheid/fibre radial diameter and large tangential wall thickness. Having narrower lumens in the wood cells, the LW is much less vulnerable to water-stress-induced xylem embolism, and so increases the safety of water conductance. The passage of one type of wood cell to another is always abrupt between two growing seasons, *i.e.* between autumn and the following spring. However, within one growing season, this passage may be relatively progressive or abrupt depending on the species.

WOOD FORMATION VARIES DURING THE AGING PROCESS

The transition from juvenile wood (formed during the first 10–20 years of a tree's life, *i.e.* in young trees and in the crown of older trees; Zobel and Sprague, 1998) to mature wood (MW) is another major transition typically found in wood during a tree's life. As demand for wood continues to increase and as new trees are developed that grow faster than their predecessors and are often logged at an early stage, the proportion of JW in the harvested timber increases. One of the characteristics of JW compared with MW is a lower density and a higher MF angle, which generally leads to such wood being considered "inferior" (lower tensile and tear strength) to MW.

REACTION WOOD: A MECHANISM BY WHICH TREES RESPOND TO STEM DISPLACEMENT

Reaction wood is generally formed in response to a non-vertical orientation of the stem caused by prevailing winds, snow, slope, or asymmetric crown shape. This abnormal type of wood forms as part of a developmental process, which aims to re-orient a leaning stem or branch, so as to enable the tree find a more favorable position. In both softwood and hardwood species, such tissue is often associated with eccentric radial growth of the leaning stem and in conifers is called CW as it often appears in localized zones of the tree held in compression, *e.g.* on the underside of a leaning stem. CW is highly lignified with more p-hydroxyphenyl subunits, and contains less cellulose than NW. The density of CW is up to 50 per cent higher than that of NW. In CW, the MFangle of the cellulose fibres in the S_2 layer of the cell wall is high ($<45°$), tracheid length is reduced, cell cross-sectional profile is rounder, and the intercellular spaces larger.

In hardwood species, reaction wood is called tension wood (TW) as it tends to form in zones of the tree held in tension *e.g.* the upper side of a leaning stem. The overall lignin content of TW is lower, the cellulose content is higher and MFangle is lower than that of corresponding NW. The wood produced on the side of a stem or branch opposite to the reaction wood (opposite wood) may also be of a special nature and can be viewed as having many properties intermediate between NW and reaction wood. The signaling pathway which controls reaction wood formation is still poorly understood but may be a gravitropic response of the tree, related to intrinsic growth direction and phytohormone distribution and interaction, particularly that of ethylene and auxin.

A high proportion of reaction wood in a trunk is considered to be a major problem for several industrial applications. CW constitutes major defects in wood quality (the increase in S_2 MF angle in CW, causes an increase in longitudinal shrinkage, and consequently, lumber with CW is more likely to warp during drying) and fibre products (decrease of pulp yield). TW is also a problem for the solid wood industry as it increases longitudinal, radial, and tangential shrinkage during the drying process.

The most important mechanism by which reaction wood allows a tree to return to the vertical, occurs during the cell maturation process. In CW (gymnosperms), the MF angle in the S_2 layer is much higher (30°–45° to the cell axis) than in NW (5°–30°), due to a greater deposit of lignin laid down between the MF chains. As a result of this change in cell wall chemical composition, the newly developed wood cells tend to expand longitudinally. However, as explained in a previous section for NW, the new cells are attached to older cells, and cannot deform fully, therefore, they too exist in a state of mechanical stress.

On cutting CW in a tree trunk, the wood therefore expands longitudinally, as these stresses are released. In TW (angiosperms), an extra layer exists between the lumen and the S_3 layer, called the gelatinous, or G layer. The G layer is almost entirely made up of cellulose, with an almost vertical MF angle. During maturation, this layer shrinks strongly in the longitudinal direction, thereby creating a very strong state of tensile stress in the cell. The combined result of reaction wood cells is to "push" the tree upright in the case of conifers, and to "pull" the tree to a vertical position in hardwoods.

This considerable plasticity in wood properties, as reflected by the coexistence of these several different types of wood within a single tree, is certainly due to natural variations in the expression patterns of genes/proteins. This variation provides a unique opportunity to dissect the molecular and biochemical mechanisms underlying such differences.

COMPARATIVE ANALYSIS OF GS GENE FAMILIES IN SEQUENCED PLANT GENOMES

To examine the evolutionary relationships of poplar GS genes we performed a cladistic analysis based on deduced amino acid sequences, including the complete GS gene families from the sequenced genomes of Arabidopsis, rice, grape, sorghum and poplar. Pine and spruce GS genes were also included in this comparative analysis. Phylogenetic reconstruction at the molecular level shows the separation of cytosolic (GS1) and chloroplastic (GS2) sequences in angiosperms as two well differentiated clusters. The poplar duplicates for GS2 and GS1 genes were distributed in the two clusters. GS1 genes from Arabidopsis, rice, grape and sorghum were distributed in three subfamilies and the PtGS1.2 and PtGS1.3 duplicates were clearly associated to two of these subfamilies. In contrast, the PtGS1.1duplicate was outside the conserved GS1 subfamilies and was more closely aligned with the GS1 isoforms of gymnosperms that group outside the main subfamilies of GS1 in angiosperms. However, these data should be interpreted with caution because the support values of the clades are moderate.

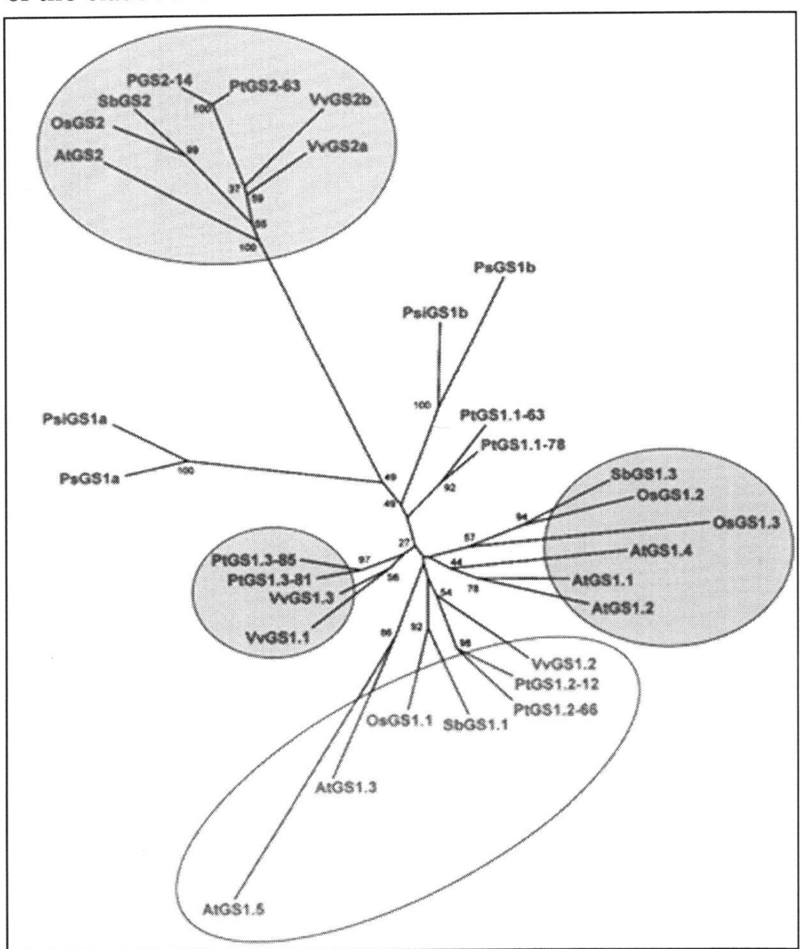

Fig. Relationships between poplar and other GS gene families in plants. Phylogenetic analyses of predicted full-length protein sequences were performed using the neighbour joining method. Tree was constructed as described. Pt: Populus trichocarpa. Os:Oryza sativa. Vv: Vitis vinifera. Sb: Sorghum bicolor. At: Arabidopsis thaliana. Ps: Pinus sylvestris. Psi: Picea sitchensis.

REGULATORY REGIONS IN THE POPLAR GS GENES

In order to get insight into the function of GS genes in poplar, the presence of regulatory elements in the 5'-upstream regions was investigated. According to results previously obtained in the structural and phylogenetic analyses, we decided to consider exclusively regulatory elements that were present in the two members of a GS duplicate. In thePtGS1.1, PtGS1.2 and PtGS1.3 genes, these common regulatory elements were found concentrated in the proximal region of the promoter (about 600 bp upstream the initiation of translation).

In contrast, the presence of common regulatory elements spanned a major region in the promoter of the PtGS2 duplicate (about 1300 bp upstream the initiation of translation). Putative regulatory elements involved in the interaction with Myb trancription factors were identified exclusively in the PtGS1.3 duplicate. Light-responsive elements such as GATA boxes were identified in all gene duplicates except PtGS1.2. Regulatory elements involved in tissue-specific gene expression (mesophyll, roots) were identified in all genes except PtGS1.3, whereas ABA response elements were present in the promoters of PtGS1.2 duplicates. Boxes specific to cytokinin response were identified in all GS genes but auxin response elements were exclusively found inPtGS1.1. The poplar GS2 promoter contains a sequence of about 200 bp showing a 90 per cent identity with light-regulatory elements that have been functionally characterized in the GS2 of pea and common bean [18]. Finally, the presence of AT-rich regions was detected in all GS promoters although they were much less abundant in the PtGS2 duplicate.

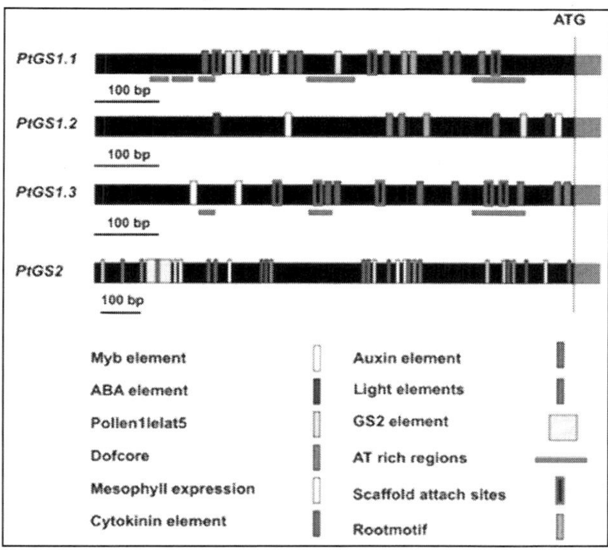

Fig. The regulatory regions of the poplar GS genes. The 5' upstream regions of GS genes are represented. Regulatory elements conserved in each pair of duplicated genes are marked in colours. The position of the ATG is marked on the right.

ORGAN-SPECIFIC EXPRESSION OF DUPLICATE GS GENES IN POPLAR

To understand the regulation of the GS gene family in poplar and obtain further insight into the biological roles of members in the gene family, GS expression was precisely quantified spatial and temporally. Total RNA was extracted from different organs and the relative abundance of GS transcripts was determined quantitatively by real-time PCR (qPCR). In all cases the transcript levels were normalized by comparison with expression levels of reference genes (as described in Material and Methods). Two month-old hybrid poplars were divided into above-ground and root-regions. The aerial region included the meristematic apex (A), young leaves and stem internodes (A1), intermediate leaves and stem internodes (A2), mature leaves and stem internodes (A3).

Aerial regions A1, A2 and A3 were further subdivided in lamina of the leaf (L), leaf vein (V) and stem (S). The root region included the main root close to the root crown (R1) and the secondary root masses (R2). The gene expression profiles of PtGS1.1, PtGS1.2, PtGS1.3 and PtGS2 differed significantly in the samples examined. PtGS1.1 transcripts were particularly abundant in the aerial regions containing intermediate and mature leaves (A2 and A3) and in R2. Interestingly, maximum levels of PtGS1.1 expression were observed in the leaf lamina (L2, L3) with decreased abundance in the leaf veins (V2, V3).

Minor levels of gene expression were observed in petioles (P2, P3) and stems (S2, S3). For the PtGS1.2 duplicate the highest transcript abundance was observed in the secondary root masses (R2), while about a half of this value was observed in petioles (P2, P3) and stems (S2, S3) of the aerial parts (A1 and A2). Much lower levels of PtGS1.2 transcripts were detected in remaining samples. The expression of the PtGS1.3 duplicate was predominant among the poplar GS1 genes, and high levels of PtGS1.3transcripts were observed in the apex, aerial and root sections. Furthermore, levels of PtGS1.3 transcripts were highest of the poplar GS gene family in the apex. It is important to note that in the aerial sections, expression of PtGS1.3 was clearly associated with samples enriched in vascular tissue, such as petioles (P1, P2 and P3) and stems (S1, S2 and S3) whereas lower levels of gene expression were observed in the leaf lamina in all sections examined. Finally, analysis of the PtGS2duplicate revealed that the transcripts of this family member were the most abundant in the young leaves (A1), and decreased progressively from the top to the bottom of the tree, with the lowest values detected in the roots.

In order to determine if there was a correspondence between the expression patterns of the GS transcripts and the distribution of GS polypeptides, we examined the distribution of GS polypeptides in different organs. Total proteins were extracted from leaves, stems and roots of two month-old poplar trees and GS polypeptides in these organs were identified by western blot analysis using antibodies raised against pine GS [19]. It has been previously reported that these antibodies were able to recognize specifically poplar GS polypeptides. The identification of two GS polypeptides, GS2 (45 kDa) and GS1 (40 kDa) in the leaf lamina. The GS1 polypeptide was predominant in stems and roots.

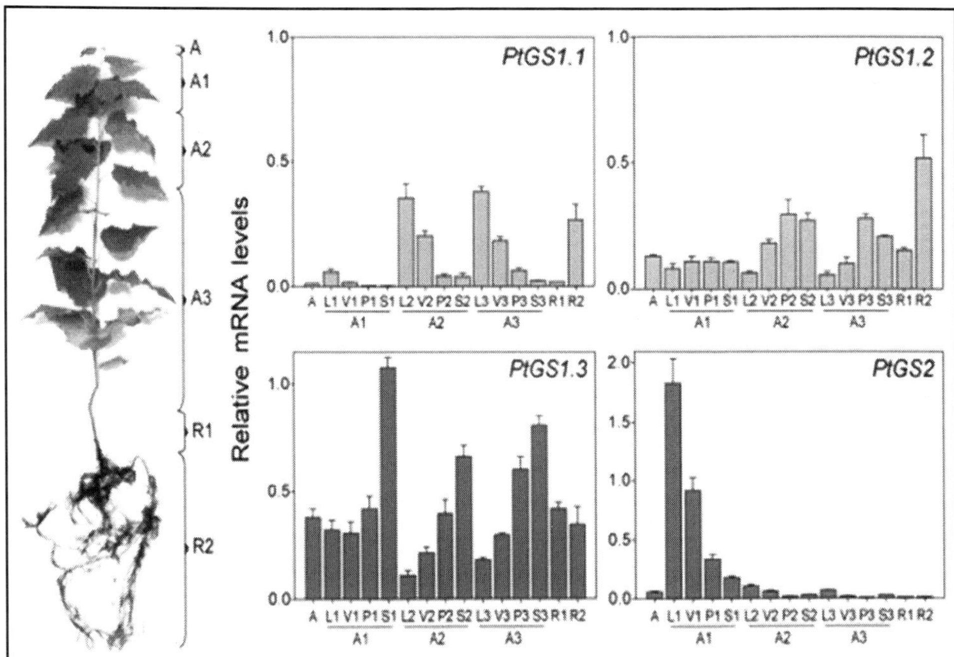

Fig. Spatial distribution of GS gene expression in poplar trees. Total RNA was extracted from different organs of 2-month-old hybrid poplar. A, meristematic apex. A1, A2 and A3, aerial sections from the top to the bottom of tree. L, leaf lamina. V, veins. P, petiole. S, stem. R1, primary root. R2, secondary root masses. Transcript levels of PtGS1.1, PtGS1.2, PtGS1.3 and PtGS2 were determined by real-time qPCR analysis as described. Expression levels are presented as relative values to reference genes (actin2 and ubiquitin). The histograms represent the mean values of three independent experiments with standard deviations.

Proteins were extracted from different organs of 2-month-old hybrid poplar. L, leaf. S, Stem. R, root. Thirty micrograms of proteins per lane were separated by PAGE and then transferred to a nitrocellulose membrane, where the proteins were probed using a specific antibody developed against pine GS [19]. A, One dimensional analysis. B, Two dimensional analysis. Spot variants in two dimensional gel separation of GS polypeptides has been previously reported [31] which could be the result of post-translational modifications. The molecular size (kDa) of protein markers are indicated on the left. Major GS spots observed in the different experiments are marked by arrows.

In order to investigate the correspondence of GS trancripts and GS polypeptides in the different organs, total proteins from the same protein samples (leaves, stems and roots) were also separated by two-dimensional gel electrophoresis (2D-PAGE), and the GS polypeptides identified by western blotting. This experimental approach allowed us to identify GS polypeptides of different charge among the family of GS polypeptides of the same size. Thus, in the leaf lamina the GS2 polypeptide was resolved as several spots with the most abundant exhibiting a calculated isoelectric point (pI) of 5.26. The GS1 polypeptide was resolved as a major spot of a pI of 5.52. In the stem, two major major spots corresponded to GS1 polypeptides of pI 5.20 and 5.81. Finally, in the roots the major GS1 spot had a calculated pI of 5.14. These experimental pI values were in the range of the predicted pI values for poplar GS polypeptides.

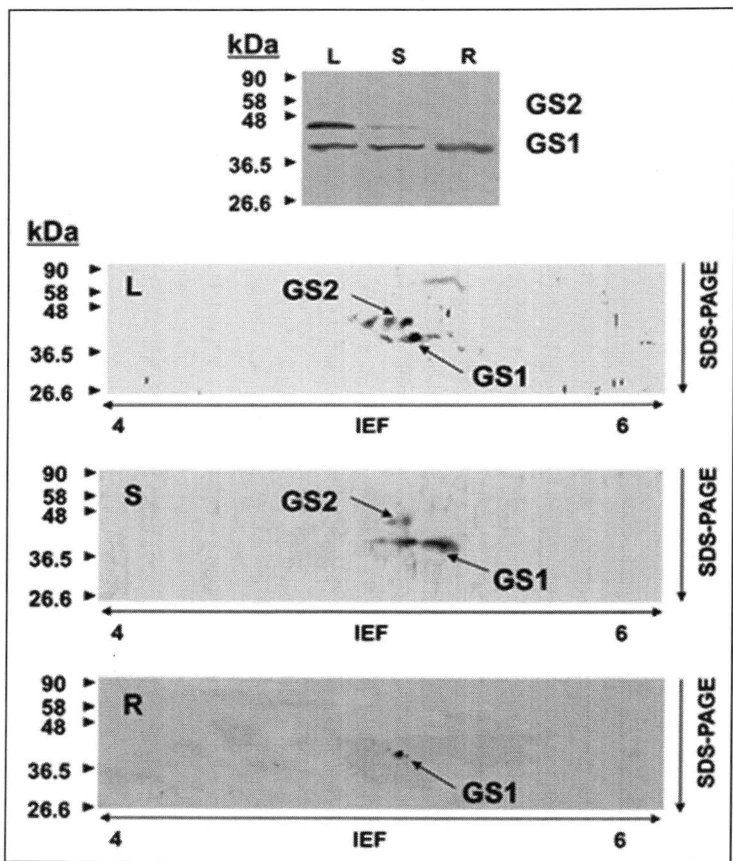

Fig. Analysis of GS polypeptides in poplar trees.

SEASONAL CHANGES IN GS GENE EXPRESSION

We were also interested to know the seasonal changes in the expression of the GS gene family in poplar. Transcript levels of PtGS1.1, PtGS1.2, PtGS1.3 and PtGS2 were quantitatively determined in RNA extracts from leaves, stem, buds and bark of 10-year-old poplar trees (Populus tremula x P. alba, clone

INRA 7171 1-B-4). GS duplicates exhibited contrasting patterns of gene expression during annual growth. The expression of the PtGS1.1 duplicate was very low during winter and increased during spring to reach the maximum values at the end of summer and autumn.

Interestingly, the peak values of transcripts were observed in leaves. Transcript abundance for the PtGS1.2 duplicate was low in all samples examined at the different seasons of the year. PtGS1.3 was highly expressed in stems buds and bark during all seasons with peak transcript levels during spring and autumn. Interestingly, the levels of PtGS1.3 transcripts were low in leaves except in autumn when levels increased significantly. Finally, high levels of PtGS2 transcripts were exclusively detected in expanding leaves in spring.

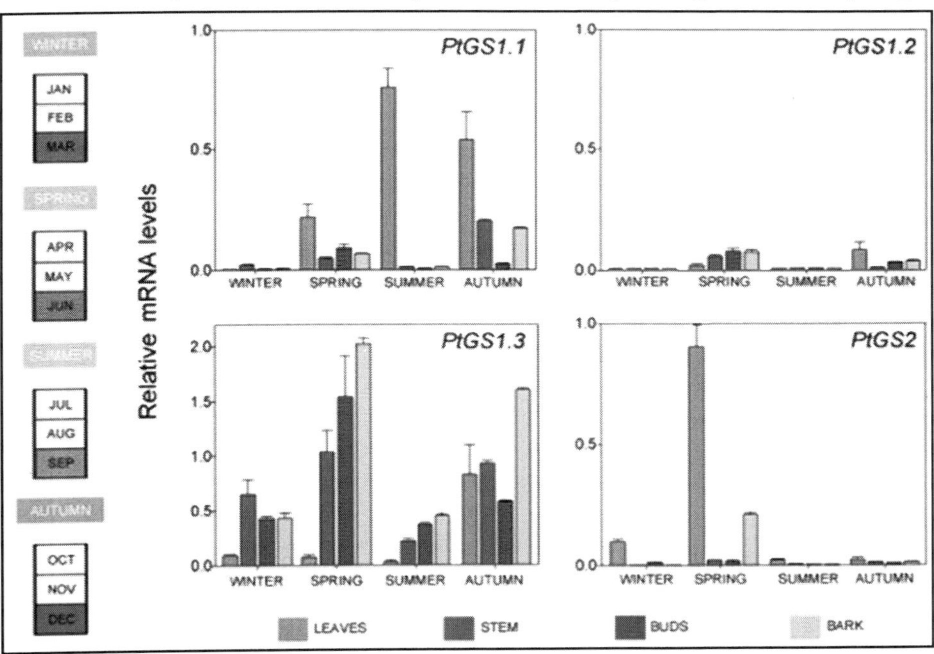

Fig. Seasonal changes of GS gene expression in poplar trees.

Total RNA was extracted from leaves, stem, buds and bark of 10-year-old hybrid poplar trees. Transcript levels of PtGS1.1, PtGS1.2, PtGS1.3 and PtGS2 were determined by real-time qPCR analysis as described. Expression levels are presented as relative values to reference genes (actin2 and ubiquitin). The histograms represent the mean values of at least three independent experiments with standard deviations.

5

Hormones and Endodormancy Induction in Woody Plants

ROOT REGROW HORMONE FOR PLANTS

Auxins are plant hormones that aid the growth of adventitious roots, those that grow from old, woody roots or from leaves, branches or stems. Plants naturally produce the auxin indoleacetic acid (IAA).

Among other growth functions in plants, IAA causes root cells to divide and grow longer and induces rooting. You can buy one of two synthetic auxins, IBA (indolebutryric acid) and NAA (napthaleneacetic acid) at most garden supply centers.

VEGETATIVE REPRODUCTION

Growing roots from cuttings is called vegetative reproduction. Plant hormones are used to stimulate the growth of roots on the cuttings of shrubs, vines and trees.

You can grow roots from softwood cuttings, shoots that are still green and soft, or from hardwood cuttings, woody, leafless winter shoots. When the soft, green outer layer of a new shoots begins turning brown and woody, it is called a half-woody cutting. Cuttings from some species, mature apples (Malus domestica), for example, will never grow roots. Cuttings from chrysanthemums (Dendranthema x grandiflora) and some other species do not need hormones to grow roots.

POWDER FORMS

Powdered hormone forms, auxin mixed with talc, are less toxic than liquid forms and are cleaner to apply. Dip a cutting in the auxin powder, then lightly tap it to remove clinging excess. To increase the amount of powder that clings to a cutting, re-cut its end or dip it in alcohol or water before application. The drawback is that this will cause the hormone to deteriorate, as well as increase the possibility of spreading disease.

LIQUID FORMS

Quick-dip liquid auxin formulations are consistent and uniform, but carry a greater risk of spreading disease than powdered forms. Keep containers sealed to prevent an increase in auxins as the alcohol or water base evaporates. This is especially important in dry, hot weather. To apply, simply dip a cutting 1/4 to 3/4 inches into liquid auxin for one to five seconds. You can also make your own liquid hormone solution by soaking cut willow (genus Salix) stems in water.

APPLICATION TIPS

Using plant hormones will not make up for poor stem cutting techniques. If you want to grow roots from a softwood cutting, make sure it has an actively growing tip. If the end of your cutting is grayish-brown or brown, cut closer to the tip of the shoot to get softer wood. If your cutting has fully-developed flowers, it may be too old to stimulate roots. Be sure to follow directions; at excessive dosage levels, auxins can be toxic to plants. The widely used weed killer 2-4-D (dichlorophenoxyacetic acid) is a synthetic plant auxin.

HOME MADE PLANT ROOTING HORMONE – WILLOW WATER

Fig. Weeping Willow (Salix babylonica).

Willows are an amazing tree that have captivated humanity since time immemorial. They appear in the ancient legends, tales, folklore and customs of the Chinese, Egyptians, Greeks, Brits, Celts and American Indians. They even feature in three of William Shakespeare's plays, Hamlet, Othello and Twelfth Night.

Some folklore associated with willows is fascinating – my two favourites are are that it is bad luck to tell a secret while standing under a willow, as the wind that blows through the leaves will reveal the secret to everyone, and that striking an animal or a child with a willow twig will stunt their growth! They did have some strange ideas way back in Medieval Europe!

Surely, there is something "magical" about these trees, for them to capture our attention sostrongly.They have some interesting and unique properties, as we'll explore in this article!

WILLOWS – A BRIEF INTRODUCTION

Willows are fast growing, deciduous trees that are mainly found found in the the Northern Hemisphere, in cold arctic and north temperate zones, in regions with moist soils. The Weeping Willow appears to be a native of extra-tropical Asia, from Japan and China to Armenia and the banks of the Euphrates, and of Egypt and North Africa.

One of the most popular and familiar willows is the Weeping willow (Salix babylonica), it has exceptional form and beauty. When mature it exhibits graceful, wide-spreading, pendulous weeping branches, with a short trunk, and a broad rounded crown. Its leaves are thin and narrow, sometimes with whitened or silky undersides. It is fast growing, and adaptable to almost any soil conditions.

Willows are an incredibly useful tree, they have many useful functions:

1. Source of Medicine – The use of willow bark dates back thousands of years, to the time of Hippocrates (400 BC) when patients were advised to chew on the bark to reduce fever and inflammation. Willow bark has been used throughout the centuries in China and Europe, and continues to be used today for the treatment of pain (particularly low back pain and osteoarthritis), headache, and inflammatory conditions such as bursitis and tendinitis. The bark of white willow contains salicin, which is a chemical similar to aspirin (acetylsalicylic acid). It is thought to be responsible for the pain-relieving and anti-inflammatory effects of the herb. In fact, in the 1800s, salicin was used to develop aspirin. White willow appears to be slower than aspirin to bring pain relief, but its effects may last longer.
2. Source of Material for Construction and Manufacturing – Willow wood is used to make furniture, tool handles, wood veneers, and toys. It is used in wood turning as it is easily worked, and is also used to make cricket bats. Willows are a source of wicker for basketry (weaving of

wicker baskets) and for making fish traps. The wood can also be used as a source of fibre for making rope, string and paper. Charcoal used by artists is exclusively made from willow.

3. Source of Energy – Willow is grown for biomass, a renewable energy source which reduces the need for fossil fuels and petroleum products. Willow can be converted into a variety of sustainable environmentally-friendly resources, including: 1. heat and electricity by direct combustion, co-firing with coal, and gasification; 2. biodegradable plastics and other polymers; 3. biofuels.
4. Willows are an ideal source of biomass because 1. Willows are easily propagated from unrooted cuttings; 2. High yields can be obtained in a few years, 3. Willow's genetic diversity and short breeding cycle can be utilized to produce improved varieties; 4.Willows vigorously re-sprout after each harvest; 5. The amount of heat in a dry ton of willow is similar to other hardwoods.
5. Large scale projects to support willow as an energy crop are already at commercial scale in Sweden, and in other countries there are being developed through initiatives such as the Willow Biomass Project in the US and the Energy Coppice Project in the UK. (Ref: College of Environmental Science and Forestry – The Willow Biomass Project)
6. Ecological/Environmental Uses – Willows have many beneficial environmental uses. They can be used in the following areas:
7. Riparian buffers – Natural barriers that prevent chemicals from entering streams, ponds, and lakes.
8. Phytoremediation – Willows clean up toxins from contaminated sites.
9. Wastewater management (biofiltration) – Willows filter contaminants from wastewater, and can be used in ecological wastewater treatment systems.
10. Environmental protection and preservation – Willows are often used for land reclamation, streambank stabilisation (bioengineering), slope stabilisation, soil erosion control, shelterbelt and windbreak construction, soil building, and soil reclamation.
11. Environmental reconstruction – Willows are used for constructing wetlands and wildlife habitat.
12. Gardening – Willows are used for in the construction of hedges, "living fences" and other living garden structures and general landscaping
13. Living snowfences – Strategically planted willows trap drifting snow.
14. Farming – Willows can used by farmers as an animal forage to feed their stock.
15. Horticultural Uses – Willow bark contains natural plant growth hormones which can be used for rooting new cuttings. This is the area that we'll be looking at in this article!

One of the most amazing properties of willows is their growth! Coppicing a willow (that is cutting it back to ground level) will result in numerous rods growing from the base that will grow at an amazing rate of 1.2-3.0m in a single season. A broken willow branch left in water will grow roots. Willows successfully root from very thick pieces of stem, this method is known as taking "trunk cuttings", and a stem as thick as a human thigh will take root of put into damp ground. Willow cuttings can even grow if put in upside-down (but please do the right thing and put them in the right way up)! This property of willows is due to the naturally occurring plant rooting hormones that they contain. We can take advantage of this naturally occurring hormone, and make extracts that we can use to induce rooting on cuttings of other plants.

"WILLOW WATER" – HOW IT WORKS

"Willow Water" is a homebrew plant rooting hormone that is easily made and can be used to increase the strike rate (growth of roots) of cuttings that you're trying to propagate. The way that it works can be attributed to two substances that can be found within theSalix (Willow) species, namely, indolebutyric acid (IBA) and Salicylic acid (SA).

Indolebutyric acid (IBA) is a plant hormone that stimulates root growth. It is present in high concentrations in the growing tips of willow branches. By using the actively growing parts of a willow branch, cutting them, and soaking them in water, you can get significant quantities of IBA to leach out into the water.

Salicylic acid (SA) (which is a chemical similar to the headache medicine Aspirin) is a plant hormone which is involved in signalling a plant's defences, it is involved in the process of "systemic acquired resistance" (SAR) – where an attack on one part of the plant induces a resistance response to pathogens (triggers the plant's internal defences) in other parts of the plant. It can also trigger a defence response in nearby plants by converting the salicylic acid into a volatile chemical form.

When you make willow water, both salicylic acid and IBA leach into the water, and both have a beneficial effect when used for the propagation of cuttings. One of the biggest threats to newly propagated cuttings is infection by bacteria and fungi. Salicylic acid helps plants to fight off infection, and can thus give cuttings a better chance of survival. Plants, when attacked by infectious agents, often do not produce salicylic acid quickly enough to defend themselves, so providing the acid in water can be particularly beneficial.

Willow water can be made from cuttings of any tree or shrub of the willow family, a group of plants with the scientific name of Salix. The more cuttings that are used and the longer they are soaked in water, the stronger will be the resulting willow water. Recommendations for the exact method of soaking vary. Cold water can be used, and soaking times of four or more weeks are often quoted. Other gardeners use boiling water to steep the willow twigs and soak the mixture for around 24 hours.

HOW TO MAKE "WILLOW WATER"

Here is the procedure for making willow water:

1. Collect young first-year twigs and stems of any of willow (Salix spp.) species, these have green or yellow bark. Don't use the older growth that has brown or gray bark.
2. Remove all the leaves, these are not used. Don't waste good green material though, compost the leaves or throw them in the garden as mulch.
3. Take the twigs and cut them up into short pieces around 1" (2.5cm) long.
4. The next step is to add the water. there are several techniques to extract the natural plant rooting hormones:
   a) Place the chopped willow twigs in a container and cover with boiling water, just like making tea, and allow the "tea" to stand overnight.
   b) Place the chopped willow twigs in a container and cover with tap water (unheated), and let it soak for several days.
5. When finished, separate the liquid from the twigs by carefully pouring out the liquid, or pouring it through a strainer or sieve. The liquid is now ready to use for rooting cuttings. You can keep the liquid for up to two months if you put it in a jar with a tight fitting lid and keep the liquid in the refrigerator. Remember to label the jar so you remember what it is, and write down the date you brewed it up, and to aid the memory, write down the date that it should be used by, which is two months from the date it was made!
6. To use, just pour some willow water into a small jar, and place the cuttings in there like flowers in a vase, and leave them there to soak overnight for several hours so that they take up the plant rooting hormone. Then prepare them as you would when propagating any other cuttings.

The second way to use willow water is to use it to water the propagating medium in which you have placed cuttings. Watering your cuttings twice with willow water should be enough to help them root.

PROPOSED ROLE FOR EACH HORMONE GROUP DURING SOMATIC EMBRYOGENESIS

Although the endogenous hormone levels by themselves do not account for all the phenomena observed during induction and development of somatic embryogenesis, a general view of the importance of each hormone group can be postulated. for each hormone group can be postulated. Auxin is considered to be the most important hormone in regulating somatic embryogenesis. Both, the endogenous contents and the application of exogenous auxins, are determiningant factors during the induction and expression phases of somatic embryogenesis. It has been reported that the culture of explants in 2,4-D-containing medium, the classic induction treatment for many species, increases the endogenous auxin levels in the explants (Michalczuk et al., 1992b).

It has also been observed that the auxin polar transport of auxin is essential for the establishment of bilateral symmetry during embryogenesis in dicotyledonous somatic (Schiavone and Cooke, 1987) and zygotic embryos, and more recently it was also demonstrated for monocotyledonous zygotic embryos (Fischer and Neuhaus, 1996).

For this gradient to be established, relatively high levels of free IAA may be necessary in the competent tissues. However, once the stimulus for the further development of the somatic embryos is given (*i.e.*, through reduction orf removal of 2,4-D from the culture medium), those levels must be reduced, to allow the establishment of the polar auxin gradient. If the levels are extremely low or high, or if they do not diminish after the induction treatment, the gradient cannot be formed, and thus somatic embryogenesis cannot be expressed. Indoleacetylaspartate as been found in high levels in embryogenic callus of 'Shamouti' orange, and it was suggested that through this mode of IAA conjugation, auxin levels in embryogenic callus are reduced to a level inductive to active embryogenesis.

Endogenous levels of ABA also appear to be significant in some monocots for initiation of embryogenic cultures (Bhaskaran and Smith, 1990). Its role as an inhibitor of precocious germination when immature zygotic embryos are used as initial explants, thus favoring indirectly callus formation, was been already discussed by Jiménez and Bangerth (2001b).

The role of ABA in somatic embryogenesis may be exerted through regulation of certain genes (*e.g.*, DC8) that are thought to be involved in desiccation and maturation phases of embryogenesis (Hatzopoulos et al., 1990). Rajasekaran et al. proposed that ABA could exert its role on somatic embryogenesis by regulating carbohydrate metabolism, via inhibitiong of a - amylase activity.

There are several instances where applied ABA has been shown to stimulate cell division and DNA synthesis, callus production and shoot morphogenesis, and to inhibit peroxidase activity, an enzyme that, as previously mentioned, causes an irreversible degradation of IAA (Rajasekaran et al., 1987a and references cited therein). Senger et al. (2001), using a homozygous transgenic line of Nicotiana plumbaginifoliaconstitutively expresing an anti-ABA single chain fragment variable antibody in the endoplasmic reticulum, clearly demonstrated that ABA is important for the formation of pre-globular structures.

The role of exogenous and endogenous gibberellins in somatic embryogenesis has not been studied in detail. The results of different reports seem to indicate a minor role for endogenous gibberellin levels, both in the initial explants and the callus cultures (Jiménez and Bangerth, 2001a,b,c,d).

There is support for the concept that cytokinins, in general, are important during the initial cell division phase of somatic embryogenesis, but not for the later stages of embryo development and maturation in carrot (Fujimura and Komamine, 1980), anise and orchardgrass. This suggests that cytokinins may have a role in cell division, but not in embryo differentiation. When analyzing the individual role of the iP- and Z-type cytokinins, Centeno et al. (1997) postulated that the role the first group in the embryogenic response might be as biosynthetic precursors to supply the large amount of active cytokinins required for the stimulation of cell division prior to somatic embryogenesis. In the general proposed pathway of cytokinin biosynthesis in prokaryotes and in higher plants, iP acts as a precursor of Z, probably the most active endogenous cytokinin.

HORMONE CONCENTRATION VS. SENSITIVITY

Several investigations, in which a lack of correlation between the endogenous hormone concentration and the response of the explants was observed, led Trewavas (1981) to postulate that the sensitivity of the tissues to a change in the hormone concentration is more important than the change in the concentration itself. This proposal generated a lot of controversy at that time, but it was supported by several observations, such as the fact that immature flowers and fruits did not respond to ethylene application, but the mature ones did.

Several reports, such as those in which no differences between the endogenous levels of most hormones evaluated in the initial explants of competent and non-competent genotypes were found (Jiménez and Bangerth, 2001b, 2001c) or that in which differences in the hormone levels did not seem to play any role in determining the morphogenetic capacity of the explants, demonstrate that there are, certainly, another factors, others than besides the endogenous levels of plant hormones, that determine the competence of the tissues to develop embryogenic cells.

This kind of results seems to support the postulate of Trewavas; however, now it is widely accepted that both, the sensitivity of the tissues to the plant hormones and, as well as the concentration of the hormones by itself, are important and modulate the responses observed in most cases. Sensitivity has been shown to contribute in a higher degree to, at least, gravitropic responses, vascular tissue regeneration, cambial growth, seed dormancy, germination, cell division, cell extension, ripening, senescence, abscission, stomatal aperture, flowering and amylase formation.

There is some evidence, that sensitivity may be important in conferring embryogenic competence to tissue culture explants. For example, it is known that only if a responsive tissue is taken as starting material, is the phytohormone content of the culture medium is a major factor regulating growth and differentiation of plant tissue in vitro only if a responsive tissue is taken as starting material. Besides, Bögre et al. (1990) postulated that the differences between embryogenic and non-embryogenic alfalfa lines are based ion their sensitivity to 2,4-D, being with the first line being more sensitive. It has also been observed that 2,4-D can modulate the level of auxin-binding proteins in the membranes of carrot cell suspension cultures and in consequence may increase the sensitivity to this class of hormones.

Guzzo et al. (1994) proposed the following model, which links together auxin response, asymmetric division and totipotency: upon environmental stimuli, cells can be made competent to respond to auxin in a morphogenetic way; if the cells have, or could be induced to produce the proper receptors, complete embryogenesis would follow; if the receptors are not the proper ones, only organogenesis or unorganized proliferation will occur. Even when the importance of cytokinin concentration in sensitivity has also been discussed, the understanding of the molecular basis of cytokinin action lags behind that of other hormones.

DIVERSE ROLES FOR PLANT HORMONES

Before we consider details of the nal consequences of hormone signalling pathways, it is helpful to think broadly about the roles of hormones in enabling organised plant development and efcient responses to alterations in the environment. The range of functions of plant hormones and responses to them can be bewildering, but most roles can be grouped under two general headings: organisers and mediators.

ORGANISERS

Organisers primarily dene the basic framework of a plant's axial structure. This includes channelling of cells into particular pathways of differentiation depending on their location within the plant. Plants tend to, even need to, maintain a balance between shoot and root development. The two systems are interdependent, so damage or loss of one upsets that balance and necessitates some developmental adjustment. We do not know exactly how complex differentiation pathways are regulated, but it seems likely that a relatively small number of primary signals are needed, with each controlling a whole suite of characters.

Auxin–Cytokinin Balance: Opposing Directional Flows of Active Signal

Tsui Sachs and Kenneth Thimann in 1967 proposed that shoot apical dominance is governed by auxin–cytokinin balance. Evidence came mainly from polar basipetal transport of shoot tip auxin and responses to applied auxins and cytokinins: auxin supplied to a decapitated shoot stump suppresses the normal lateral bud growth response, but cytokinin supplied directly to lateral buds promotes outgrowth of intact plants. More recent studies on transgenic plants and branching mutants suggest that there are probably other regulatory signals in addition to auxin and cytokinin.

Overall, however, this simple theory, along with auxin and cytokinin responses in tissue cultures, gives us the foundations of control of root:shoot development ratios, and enables comprehension of plant developmental homoeostasis. This balancing act comprises several developmental elements, but all potentially trace back to auxin:cytokinin concentration ratios. Even in intact plants, shoot branching is limited if root growth is poor or if roots are stressed. Conversely, a vigorous root system depends on carbon supply from shoot photosynthesis. Supercially, root:shoot balance appears resource limited, but the role of hormones overlays an ability to signal in advance of crisis, and enables stochastic (modular) adjustment of units of plant development: number of active shoot branches and number of lateral roots, in addition to modication of the growth rate of each.

Mechanical damage, whether removal of just a shoot apex, or cutting off a stem at ground level, may invoke similar hormone-driven responses. Shoot apex replacement is rapidly achieved by outgrowth of an existing lateral meristem, in theory stimulated by auxin depletion and cytokinin accumulation around the top of a cut stem. A tree stump lacking reserve buds may still possess active cambium cells, which can respond to the same cytokinin enhancement by initiating rapid cell division and subsequent shoot organogenesis.

A stem cutting continues to transport auxin to the cut base, but lacks its normal cytokinin supply from the roots. This high auxin:cytokinin ratio stimulates cell activation leading to adventitious root organisation, and in commercial propagation is accelerated by supplying additional auxin in rooting powders and solutions. In addition, there are strong links between cytokinins and delay of senescence. A plant with damaged, diseased, water-stressed or mineral-decient roots will export less cytokinin in the xylem, one consequence being premature leaf senescence usually from the stem base upwards.

Seed-Derived Hormones Regulate Pattern of Fruit Development

Although fruit and seed tissues are genetically different — the former is parental, the latter is progeny — the two develop in a coordinated manner. In most species, if ovules are not fertilised or the embryo aborts, fruit tissues stop growing and are usually shed prematurely. Because seeds represent the next generation, it makes little sense for a plant to continue investing resources in a package that contains no propagules. Exceptions to this are parthenocarpic (seedless) fruits, some of which have genetic causes, and others which are induced chemically by application of growth-promoting hormones: auxin, gibberellin, cytokinin or combinations of these. Parthenocarpic fruit are prized by humans and include seedless or semi-seedless commercial varieties of grape, citrus, banana, watermelon, pineapple and lychee. The relationship between seed and fruit growth appears to be driven by hormones synthesised in the developing endosperm and embryo, and is neatly illustrated by the relationship between auxin levels and fruit growth rates in blackcurrant.

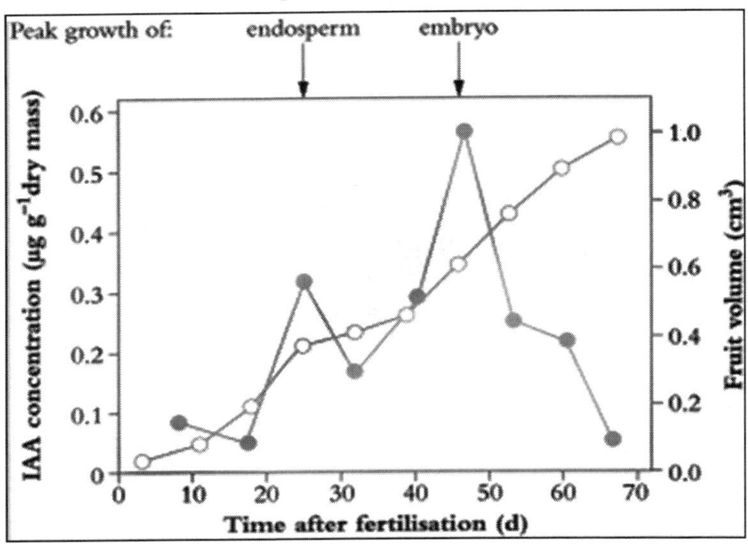

Fig. During seed and fruit development in many species there is a phase of endosperm development followed by embryo growth. These two tissues are thought to be the source of hormones that promote fruit growth. Here, the two rapid phases during the double sigmoid fruit growth curve of blackcurrant (Ribes nigra) coincide with peaks of IAA content (solid circles) and with maximal rates of endosperm then embryo development (open circles).

MEDIATORS

The second broad role of hormones is as mediators of environmental signals, often stress factors, which lead to modication of physiology and patterns of development. For example, as discussed in the preceding chapter, photoperiod perception in leaves leads to flowering at the shoot apex. A light signal is translated into a chemical one.

The route of signal trans-mission from leaf to apex appears to be in the phloem sap, and although we do not know of a universal 'florigen' hormone, part of the signal in some species may be specic types of gibberellin. Gibberellins also have a wider role in mediating some types of phytochrome responses, such as stem elongation in long-day plant rosette species. Entry into and exit from dormancy often depends on external inputs such as fluctuation in water availability: some responses to dehydration during seed maturation and imbibition during germination are mediated by ABA and gibberellins, respectively. Low temperature is another factor which can break endodormancy or induce flowering, and may be mediated by hormones such as gibberellins and cytokinins.

ABA as a Mediator of Water Status Information

The role of ABA in transmitting information about plant water status was discovered in the early 1970s. Here, we take a detailed look at one of the best studied of all 'mediator' roles of hormones. When water loss from leaves is accelerated by exposing them to a stream of warm air, ABA concentration rises dramatically, by about 10- to 50-fold and stomata close. Similarly, a low concentration of ABA supplied exogenously to excised leaves via the transpiration stream induces stomatal closure.

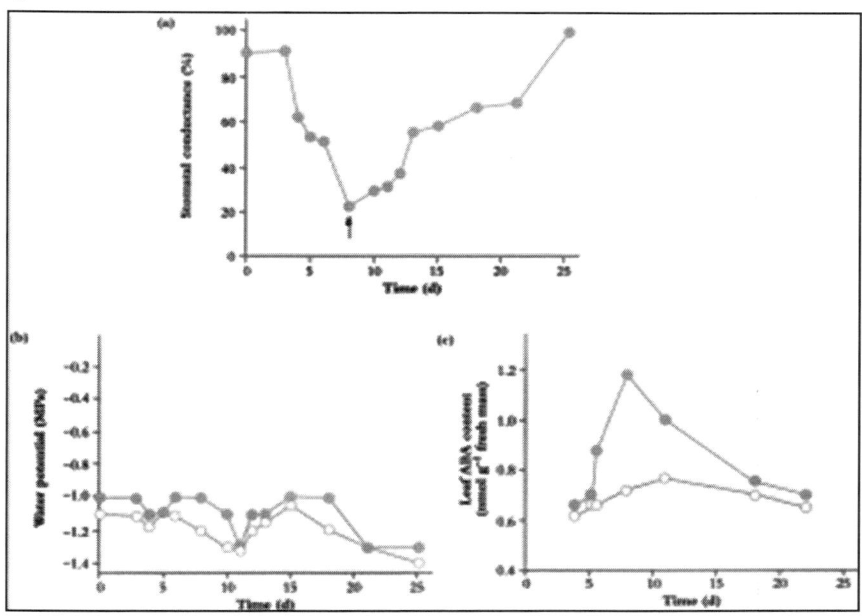

Fig. ((a), (b), (c)) Response of grapevines to hydraulic and non-hydraulic signals during water stress applied to split root systems. Root systems can be split vertically (surface v. deep) or horizontally (left-right, as in this experiment (d)) and different water stresses applied to each half. If one half is kept well watered, this is sufficient to maintain normal shoot water status and no leaf water potential difference is detected (solid circles) compared with control fully watered plants (open circles) (b). If the other half root system is dry, any drought signal induced may be transmitted to the shoot. A prime candidate for this root signal is ABA, which is detected either chemically (c), or by its effects on stomatal aperture (a). In many species, root-generated ABA can cause stomatal closure in the absence of any water deficit in the shoot. This is interpreted as an early warning system, enabling plants to reduce water use under imminent drought conditions. In nature, during periods without rain, surface roots would normally become dry before deep roots.

It was concluded that ABA synthesis in leaves, induced by water stress, is the cause of stomatal closure. Further evidence for the involvement of ABA in stomatal regulation came from studies of ABA-decient mutants such as flacca in tomato, wilty in pea anddroopy in potato, which wilt rapidly when exposed to only mildly stressful conditions but regain a normal phenotype if treated with ABA. Synthesis of ABA in wilting leaves is enhanced as turgor approaches zero. Conjugated forms of ABA such as the b-glucoside can be present in leaves at quite high concentration and represent a potential source of free ABA, but actually appear quite stable and do not break down under stress. Therefore de novo synthesis of ABA during stressful conditions is responsible for stomatal closure, and acts as a protective mechanism against the potentially damaging effects of water loss. ABA-induced stomatal closure pre-empts hydraulically driven stomatal closure which would eventually occur as stomatal guard cells lose turgor. Hydraulically driven closure occurs far later than closure induced by ABA and usually occurs too late to prevent excessive and damaging levels of water decit.

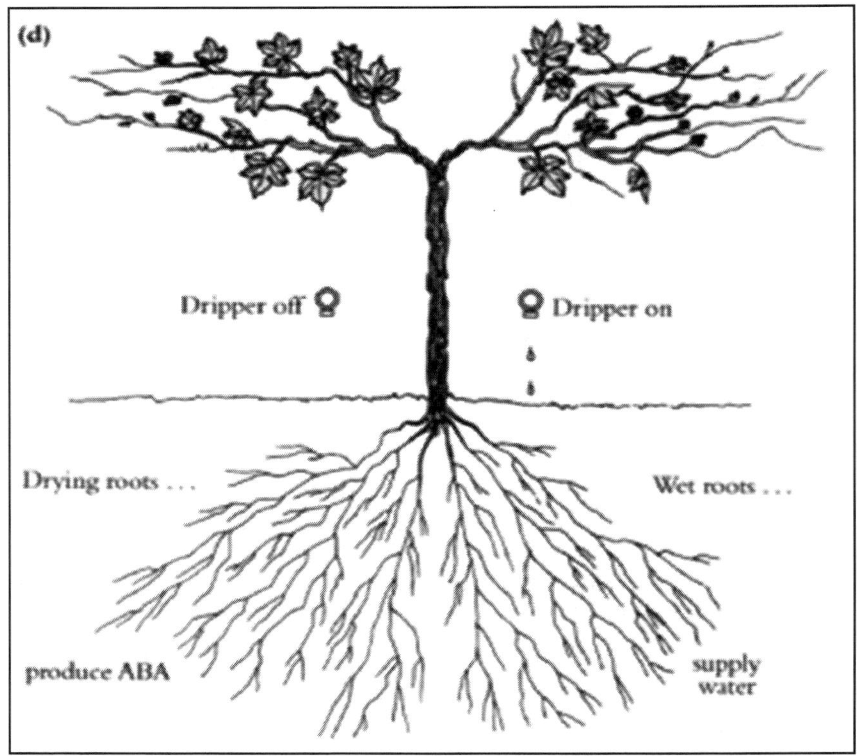

Stomatal closure in response to increased levels of foliar ABA provides a solution to one of the major problems faced by mesophytic plants, that is, the compromise between maintaining sufcient gas exchange to satisfy the CO_2

requirements for carbon assimilation but at the same time limiting water loss when conditions become unfavourable. However, this rather simple interpretation of plant response to stress is not the whole story. For example, water-stressed plants can have leaf water potentials which are similar to or even higher than those of well-watered plants and yet the stomata are fully closed. Shoot extension and leaf expansion are also highly sensitive to stressful conditions but they are not always accompanied by low leaf water potentials. Clearly, ABA synthesis in leaves is not the only process occurring during water stress.

Roots as a Source of ABA

Part of the answer to this puzzle came from experiments using plants with divided root systems. For example, if a piece of grapevine cane bearing six or seven nodes with dormant buds is sawn along its length from the base for about two internodes, it is possible to induce root formation on each of the two halves. These split root systems can be planted in separate pots or in the eld, which allows independent manipulation of the soil moisture status of each root. It has long been known that xylem sap contains ABA, and that increased ABA in droughted roots might thus be transmitted to the leaves. However, simply drying the roots of a plant with a single root system affects the water relations of the whole plant and it is then difcult to distinguish the effects of lowered leaf water potentials from the effects of root-derived chemical signals. Split-root plants allow study of the effects of drying soil without the complications of changed water relations because the soil around one root system is maintained fully watered.

This root system supplies as much water as the canopy needs. Normally, the second root system is then dried and the effects of any chemical signals studied. Here we show the effect of withholding water from one root system of twin root grapevines. Stomatal conductance fell rapidly, and within 8 d was only 22 per cent of that in fully watered control vines yet water potential of the leaves remained unchanged. Leaf ABA content also changed in response to partial root drying. When conductance was at its lowest, ABA levels had doubled when compared with fully watered controls. ABA levels returned to control values 10 d after rewatering the dry pot, but conductance took somewhat longer to recover.

The leaves did not receive any hydraulic (water decit) signal which may have initiated local ABA synthesis. We conclude that the drying roots produced a chemical signal which is transported to the leaves in the transpiration stream and which induces stomatal closure. The chemical signal is most likely to be ABA. Zhang and Davies (1990) took a direct approach by supplying different solutions to excised maize leaves and measuring stomatal conductance. They tested xylem sap from well-watered plants, sap from stressed plants, sap from which most of the ABA had been removed by passage through a column containing anti-ABA antibodies and a series of synthetic ABA solutions. In every case, the anti-transpirant activity of each solution was explicable in terms of its ABA content. Further evidence that it is a closing stimulus arising from drying roots and not a lack of an opening stimulus comes from the observation that stomata re-open after drying roots are excised.

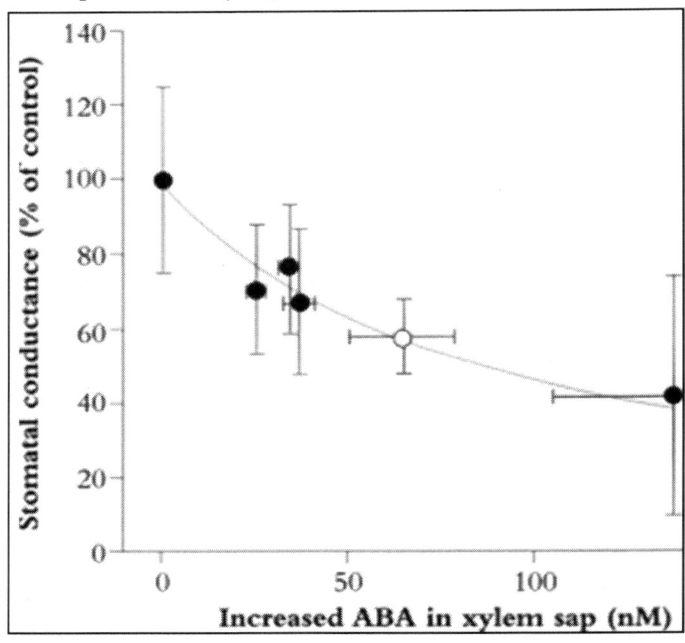

Fig. Large fluctuations are often seen in ABA concentrations in xylem sap moving from root to shoot. In some species such as maize (but not others such as wheat and apricot), drought-induced stomatal closure can be accounted for entirely by the increased amount of ABA signal. In this experiment, increased ABA was generated by withholding water for up to 20d. The error bars on each point are standard deviations and indicate the range of both the increase in ABA content and the effect on stomatal conductance. The open circle shows the xylem ABA concentration and leaf conductance resulting from feeding 10^{-5} M ABA to part of the root system.

Experiments like this help us understand how plants in the eld deal with everyday fluctuations in soil water, sustained drought and other environmental conditions. Surface layers of soil, which usually have the highest root densities, dry rst and roots in this zone will be stimulated to send enhanced ABA signals to the leaves, slowing transpiration and thus providing the rst indication that soil conditions are not ideal.

At this time, the deeper roots may still have access to water and so no hydraulic signal has been generated. Such ABA signalling from roots does not result in large increases in leaf ABA and that which does accumulate is soon dissipated through metabolism and translocation once the dry root signal is removed.

This enables leaves to monitor continuously root water stress and to adjust stomatal apertures according to distant and local water availability. If drought continues and more of the soil prole dries, then leaf water potentials will fall and trigger new synthesis of ABA in leaves, reinforcing and extending the stomatal closure already set in train by the roots. The large increases in ABA which then result may have more far-reaching consequences because expression of certain genes is regulated by ABA. Some of these have sequences which are predicted to confer heat stability to their resulting protein products. Unexpected relationships between conductance and ABA content

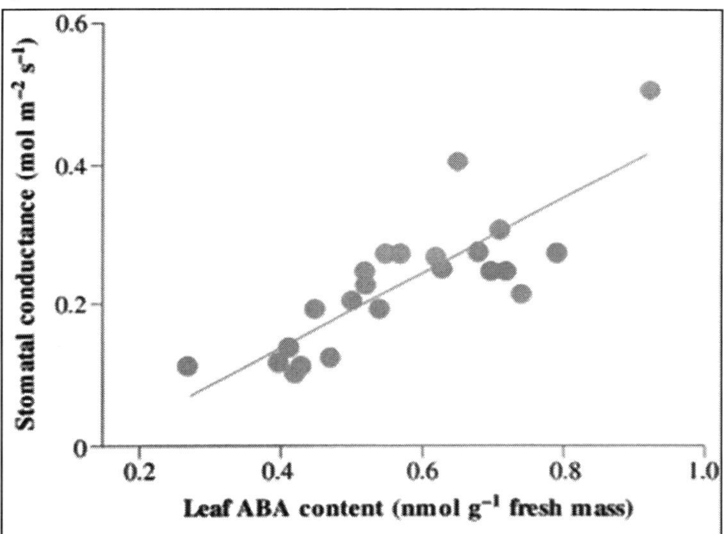

Fig. In an unusual response, stomatal conductance was postively correlated with leaf ABA concentration and not inversely correlated as expected. This study used apricot plants, which are able to osmoregulate during drought and thereby maintain cell turgor and hence open stomata. The increase in ABA is probably the result of increased supply from the roots during drought, but in this case the ABA does not result in stomatal closure.

The picture of ABA derived from roots causing reduced stomatal conductance during periods of water decit is true in many, but not all, cases. For example, this correlation does not hold in apricot which instead can osmoregulate and thereby maintain stomatal opening. In a study comparing the drought responses of grapevine, which largely conforms to the normal model, with apricot, another drought-tolerant plant often grown in close proximity to grapevine, xylem ABA content in apricot was only about 5 per cent of that needed to induce stomatal closure. Moreover, ABA levels in leaves showed a positive relationship with stomatal conductance, contrary to normal expectations.

ABA was accumulating with increased transpiration but was having no effect on stomatal conductance. Unlike grapevine, which operates over a fairly narrow range of leaf water potentials, apricot leaf water potential fell progressively throughout the season, yet stomata remained open. The key to these apparently anomalous results was that leaf osmotic potential fell along with the water potential, thus maintaining leaf turgor and stomatal opening. By the end of the growing season, sorbitol, the major organic osmoticum in apricot leaves, had accumulated to a concentration of 400 mM. Apricot uses osmotic adjustment to protect itself during drought and ABA appears to play little part. Indeed, it was found that even when apricot leaves were deliberately wilted, their ability to synthesise ABA was almost totally eliminated when sorbitol concentrations were high.

WINTER DORMANCY AND CHILLING IN WOODY PLANTS

Since most plants do not grow during the winter, we say they are dormant. There are actually two types of dormancy during the winter. One is called endo-dormancy. In endo-dormancy, the plant will not grow even under good, warm, growing conditions. Endo is a Greek word meaning inside. In endo-dormancy, something inside the plants is inhibiting growth. The other is called eco-dormancy and occurs when the plant is ready to grow but the environmental conditions are not right, usually too cold. Endo-dormancy occurs first. Short days and freezing temperatures in the fall induce endo-dormancy in the plant.

As the plant enters endo-dormancy, it tracks chilling units to track the passage of the winter. Chilling units are hours of time spent above freezing. The number of hours required for chilling varies for different plants from less than 500 to 1,500 hours or more. Many people think the plant is tracking hours below freezing. It is not. Hours below freezing have no effect on chilling, but will increase cold hardiness. If warm weather occurs before the plant completes its chilling requirement, no growth occurs. Chilling and endo-dormancy normally prevent plants from beginning growth during warm spells in the middle of the winter. Not all hours above freezing are equal. Temperatures between 40 and 50 degrees Fahrenheit (5 to 10 degrees Celsius) are most effective. Temperatures just above freezing and above 50 F are less effective and temperatures above 60 F often have a negative effect on chilling.

These peach buds appear dormant, but have completed their chillingrequirement and are waiting for warmer weather to begin growth. Photo credit: Mark Longstroth, MSUE

Plants from the south or far north have relatively short chilling requirements. In the far north, it is below freezing for a long time and the spring warm-up is relatively short. Likewise winters in the south are short and mild. Plants from the middle temperate regions like Michigan have relatively long chilling requirements that keep them dormant through the long stretches when the temperatures cycle above and below freezing in a Michigan winter. Most of the fruit crops we grow in Michigan have chilling requirements of 700 to 1,300 chilling units. We normally complete endo-dormancy here in Michigan in January, early January in the south and late January in the north. Of course, there are big differences between winters. Some are long and cold, others are warmer. The relatively warm winter we are experiencing in 2013 is allowing many plants to accumulate their chilling earlier than normal.

Another important thing happens during endo-dormancy. The plants are cold hardy. As long as the trees, bushes or vines are in endo-dormancy, they have the ability to acclimate to cold weather; we call this cold hardiness. As long as the temperatures are below freezing, the plants are ready for really cold temperatures. Maximum cold hardiness occurs when plants have been subject to cold, subfreezing temperatures for several days or more. As long as the plants are in endo-dormancy they have the ability to acclimate to colder temperatures and withstand winter cold.

After chilling is completed the plants are no longer in endo-dormancy. They are now in eco-dormancy. The plants are dormant only because of cold or cool weather. Warmer temperatures into the mid-40s will cause them to begin growth. Once the plants start to grow, they lose the ability to readjust to colder temperatures. There is usually a slow progression of development when the plant begins to grow as the temperatures slowly rise. Growth first becomes apparent when buds swell and then green tissue emerges from the bud. The plants actually begin growing before we notice the buds swelling.

FALL COLOUR SHOW AND WINTER DORMANCY IN WOODY PLANTS

The brilliant fall foliage we see is the results from the breakdown of the chemical machinery in the leaves as the plant stores those materials for growth next spring. Leaves are just temporary organs; the plant uses them to make sugar from sunlight by photosynthesis. Now that winter is coming, the deciduous perennials breakdown the proteins and other chemicals in the leaves and store them in the buds, bark and wood for growth next spring. The colours are accessory pigments that helped protect the chlorophyll in the leaves from breakdown by the sunlight during the season.

Fig. Bluecrop blueberries are a deep red by the end of October.

The plant's first clue that winter was coming is when the days began to get shorter. Plants track the hours of daylight during the day. In late summer (August), the day length really begins to change and the days rapidly begin to shorten.

By the first day of fall when the day and night are of equal length, perennial plants are getting ready for winter. Cooler temperatures are also an indicator that winter is on the way. The fats and proteins in the cells of the wood and bark that will overwinter are changed from forms that work best in the warm summer to forms that function when the temperatures are near freezing and can survive freezing and thawing in the winter.

Freezing temperatures are the plants final clue that winter is coming. Many woody perennials lose their leaves as they become dormant, such as maples and apples. Evergreen plants such as pine trees, strawberries and cranberries keep their leaves all winter. For evergreen plants, water loss during the winter can be a big problem if the ground is frozen.

As the temperatures get colder, plants acclimate to the cold, entering a state of deep dormancy when they will not grow, even if the conditions are good for growth. You can take cuttings from a plant in the late fall or early winter and these cuttings will not grow.

Horticulturists used to call this rest, but now use the term endo-dormancy (endo is Greek for inside), meaning that something inside the plant is causing it to remain dormant. The plants that live through Michigan winters track the cold of winter to keep them from growing during warm spells in early winter. Many plants have a winter chilling requirement and will not grow until chilling is completed.

FORCING CUTTINGS TO DETERMINE THE END OF DORMANCY IN FRUITS AND OTHER PLANTS

Since most plants do not grow during the winter, we say they are dormant. There are actually two types of winter dormancy. One is often called endo-dormancy and is when the plants will not grow even if the conditions are warm enough for growth. The other is eco-dormancy and is when the plant does not grow because the conditions are too cold. Endo-dormancy typically prevents plants from growing during winter warm spells.

During endo-dormancy, plants accumulate chilling units when air temperatures generally are above 35 degrees Fahrenheit and below 50 F. Temperatures below freezing or warm temperatures above 55 or 60 F have little effect on chilling hour accumulation. The chilling hours required varies for different plants from 700 to 1,300 hours or more. Chilling and endo-dormancy normally prevent plants from beginning growth during warm spells in the middle of the winter.

The mild weather we have had this winter makes me think that some plants may have already completed their chilling requirement and are ready to start growing. The return of seasonably cold temperatures may keep growth from occurring. Once growth begins, the plant cannot increase its ability to withstand cold and can be injured by very cold weather. In the deep winter when plants are in endo-dormancy, they can become cold hardy to -10 or -20 F or below. Once growth begins, they lose the ability to withstand these extreme cold events.

Fig. There is no doubt these buds are swollen and the plant is growing.

According to Michigan State University Extension, there is one very easy way to know if endo-dormancy has been completed. You can take cuttings from the plants you are interested in and bring them inside to see if they will grow under warmer conditions. Collect several healthy shoots from the plants and place them in a vase or glass of water to provide consistent warm temperatures. If the buds begin to swell and grow within a week to 10 days, then you know the plants have completed their chilling requirement and warm weather will cause them to grow. You may need to do this several weeks in a row. I usually start collecting shoots in early to mid-January and generally see growth here in southwest Michigan in mid- to late January. Often the first time I see growth, the growth is ragged and not all the buds break and start to grow. This indicates that not all the buds have completed their chilling requirement, but several have and are ready to grow.

Fig. It is hard to tell if these buds are swollen or not. Forcing them will give you an answer in a few days.

Once the plants have completed their chilling and moved into eco-dormancy, growth depends on the heat units they accumulate. If we get warm temperatures and growth begins, then the temperatures falling into the teens or below might cause damage. If you force some cuttings, you will have a good idea of how worried about winter cold you need to be.

6

Physiology and Regulation of Seasonal Nitrogen Cycling in Woody Plants

NITROGEN ASSIMILATION IN PLANTS

Plants absorb nitrogen from the soil in the form of nitrate (NO_3^-) and ammonia (NH^{4+}). In aerobic soils where nitrification can occur, nitrate is usually the predominant form of available nitrogen that is absorbed. However this need not always be the case as ammonia can predominate in grasslands and in flooded, anaerobic soils like rice paddies. Plant roots themselves can affect the abundance of various forms of nitrogen by changing the pH and secreting organic compounds or oxygen. This influences microbial activities like the inter-conversion of various nitrogen species, the release of ammonia from organic matter in the soil and the fixation of nitrogen by non-nodule-forming bacteria.

Ammonium ions are absorbed by the plant via ammonia transporters. Nitrate is taken up by several nitrate transporters that use a proton gradient to power the transport.Nitrogen is transported from the root to the shoot via the xylem in the form of nitrate, dissolved ammonia and amino acids.

Usually (but not always) most of the nitrate reduction is carried out in the shoots while the roots reduce only a small fraction of the absorbed nitrate to ammonia. Ammonia (both absorbed and synthesized) is incorporated into amino acids via the glutamine synthetase-glutamate synthase (GS-GOGAT) pathway. While nearly all the ammonia in the root is usually incorporated into amino acids at the root itself, plants may transport significant amounts of ammonium ions in the xylem to be fixed in the shoots. This may help avoid the transport of organic compounds down to the roots just to carry the nitrogen back as amino acids.

Nitrate reduction is carried out in two steps. Nitrate is first reduced to nitrite (NO_2^-) in the cytosol by nitrate reductase using NADH or NADPH. Nitrite is then reduced to ammonia in the chloroplasts (plastids in roots) by a ferredoxin dependent nitrite reductase. In photosynthesizing tissues, it uses an isoform of ferredoxin (Fd1) that is reduced byPSI while in the root it uses a form of ferredoxin (Fd3) that has a less negative midpoint potential and can be reduced easily by NADPH. In non- photosynthesizing tissues, NADPH is generated by glycolysis and the pentose phosphate pathway.

In the chloroplasts, glutamine synthetase incorporates this ammonia as the amide group of glutamine using glutamate as a substrate. Glutamate synthase transfer the amide group onto an 2-oxoglutarate molecule producing two glutamates. Further transaminations are carried out make other amino acids (most commonly aspargine) from glutamine. While the enzyme glutamate dehydrogenase (GDH) does not play a direct role in the assimilation, it protects the mitochondrial functions during periods of high nitrogen metabolism and takes part in nitrogen remobilization.

PH AND IONIC BALANCE DURING NITROGEN ASSIMILATION

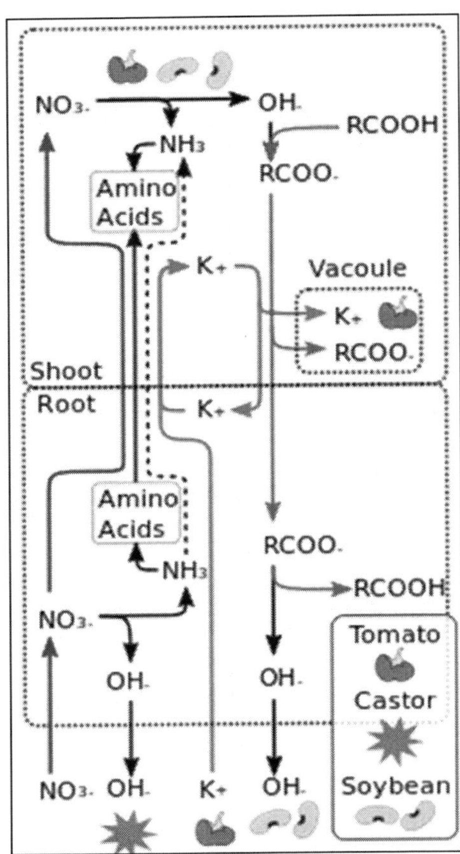

Fig. Different plants use different pathways to different levels. Tomatoes take in a lot of K^+ and accumulate salts in their vacuoles, castor reduces nitrate in the roots to a large extent and excretes the resulting alkali. Soy bean plants moves a large amount of malate to the roots where they convert it to alkali while the potassium is recirculated.

Every nitrate ion reduced to ammonia produces one OH^- ion. To maintain a pH balance, the plant must either excrete it into the surrounding medium or neutralize it with organic acids. This results in the medium around the plants roots becoming alkaline when they take up nitrate.

To maintain ionic balance, every NO_3^- taken into the root must be accompanied by either the uptake of a cation or the excretion of an anion. Plants like tomatoes take up metal ions like K^+, Na^+, Ca^{2+} and Mg^{2+} to exactly match every nitrate taken up and store these as the salts of organic acids like malate and oxalate. Other plants like the soybean balance most of their NO_3^- intake with the excretion of OH^- or HCO_3^-.

Plants that reduce nitrates in the shoots and excrete alkali from their roots need to transport the alkali in an inert form from the shoots to the roots. To achieve this they synthesize malic acid in the leaves from neutral precursors like carbohydrates. The potassium ions brought to the leaves along with the nitrate in the xylem are then sent along with the malate to the roots via the phloem. In the roots, the malate is consumed. When malate is converted back to malic acid prior to use, an OH^- is released and excreted. ($RCOO^- + H_2O \rightarrow RCOOH + OH^-$) The potassium ions are then recirculated up the xylem with fresh nitrate. Thus the plants avoid having to absorb and store excess salts and also transport the OH^-.

Plants like castor reduce a lot of nitrate in the root itself, and excrete the resulting base. Some of the base produced in the shoots is transported to the roots as salts of organic acids while a small amount of the carboxylates are just stored in the shoot itself.

BIOSPHERE

The biosphere consists of all of the earth's organisms living in the geosphere, hydrosphere and atmosphere. Research in recent decades has shown that the organisms participating in the nitrogen (N) cycle are essentially ubiquitous - living in guts of humans, animals, insects, worms, in plants, in dust and rain, to the bottom of the oceans, and down to many 100s of meters beneath the surface of the earth. Many of these recent research findings have yet to be incorporated into estimates of N budgets and reservoirs.

Nevertheless, it is clear that the biosphere's N reservoir is by far the smallest of the four spheres but its cycling of N is by far the largest (*i.e.*, the turn-over rate of N is much greater in the biosphere than in any other sphere). The relatively large size of biospheric N cycling is fortunate because N is the limiting nutrient for much (if not most) life on earth and cycling increases the availability of N for growth.

The biosphere appears well designed from the viewpoint of energy efficiency in its use of N. Massive amounts of energy are required to reduce oxidized (nitrified) forms of N (*e.g.*, NO_2^- and NO_3^-) to the ammoniacal forms of

N which make up the proteins, enzymes and other essential biocompounds. Most of the N acquired and cycled is internal to the biosphere, with fixed, reduced forms of N making up the bulk of transfers within the food web of the biosphere's universe of plants, animals, and microorganisms.

An example of above-ground N transfer would be a plant producing a flower whose pollen is eaten by a butterfly. The butterfly is, in turn, eaten by a dragonfly which then gets eaten by a frog. The frog gets eaten by a snake which then gets eaten by a hawk. Each organism of this food chain represents a trophic level - level one being the plant and level six the hawk.

N transfer in the biosphere is more accurately depicted as a web than as a ladder or pyramid. The living tissues of all six trophic levels of the food chain are fed on by parasites. And generally 90 per cent of the food eaten by any one tropic level is not passed up to the next highest level but is excreted as waste organic matter. And, as will be discussed, the N in these wastes feed whole communities of their own. Organisms can act on different trophic levels. For example, the frog can eat either the butterfly or the dragonfly. And a highly successful omnivore, such asHomo sapiens, can acquire N from any trophic level.

Even the first trophic level (plants) acts on different trophic levels, *e.g.*, plants utilize both inorganic- and organic-N. And organisms in the second trophic level- plant eaters (herbivores) - vary in the number of trophic levels capable of eating them. This is illustrated by the herbivores living on Illinois' most prevalent natural landscape element, the prairie:

"A considerable portion of the above ground biomass of a prairie was consumed each year by the grazing of a wide range of grazing animals, such as bison, elk, deer, rabbits and grasshoppers". The number of trophic levels (levels of predators) above the bison and elk are different from the number existing above grasshoppers and rabbits. Most of the N eaten by the herbivores, predators, and parasites was returned to the soil as organic wastes:

"Grazing increased growth in prairies, recycle[d] nitrogen through urine and feces, and trampling open[ed] up habitat for plant species that prefer some disturbance of the soil". These organic wastes, along with dead biomass from above ground, and the roots of plants growing below ground - the roots of prairie plants can grow deeper into the soil that their aboveground parts grow into the air -supply the organic matter which supports the complex world of subterranean organisms.

Living in the soil are vast numbers of microorganisms such as bacteria, fungi, actinomycetes, protozoans, nematodes, and algae. A cup of soil can contain as many bacteria as there are people living on earth. Less numerous microorganisms (such algae and protozoans) typically number only 1 to 10 billion in the 10 cm. surface slice of a m^2 of soil. Given their short lifetimes and extremely high potential reproductive rates, living and dying microbial biomass turns over large amounts of N, more than half of the 5.8 billion metric tons/yr estimated to occur in the top 1 m. of world soil. As in the above-ground world, microbial herbivores (and parasites) are fed on by at least three trophic levels of microbial and soil animal predators.

The density of organisms living in the immediate root zone (rhizosphere) ranges from 10 to 100 times that of the bulk soil. Roots excrete readily decomposable organic substances and slough off tissue, thereby stimulating a high degree of microbial activity in the neighbouring soil. High numbers of highly active free-living microorganisms attack soil particles to release plant nutrients which ultimately become available to the root. Other organisms infect the root and send strands well out into the soil. Dissolved soil nutrients pass through the microbial strands into the root and organic matter passes from the root into the strand to feed it.

A similar relationship exists between roots and N-fixing microorganisms. Organic matter exterior to the root stimulates free-living, N-fixing microorganisms. Other N-fixers infect roots and live in symbiosis with the plant. The symbiotic N-fixers generally fix more N that their free-living counterparts because the plant provides not only food but also a reducing environment to protect the N-fixing enzyme (nitrogenase) from the deleterious effects of O_2 gas.

Clearly, the biosphere is complex. The difficulties this complexity imposes upon our understanding of the biospheric N cycle are compounded by the fact that so many units of the biosphere have virtually complete N cycles unto themselves. The typical plant growing in the soil of the geosphere stimulates N fixation. This typical plant also stimulates N mineralization, and nitrification by providing complex root exudates of carbohydrate and hormone-like substances, which stimulate microbial growth, and the growth of worms and other soil animals.

The mucus, wastes, and other excretions of soil animals also promote N fixation, mineralization, and nitrification, and denitrification. Conversely N-fixing bacteria not only supply fixed N, they also supply plant growth stimulating substances and stimulate the growth of N-fixing nodules in legumes. Furthermore, "Root infective arbuscular mycorrhizal fungi (AMF) increase root surface area thereby assisting the roots in exploring a large soil volume. AMF infection is known to increase nutrient uptake, N_2fixation, plant tolerance to soil chemical constraints (acidity, alkalinity, salinity), toxic elements and drought. They also help in biological control of root pathogens and are involved in nutrient cycling (solubilization, mineralization)" (Baligar and Fageria, 1999, p. 199).

Aquatic ecosystems present an even more complex picture than do the plant-based ecosystems of the geosphere. This is because the rooting zone of aquatic vegetation not only presents the same complex N cycle picture as does terrestrial vegetation, but also the same suite of interactions exists to a significant extent on the plant surfaces exposed to water - the aquatic surfaces of plants being mini-ecosystems unto themselves and in free-living (planktonic) algae living in the water.

For example, planktonic algae of an productive (eutrophic) lake can fix an amount of N equal to nearly half that received annually in run-off and atmospheric deposition. It is not unusual for aquatic plants (macrophytes) to have amounts of algae and bacteria living on them equal to the total weight of the plants themselves. The productivity of algae living on aquatic plants (epiphytic) occupying 1/4th of the area of a lake can account for 3/4ths of the total algal productivity of even a productive lake in a limestone watershed. "Nitrogen fixation by epipelic [bottom living], as well as epiphytic, blue-green algae and bacteria is common...". Blue-green algae living on the surfaces of vascular aquatic plants have been reported as fixing N at rates from 15 kg N/ha-yr to greater than 500 kg N/ha-yr at plant densities of 200 g plant dry weight/m^2.

Individual wetlands can have vascular plant densities that range from 0 to 1,000s g plant dry weight/m^2. N-fixation may be appreciable across the whole range of values. For example, N-fixing microorganism living in and on the stems of living and dead Spartina (2200 g plant dry weight/m^2) fixed an amount of N during the month of July alone that "...was at least 1550 kg N_2/ha. The barren zone, during its peak fixation month of July had a potential nitrogen input of 210 kg N_2/ha. In comparison, the growing season of an alfalfa crop encompasses at least two months, and during this period approximately 250 kg N_2/ha are produced. During the growing season, a crop of soybeans fixes about 150 kg N_2/ha."

So-called barren zones of wetland areas lack growth of vascular plants but often have appreciable growths of algae. Algae living in the top 0.25 cm. of marsh soil have been shown to fix 64 Kg N_2/ha-yr and blue-green algal mats living on top of marsh soil have been shown to fix over 200 Kg N_2/ha-yr. N-fixation in the top 8 in. of wetland soil at 15°C has been shown to be 144 kg N/ha in a 180-day period (Tjepkema and Evans, 1976).

Furthermore, aquatic and wetland sediments undergo especially intense N cycling. For example, populations of N-fixing bacteria are especially large in oxygen-free, waterlogged sediments. In such environments N-fixing microorganisms do not have to expend as much energy to protect the N-fixing enzyme (nitrogenase) as they would in oxic sediment. This, plus a usually plentiful supply of organic matter to use as sources of energy, make for relatively intense N-fixation on the order of 10s to 100s of kg N/ha-yr in natural wetlands and aquatic sediments.

This has also been also been demonstrated experimentally. For example a review of the literature reported, "In waterlogged soils amended with 1 per cent straw, or less, nitrogen fixation rates up to 150 kg ha^{-1} a^{-1} were achieved; with 5 to 20 per cent straw and waterlogged conditions 500 to 1000 kg ha^{-1} a^{-1} were fixed. The responsible organism was Clostridium butyricum and Meiklejohn (1967) also found that the number of clostridia increased considerably when approximately 678 to 1356 kg/ha of compost was added to the soil.".

N fixation has been reported to be especially intense in the rhizosphere of aquatic plants, *e.g.*, "For a typical T. testudinum stand, N_2 fixation is estimated to be 100 to 500 kg N/hectare per year. Numbers of N_2-fixing in the rhizosphere sediments were roughly 50 to 300 times more abundant than those in the non-rhizosphere sediments..."

And for a stand of maximum productivity, N-fixation was estimated to be "...350 to 1700 kg N/hectare per year. These estimates are comparable to estimates of N_2 fixation associated with legumes, which are typically in the range 110 to 220 kg N/hectare per year"

These reducing aquatic and wetland sediments also are the site of appreciable denitrification of NO_3-N produced in the surface oxidized sediment layer (if present) and/or brought in from overlying oxygenated water (if present) to the reducing environment of the underlying waterlogged sediments. However some of this N gas is recycled by N fixation. Whereas the biosphere appears to be energy and material inefficient in utilizing only a small part of available N - that portion which undergoes nitrification/denitrification - these apparent inefficiencies are also part of an excellent design. Namely, the leakage of N through nitrification/denitrification allows N to spread out from N-rich environments in solution as NO_3^- and as gases - much as seeds can spread out and away from trees. In this way the N-rich portions of the biosphere "seed" the entire earth with N.

People are part of the biosphere. Since the harnessing of fire, long before the dawn of recorded history, essentially wherever people have lived they have had a profound influence on the biosphere and its N reservoir and N cycle. Fire generally promoted the growth of N-rich vegetation which, in turn, promoted the accumulation of soil N through the humification of the N-rich organic matter. Fire also stimulated symbiotic and asymbiotic microbial N fixation directly. N fixation was indirectly promoted by fire as it enhanced the biomass to support large herds of grazing animals to live on the N-enriched landscape.

Fire also enhanced the flow of terrestrial N to the atmosphere and the hydrosphere (surface and ground waters). Nevertheless, in spite of the increased transfers, the fire-induced gains in terrestrial N were generally greater than the fire-induced losses to the atmosphere and hydrosphere.

In Illinois, and much of the Midwest, annual burnings by Native Americans kept the N cycle (and other nutrient cycles) at high rates of fixation, transfer and accumulation. Fire also shaped the vegetation. Whereas now Illinois is ecologically mapped as being in the eastern hardwoods ecoregion (if you abandon land, trees grow on it) when Europeans began settling the state, 9 million ha. of Illinois' 14 million ha. of land was prairie due to repeated burning by Native Americans and intense grazing by buffalo and other animals. And the one-third of Illinois that was forested had more park-like forests than the forests of today -the forest floor being rich in grasses and legumes, and the species composition of the forest overstory was different.

Early explorers and settlers noted than once Native Americans were cleared off the land in advance of European settlement, prairies soon stated growing up into trees. And the large herds of buffalo and other animals whose dung and bones littered the landscape also disappeared within 20 years after the departure of the herds. As with the forests, the remaining prairies changed in plant composition and lost most of their N-fixing legumes.

The clearing of land by the European settlers went slowly at first. Populations were low relative to today's standards and modification of the land had to be done by hand and animal power, not machines as are used today. By 1900 only about 4 million ha. of Illinois was plowed and growing row crops. Machine power enabled the drainage of about 4 million additional ha. of land (mostly in the 20th century) and the total area of Illinois in crop land increased to 9.3 million ha. Drainage and leveeing reduced the organic and nutrient loadings that aquatic and wetland vegetation imposed on Illinois' surface waters.

At first, the prairie soils were too rich in N and other nutrients to grow crops well. After some years fertility declined but bumper crops could still be grown for decades without addition of N and other nutrients. For decades there was still so much N in the soils that crusts of nitrate salts were an unremarkable phenomenon in Midwest soils. And so much nitrate could accumulate in animal forage that animals eating it were poisoned.

However, over time soil-N levels and crop yields dropped to low levels. In the second half of the 20th century crop yields increased to record levels due to improved soil and crop management techniques, development of new plant varieties, and the use of chemical fertilizers.

There are major challenges to estimating historical mass balances for the biosphere and human impacts on it. For example, in estimating the impacts of agriculture to Illinois' N mass balance the effect of removing the N-fixing prairie ecosystem needs to be taken into consideration. Such mass balance estimates need to take into account the agriculturally-induced decrease in the soil-N reservoir and concomitant decreases in natural soil-N cycling. Human impacts must consider both anthropogenically-induced reductions as well as additions. So far, only additions are considered in N mass balances.

For example, today's natural N cycle is generally considered only from the viewpoint of its being an imperfect filter against the removal (by denitrification) of anthropogenic N additions. However, today's natural ecosystem still has a N-fixing component which needs to be taken into consideration. Mass balance studies in Illinois have yet to consider how anthropogenic N additions interact with the whole of the remaining natural N cycle: an example being that N additions will reduce asymbiotic and symbiotic N fixation in both terrestrial and aquatic ecosystems.

Conversely, massive pollution of surface waters by phosphorus (P) in detergents and other pollutants greatly increased blooms of N-fixing algae which contributed to the N enrichment and eutrophication of lakes and rivers. Fortunately, timely recognition of the importance of controlling phosphorus pollution in the 1960's and 1970's led to a subsequent reversal in eutrophication and associated N enrichment by blooms of N-fixing algae. The recognition of the relationship between P-enriched environments and concentration of NO_3^- in water goes back to the 1920s (McHargue and Peter, 1921). But such interaction of N with P and other elemental cycles in the biosphere has yet to be considered in Illinois mass balance studies (*e.g.*, David and Gentry, 2000a, b) nor have they been used to explain trends in water quality (Krug and Winstanley, 2000).

The challenges to estimating historical mass balances for the biosphere and human impacts on it are formidable; and we have a long way to go in recognizing and overcoming them.

SOIL ORGANIC MATTER DECOMPOSITION AND NITROGEN AVAILABILITY

Temperature, the quality of organic matter inputs, and soil water have been identified as the primary controls on decomposition rates. Most studies, however, treat SOM as an amorphous black box that mineralizes C and N at varying rates in response to biotic and abiotic controls. As a result, our ability to predict the magnitude and variability of changes in mineralization across a warmer future landscape is still limited by our poor understanding of how these factors control SOM decomposition.

The notion that decomposition in arctic tundra soils will increase substantially with warming assumes that the breakdown of this material is limited primarily by environmental conditions, rather than by the inherent recalcitrance of the organic matter. This has been confirmed by laboratory incubations, which have shown that this organic matter has the potential to decompose rapidly, and that some of it may mineralize significant quantities of N (Weintraub and Schimel 2003).

Thus, given more favorable conditions for decomposition, tundra SOM can decompose rapidly and release stored C to the atmosphere and N to the soil. As a result, whether or not tundra ecosystems become a net source for atmospheric carbon dioxide with warming will depend on whether increases in N availability to plants, and the resulting gains in primary productivity, can offset C losses from SOM. Thus, the controls on plant N uptake in the tundra are likely to be the factors determining changes in C storage in arctic tundra ecosystems.

Given its important role in constraining potential changes to the C balance of arctic tundra ecosystems, N availability to plants in tundra soils is poorly understood. The classical model in plant ecology was that plants can only take up inorganic N, which is made available by microbial activity. In addition, it was thought that plants competed poorly with soil microbes, and therefore only captured soil resources that soil microbes didn't use (Schimel and Bennett 2004). Studies on N mineralization in arctic tundra soils, however, have shown that net mineralization rates are too low to account for the amount of N taken up by plants (Giblin et al. 1991, Nadelhoffer et al. 1991). Thus, assessing plant N uptake in tundra soils has proved difficult.

Research over the last decade suggests that amino acid uptake is likely to be an important component of plant N budgets in tundra systems, and that plants can bypass the microbial N mineralization step by taking up organic N. However, the role of soil amino acids and other organic N forms as components of the N cycle and as N sources to plants has not been well quantified. In part, this is because little is known about the seasonal dynamics of amino acids and dissolved organic N in soil, and how they relate to the dynamics of dissolved inorganic N and plant growth.

Furthermore, it has been demonstrated that at least one tundra sedge, E. vaginatum, can take up the adenine (a nucleic base) and choline (an amine) as intact molecules, in addition to a range of amino acids (Weintraub and Schimel 2005a). Thus, depending on their availability in soil, it is possible that other organic N forms beside amino acids may also be components of the N economy of tundra plants, but their importance is unknown. That plants may be using a wider variety of organic N forms than just amino acids, however, makes quantifying the overall importance of organic N in the N economy of tundra plants a significantly more difficult task.

The concentrations of biologically available N forms in soil are controlled by the balance of their production and consumption rates. The release of biologically available N from complexes of insoluble organic matter is mediated by the depolymerization of SOM by microbial extracellular enzymes. The rapid turnover of soil amino acids suggests that extractable concentrations are a snapshot of the balance between production and consumption at any particular time, and are therefore a short-term measure of the amino acids' availability. For amino acids, production rates are controlled by the activities of protein-degrading extracellular enzymes, proteases, which break down proteins into soluble peptides and individual amino acids, and by the direct release of amino acids from soil microbes in response to osmotic changes or as a result of cell lysis.

Microbial turnover and the input of fresh plant detritus are also likely to increase the production of amino acids by providing proteins to proteases.

Thus, proteolysis is the rate-limiting step in the release of peptides and amino acids from the breakdown of soil proteins, the most prevalent N form in soil. Proteolytic activity can be controlled by protein supply to protease enzymes, if they are substrate limited, or by the activity of the enzymes, if they are saturated by a substrate. As microbes produce more extracellular enzymes that must bind to solid substrates, the enzymes have to diffuse farther out from the cells, the substrates must diffuse farther back, and the enzymes can compete with one another for binding sites. This results in substrate limitation unless the enzyme pool is very small.

NITROGEN UPTAKE FROM SOIL

The consumption of biologically available N from the soil by plants and microbes depends on the organisms' physiological capacities for uptake, and on the concentrations of these biologically available N forms in the soil. The controls on the magnitude and timing of nutrient uptake in soil are poorly understood, but microbial N demand is likely to be stimulated by high C availability, whereas nutrient uptake by plants is likely to be controlled by growth form and phenology. Although plant uptake is a direct sink for soil N, plants can also stimulate microbial N immobilization and thereby increase microbial sinks through root exudates and litter inputs. As a result, species-specific patterns in the timing and magnitude of plants' nutrient uptake and C inputs to the soil have the potential to create different patterns of nutrient availability in different plant communities.

It has been hypothesized that for a given species, plant uptake of different N forms is controlled by the relative differences between soil and root uptake rates, with plants competing best for the N forms that microbes take up most slowly. The idea is that C-limited microbes compete better for more C-rich organic N forms. It has also been suggested that plants may take up N at times when microbes are less active. A recent study byMcKane and colleagues (2002) also suggests that niche separation in N uptake may occur across different N forms, with different plant species competing better for different forms of N. They suggest that the more productive tundra species take up the most abundant N forms available in the soil, while the less productive tundra species depend on scarcer N compounds. These ideas suggest that there should be differences in the uptake rates of different N forms between plant species, and between plants and soil.

However, there are challenges to the hypotheses about nutrient partitioning and the importance of amino acid uptake. First, most studies examining organic N uptake have used a single amino acid (or at most two) as a model. Typically, the model amino acid has been glycine, because it is taken up rapidly by plants and slowly by soil microbes, is present in relatively high concentrations in the soil solution, and is therefore hypothesized to be important in plant N nutrition. Although these factors do suggest that glycine may be one of the more important amino acids in soil solution, it comprises less than 9 per cent of the amino acids in both plant structural protein and SOM. Thus, fully testing hypotheses about amino acid uptake and partitioning will require understanding the dynamics of a wider range of amino acids.

A more direct challenge to theories about differential partitioning of N forms comes from studies that have found that competitive N partitioning between tundra plants and soil differs more by plant species than by N form or sampling date, and that plants compete for a relatively constant fraction of available N. These results suggest that differences in root architecture and rooting volume may be more responsible for differences between plant species' abilities to compete for soil N than is partitioning by N form. For example,Weintraub and Schimel found that the sedge E. angustifolium took up about 0.5 per cent of added N, regardless of which compound the N was in, and Schimel and Chapin (1996) found that C. aquatilis, a co-occurring wet meadow species with a much more extensive fine root network, took up 12 per cent to 16 per cent of added N. Although the uptake experiment in Schimel and Chapin (1996) ran longer than that ofWeintraub and Schimel, their results for E. vaginatum, the predominant moist tundra sedge, were comparable. Taken together, the results from these studies suggest that even within a particular plant community, plant N uptake varies more by species than by N form, and that these differences are probably caused by differences in their roots' access to available N in soil. These results therefore contradict the hypothesis that differences in the uptake rates of different N forms between plant species control their N partitioning.

For individual plant species, Weintraub and Schimel found that competitive N partitioning in two tundra sedge species was more consistent than would have been predicted by relative differences in soil and root uptake rates for a variety of different amino acids and other N compounds. This makes sense in light of recent research that suggests that root amino acid transporters have broad specificity (Persson and Näsholm 2002) and that in an N-limited environment, physical access is likely to regulate uptake (Schimel and Bennett 2004) and therefore to be the most important control on plant N acquisition for a given species.

SEASONAL DYNAMICS OF NITROGEN AVAILABILITY

If plant uptake of different N forms in tundra soils depends on their availability, then, to understand plant uptake patterns, it may be important to consider the seasonal dynamics of biologically available soil N pools.Weintraub and Schimel found that concentrations of soil amino acids and dissolved inorganic N all abruptly decline at the height of the arctic growing season in July. This effect is particularly pronounced in the tussock community, where soil N availability is relatively high before the onset of root growth in E. vaginatum, the dominant plant species. After the onset of root growth in July, extractable N concentrations rapidly decline, and remain extremely low for the rest of the growing season.

This pattern suggests that low N concentrations in tundra soils at the height of the growing season are probably the result of increased N uptake associated with the peak in root growth (Weintraub and Schimel 2005b). However, Weintraub and Schimel found that E. vaginatum actually competed slightly better for N in June than in July, and that plants were consistently able to compete for soil N when it was available. Thus, plant N acquisition may have declined when soil N availability was decreasing (Weintraub and Schimel 2005b), despite increased root growth. If plant N uptake did not increase with root growth, then the declines in biologically available soil N pools may not have been caused entirely by increases in plant N uptake, but may also have resulted from significant N immobilization, possibly stimulated by root C inputs to the soil.

The seasonal dynamics of available N in arctic tundra soils therefore indicate that there is increased N demand at the height of the arctic growing season, the result of N uptake by both plants and soil microbes. At the height of the growing season, when amino acid and ammonium concentrations were at their lowest, soil protease activity and soluble protein concentrations also increased. The coincidence in timing suggests that increased soil N demand stimulates microbial N acquisition, causing microbes to increase production of proteases. Despite the increase in enzyme activity, proteolysis becomes substrate limited at this time, as the increase in the activity of these enzymes exceeds the availability of soil proteins (Weintraub and Schimel 2005c). This increase in protease activity also causes the appearance of high concentrations of soluble proteins in the soil solution, as they are liberated from the breakdown of larger, insoluble protein complexes (Weintraub and Schimel 2005c).

The period during mid-July when N pools and processes are changing so rapidly is an important period for soil phosphate ($PO^{3-}{}_4$) dynamics as well. As N pools crash and protease activities spike, soil $PO^{3-}{}_4$ concentrations also spike. Previous research suggests that this is caused by phosphatase enzymes in soil that mineralize organic phosphorus (P) into $PO^{3''}{}_4$, and that these enzymes can be produced both by plant roots and by soil microbes. Thus, increases in soil P demand and N demand coincide, resulting in increases in the production of enzymes that microbes (and, in the case of phosphatase, plants) use to scavenge these nutrients from organic pools.

The model of nutrient availability that emerges for tundra soils is one in which plants can take up not only mineralized N but also amino acids and other organic N forms released by the breakdown of SOM, which is carried out largely by microbial extracellular enzymes. The main controls on N partitioning between plants and soil appear to be plant community composition and the availability and accessibility of N to plant roots. The major transitions in soil N and P pools both occur in mid-July, at the height of the arctic growing season.

Thus, fluctuations in soil N and P availability appear to be seasonally driven. The most likely explanation for the rapid shifts in soil nutrient concentrations is that the changes are driven by the onset of rapid root growth. Across the different tundra communities, plant nutrient uptake and root C inputs to the soil at the height of the growing season cause high microbial nutrient demand, stimulating the production of proteases and phosphatases to increase N and P supply from organic matter breakdown, which in turn causes rapid increases in soluble protein and $PO^{3-}{}_4$ concentrations in soil. Thus, it appears likely that nutrient pool sizes are driven more by sink than by source processes in tundra soils.

That no increases in soil amino acid availability are observed when protease activity increases suggests that amino acid uptake is extremely rapid at this time, and further suggests that the increases in soil enzyme activity are stimulated by high microbial N demand at the peak of the growing season. The timing and magnitude of plant root growth and nutrient uptake appear to be the major factors determining the seasonal dynamics of available nutrients in tundra soils, suggesting that changes in plant community composition have the potential to substantially alter overall nutrient cycling in tundra ecosystems.

SEASONALITY AND LIFE CYCLES

First let's define some common terms such as annual, perennial, grass, forb and shrub. An annual plantis one that starts from seed each year. A perennial plantsurvives for several years. While perennials may produce seeds they invest a certain amount of energy to storing carbohydrates in roots and crowns for use in respiration during dormant (cold or dry) periods and initial support of regrowth at the beginning of a new growing season.

Grasses are monocotyledonous, usually herbaceous plants with narrow leaves growing from the base. Monocotyledonous plants or monocots are one of two major groups of flowering plants (angiosperms) that are traditionally recognized, the other being dicotyledonous plants or dicots. Monocot seedlings typically have one cotyledon (seed-leaf), in contrast to the two cotyledons typical of dicots. Graminoids include the grasses of the Poaceae family, as well as the sedges of the Cyperaceae family and the rushes of the Juncaceae family.

The grasses dominate most of the world's grasslands but also include cereals, bamboo, and turf grasses that are cultivated for food, fibre and recreation. Sedges include many wild marsh and grassland plants, and some cultivated ones such as water chestnut (Eleocharis dulcis) and papyrus sedge. Forbs are herbaceous flowering plants that are not grasses, sedges or rushes. Forbs are dicotyledonous and non-woody. The term, forb, is frequently used in vegetation ecology, especially in relation to grasslands. A shrub or bush is a horticultural rather than a strict botanical category of woody plant, distinguished from a tree by its multiple stems and lower height, usually less than 5–6 m tall. A large number of plants can be either shrubs or trees, depending on the growing conditions they experience.

Fig. Monocotyledonous (left) and dicotyledonous (right) seedlings.

Fig. True grass, sedge and a rush.

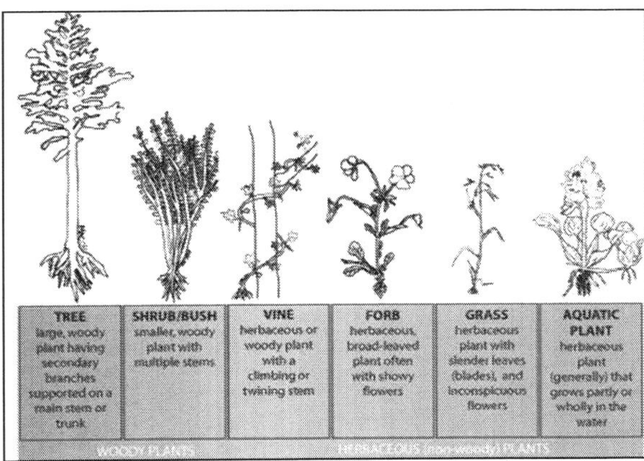

Fig. Perennial plants include herbaceous grasses and forbs and woody plants include shrubs and trees.

LIFE CYCLES

Phenology is the study of periodic plant life cycle events and how these are influenced by seasonal and inter-annual variations in weather. Examples of life cycle events include the date of germination or seedling emergence, or the date of flowering or seed set. A listing of phenological stages normally includes vegetative, flowering and dormancy stages for perennials. 12 phenological stages or stages of maturity that have been used to study seasonal changes in forage quality of annual grasses.

Table. Numerical stage of maturity used to predict crude protein, crude fibre, phosphorus and calcium content of annual grasses, filaree and bur clover.

Stage number	Stage description
1	germinated
2	early vegetative
3	late vegetative
4	early bloom
5	mid bloom
6	full bloom
7	late bloom
8	milk stage
9	dough stage
10	mature
11	dry
12	dry leached

Each year annual plants, germinate, become established and proceed through vegetative and reproductive stages. During the winter when moisture is adequate but temperatures are low, photosynthesis and plant growth are slow. With the arrival of spring, photosynthesis and plant growth rates increase. As soil moisture is depleted plants begin to dry and die becoming litter. Variation in seasonal temperatures and precipitation influence the seasonality of plant growth. Perennial plants live for several years and re-grow each year. Therefore you will be managing the same plant year after year. They reproduce from seed or vegetatively with tillers, stolons and rhizomes. Short lived perennials last 3-5 years whereas properly managed long-lived perennials can survive much longer.

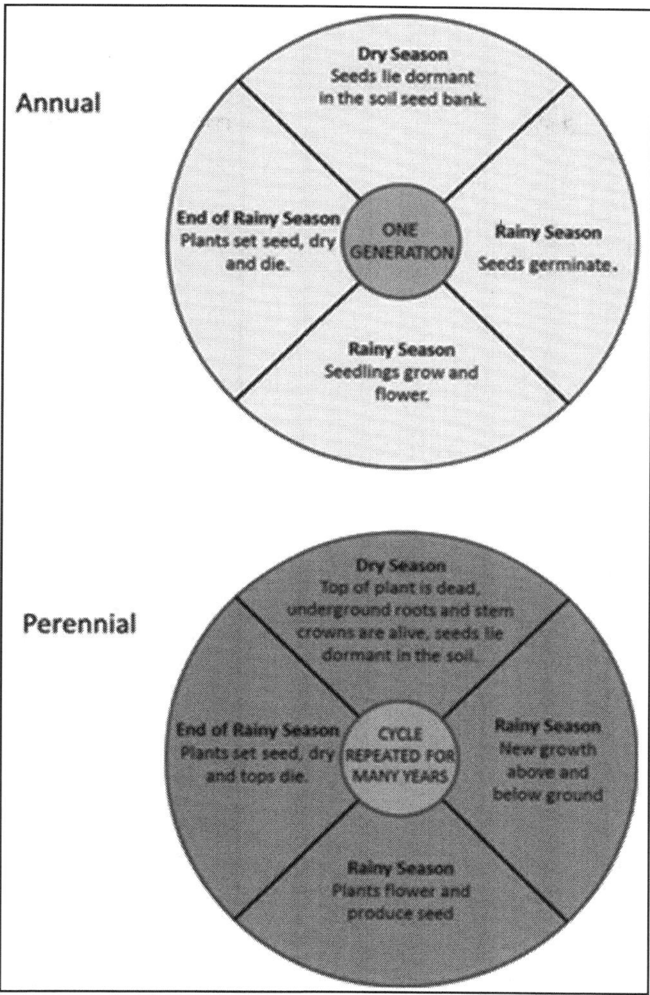

Fig. Annual and perennial plant life cycles.

Woody perennials can live for decades and centuries. In temperate regions many perennial plants enter dormancy to survive freezing winter temperatures. In Mediterranean regions where there is a pronounced summer dry season and mild winter temperatures, perennial grasses and forbs may enter a dry season dormancy, regrowing with the fall rains.

Much of the aboveground biomass of perennial grasses and forbs die as the cold or dry season approaches. The remainder of the aboveground and near surface portions of these plants enter a dormant phase until the cold or dry season is over. During cold dormancy (winter) soil moisture is stored during rainy periods and snow melt. As spring approaches these plants use this soil moisture to begin to grow as temperatures increase. These plants will remain vegetative for several weeks but will eventually flower and develop seeds. As the growing season progresses seed is set and eventually dispersed. With cooling temperatures the plants begin to enter dormancy and much of the aboveground biomass dies and dries. Most perennial grasses and forbs in the western U.S follow this winter dormancy life cycle pattern.

SEED BANKS

When thinking about seed banks in California annual rangelands, it is important to make a distinction between short-term (*i.e.* transient) seed banks and long-term (*i.e.* persistent) seed banks. Transient seed banks refer to the seeds that spend a short time in the soil, usually the time between their production and dispersal in late spring and their subsequent germination with the onset of fall rain. In contrast, persistent seed banks refer to seeds that remain in the soil for multiple years; in fact, these seeds can remain viable in the soil for many decades. The degree of difference between the species composition of the aboveground grassland community and the community hidden underground in the seed bank can be quite striking and varies among species and grassland types.

Although the relative contribution of different grassland species to transient and persistent seed banks can vary widely, there are some general trends. Grasses, although they are often the dominant component of transient seed banks, are much less likely to contribute to persistent seed banks. The seed of most grass species germinates in the year of its production and rarely survives more than a year or two in the soil. Even when focusing specifically on transient seed banks, the relative contribution of annual and perennial grasses to these short-lived seed banks can be very different.

A study of a mixed annual and perennial (Stipa sp.) grassland in the Central Valley found that, even in areas dominated by perennial grass cover, there were essentially no perennial seeds in the soil seed bank. In contrast, annual grasses had a well-developed transient seed bank even in areas where they were a very minor component aboveground. Compared to grasses, forbs have a tendency to produce a more persistent seed bank. A five year study in a California annual grassland indicated that seed carry over rates (a measure of seed bank persistence) were more than 10 times greater in forb species than in annual grasses. Among forbs, legumes have the greatest rates of seed carryover and thus can often form very long-lived persistent seed banks.

Seed coat impermeability to water (hard seed) is a form of persistent seed dormancy that is widespread in legumes and is further described below under the section on Germination. Seed longevity may explain the dominance of legumes in persistent seed banks in grasslands. Hull (1973) compared germination rates for a number of North American rangeland species that had been stored in unheated sheds for 14 to 41 years. Seeds of legumes retained their viability longer and had much higher rates of germination than any of the grass and forb species tested, regardless of storage time.

Spatial variation in the longevity of soil seed banks can depend on the frequency of soil disturbance and the formation of gaps in both plant canopy and litter layers. Germination cueing represents the capacity of a seed to detect a potential "opening" for establishment and may involve a number a physical cues such as light quality or soil temperature fluctuations. For example, Rice (1985) reported that diurnal temperature variation among three types of microsites in annual grassland (under grass litter, bare soil, and buried under gopher mounds) significantly affected rates of dormancy release in broad-leaved filaree (Erodium botrys). Microsite variation in soil temperature germination cues in this hard seeded forb might have a strong influence on seed bank depletion and longevity by affecting the loss rate due to germination.

GERMINATION

Seed germination initiates a series of changes that ultimately lead to a mature plant and reproduction of the species. Favorable temperature and moisture are essential for successful development of the seedling during the first critical stages of growth. Rapid germination and growth results in a high demand for light, moisture, nutrients and other plant growth requirements.

Fully developed seeds contain an embryo and food reserves, wrapped in a seed coat. Under favorable conditions, the seed begins to germinate and the embryonic tissues resume growth, developing towards a seedling. Some plants produce varying numbers of seeds that lack embryos, these are called empty seeds, and never germinate.

While water is required, temperature, oxygen and light quality may also influence germination. Mature seeds are often extremely dry and need to take in significant amounts of water, relative to the dry weight of the seed, before cellular metabolism and growth can resume. The uptake of water by seeds is called imbibition, which leads to the swelling and the breaking of the seed coat.

When seeds are formed, most plants store a food reserve with the seed, such as starch, proteins, or oils. This food reserve provides nourishment to the growing embryo. When the seed imbibes water,hydrolytic enzymes are activated which break down these stored food resources into metabolically useful chemicals. After the seedling emerges from the seed coat and starts growing roots and leaves, the seedling's food reserves are typically exhausted; at this point photosynthesis provides the energy needed for continued growth and the seedling now requires a continuous supply of water, nutrients, and light. When a seed germinates the new seedling leaf grows towards light. This is called phototropism.

Oxygen is required for respiration during germination. Oxygen is found in soil pore spaces but if a seed is buried too deeply within the soil or the soil is waterlogged, the seed can be oxygen starved. Some seeds have impermeable seed coats that prevent oxygen from entering the seed, causing a type of physical dormancy which is broken when the seed coat is worn away enough to allow gas exchange and water uptake from the environment. Hard seed produced by some legumes, such as rose clover, can allow seed to survive in soil for more than 20 years.

Temperature also influences germination. Seeds from different species and even seeds from the same plant germinate over a wide range of temperatures. Seeds often have a temperature range within which they will germinate, and they will not do so above or below this range. Many seeds germinate at temperatures slightly above room-temperature 60-75 F (16-24 C), while others germinate just above freezing and others germinate only in response to alternations in temperature between warm and cool. Some seeds germinate when the soil is cool 28-40 F (-2 - 4 C), and some when the soil is warm 76-90 F (24-32 C).

Some seeds require exposure to cold temperatures (vernalization) to break dormancy. Seeds in a dormant state will not germinate even if conditions are favorable. Some seeds will only germinate following hot weather and others must be exposed to hot temperatures during a forest fire which cracks their seed coats. Germination in many seeds, especially small seeds, is regulated by light and many seeds, including species found in forest settings, will not germinate until an opening in the canopy allows sufficient light for growth of the seedling. Some seeds need to pass through an animal's digestive tract to weaken the seed coat enough to allow the seedling to emerge.

Variability in the rate of germination exists between and within species. Seed size has been shown to be a critical factor in promoting seedling vigour. In legumes and other forbs, seed coat hardness or impermeability often retards germination but spreads germination over years which is a survival advantage for the species. In general, germination is reduced with increasing age of seeds.

SEEDLING ESTABLISHMENT

With emergence of the radical during germination, seedling establishment begins and may not be considered successful until an adequate root system and leaf area has developed to sustain a high rate of growth. While there is no single attribute that influences seedling vigour and establishment, seed size and weight, rapid germination, seed age, high levels of biochemical and physiological activity, and rate of root and shoot growth are all potential indicators of seedling vigour. Rapid root growth is fundamental to establishment and development of annual rangeland plants. Individual plants and species may gain an advantage over competitors if they are able to maintain both rapid root and top growth. In California, annual grasses frequently exhibit root growth rates greater than native perennial grasses. This is one of the reasons that native perennial grass establishment is so difficult in California's annual rangelands.

SEASONAL GROWTH RATES

Growth rates in the annual rangelands following germination are rapid if temperatures are warm and slow if temperatures are cold. The average germination date at the UC Sierra Foothill Research and Extension Center (UC SFREC) in Yuba County, California is October 20 and the average standing crop on December 1 is 347 lbs/acre or less than 12 per cent of peak standing crop in May.

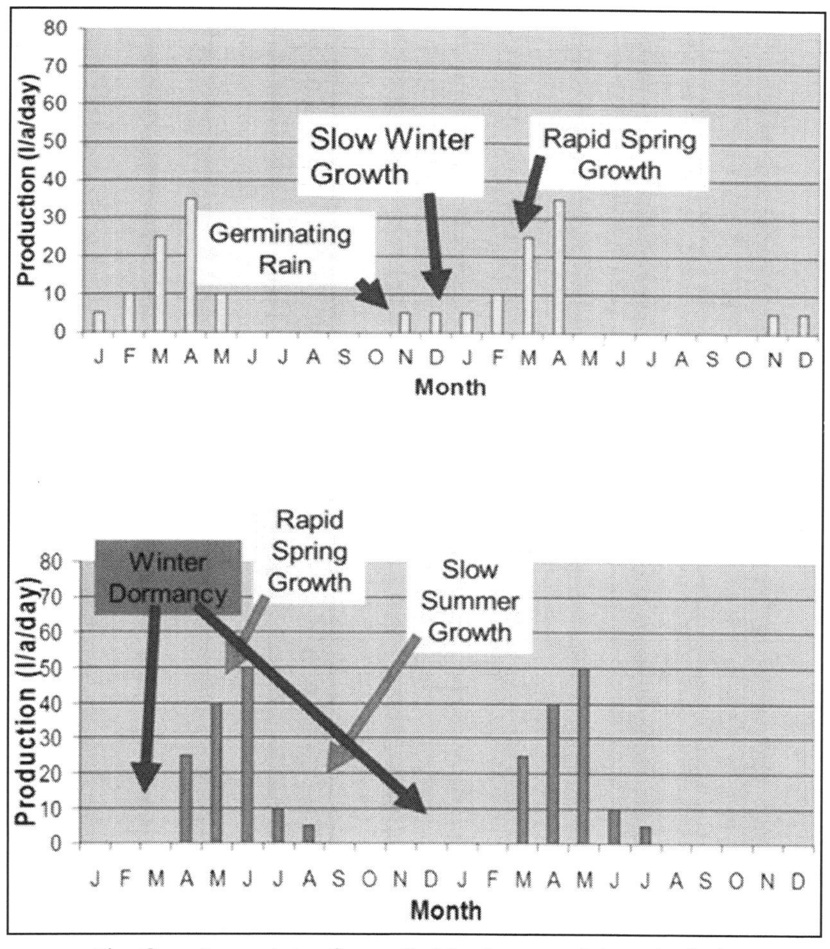

Fig. Growing points often called buds or meristems include apical meristems, axillary buds and intercalary meristems.

During the winter growth is slow such that the average standing crop at UC SFREC on March 1 is only about 700 lbs/acre which is less than 25 per cent of standing crop of 2984 lbs/acre on May 1. Thus in this example daily growth rates average about 5 lbs/acre/day from October 20 to March 1. During rapid spring growth the average rates of growth are about 37 lbs/acre/day resulting in an average standing crop on May 1 of 2942 lb./acre. On average, little production occurs during May at UC SFREC resulting in only small differences between average standing crop on May 1 and on average peak standing crop.

On intermountain rangelands, grass growth begins with warming temperatures after a period of winter dormancy. For example, in northeastern California there is little or no grass production from October through February or March. Only about 10 per cent of the annual production occurs in April as plants begin to grow. In May and June growth is rapid often accounting for 50 to 75 per cent of the annual production. Growth slows for the rest of the summer with increasing temperatures in July and reductions in soil water availability.

In California's annual rangelands the grasses and forbs produced during the growing season dry and become litter as the growing season ends. University of California has published guidelines for how much litter or residual dry matter (RDM) should be left at the end of the grazing season for soil protection and to provide mulch to protect germinating seeds.

FORAGE QUALITY

Forage quality decreases as plants progress through their yearly life cycle. During theearly vegetative stage of growth, before stem elongation and flowering, forage quality is greatest because cell contents and nutrient concentrations in metabolically active tissues are greater and contain less cell wall structure. For annual plants, this stage follows germination. For perennial plants, this is the new plant growth following dormancy or regrowth following harvest. As the season progresses cell wall increases and cell content decreases resulting in a gradual decline in protein content and digestibility.

In the late vegetative stage when stems are beginning to elongate just before flowering, nutrient concentrations are usually lower than at early vegetative stages. This occurs during the adequate-green season's spring flush of growth.

As plants begin to flower nutrients are being translocated to the flowers and nutrients in the forage continue to decline. By the late flowering stage when the dough stage in grass seeds occurs, nutrients have accumulated in flowers and seed, resulting in a loss of nutrients in leaves and stems. This stage occurs late in the adequate-green season (Bentley and Talbot 1951).

Fig. Protein, energy, vitamins and minerals decrease fibre and lignin increase as plants mature.

As plants mature and begin to dry, seeds are dispersed and forage quality has declined to such an extent that it does not meet the nutritional requirements of some kinds and classes of livestock. In the dry stage plants are cured, seed has been dispersed, and weathering is in progress. Plant nutrients are low and fibre is high. Weathering is accelerated by rainfall that leaches nutrients from the dry residual forage. This is the dry leached stage when forage quality is lowest.

MORPHOLOGY AND DEVELOPMENT

GRASS ANATOMY

In this section we will discuss the morphology and development of grasses and forbs and plant reproduction.

Growing Points (Buds, Meristems)

There are several growing points on a grass plant. Apical meristems or buds develop into the flower and are elevated during the flowering process. Axillary buds give rise to tillers, rhizomes and stolons.

Growing points often called buds or meristems include apical meristems, axillary buds and intercalary meristems, then select:

- Select Shoot Development/Crown to see apical meristem and axillary buds on the crown of a grass plant.
- SelectShoot Development/Leaf Expansion Dynamics to see the location of the intercalary meristem.
- SelectShoot Development/Flowering to see an animation of the raising of the floral bud.
- SelectShoot Development/Tilleringto see an animation of tiller growth from axillary buds.
- SelectShoot Development/Rhizome and Stolon Development to see an animation of rhizome and stolon growth from axillary buds

Intercalary meristems allow leaves to expand following grazing or mowing. Buds near the ground are less likely to be grazed or mowed but some buds become elevated as the season progresses increasing the risk of removal during grazing or mowing. Delaying bud elevation reduces risk of bud removal.

Developmental Anatomy

Grasses and other plants progress through a vegetative phase, a transition phase and a reproduction phase. In the vegetative phase grass shoots are mostly leaf. Leaf blade collars remain nested in the base of the shoot and there is no evidence of sheath elongation or culm development. In response to day-length, temperature or other environmental variables the apical meristem is gradually converted from a vegetative bud to a floral bud. This is called floral induction. This conversion phase is termed the transition phase.

During the transition or elongation phase floral induction begins, leaf sheaths begin to elongate and culm internodes also elongate raising the floral buds and leaf bases to a grazable height. During the reproductive phase the conversion from vegetative to floral bud production is completed and the unseen inflorescence emerges from the leaf sheath.

Fig. Vegetative, elongation and reproductive stages of annual plant life cycle.

Just before the inflorescence emerges it is covered by the leaf sheath and this is commonly called the "boot stage" of development. Successful regrowth following defoliation depends on productive plant meristems or buds. Plant species with growing points elevated are more susceptible to grazing than plants that keep their growing points close to the ground during most of their life cycle.

FORB ANATOMY

Growing Points (Buds, Meristems)

Forb anatomy varies between species. This diagram of legumes identifies some common forb plant parts. Like grasses and other plants, forbs have apical buds that may develop into flowers and axillary buds that produce stems, rhizomes and stolons.

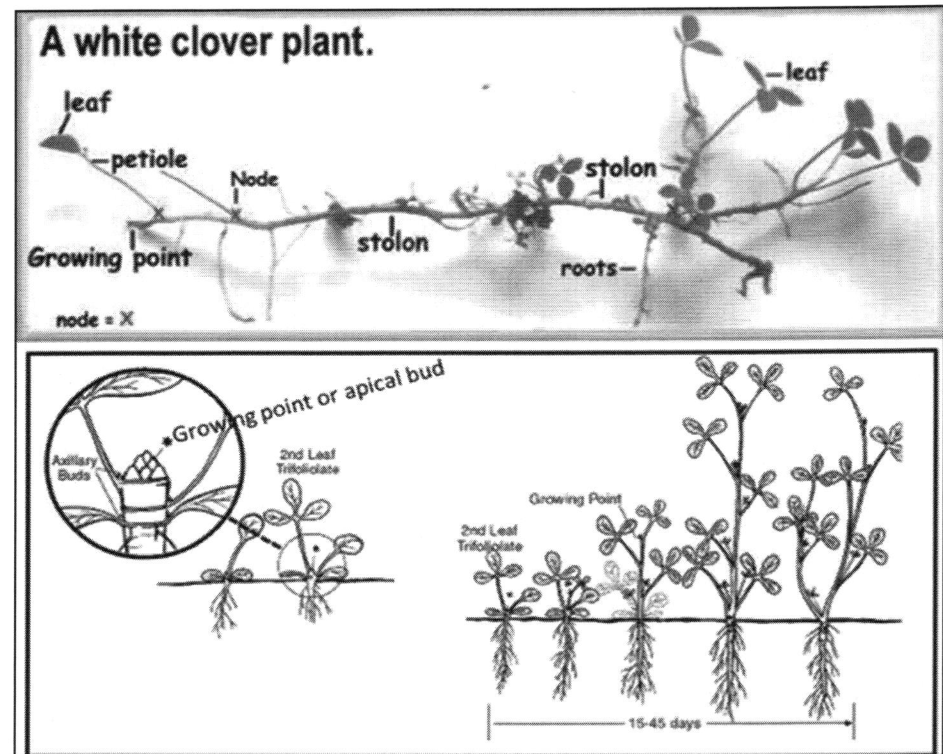

Fig. Location of growing points on a clover plant.

Woody plants have apical and axillary buds like those of forbs. They also have buds on the root crown or roots that resprout following damage or loss of the aboveground stems as occurs during fire or following wood cutting. Chamise and some oaks are strong resprouters following fire or top removal.

REPRODUCTION

The reproductive phase is triggered primarily by photoperiod (Leopold and Kriedemann 1975, Dahl 1995) but can be slightly modified by temperature and precipitation. Some plants are long-day plants and others are short-day plants. The long-day plants reach the flowering phenological stage after exposure to a critical photoperiod and during the period of increasing daylight between mid April and mid June. Generally, most cool-season plants are long-day plants and reach flower phenophase before 21 June.

The short-day plants are induced into flowering by day lengths that are shorter than a critical length and that occur during the period of decreasing day length after mid June. Short-day plants are technically responding to the increase in the length of the night period rather than to the decrease in day length (Leopold and Kriedemann 1975). Generally, most warm-season plants are short-day plants and reach the flower phenophase after 21 June. The annual pattern in the change in daylight duration follows the calendar and is the same every year for each region.

Plant populations persist through both asexual (vegetative) reproduction and sexual reproduction (Briske and Richards 1995). Annual plants are dependent on sexual production (seed) each year for survival. Likewise, short-lived perennials depend on seed production. Vegetative growth is the dominant form of reproduction in semiarid and mesic grasslands, including the tallgrass, midgrass, and shortgrass prairies of North America (Briske and Richards 1995).The frequency of true seedlings is low in perennial grasslands and occurs only during years with favorable moisture and temperature conditions (Wilson and Briske 1979, Briske and Richards 1995), in areas of reduced competition from older tillers, and when resources are easily available to the growing seedling. Sexual reproduction is necessary for a population to maintain the genetic diversity enabling it to withstand large-scale changes (Briske and Richards 1995).

Reproductive shoots are adapted for seed production rather than for tolerance to defoliation (Hyder 1972). Grass species that produce a high proportion of reproductive shoots are less resistant to grazing than are those species in which a high proportion of the shoots remain vegetative.

PHOTOSYNTHESIS AND CARBOHYDRATES

FACTORS THAT INFLUENCE PHOTOSYSNTHESIS

When considering grazing and plants it is important to remember that 1) Plants are the only source of energy for grazing animals, 2) the formation of sugars, starches, proteins and other foods is dependent on photosynthesis, 3) plants do not get food from the soil but they obtain raw materials needed for photosynthesis and subsequent food production, and 4) when leaves are removed from plants, food-producing capacity is reduced.

Photosynthesis is the bonding together of CO_2 (carbon dioxide) with H_2O (water) to make $C_6H_{12}O_6$(sugar) and O_2 (oxygen), using the sun's energy. The sugar contains the stored energy and serves as the raw material from which other compounds are made. Respiration is the opposite of photosynthesis — the stored energy in the sugar is released in the presence of oxygen, and this reaction releases the CO_2 and H_2O originally bonded together by the sun's energy.

Stomata are the "pores" in leaves (and stems) through which CO_2 is taken in and O_2 is released during photosynthesis. Plants control when stomata are open or closed and the width of the opening. The width of the opening is controlled by two guard cells that expand and contract to open and close the space between them. Transpiration is the process of water loss (evaporation) through the stomata when they are open. This pulls more water and nutrients up to the top of the plant, but causes the plant to lose water and potentially dehydrate. Water Use Efficiency (WUE) refers to how good the plant is at bringing in carbon dioxide for photosynthesis without losing much water out of its stomata. More specifically, it is the ratio of carbon dioxide intake to water lost through transpiration.

Numerous factors influence photosynthesis including leaf area, light intensity and quality, carbon dioxide content of the air, physiological efficiency, soil nutrients, water supply and temperature. Light interception increases with leaf area. Photosynthesis increases with increasing light intensity. Thus photosynthesis increases with increasing leaf area. And it follows that forage yield resulting from photosynthesis increases with leaf area.

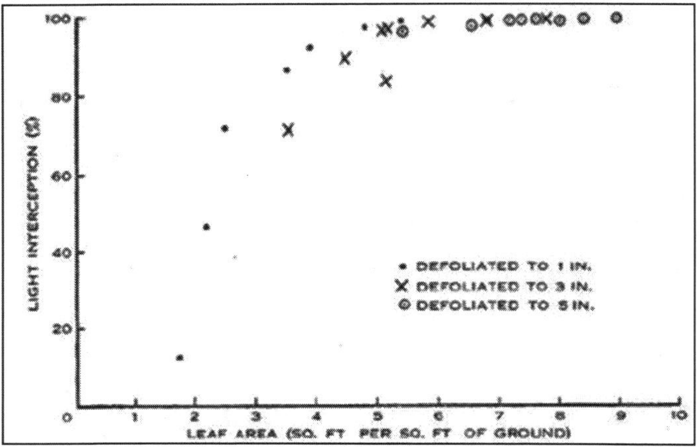

Fig. Relationship between light interception and leaf area.

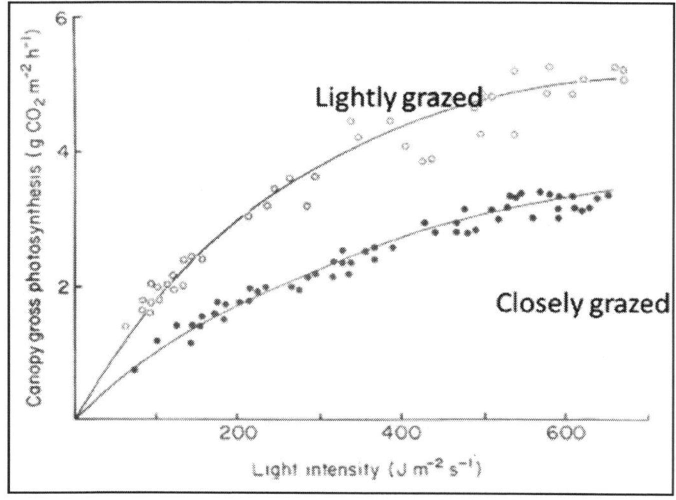

Fig. Photosynthesis increases with increasing light intensity.

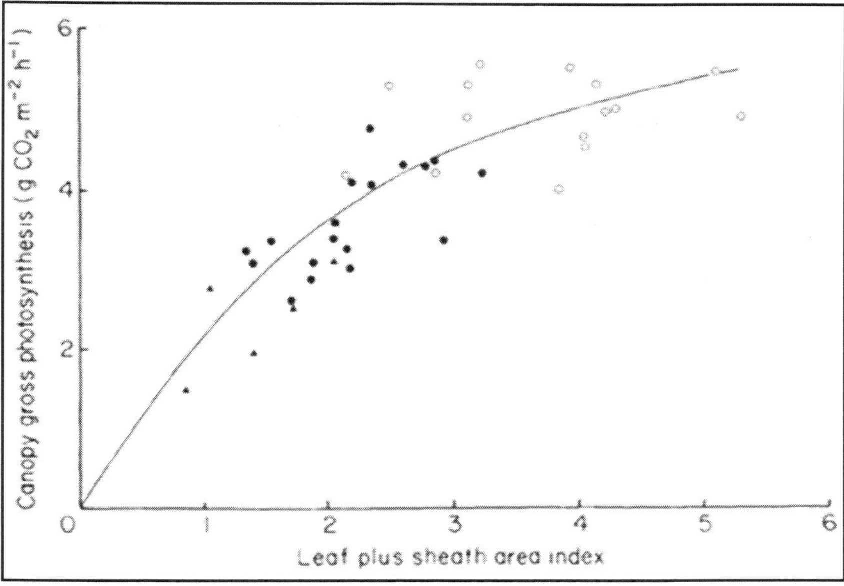

Fig. Thus photosynthesis increases with increasing leaf area.

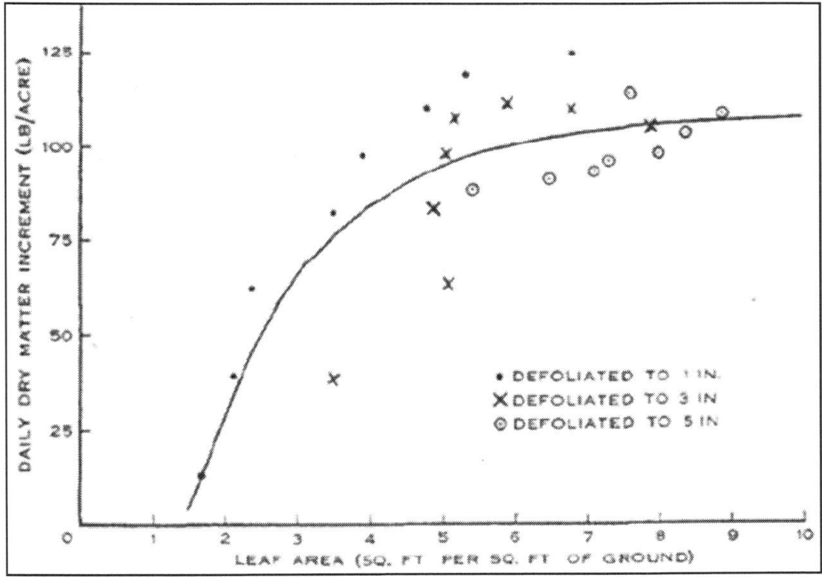

Fig. Relationship between leaf area and herbage yield.

Production resulting from photosynthesis is expressed as gross primary production (GPP) and net primary production (NPP). NPP is GPP minus respiration (R). GPP and NPP initially increase as leaf area increases but as upper leaves begin to shade lower leaves respiration increases resulting in a decrease in NPP.

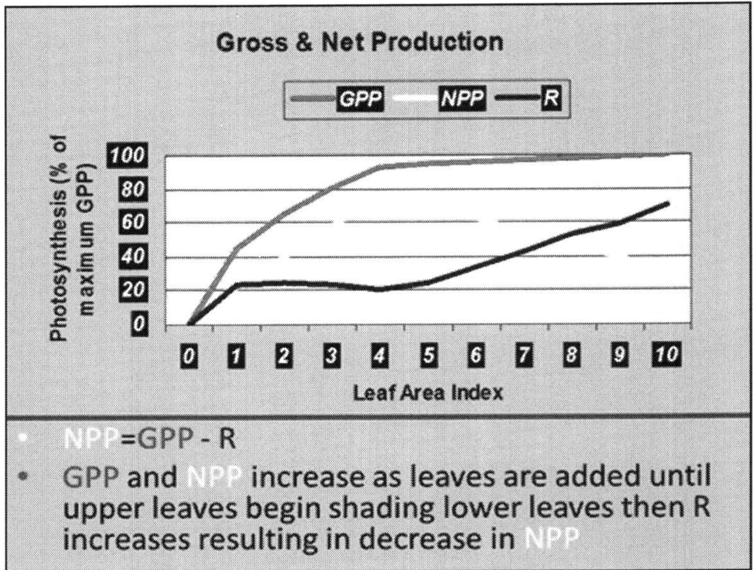

Fig. Change in gross primary production (GPP), net primary production (NPP) and respiration (R) with increasing leaf area.

CARBOHYDRATES AND CARBOHYDRATE ALLOCATION

Carbohydrates stored in roots and stems are the "savings account" of many perennial forage plants. They are energy stores used for survival during dormancy and to start growth following dormancy, although photosynthesis takes over fairly quickly. Sugars produced during photosynthesis are used as an energy source immediately or stored or converted to starch and then stored.

These stored carbohydrates are an energy source that the plant can draw on when photosynthesis is inadequate to meet current plant energy needs. Dormancy is one period when photosynthesis is low or non-existent. Thus the plant draws on these reserves to start growth as dormancy ends. The plant uses this energy for such activities as 1)root replacement, 2) leaf and stem growth following dormancy, 3) respiration during dormancy, 4) bud formation and 5) regrowth following top removal.

Plant scientists use the term 'source' for tissues where carbohydrate is produced and 'sink' for tissues where carbohydrates are utilized. Plant organs can be either sources or sinks depending on stage of growth and environmental conditions.

In early spring, carbohydrates stored in seed, crown, stem base, root or rhizome tissues are the source for carbon and energy utilized in the formation of the first new leaves; which in this case are the sink. When enough leaf area has formed such that the surface area has sufficient photosynthetic capacity to produce more carbohydrate than required for growth, that leaf then becomes a source of sugar. Once the leaf is fully extended, the sink for growth is removed.

Thereafter, sugars produced in excess of respiratory needs are available for translocation to sinks in other parts of the plant. Meristematic tissues, which are undifferentiated growth points throughout a plant, have priority for allocation of carbohydrates. The sink for excess carbohydrates might be new leaves, tillers, roots, stems or seed production. During the stem elongation phase, the developing reproductive organs inside the stem are the sink. During seed filling, the stem is then the source and the seed is the sink. If adverse conditions limit seed filling, excess sugars may be leftover in the stem. High respiratory rates in cool season grasses during hot weather may become a sink, burning up sugars that might otherwise go towards growth or seed production. When growth slows or stops due to cold temperatures, lack of water or other nutrients, the sink is removed. As long as there is green leaf tissue and adequate sunlight to allow production of photosynthates, accumulation may occur whenever carbohydrate production exceeds utilization.

Fig. In early spring, carbohydrates stored in seed, crowns, stem bases, roots or rhizomes are the source for carbon and energy utilized in the formation of the first new leaves which are initially a sink.

Fig. Once photosynthesis starts sugars are produced in excess of respiratory needs fairly quickly and excess sugars are translocated to sinks in other parts of the plant (new leaves, tillers, roots, stems or seed production).

The source-sink relationship between various plant organs is very dynamic, and can change hourly as environmental conditions affect photosynthetic capacity, respiration, and growth. Polysaccharides are too large for transport, so they are hydrolyzed to simple sugars for translocation. Much of the translocation of sugars from source to sink occurs in stem tissue. This is why stems are often higher in sugar concentration than leaves.

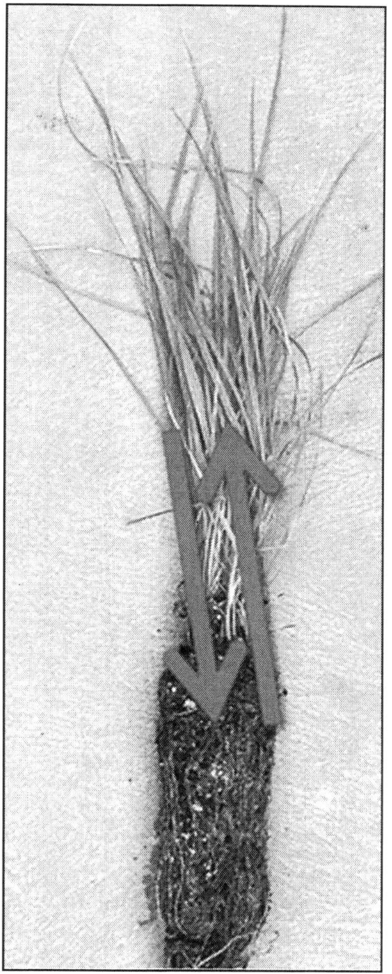

Fig. The source-sink relationship between various plant organs is very dynamic, and can change hourly as environmental conditions affect photosynthetic capacity, respiration, and growth.

WATER AND NUTRIENT UPTAKE

Roots take up water containing mineral nutrients (N, P, K, S, Ca, etc.) from the soil. When soil water content exceeds the permanent wilting point water is available to plants and nutrient uptake occurs. In crop plants permanent wilting point is about 15 atm. of tension. However, many arid land plants can extract soil water well below the permanent wilting point for crop plants. However, most nutrient uptake occurs during periods when soil moisture exceeds 15 atm. of pressure.

Complex interactions involving decomposition of rocks, organic matter, animals and microbes take place to form inorganic nutrient ions in soil water.

Roots absorb these mineral ions if they are readily available. They can be tied up by other elements or by alkaline or acidic soils. Soil microbes also assist in ion uptake. Mycorrhizae are a mutualism between plants and fungi. The plant provides the fungus with carbohydrates and the fungus helps the plant get nutrients from the soil, like phosphorus and nitrogen. Plants make carbohydrates from carbon dioxide and sunlight and their growth is usually limited by nitrogen and phosphorus. While fungi can absorb nitrogen and phosphorus from the soil, they can't make their own carbohydrates.

SECONDARY COMPOUNDS/TOXINS

Secondary products or metabolites are compounds produced by plants that appear to have no function in photosynthesis, respiration, solute transport, translocation protein synthesis, nutrient assimilation, differentiation or the formation of carbohydrates, proteins and most lipids. However, secondary compounds have important ecological functions in plants. They protect plants against herbivores and pathogens and they serve as attractants for pollinators and seed dispersing animals.

Secondary compounds have been divided into three groups: terpenes, phenolics and nitrogen-containing compounds. Terpenes are the largest class and include diverse substances that are generally insoluble in water. Terpenes defend against herbivores in many ways. Pyrethroids are non-oterpenes that occur in the leaves and flowers of the Chrysanthemum species demonstrate insecticidal activity and are the ingredients of some commercial insecticides. Conifers accumulated monoterpenes in resin ducts found in needles, twigs and the trunk. These compounds are toxic to many insects. Some terpenes are associated with odors that repel herbivores and toxins that are poisonous to herbivores.

Phenolic compounds from leaves, roots and decaying litter are sometimes the source of allelopathic compounds that reduce germination and growth of nearby plants. Lignin is a complex phenolic compound found in cell walls of xylem and other conducting plant tissues. While lignin strengthens and protects plants it deters feeding by animals because it is relatively indigestible. Flavenoids are a large class of phenolic compounds that serve to attract animals for pollination and seed dispersal. Some isoflavenoids in legumes have anti-estrogenic effects resulting in infertility of sheep with clover rich diets. Tannins are also phenolic compounds that are common in woody plants. Tannins are general toxins that may significantly reduce growth and survivorship of many herbivores when added to their diets. Cattle and deer commonly avoid plants and plant parts with high tannin contents. Tannins and other phenolics can bind dietary protein in cattle and other animals.

Nitrogen-containing compounds include alkaloids and cynogenic glycosides which are toxic to humans and other animals. Most are biosynthesized from common amino acids. Large numbers of livestock deaths are caused by ingestion of alkaloid-containing plants such as lupines, larkspur and groundsel. Likewise cyanogenic glycosides are widely distributed in the legume family and in sorghum (Sorghum spp.) and corn (Zea mays) as well as some species in the rose family.

Some secondary compounds inhibit growth of other plants. Allelopathy is the inhibition of the growth and development of one plant by another. Plants communicate with each other in a variety of ways. Plants use allelopathy as a means to guard their own space and protect their resources. Allelopathy is a strategy to reduce competition. For example, one way for a tree to protect its root space is to make other trees' roots die off using allelopathy. The tree can then pull more water from the soil for itself.

GRAZING AND PLANT GROWTH

DETRIMENTAL GRAZING EFFECTS

Grazing removes leaves where photosynthesis occurs. Photosynthesis is required for growth of new buds, leaves, stems, and roots, Photosynthesis is required for production of seeds, and for storage of carbohydrates. Consequently, the removal of photosynthetic tissue by grazing can have detrimental effects including: 1. Reduced carbohydrate production and storage, 2. Reduced leaf and stem growth, 3. Reduced seed production, and 4. Reduced root growth. Reduced growth can result in reduced competitive ability.

Grazing effects on the productivity of a plant are influenced by the season, intensity, frequency and duration of grazing. Competition from neighbouring plants can also influence productivity of individual plants. A grazed plant whose neighbours are not grazed may be at a competitive disadvantage. Thus grazing of surrounding plants can influence the productivity of an individual plant.

Annuals

Grazing of annual grasses often results in reduced flowering and seed production with little detrimental effect on vegetative components of the plants. Greater tillering following defoliation often compensates for the loss of photosynthetic tissue following defoliation. The large investment of annual plants in seeds ensures its annual regeneration under moderate grazing and, possibly, even under intense grazing in the vegetative phase. However, intense grazing into the reproductive phase can severely reduce the survival of annual grasses to maturity and seed production in the same year (Noy-Meir and Briske 1996).

Season of defoliation can influence the productivity of annual grasses. Leaf elongation in soft chess brome (Bromus hordeaceus) is complete by the time the leaf blade emerges from the sheath. Removal of emerged leaves is not followed by regrowth of the leaf. Instead only young leaves that have not emerged from the sheath regrow following clipping. If clipping is delayed until flowering, removal of the terminal bud will result in cessation of growth of that shoot. If a portion of the terminal bud remains the shoot continues to grow. While other grasses and forbs may react differently to clipping during the vegetative and flowering period, this illustrates the importance of season of defoliation.

The growing season on annual rangelands is short. During the growing season annual plants move from the vegetative state to flowering and maturity rapidly. The effects of rest following grazing depends on the phenological stage and the amount of time remaining in the growing season. Cold weather may slow regrowth following winter grazing. During rapid spring growth regrowth following grazing is rapid but by the time a normal rest period is over the plants may have flowered and began to mature as they near the end of the growing season.

Perennials

Holochek et al. (2004) reviewed several North American grazing studies and concluded that perennial grasses can be grazed without damage if 50 to 70 per cent of the leaf and stem material by weight is left intact as a metabolic reserve to support regrowth. Without this reserve, plant productivity and growth can be reduced. Grazing that is too close and too frequent can slow recovery from grazing and in the long run is detrimental to plant productivity, competitive ability and survival. Grazing that is close but followed by an adequate rest period that allows for regrowth and recovery is not detrimental but each plant species differs in the intensity and frequency of grazing it will tolerate.

Rotational grazing provides rest following grazing. Continuous grazing can be supported by many species if grazing intensity is low enough to maintain adequate leaf area. Long grazing periods that result in grazing of regrowth shortly after it is produced can suppress regrowth and recovery rates, especially when grazing is close. Long or continuous grazing periods that maintain adequate leaf area can be supported by many perennial grasses and forbs. The three ryegrass plants the effect of frequency and intensity of defoliation on individual plants.

- Plant A was allowed to grow for three months without grazing, note the healthy root system.
- Plant B was clipped to 3 inches every three weeks for three months, it also has a relatively healthy root system.
- Plant C was clipped to 1 inch every week for 3 months, note the weak root system.
- Plant B was properly managed. It was not clipped too intensely (closely) and it had a three week regrowth or recovery period between each clipping.

- Plant C was clipped to closely and too frequently to maintain adequate rooting depth and may not survive a drought.

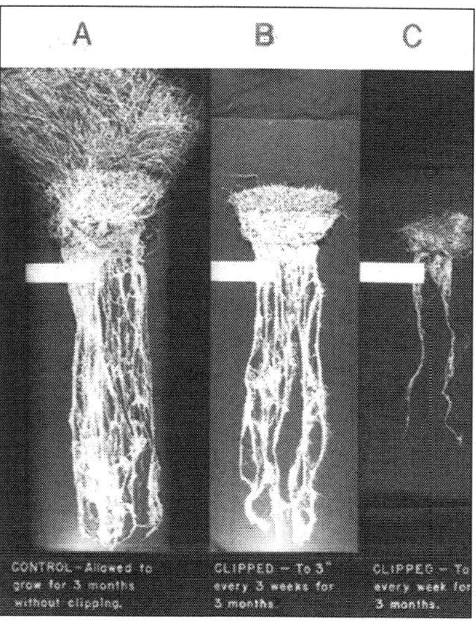

Fig. Effect on productivity of different frequencies and intensities of clipping.

Plants that are grazed or clipped too closely (intensity), leaving little or no residual leaf material and removing growing points from tillers, are slow to regrow as illustrated by the purple needlegrass plant. This results in delayed regrowth and may result in use of stored carbohydrates. Root growth may stop in response to heavy grazing and flowering may be suppressed. Reduced root growth and root death can result in reduced drought tolerance. The purple needlegrass plant illustrates that leaving adequate residual leaf area following grazing or clipping supports regrowth. This plant was clipped toa stubble height of 10 cm (4 inches) leaving adequate leaf area for regrowth.

Fig. Regrowth of purple needlegrass following weekly clipping to ground level for one growing season.

Fig. Regrowth of purple needlegrass following weekly clipping to 10 cm (4 in).

Season of grazing can influence productivity following grazing. Regrowth rates change as plants progress from vegetative states, to flowering, seed production and maturity. Regrowth rates are faster during the vegetative state but are often slowed during flowering and seed production. Regrowth rates slow with the approach of dormancy. Dormant season grazing is usually not detrimental. For perennial plants with long growing seasons, grazing followed by rest may be beneficial to plant productivity, competitive ability and survival. Long growing seasons occur in regions with dependable moisture throughout the year and short cold or dry seasons such as New Zealand and in irrigated pastures in California.

Most rangelands have short growing seasons. For perennial plants with short growing seasons the effects of rest following grazing may not be realized because regrowth is slowed as the plant matures and approaches the end of the growing season. In other words the growing season is too short for rest to be as effective as in a longer growing season.

Grazing at intensities and frequencies that reduce plant growth may also reduce the competitive ability of the plant, especially if the competitor is not being grazed. Grazed plants may be shaded by adjacent competitors. Grazed plants with reduced root systems may be less capable of extracting water and nutrients than an adjacent ungrazed plant. Grazed plants may produce fewer seeds. Vegetative reproduction from tillers, stolons and rhizomes may be suppressed by grazing.

ELEMENT INTERACTIONS AND THE GLOBAL CARBON CYCLE

The global carbon cycle is linked to other element cycles in many complex ways. For example, the burning of fossil fuels not only releases large amounts of carbon to the atmosphere, but it also increases the input of nitrogen, phosphorus, and sulphur to the atmosphere. Some of this nitrogen, phosphorus, and sulphur may enter terrestrial ecosystems in bulk precipitation, resulting in an increase in nutrient availability in these systems. This rise in available nutrients may in turn stimulate both carbon fixation and storage in terrestrial ecosystems, as has been suggested by Deevey (1970) and Simpson et al.(1977), thereby altering the dynamics of the global carbon cycle. In this chapter of the paper we consider how man's alteration of the global cycles of nitrogen, sulphur, and phosphorus could potentially increase the carbon storage capacity of the world's forests and thereby alter the global carbon balance.

THE GLOBAL CARBON CYCLE: AN OVERVIEW

The carbon dioxide concentration of the atmosphere has risen at least 40 ppm since the beginning of the industrial revolution. The present annual rate of increase is between 1.0 and 1.5 ppm, translating to an increase in the atmospheric carbon load of about 2700 Tg of carbon per year.

The annual carbon budget for the atmosphere can be formally stated as a mass balance equation with two source terms and two sink terms. The two source terms are: (1) the release of carbon dioxide to the atmosphere from the combustion of fossil fuels; and (2) the net release of carbon dioxide to the atmosphere resulting from land use changes (*e.g.*, forest to cultivated field, pasture to forest) and the oxidation of harvested renewable resources. The two sink terms are: (1) the net uptake of carbon from the atmosphere by a variety of processes in the world's oceans; and (2) the net uptake of carbon from the atmosphere by terrestrial ecosystems due to 'fertilization' of these systems with carbon dioxide or nutrients, or both. In the mass balance equation, AI is the annual increase in the carbon stock of the atmosphere.

$$AI = FFR + TR - OU - TU$$

The current best estimates of the variables. The magnitude of the release of carbon dioxide to the atmosphere from the combustion of fossil fuels is well known; This process is now estimated to release about 5200 Tg of carbon annually. Estimates have ranged over an order of magnitude for the net release of carbon dioxide to the atmosphere from terrestrial vegetation and soils as a consequence of land use changes and the oxidation of harvested renewable resources. To date, the most systematic analysis of the terrestrial source term has been conducted by Houghton et al (1983). According to their 'population' based estimate, the magnitude of this source term is currently 2600 Tg of carbon annually. The net annual uptake of carbon dioxide from the atmosphere by the world's oceans is now estimated to be 2100 Tg of carbon (40 per cent of the amount of carbon released from the combustion of fossil fuel). With four of the five terms in the mass balance equation defined, we can calculate TU, the net annual storage of carbon by terrestrial ecosystems due to 'fertilization' of these systems with carbon dioxide or nutrients, or both. By difference, the 'fertilization' factor required to balance the global carbon budget is 3000 Tg of carbon. A central question in the global carbon cycle is: Will carbon storage on land increase in response to man's acceleration of the global cycles of N, S, and P? We will assume that N, S, and P added to forests in bulk precipitation act as fertilizer. In this chapter of the paper we attempt to evaluate the consequences of such a fertilization.

We will use a simple element-matching approach to evaluate the expected increase in carbon storage in a terrestrial ecosystem following the addition of a given amount of a plant nutrient. Two assumptions are made in an element-matching analysis: (1) carbon will be stored in some constant proportion to nitrogen, sulphur, and phosphorus; and (2) the concept of a single limiting nutrient for plant growth and organic matter decomposition is valid.

Table. Components of the atmospheric carbon budget for 1980.

		Amount
	Symbol	**(Tg C/yr)**
Inputs to atmosphere	FFR	5200
Fossil fuel CO_2		
Net CO_2 flux due to forest cutback, etc.	TR	2600
Outputs from atmosphere		
CO_2 uptake by oceans	OU	2100
CO_2 taken up and stored in plants and		
organic residues	TU	3000
Accumulation in atmosphere		2700

Table. Estimates of annual net carbon exchange between terrestrial ecosystems and the atmosphere in or about 1980. Positive values indicate net terrestrial releases to the atmosphere.

Author	**Amount (Tg C yr^{-1})**
Adams et al. (1978)	400 to 4,000
Bolin (1977)	400 to 1,600
Wong (1978)	1,900
Hampicke (1979)	1,500 to 4,500
Woodwell et al. (1978)	2,000 to 18,000
Moore et al. (1981)	2,200 to 4,700
Houghton et al. (1982)	2,600 population-based estimate
	(range 1,800–4,700)

ELEMENT COMPOSITION OF FOREST ECOSYSTEMS

The mean element composition (by weight) of the three major components of forest ecosystems – vegetation, surface litter (*i.e.*, forest floor) and mineral soil. In computing the element composition of the forest components, only the organic fractions of the various elements were used. Also contains the carbon to element ratios, which are greatest in the vegetation and smallest in the soils.

Table: Element ratios (by weight) in the three major components of forest ecosystems. Values for vegetation are for woody tissue only. They were derived from a broad survey of the literature, with heavy reliance on Rodin and Bazilevish (1967)

	Element								**Ratio**					
System														
component	C		N		S		P		C:N		$C:S_o$		$C:P_o$	
Vegetation	1500		10		1		1		150		1500		1500	
Litter	500		10		1		1		50		500		500	
Soil	120		9	.4	1		1		13		120		120	

These ratios are the heart of the element-matching analysis. For example, if one unit of nitrogen is added to a forest ecosystem and it is stored in the vegetation component which has a C:N ratio of 150:1, we would predict the storage of an additional 150 units of carbon in the vegetation component of the forest ecosystem.

Although element matching is a simple form of element interactions analysis, it can lead to significant insights. With respect to the analysis that follows, the power of the element matching technique is in its implication of constraints on the increase in the ability of forest ecosystems to act as sites of carbon storage, as a consequence of inadvertant eutrophication.

FOSSIL FUEL COMBUSTION AND THE ACCELERATION OF THE N, P, AND S CYCLES

The activities of industrial man are accelerating the global cycles of nitrogen, sulphur, and phosphorus. Through the burning of fossil fuels, the industrial fixation of nitrogen, and the mining of phosphate, man is increasing the inputs of nitrogen, sulphur, and phosphorus to the land. The estimates of the amounts of C, N, S, and P introduced to the biosphere annually through man's activities.

A major portion of the industrially fixed nitrogen and mined phosphorus is applied directly to agricultural fields. Very little N and P fertilizer is added directly to forests. Fossil fuel emissions of nitrogen, phosphorus and sulphur are dispersed much more widely over the biosphere, and some fraction of the fossil fuel N, S, and P finds its way into forest ecosystems.

Table. Element loading of the biosphere by industrial activity (in Tg) (modified from Peterson, 1981)

	C	N	S	P
Fossil fuel emissions	6000	24	65	1*
Industrial nitrogen fixation		50		
Phosphate mining				10

Note:

*All values rounded to nearest whole number.,

The forests of the world cover a land area of approximately 57×10^{12} m^2. If, each year, all of the fossil fuel N, S, and P were to be evenly distributed over the world's forests, the input rates would be 0.4 g N m^{-2} yr^{-1}, 1.1 g S m^{-2},and0.02 g P m^{-2} yr^{-1}.These values are very similar to the N, S, and P bulk precipitation input values reported for a variety of forests around the world.The mean annual bulk precipitation input values for N, S and P are 0.6 g m^{-2}, 1.1 g m^{-2},and 0.02 g m^{-2} respectively. Certainly, fossil fuel burning is not the sole source of the N, S, and P found in bulk precipitation; moreover, fossil fuel N, S, and P are not uniformly distributed. For example, nitrogen input at the Solling beech forest (2.26 g N m^{-2} yr^{-1}), which is in the heart of one of the industrial regions of West Germany, is approximately eleven times higher than nitrogen input at the H. J. Andrews Douglas fir forest (0.2 g N m^{-2} yr^{-1}), which is in a rural, heavily forested region of the United States.

Table. Nutrient budgets for various terrestrial ecosystems of the world (g m^{-2} yr^{-1})

	Nitogen Location	Precipitation input	Stream -water output	Net gain or loss	Net gain Input
Temperate: mostly angiosperm and deciduous forest	Coshocton, OH, U.S.A.	2.00	0.25	+1.75	
	Hubbard Brook, U.S.A.	0.65	0.40	+0.25	
	S.E., U.S.A.	0.20	0.10	+0.10	
	Silverstream, New Zealand	0.22	0.18	+0.04	
	Taughannock Creek, NY, U.S.A.	0.97	0.56	+0.41	
	Walker Branch, TE, U.S.A.	0.87	0.18	+0.69	
	Soiling, W. Germany	2.26	0.60	+1.66	
					Mean 0.55
Temperate: mostly coniferous and evergreen forest	Birkenes Watershed, Norway	1.45	0.22	+1.23	

	Carnation Creek, Vancouver Island, Canada	0.27	0.11	+0.16
	Cedar River, WA, U.S.A.	0.11	0.06	+0.05
	ELA, Ontario, Canada	0.64	0.09	+0.55
	Finland	0.60	0.20	+0.40
	Storsj6n, Sweden	1.00	0.23	+0.77
	Velen, Sweden	0.59	0.04	+0.55
	Western Cascades Range, OR, U.S.A.	0.25	0.12	+0.13
	H. J. Andrews	0.20	0.17	+0.03
	Coweeta	0.55	0.02	+0.53
	Mean	0.71		
	Tropical: angiosperm mostly evergreen forest	0.16		
	Rio Negro, Brazil	0.56	0.47	+0.09
	Mean	0.63		
		PHOSPHORUS		
Temperate: mostly angiosperm and deciduous forest	Coshocton, OH, U.S.A.	0.018	0.005	+0.013
	Hubbard Brook, U.S.A.	0.0036	0.0019	+0.0017
	Pago Catchment, Australia	0.033	0.026	+0.007
	Silverstream, New Zealand	0.020	0.003	+0.017
	Taughannock Creek, NY, U.S.A.	0.007	0.020	-0.013
	Walker Branch, TE, U.S.A.	0.054	0.002	+0.052
Temperate: mostly coniferous and evergreen forest	Blue Range Catchment, Australia	0.039	0.042	-0.003
	Boundary Waters Canoe Area, MN, U.S.A. (24)	0.014	0.0015	+0.013
	Carnation Creek, Vancouver Island, Canada	0.011	0.005	+0.006
	Cedar River, WA, U.S.A.		0.002	–
	Clear Lake, Ontario,	0.035	0.009	+0.026

	Canada			
	ELA,Ontario,Canada	0.032	0.005	+0.027
	Finland	0.001	0.003	-0.002
	Storsjön, Sweden	0.014	0.002	+0.012
	Western Cascades Range, OR, U.S.A.	0.029	0.051	-0.022
Tropical: angiosperm mostly evergreen forest	Rio Negro, Brazil	0.020	0.010	+0.010
	Mean	0.023		
		SULPHATE-SULPHUR		
Temperate: mostly angiosperm and deciduous forest	Hubbard Brook, U.S.A.	1.88	1.76	+0.12
	S.E., U.S.A.	0.80	0.70	+0.10
	Silverstream, New Zealand	0.70	1.30	-0.60
	Taughannock Creek, NY, U.S.A.	2.10	3.80	-1.70
	Walker Branch, TE, U.S.A.	1.88	1.13	+0.75
Temperate: mostly coniferous and evergreen forest	Birkenes Watershed, Norway	1.56	2.69	-1.13
	Carnation Creek, Vancouver Island, Canada	0.87	2.80	-1.93
	ELA, Ontario,Canada	0.30	0.32	-0.02
	Finland	0.14	0.47	-0.33
	Storsjön, Sweden	1.15	2.53	-1.38
	Velen, Sweden	1.03	0.94	+0.09
	Mean	1.13		

At present we lack a detailed understanding of what fraction of the bulk precipitation inputs of N, S, and P to various forests result from the burning of fossil fuels.

For illustrative purposes, we will begin our element-matching analysis by assuming that 25 per cent of the fossil fuel N, S, and P is evenly distributed over the world's forests. This assumption results in annual nutrient inputs of the following magnitudes to the world's forests: 6.00 Tg N, 16.25 Tg S and 0.25 Tg P.

CARBON-NITROGEN INTERACTIONS

Nitrogen is frequently a limiting factor for forest growth. The application of nitrogen fertilizers to forest stands often results in dramatic increases in carbon storage in forests (*e.g.*, Miller et al., 1976). The amount of carbon stored per unit of nitrogen applied depends ultimately on how much of the nitrogen remains in the forest system and how the nitrogen is distributed among the forest's three components: vegetation, litter, and soil.

The maximum carbon storage in forests would occur if all added nitrogen remained in the system and if all of the added nitrogen were stored in the vegetation, since it has the largest carbon to nitrogen ratio of the three forest components. Under these conditions, addition of the 6 Tg N fixed each year through fossil fuel combustion would result in the storage of 900 Tg C in trees.

But not all of the nitrogen entering a forest in bulk precipitation will be retained; some of it will be leached from the system and some, generally a much smaller amount, will be lost through denitrification. To estimate the efficiency with which forests retain nitrogen entering them in bulk precipitation. A word of caution is warranted at this point. The measurement of nitrogen entering a forest ecosystem is relatively straightforward. Measurements of gaseous losses of nitrogen are very few and difficult to interpret and measurements of solution losses of nitrogen from forests are difficult to make. Data on leaching losses are often scanty and derived from systems with poorly defined hydrology. Therefore, the efficiency calculations we derive must be considered as suggestive, not definitive.

Nitrogen retention efficiencies for forest systems were calculated by dividing the net gain of nitrogen by the input of nitrogen. The mean retention efficiency value for all forest systems is about 60 per cent. Using the 60 per cent retention efficiency, we can recalculate the estimated carbon storage per unit nitrogen due to forest fertilization. We estimate a nitrogen-fertilizer induced carbon storage in the world's forests of 540 Tg C/yr given the following assumptions: 1) of the 6 Tg N entering the world's forests, 60 per cent or 3.6 Tg N is retained; 2) all of the added nitrogen is stored in the vegetation; and 3) the storage of one unit of nitrogen results in the storage of 150 units of carbon.

When a forest is fertilized, the total amount of fertilizer retained is more than actually ends up in the vegetation. Some will end up in the litter (surface organic horizon), and some will end up in the soil (Mead and Pritchett, 1975a, b). We therefore needed a set of fractionation factors that will allow us to distribute the fertilizer among forest components. We chose to use the relative distribution of carbon within the system, reasoning that this distribution integrates a variety of plant and soil processes responsible for element distribution.

We have not included the more subtle components of fractionation analysis. Since the major forest types of the world have distinctly different carbon distributions, we considered it necessary to regionalize our analysis.

The mean values for the absolute and relative distributions of carbon in the world's four major woody vegetation types, and the total area of each type.

These relative distributions are then used in conjunction with the carbon to nitrogen ratios of the three components and the nitrogen input per unit area to estimate carbon storage per unit nitrogen due to forest 'fertilization'. Assuming that 6 Tg N is uniformly distributed across the world's forests with 60 per cent retained in the forests in some organic form (an effective nitrogen fertilizer addition to the world's forests of 3.6 Tg N or 0.06 g N m^{-2}) the net rate of carbon storage in the world's forests due to nitrogen fertilization is 320 Tg C.

It is clear that the inadvertent nitrogen enrichment of forests is patchy; that is, some systems receive high nitrogen inputs while others receive low inputs. In an attempt to improve our estimate of increased carbon storage resulting from inadvertent nitrogen fertilization, we weighted the nitrogen inputs to the world's four major forest types. We again used a nitrogen input to the world's forests of 6 Tg.

Given that much of the fossil fuel use occurs in close proximity to temperate forests, they were allotted an annual input of 4 Tg N or 0.3 g N m^{-2}. The annual nitrogen input for the boreal forest was set at 1 Tg or 0.08 g N m^{-2} and that for the tropical forest was set at 0.5 Tg N each year or 0.02 g N m^{-2}. Like the tropical forest, the annual nitrogen input for the woodlands and shrublands was set at 0.5 Tg, resulting in an enrichment rate of 0.06 g N m^{-2} yr^{-1}. And once again we used a 60 per cent retention efficiency for all systems and the fractionation factors to allocate nitrogen and new carbon among the vegetation, litter, and soil of each of the four forest types. Based on these assumptions, the annual rate of fertilizer-induced carbon storage in the world's forests was about 310 Tg.

Table. Absolute and relative distributions of carbon in the world's forests, and estimates of forest area

Forest components	Tropics		Temperate		Boreal		Woodland and shrubland	
	Absolute*	Relative	Absolut*	Relative	Absolute*	Relative	Absolute*	Relative
Vegetation[a]	20,969	0.665	16,042	0.552	10,000	0.372	6,000	0.455
Litter[a]	147	0.005	1,208	0.042	2.000	0.074	282	0.021
Soil[b]	10,400	0.330	11,800	0.406	14,500	0.554	6.900	0,523
Total	31,516	1.000	29,050	1.000	26,500	1.000	13,182	1.000
Forest Area†	24.5		12		12		8.5	

*g C m^{-2}

†$10^{12}m^2$.

[a]Whittaker and Likens (1973).

[b]Schlesinger (1977).

Table. Potential carbon storage in the world's forests as a consequence of nitrogen loading from fossil fuel combustion (assuming all nitrogen entering forests is stored in organic form – see text for details of calculations)

		Carbon storage		Ecosystem mean C density	Ratio of ecosystm C density to annual C storage
	Componet	C/regn (Tg C)	C/m² (g C m⁻²)	(g C m⁻²)	
Tropics					
	Vegetation	29.9	1.2		
	Litter	0.1	Trace		
	Soil	1.3	0.1		
	Total	31.3	1.3	31,500	24,200
Temperate					
	Vegetation	198.7	16.6		
	Litter	0.5	Trace		
	Soil	12.6	1.1		
	Total	211.8	17.7	29,100	1,600
Boreal					
	Vegetation	33.5	2.8		
	Litter	2.2	0.2		
	Soil	4.3	0.4		
	Total	40.0	3.4	26,900	7,900
Woodland and Shrubland					
	Vegetation	20.5	2.4		
	Litter	0.3	Trace		
	Soil	2.0	0.2		
	Total	22.8	2.6	13,200	5,100
Grand Total		305.9			

In this analysis, the temperate forests accumulate the largest amount of carbon and the tropical forests accumulate the least amount of carbon as a consequence of inadvertant nitrogen fertilization. The rates of annual carbon increment are small relative to the standing stocks of carbon in forests. This is most obvious for tropical forests, where an annual carbon increment of 1.3 g m^{-2} represents a change in carbon stocks of about 0.0041 per cent or 1 part in 24,000. Such a small change in a large store of carbon will be undetectable in field measurements for many decades.

Annual net carbon accumulation per unit area is equivalent to the ecologist's net ecosystem production term. Several measurements of net ecosystem production (NEP) have been made in the temperate forest regions. These values represent the total amount of net carbon storage in these ecosystems in a single year. The mean NEP for these four sites is 200 g C m^{-2} yr^{-1}. If we assume that these forests have been subjected to nitrogen fertilization from the combustion of fossil fuels, we would have to argue that approximately 8.8 per cent of the NEP was due to fertilization (17.7 g C m^{-2}divided by 200 g C m^{-2}).

Table. Net ecosystem production estimates for four temperate zone forests.

Site	g C m^{-2} yr^{-1}	Reference
Hubbard Brook	218	Whittaker *et al.* (1974)
Walker Branch	160	Reichle *et al.* (1973)
Brookhaven	270	Whittaker and Woodwell (1969)
H. J. Andrews	155	Grier and Logan (1977)
Mean	200	

Our analysis suggests that man can have an impact on the global carbon balance by changing the flows of other elements such as nitrogen. 'Fertilization' of forests with nitrogen from fossil fuel sources will atmost result in the storage of about 300 Tg C in these systems annually. This amount of carbon storage, an upper estimate, is approximately 10 per cent of the amount needed to balance the global carbon budget as we currently understand it.

Phosphorus and Sulphur Inputs and Carbon Storage

Phosphorus is the one major element that must be supplied almost entirely by the parent material of unfertilized soils because of the low atmospheric inputs. In tropical forests with highly weathered soils, phosphorus may be a limiting nutrient for plant growth. In northern forests, massive surface organic matter accumulations may isolate plants from unweathered mineral soils, thereby depriving them access to phosphorus. Carbon accumulation in plants and soils of both regions may be controlled by phosphorus availability.

The regional summary of amounts of carbon storage, assuming that 0.25 Tg P is uniformly distributed across the world's forests and retained in the forests in organic form in proportion to mean carbon distribution by forest type. The net carbon storage in forests due to P fertilization is about 220 Tg C. There is probably relatively little chance that this potential will be realized, since most of the phosphorus that enters a forest will probably be bound chemically in soils as compounds of Al, Fe, and Ca.

Sulphur has been identified as a limiting nutrient in only a few forest types. Thus while sulphur loading of the atmosphere is great, there is little chance that it will stimulate forest growth on the global scale. And, in fact, this high sulphur loading may be limiting forests' ability to respond to either nitrogen or phosphorus fertilization due to the acid precipitation problem associated with sulphur loading of the atmosphere.

Table. Potential carbon storage in the world's forests as a consequence of phosphorus loading from fossil fuel combustion (assumptions stated in the text).

		Carbonstorage		Ecosystem	Ratio of ecosystem
		C/region	C/m²	mean C density	C density to annual C storage
	Componet	(Tg C)	(g C m²)	(g C m⁻²)	mass
Tropics					
	Vegetation	107.2	4.3		
	Litter	0.3	Trae		
	Soil	4.3	0.2		
	Total	111.8	4.5	31,500	7,000
Temperate					
	Vegetation	43.6	3.6		
	Litter	1.1	0.1		
	Soil	2.6	0.2		
	Total	47.3	3.9	29,100	7,500
Boreal					
	Vegetation	29.4	2.4		
	Litter	1.9	0.2		
	Soil	3.5	0.3		
	Total	34.8	2.9	26,900	9,300
Woodland and Shrubland					
	Vegetation	25.5	3.0		
	Litter	0.4	Trac e		
	Soil	2.3	0.3		
	Total	28.2	3.3	13,200	4,000
Grand Total		222			

SUMMARY

We have considered the possibility that carbon storage in forest ecosystems is stimulated by the increased inputs of N, S, and P that result from the combustion of fossil fuels. Our most extensive analysis related elevated N inputs with increased carbon storage in forests.

From this analysis we have concluded that the maximum amount of additional carbon storage that could be promoted by this form of N fertilization is about 300 Tg C per year. As we currently understand the global carbon budget, the fate of 3000 Tg C that fluxes into the atmosphere each year cannot be accounted for.

If 300 Tg C per year were stored in the world's forests as a result of inadvertent N fertilization, the amount of carbon unaccounted for would be reduced by 10 per cent.

Finally, we must stress that the inadvertent nitrogen fertilization of the world's forests may not promote an annual increment of carbon storage as large as 300 Tg/yr for a variety of reasons, several of which are listed below:

1. Other limiting factors – Our analysis has not fully considered the possibility that water availability and the availability of nutrients such as phosphorus may limit the effectiveness of N fertilization.
2. Toxic substances – The N fertilization of forests that is caused by fossil fuel combustion is accompanied by hydrogen ion loading (*i.e.* acid precipitation) and heavy metals input. These factors may reduce the ability of forest ecosystems to respond to N fertilization.

While the inadvertent N fertilization of the world's forests will probably not promote a carbon storage as large as 300 Tg per year, an N-fertilization effect may be of sufficient magnitude to be important in the global carbon budget. Further analysis of this problem is necessary.

PHOSPHORUS–'THE MASTER ELEMENT'

As soils develop through geological time, there is an extended period during the early and middle stages of pedogenesis when carbon accumulates. How phosphorus availability in developing soils is thought to control this carbon accumulation. We also explore, in a very preliminary way, how important this mechanism of carbon accumulation is in the context of the global carbon budget.

PHOSPHORUS AVAILABILITY AND CARBON, NITROGEN AND SULPHUR ACCUMULATION IN SOILS

A. C. Redfield (1958), in his classic paper 'The biological control of chemical factors in the environment', hypothesized that in ocean systems, phosphorus is the master-element. Redfield argued that through its influence on the oceanic carbon, nitrogen and sulphur cycles, phosphorus controls the quantity of nitrate in the sea, and the partial pressure of oxygen in the atmosphere.

T. W. Walker and his co-workers have hypothesized that in terrestrial systems, phosphorus is also the master element, regulating the accumulation of carbon, nitrogen and organic sulphur in soils (Walker, 1964; Williams and Walker, 1969a; Syers et al., 1970; Walker and Syers, 1976). They have shown that the total amount and chemical forms of phosphorus in an ecosystem change predictably during soil development. The total amount of phosphorus declines with time as leaching losses exceed inputs. In their scheme the soil's total phosphorus pool is divided into four components: (1) easily weathered (primary) minerals such as apatite, Ca-P; (2) available P or non-occluded P; (3) difficult-to-weather (secondary) minerals or occluded P; and (4) organically bound P. At the initiation of soil development, phosphorus is present in weatherable minerals. In the early and middle stages of soil development, phosphorus is present in all four forms, with available P making up a sizeable fraction of the total phosphorus pool. Late in soil development phosphorus is present mainly as difficult-to-weather mineral forms or as organically bound phosphorus.

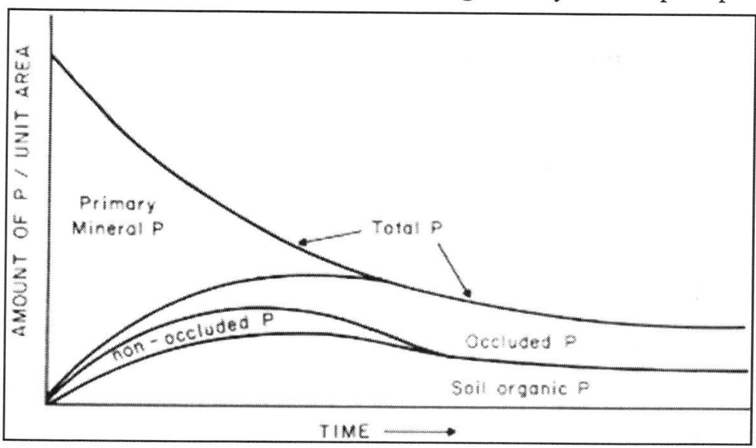

Fig. Changes in total phosphorus and phosphorus fractions during soil development. Non-occluded P is basically plant-available P. Occluded P is highly recalcitrant secondary mineral P and inaccessible primary mineral P. Modified from Walker and Syers (1976).

Phosphorus exerts control over nitrogen accumulation by influencing nitrogen fixation. An ample supply of phosphorus and a scarcity of nitrogen are necessary for high rates of nitrogen fixation. In the very early stages of soil formation on parent material devoid of nitrogen, nitrogen fixation is an important process. With high phosphorus availability and increasing nitrogen availability, plant production increases and organic matter begins to accumulate in the soil. In the middle stages of soil formation, losses of P are equalled by P input from weathering, the N:P ratio increases and non-N-fixers compete successfully for the N and P being mineralized from soil organic matter.

The amounts of available N and P are in the optimum range for maximum plant production and organic matter continues to accumulate in the soil. Late in soil development, soil organic matter begins to decline. This occurs when apatite has disappeared or fallen to such a low value that the rate of release of P by dissolution of apatite is less than the loss of P from the system either by leaching or conversion to unavailable forms or both (Williams and Walker, 1969b, Syers et al., 1970). Further development of the ecosystem in climates where leaching occurs causes additional loss of P and leads to declining levels of unavailable inorganic P and organically bound P as well as organically bound C, N, and S.

Pedogenesis and The Global Carbon Cycle

Given the control exerted on C, N, and S soil stocks by P on a geological time scale, the question arises as to the mean position of the world's soils on the Walker curve. Is the mean pedogenic position of the world's soils in an early enough stage of development to be accumulating carbon even though external P inputs are insignificant? And if soil C accumulation is regulated by the rate of supply of available P through weathering, what is the magnitude of the resulting C storage on an annual basis? Is the C storage rate large enough to be significant in short term global carbon balance considerations?

Let us address these questions by attempting to establish the order of magnitude of carbon accumulation that could possibly result annually if the world's soils were considered to be in the middle stages of pedogenesis; that is, if phosphorus were not limiting the rate of C accumulation. One such estimate can be derived from Syers et al. (1970). They studied changes in C and organic stocks of N, S, and P along a 10,000 yr chronosequence of soils developed on windblown sands in New Zealand. During the middle stages of pedogenesis (years 3,000–10,000) they calculated a mean carbon accumulation of 1.4 g C m^{-2} yr^{-1}. If the 57×10^{12} m^2 of the world's forests were accumulating C at this rate, a total of 79 Tg C would be accumulating each year. This amount of carbon storage in soils is small in the context of the overall global carbon budget. A storage of 79 Tg C per year in the soils of the world's forests identifies the fate of only about 2 per cent of the 3000 Tg C that is unaccounted for in the global carbon budget as we currently understand it.

CONCLUDING STATEMENT

We consider this chapter of the paper important not for the specific questions it has raised, but rather because of the general class of questions it has raised. Is it possible that the terrestrial biosphere is on a carbon accumulation trend that is independent of the activities of man? If yes, what are the mechanisms and the magnitude of the accumulation? Do element interactions play an important role in controlling the rate of the accumulation? These are questions we must address to make complete an analysis of the role of terrestrial biosphere in the global carbon cycle.

Bibliography

A S Sachdeva: *Molecular Biology of Evolution*, Vista International Publishing House, Delhi, 2008.

A S Sachdeva: *Molecular Biology of Genetics*, Vista International, Delhi, 2008.

A S Sachdeva: *Molecular Biology of Life*, Vista International Publication, Delhi, 2008.

A. Hemantaranjan: *Physiology of Nutrition and Environmental Stresses on Crop Productivity*, Scientific Publication, Delhi, 2014.

A. Hemantaranjan: *Plant Physiology, Biochemistry and Plant Molecular Biology in New Millennium*, Scientific Publication, Delhi, 2003.

Charlotte Jhonson: *Plant Molecular Biology*, Oxford Book Company, Delhi, 2009.

D.K. Tharyani, Rekha More, Varsha Gathoo, S. Santhi Prakash, Asawari Shinde, Smita Kamerkar, Anuradha Batwal, Smita Pais, Gitanjali Wadekar, Asmita Huddar and Suni Mathew: *Curricular Strategies and Adaptations for Children with Hearing Impairment*, Kanishka Publication, Delhi, 2006.

E.D. Tripathi, Kamla Kulshreshtha, K.J. Ahmad, Madhoolika Agrawal, Sagar Krupa, C.K. Varshney and P. Pushpangadan: *Plant Response to Environmental Stress*, International Book Distributing, Delhi, 2006.

Indubala Singh: *Gender Relations and Cultural Ideology in Indian Cinema : A Study of Select Adaptations of Literary Texts*, Deep and Deep Publication, Delhi, 2007.

L.V. Gangawane and V.C. Khilare: *Molecular Biology of Plant Pathogens*, Daya Publication, Delhi, 2010.

M Prakash: *Molecular Biology of Evolution*, Discovery Publishing House, Delhi, 2008.

M Prakash: *Molecular Biology of Genetics*, Discovery Publishing House, Delhi, 2008.

M Prakash: *Molecular Biology of Life*, Discovery Publishing House, Delhi, 2008.

Madan Pal Singh, Sangeeta Khetarpal, Renu Pandey and Pramod Kumar: *Climate Change : Impacts and Adaptations in Crop Plants*, Today and Tomorrow Publication, Delhi, 2011.

Madhu Shankar Gupta: *Objective Genetics Biotechnology and Molecular Biology*, Manglam Publishers, Delhi, 2011.

Marine Carrin and Harald Tambs-Lyche: *People of the Jangal : Reformulating Identities and Adaptations in Crisis*, Manohar Publication, Delhi, 2008.

Moore: *Biochemistry and Physiology of Plant Hormones, 2e*, Springer, India, 2003.

Nafees A. Khan and Samiullah: *Phytohormones in Crop Productivity under Different Environments*, Scientific Publication, Delhi, 2001.

Prakash S Lohar: *Endocrinology : Hormones and Human Health*, MJP Publication, Delhi, 2005.

R. K. Saxena and Sumitra Saxena: *Animal Adaptations: Evolution of Forms and Functions*, MV Learning an imprint of Viva Books, Delhi, 2015.

R. Ranjan, S.S. Purohit and V. Prasad: *Plant Hormones : Action and Application*, Agrobios Publication, Delhi, 2008.

R. Ranjan: *Molecular Biology of Phytochrome*, Agrobios Publication, Delhi, 2002.

Ramphal Sharma: *Molecular Biology of the Cell*, RBSA Publication, Jaipur, 2006.

S.N. Chaturvedi and K.P. Singh: *Plant Reproductive and Molecular Biology : Festschrift Volume I to Felicitate Prof. S.V.S. Chauhan*, Aavishkar Publication, Delhi, 2005.

Samuel Delvin: *Vitamins, Minerals and Hormones*, Ivy Publication, Delhi, 2003.

Shubhrata R Mishra: *Understanding Plant Hormones*, Discovery Publishing, Delhi, 2011.

Srikumar Chattopadhyay and Richard W. Franke: *Striving for Sustainability Environmental Stress and Democratic Initiatives in Kerala*, Concept Publication, Delhi, 2006.

Index

N

P

Q

R

S

T

U

V

X